The Economics of Personal Choice

THE ECONOMICS OF PERSONAL CHOICE

James N. Morgan

Professor of Economics and Research Scientist
Institute for Social Research
The University of Michigan

Greg J. Duncan

Associate Research Scientist
Institute for Social Research
The University of Michigan

Ann Arbor The University of Michigan Press

HB
801
.M6925
1980

Copyright © by The University of Michigan 1980
All rights reserved
Published in the United States of America
by The University of Michigan Press
and simultaneously in Rexdale, Canada,
by John Wiley & Sons Canada, Limited
Manufactured in the United States of America

Library of Congress Cataloging in Publication Data

Morgan, James N
   The economics of personal choice.

   Includes bibliographies and index.
   1. Consumers. 2. Economics. 3. Finance,
Personal. I. Duncan, Greg J., joint author
II. Title.
HB801.M6925   1980   330   80–15389
ISBN 0–472–08007–5

Preface

Beware of the biases, special interests, and axes to grind of any person who is bent on helping you. Our own prejudices may become apparent as you read this book, but with some advance information you should be able to recognize them more readily.

One of our biases is toward the notion that everybody needs to understand some economics, since economics underlies many of the decisions individuals have to make in their lives. A relatively few principles, applied in a variety of ways and situations, can serve to inform a great many important decisions and help to avoid later regret.

We have been teaching a course in consumer economics at the University of Michigan, one of us for more than a quarter of a century, using various textbooks, including two that Morgan wrote. Students find many texts preachy, dull, and analytically inadequate. We frequently find them economically unsophisticated, full of dated facts but little analysis, loaded with trite advice (such as "Be careful"), and focused on the process of buying major consumer products.

We thought we could write a book that would be understandable to any intelligent reader without prior training in economics and without the discipline and stimulation of a formal class. But we intend it also for use in college-level classes.

Detailed facts about the marketplace are not to be stressed here. They will need to be studied at the time that major decisions are made. Discussions of consumer protection laws are relegated to the end of the book because it seems to us that beyond the ordinary safety, sanitation, health, and weights-and-measures regulations, many government attempts to protect the consumer have done more harm than good.

You may miss the pillorying of the bad guys and the passionate indignation about treatment of the average consumer. It is not that there are no problems, nor that we do not care; but easy indignation often tends to mask a failure in judgment or information-gathering. The seller may or may not be the "guilty party," but the buyer need not be naive, and a clear head is better than a head of steam.

Our main work has been personal interview survey research at the Survey Research Center, Institute for Social Research, The University of Michigan, mostly on household behavior, attitudes, and conditions. That background has guided the focus of this book insofar as it leads to an understanding of how the majority of consumers behave; but we have tried to avoid burdening the reader with facts about consumer behavior in general. Indeed, human behavior is so varied that attempting to analyze it provides little guidance in terms of what the "average person" does. We have included enough about the processes of survey research to allow the reader to understand, and not be deceived by, the plethora of "facts" reported in the press.

We try to be cautious about leaping to conclusions about economic policy, since these require a combination of facts, understanding of people's behavior, analysis of the economic system, and knowledge of the political process. You will find a number of suggestions in the book, some of them for social reforms of dramatic dimension. But more than economics is required to get from here to there.

We have attempted to retain the idea that economics is a set of "If . . . , then . . ." propositions, not a religion or a philosophy, and hence have tried to avoid telling the reader what to do. There are many noneconomic considerations that enter into any economic decision, and vast differences between people as to their goals, even in strictly economic terms. Most people at one time or another spend money or time on some luxury dear to their hearts. This book can help to determine what that luxury costs, but it cannot help to determine what it is worth to you.

Like any other investment, the time, energy, and thought invested in assembling information and making economic choices may or may not pay off. We have suggested some simplifications and shortcuts to minimize the time and energy and to make sure that the end result is worth it. Perhaps making a few large calculated decisions will allow you to relax and make the smaller choices more casually.

We hope you will come to think a little more like an economist and even to enjoy it. To add to your enjoyment, remember that careful consumers benefit others as well as themselves by making markets work better and by improving the correlation between price and quality.

It may appear from the examples given that the principles being illustrated are useful only to upper-middle-income, well-educated people. That is not true. The lower your income, the more constraints you face, and the more crucial it is that your economic decisions be the right ones for you. The same principles apply at all income levels. The very affluent may believe they can afford to ignore all this and simply enjoy their money. This is true for the small expenditures and minor decisions; but more money allows bigger mistakes, and exposes you to more alluring opportunities to make them. It is impossible to give examples that cover everyone's particular situation, so you should try continually to apply the principles to the choices or problems you are actually facing or likely to face soon. When the book talks about cars, for example, the same principles can apply to motorcycles or bicycles, as well as to snowmobiles, yachts, or even second homes.

Since the best way to enjoy any subject is to become an expert in one small area of it, we have suggested some projects at the end of each chapter through which you can learn a lot more. Whether you simply read more critically, or go out to collect local market information, or talk to some experts, you should try to apply some of the economic principles that pervade this book. If you price ten-speed bicycles or washing machines at all of the retail outlets in your town, think of the implication of the price ranges for optimal shopping behavior, and of why the price differentials exist. If you talk with experts, many of whom have their own biases, perhaps the insights that you will have gleaned from this book can help you to ask the right questions, interpret what you learn from them, or avoid accepting incomplete or incorrect answers.

Finally, some things not stressed in this book, and why:

1. *Details of the federal income tax and its computation.* This is so complex, changing, and subject to interpretation that a brief treatment would be superficial, and a more complete treatment would soon be out of date. We have included tax considerations where they seem appropriate, pointing out that most strategies attempt to change the amount of one's *taxable* income. The benefits of this depend on one's tax bracket, more precisely the tax rate in that bracket, called the marginal tax rate.

2. *Details of the Social Security system.* This is another extremely complex system, subject to rapid changes in detail as taxes, benefit levels, and even special coverages are changed. We have given a general discussion of its logic and pointed out the ways its survivor provisions affect the choice of life insurance.

3. *Details of the operation of the stock market and other financial markets.* It is more important to understand general principles—such as the risk-yield mix, leverage, and the capitalization (calculation of present values) of expected future yields—than it is to know how a particular market functions or what a stockbroker does. Indeed, a basic knowledge of the theory of capital and interest will protect most people from the nonsense that is written and spoken about the stock market and other financial investments.

4. *The use of trusts and other devices to minimize income, estate, and inheritance taxes.* These details are of concern only to the affluent, involve rapidly changing laws and interpretations of laws, and require expert professional help. We have warned that they sometimes cost more to set up and to have administered than they save. The 1976 Tax Reform Act makes such devices unnecessary for estates below half a million dollars.

5. *Detailed facts on consumer behavior, expenditures, and assets.* These are complex and require a great deal of

interpretation to be of much value to anyone. As guidance for an individual, they are nearly useless: there is no average consumer.

6. *Technical details on nutrition, how appliances work, how to repair your car, etc.* These are again voluminous, changing, and of interest only when you have specific questions. We have attempted to list some sources which would help you to locate the details you need.

This emphasis on understanding and insight more than on factual details is the intentional result of our belief that the mass of detailed information available may leave us too little time to think about what we are trying to do and how best to do it. A Nobel prizewinner makes the point:

In a world where information is relatively scarce, and where problems for decision are few and simple, information is almost always a positive good. In a world where attention is a major scarce resource, information may be an expensive luxury, for it may turn our attention from what is important to what is unimportant.[1]

With some effort and imprecision we have compressed the list of important economic insights to five items. These are explained briefly in the introductory chapter and are clarified as we apply them in one way or another in all subsequent chapters. Study them carefully, because once learned they will serve you well in almost every consumer decision you make.

1. Herbert Simon, "Rationality as Process and as Product of Thought" (The Richard T. Ely Lecture), *American Economic Review* 68 (May, 1978): 13.

Acknowledgments

The Economics of Personal Choice was written in response to the enthusiasms, questions, arguments, and confusions of hundreds of students spanning many years. We hope that new generations of students and the general public will find the book clear, useful, and even enjoyable.

We are indebted for welcome suggestions and encouragement from Georgianne Baker of Arizona State University, Carolyn Shaw Bell of Wellesley College, Marjorie East of Pennsylvania State University, E. Scott Maynes of Cornell University, and Richard Porter of the University of Michigan. Some chapters benefited from reading by specialists including Alfred Conard in law (University of Michigan), Jeffrey O'Connell in law (University of Illinois), Sandra Newman in urban planning (University of Michigan), and Jennifer Gerner in housing (Cornell University). Thomas Gies (University of Michigan) informed us on mortgages and banking. Two "lay" readers, Alfred Hassler (former editor of *Fellowship*) and Renate Farmer, convinced us that the book should be made readable to noneconomists and nonstudents.

Many improvements in style and wording came from careful editorial reading by Joan Brinser and Richard Barfield. We also profited from comments by Charles Stallman, Susan Augustyniak, Ronnie Silverberg, Elwin Duncan, and a variety of readers of earlier versions. Our excellent typist, Barbara Browne, not only improved the appearance of the manuscript but also spotted inconsistencies and errors for us.

Contents

1 CHAPTER ONE
INTRODUCTION: PRINCIPLES AND STRATEGY
1 Five Principles
4 Social Considerations
4 A Note on Jargon
4 An Encouraging Word
5 More Information?
5 Some Projects to Learn More

7 CHAPTER TWO
INVESTMENT IN YOURSELF
7 Capital Theory
8 Present Values
10 Alternative Futures and Uncertainty Corrections
12 Factual Evidence on the Payoff
13 On-the-Job Training
13 Other Investments
14 Private and Social Considerations in Education and Similar Investments
16 Summary
16 More Information?
17 Some Projects to Learn More
18 Appendix 2.1: Consumer Decisions Involving Costs and Benefits at Different Times

23 CHAPTER THREE
EARNING, SHARING, HAVING CHILDREN, AND THE ECONOMIC STATUS OF THE HOUSEHOLD
23 Selecting a Job
24 How Much Work?
25 Marriage and Other Partnerships
26 Having Children
28 Measuring Family Well-Being
30 Family Needs Standards and the Official Poverty Line
31 Measuring Inequality
32 The Redistribution of Income
   Noncontributory Transfers
   Contributory Transfers
   Taxes and Redistribution
   Effects of Redistribution on Behavior
   Proposed Reforms
38 Summary
39 More Information?
40 Some Projects to Learn More

	CHAPTER FOUR		CHAPTER FIVE		CHAPTER SIX
41	**HOUSING AND RESIDENTIAL LOCATION**	65	**LONG-TERM FINANCIAL PLANNING AND DAY-TO-DAY BUDGETING**	91	**BORROWING AND CONSUMER DEBT**
41	How Much Housing?	65	A Simple Budgeting Scheme	91	Amortization Algebra
42	The True Costs of Owning	67	Long-Range Planning	93	Varieties of Lenders
44	Own or Rent?	67	Setting Saving Goals	94	Sources of Loans
49	Legal Traps and Tax Issues	68	The Algebra of Annuities	96	The Timing of Purchases and Debt
51	Buying and Selling	72	Social Security, Private Pensions, and Saving Goals	96	Credit Ratings
52	Where—The Question of Neighborhood	73	Summary of Budgeting Steps	97	Trouble: Repossession, Garnishment, and Bankruptcy
53	Homeowner's Protection	74	Detailed Financial Analysis	100	Aggregate Debt and Economic Policy
54	Design, Style, and Site	77	Sources of Income	100	A Cashless and Checkless Society?
54	The Social Approach to Housing and Community	77	Estimating Savings	101	Summary
	Housing Costs Too Much?	78	Monitoring Current Expenditures to Achieve Saving Goals	101	More Information?
	Urban Development	79	Monitoring Consumption to Achieve Saving Goals	102	Some Projects to Learn More
	Slums—Cause or Effect?	80	Detailed Expenditure Monitoring	103	Appendix 6.1: FTC Buyers Guide No. 7, Fair Credit Reporting Act
	Property Values and Race	80	Still More Detail		
	The Role of Government	81	Outside the Budget		
60	Summary	82	Consumer Saving Behavior		
61	More Information?	83	Aggregate Implication of Spending-Saving Decisions		
63	Some Projects to Learn More	84	National Fiscal and Monetary Policy and the Consumer		
		84	Social Security		
			The Importance of Interest		
			The Trust Fund Issue		
		87	Sex and Policy		
		88	Summary		
		89	More Information?		
		89	Some Projects to Learn More		

CHAPTER SEVEN
THE INVESTMENT OF SAVINGS

- 105 Theory of Investment
- 109 Desirable Characteristics of Investments
- 110 Tax Considerations
- 111 Information and Management Costs
- 111 Social and Ethical Considerations
- 111 Characteristics of Available Investments
  - Savings Banks or Savings and Loan Associations
  - Government Bonds
  - Real Estate
  - Common Stock
  - Mutual Funds or Investment Trusts
  - Puts and Calls: The Options Market
  - Commodity Futures
  - Small Businesses
  - Preferred Stock, Corporate Bonds, Debentures
  - Checking Accounts and Checking-Saving Combinations
  - Money Market Funds
  - Odds and Ends
- 120 Some Technical Details
- 121 What People Do
- 122 Some Social Aspects of Private Investment
- 123 Summary
- 123 More Information?
- 125 Some Projects to Learn More

CHAPTER EIGHT
INVESTMENTS IN CONSUMER DURABLES

- 127 Theory Again
- 129 Automobiles
  - When During the Year?
- 131 Other Durables
- 132 Benefits
- 133 Shared Ownership or Renting of Durables
- 133 Do-It-Yourself Repair and Maintenance of Appliances
- 134 Additions and Repairs to the Home
- 135 Sources of Information
- 136 The Timing of Acquisitions
- 136 Household Behavior
- 137 Summary
- 137 More Information?
- 138 Some Projects to Learn More

CHAPTER NINE
RISKS, INSURANCE, AND ESTATE PLANNING

- 139 Some Principles
- 139 Major Risks
- 140 How Much Insurance?
- 140 Availability
- 141 Life Insurance Needs
  - The Family Life-Cycle Pattern of Needs
  - Life Insurance Needs for Equal Spouses
- 146 Types of Life Insurance
  - Term Insurance
  - Whole Life Insurance
- 149 Evidence on Life Insurance Costs
- 150 Rules of Thumb
- 151 More Details about Life Insurance
- 153 Automobile Liability Insurance
- 156 Insurance for Damages to Your Own Car or Its Occupants
- 156 Buying Auto Insurance
- 157 Medical Insurance
- 158 Worker's Compensation Insurance
- 159 Household Insurance
- 159 Household Behavior
- 160 Regulating the Insurance Industry
- 160 Gambling
- 161 Funerals
- 161 Prepare Now, Go Later
- 163 Summary
- 164 More Information?
- 166 Some Projects to Learn More

167	**CHAPTER TEN** **MEDICAL CARE**	**199**	**CHAPTER ELEVEN** **OTHER ITEMS IN THE BUDGET**	**221**	**CHAPTER TWELVE** **CONSUMER DECISION MAKING, CONSUMER INFORMATION, AND CONSUMER PROTECTION**
167	Reducing the Need for Care	199	Priorities and Shopping		
	Nutrition	201	Food		
	Exercise	204	Clothing	221	Motivation
	Safety, Prevention, and Strategy	205	Transportation and Recreation	223	Family Decision Making
	Mental Health	209	Recreational Equipment	223	Communication and Consensus
	Public Policy Aspects	211	Recreational Facilities	224	Social Optimum
171	Getting Medical Care	211	Philanthropy	226	Household Economic Information
172	Malpractice	213	Other Expenditures	231	Shopping and Bargaining
172	Costs of Medical Care	213	Services (Particularly Repairs)	232	Consumer Protection by Government
173	Drugs	215	More Information?		Fraud
174	Paying for Medical Care	216	Some Projects to Learn More		Dangerous Foods, Drugs, and Products
175	Handling the Income Loss	218	Appendix 11.1: Federal Food Standards		Monopoly and Restraints on Competition
176	Public Policy				Deception, Misleading Advertising, and Defective Products
178	Fads, Quacks, Nostrums, Food Additives, New Nonprescription Drugs			235	Seduction of the Consumer
179	Summary			235	The Consumer Interest
180	More Information?			238	Research on Consumer Behavior
182	Some Projects to Learn More			238	Survey Research
183	Appendix 10.1: A Primer on Vitamins			239	How Survey Research Can Benefit Consumers
186	Appendix 10.2: Nutrition Labels: A Great Leap Forward			240	Summary
191	Appendix 10.3: Fats in Food and Diet			240	More Information?
196	Appendix 10.4: Recommended Daily Dietary Allowances			243	Some Projects to Learn More
				245	GLOSSARY
				251	INDEX

CHAPTER ONE
INTRODUCTION: PRINCIPLES AND STRATEGY

Consider the following bits of consumer advice:

☐ It pays to buy a new car when the repair costs on the old car exceed its depreciation costs.
☐ You are better off buying than renting a house if the mortgage payments are no larger than the rent you would be paying, because you end up owning a house.
☐ The interest rate on an installment loan is determined by simply dividing the interest charges by the amount of the loan.
☐ It is better to buy life insurance when you are younger because the rates are much lower.
☐ It pays to stock up when something is on sale.

Each of these statements may sound plausible, and yet each is either misleading or simply incorrect. Each ignores some elementary economic principles. The principles are neither difficult nor numerous, and once they are learned, they can provide the basis for informed consumer decisions in a wide variety of situations.

Economics has the reputation of being a "dismal science" that reduces everything to market values and measurable quantities. Even getting educated becomes an "investment in human capital," its benefits analyzed as a "rate of return" on the investment in terms of later earnings. Other human considerations—pleasure, aesthetics, lifelong friendships, learning for its own sake—are thought to be ignored or even scorned.

The premise of this book is quite different. Rather than reducing everything in life to economic terms, it sees the economist's ways of looking at things as a means of enriching life by providing a background against which life's necessary choices can be made. Virtually all choices have some economic implications—costs, or benefits, or both. The question is whether the person making the choice is able to evaluate those costs and benefits easily and effectively.

Business executives constantly use economic insights in making choices, and the same principles can apply to individual and family decisions. It is equally important that they do so, but more complicated, because individual decisions have more noneconomic and nonmeasurable costs and benefits. This book should make it easier to see how getting and organizing information will pay off in terms of better decisions. A "better decision" is not one that the authors endorse, but one that is based on enough information and insight so that the person making the decision will not regret it later.

The purpose of this book is not to impose on you any values about how to spend time or money, or even about how much effort to put into improving your choices; it is to show what economics has to say about how choices can be made, so that you can decide how much time and energy to spend on improving your capacity to reach your goals.

Principles are dull without examples and become clear only by application in a variety of situations. Hence, this book is organized around a series of typical choice situations, in which the same principles can be used. Throughout, we shall try to suggest simplified ways of applying these principles, avoiding complex calculations or unnecessary precision.

Five Principles

Any choice has both benefits and costs, and our goal is to select the alternative with the largest surplus of benefits over costs. It helps if we can measure as many of the costs and benefits as possible in the same units, namely, dollars. Then, in thinking about any particular course of action, we can ask ourselves whether its total benefits, measurable or not, exceed the total benefits of the most appealing alternative use of equivalent time and money. There are five kinds of translations or adjustments used in converting costs or benefits into dollars. Here, they are only described briefly, but they will come up again and again, becoming clearer through use:

1. *Only today's dollars are comparable*. The costs to be incurred or benefits to be received at some future date must be converted to present values to allow for interest and inflation. A benefit that will be worth $100 twenty years from now is worth only $55 today, because in twenty years, at a 3 percent interest rate, $55 now plus compound interest would accumulate to $100. Inflation makes money worth less in the future, but inflation also causes market interest rates to be higher by about the rate of inflation. Therefore we can often use 3 percent as the real inflation-adjusted interest rate and take care of inflation without needing to predict it. As explained in chapter 2, the 3 percent rate used in this example has been chosen with care and will be used in most present-value calculations in this book.

2. *Time is worth money*, and a decision that saves time or takes time has a benefit or cost. Sometimes it is helpful to value time at the amount you would make by working an extra hour on your job. (Sometimes you can earn double for overtime, or you may have no chance to earn more at all.)

3. *Costs or benefits that do not involve actual money payments can often be converted into dollar "imputations."* The cost of having your money tied up in owning a house is the interest you could otherwise be earning on it—the imputed interest. Cars and houses depreciate in value, and that depreciation is part of their cost—the imputed cost. Durable goods that you own also provide a stream of benefits as though you were renting them—the imputed rent.

4. *An uncertain dollar is not as good as a sure thing.* Where we can estimate probabilities, the dollar equivalent of an anticipated amount to the sure thing is the "expected value," that is, the dollar amount times the probability of realizing it. Thus, the expected value of an investment that has an even chance of paying $10,000 and an even chance of paying nothing at all is $5,000. If risk itself is something you want to avoid, then the expected value of this investment to you is less than $5,000.

5. *Costs and benefits count only after taxes*. Taxes are so pervasive and so large these days that, in making decisions which result in economic costs or benefits, it is worthwhile to consider the tax effects of each alternative. A decision to spend a sum of money may actually cost you less than the value of the entire sum, since it may reduce your tax bill; conversely, a decision which will add to your income may be worth less than its face value because it increases the tax you must pay. You may even gain more by saving money you have already earned than by earning more money; for example, saving $100 in fuel bills by turning down the heat while you are away from home results in a nontaxable benefit to you of $100, while adding an extra $100 to your income increases the amount of income tax you must pay. Tax considerations make the motto "A penny saved is a penny earned" an understatement!

Implicit in these five rules for converting costs and benefits into comparable dollars is an important, counterintuitive principle: the past is irrelevant; past costs are "sunk costs" to be ignored. Money already overbet on a poor poker hand is irrelevant in a shrewd choice about dropping out of the game. Decisions about entering a new field of study are not to be based on the amount of time and money already invested in learning other fields, although that may affect the potential future benefits from more education. And even if I have just spent a lot fixing up my old car, an analysis of future benefits and costs may reveal that I should trade it in or junk it. The sunk cost principle is more than a matter of not "throwing good money after bad," however. If I pay an ex-friend $1,000 for a car that I discover is really only worth $200, then it still may be worthwhile to spend money fixing it up if the car's value could be raised above $200 by more than the cost of the repairs.

Now consider the decision to purchase and read this book, and the possible complementary decision to spend the time and tuition required for a class in which to study it. How far can we go in examining the costs and benefits of that decision, using our five principles?

Table 1. Marginal Tax Rates at Different Levels of Taxable Income (1979 Figures)

Taxable Income	Marginal Tax Rate for: Married Persons Filing Jointly	Single Persons
$ 5,000	14%	18%
10,000	18	21
15,000	21	30
20,000	24	34
25,000	32	39
30,000	37	44
40,000	43	49
50,000	49	55
100,000	59	68

The costs are incurred in the present, but the benefits stretch into the future. Since the time of decision is now, it makes sense to convert all the costs and benefits to present values. Suppose the knowledge you gain from studying the book might save you $100 each year for the next fifty years. What is the present value of that benefit? At an interest rate of 3 percent, it is now worth not $5,000, but $2,573. In fact, any fifty-year stream of costs or benefits has a present value of about half its total amount. (See the appendix to chapter 2.) What about inflation? If prices rise, presumably you could expect to save more than $100 each year, but in that case the market interest rate will also tend to be higher by approximately the rate of inflation. A 10 percent inflation rate means a 13 percent interest rate, so the low 3 percent rate remains valid in today's dollar values. A lot of confusion and difficulty can be avoided by using the 3 percent "real" rate and not attempting to forecast the rate of inflation.

Our second principle converts the time you might spend studying this book into a money cost, using the pervasive principle that the value of anything is the cost of its alternative opportunity. What else could you do with this time? Could you be working and earning money? Would you insist on premium pay for overtime, because you value your leisure? In that case, perhaps the cost of studying this book should be evaluated at 150 percent of your hourly wage rate! On the other hand, if you have little else to do, you may feel the time invested costs you little or nothing. However, unless the value you place on your time is very low, *the major cost of reading this book is the value of the time spent reading it*. If you value your time at $3.00 per hour and spend 100 hours reading the book, then the time cost of reading it is $300.

Our third principle, converting noncash items to dollars by imputation, has already been demonstrated in estimating the value of the time you might invest in learning.

The fourth principle is that uncertain benefits can be converted to an expected value by multiplying by the probability that they will be realized. Going back to our $100 per year for fifty years, you might feel that you have only a fifty-fifty chance of making these money-saving decisions, so you should cut that $2,573 estimate of the present value of benefits in half. The logic behind using probabilities is that if one chose that alternative many times, the average result would be the benefit times the probability. People object that they are making the choice only once, and they also sometimes distort the probabilities in biased ways, but the principle remains valid.

Fifth, and last, what part do taxes play in these calculations? If better consumer decisions save you money, there is no income tax on that saving, as there would be on an earned amount. Since most decisions have dollar effects that are small relative to your income, you can estimate federal income tax effects by using the marginal tax rate—the fraction of one additional dollar of income that would be taken or, in this case, saved in taxes. Table 1 gives some illustrative rates for single and joint (husband-wife) returns at different taxable incomes; the rate varies from about 14 percent to 70 percent. The marginal income tax rate you face is a crucial number. If it is 30 percent, then each dollar of tax-free income is worth a full dollar rather than the seventy cents you would receive after taxes, or 43 percent (100/70) more than the taxable dollar. If your marginal tax rate is 50 percent, tax-free dollars are worth twice as much, and if your rate gets to 70 percent, they are worth two-and-a-third times as much! In general, dollars of tax-free income are worth $x/(1-x)$ percent more, where x is the marginal tax rate.

In summary, if you convert a future benefit to present value, reduce it because it is uncertain, increase it because it is a tax-free benefit, and subtract the cost of the book, the tuition, and the value of your time, you might have an estimate of the net benefits of learning some elementary economics. The final question is whether some other way of spending that time and money promises a higher net benefit.

Even if you do not go through such calculations, some

obvious rules of thumb derive from these general methods of comparing close alternatives and translating everything to present values. Anything with costs now and benefits in the distant future must provide a lot of benefits to cover the interest on the investment. Benefits that are not taxable, or (if you itemize deductions) costs that are deductible from taxable income, are better than taxable benefits or nondeductible costs.

There are a few other shortcuts. Decisions made by friends with similar tastes and incomes are clues as to what their information-getting and decision making led to, and this is useful information. This is a good way of guessing what you would find if you went through the same process. If a mechanically alert friend has just bought a particular brand of appliance and is satisfied with it, this may be all the information you need. On the other hand, people who spend other people's money—for instance, on expense accounts—may not make choices that you would want to make using your own money. You might also want to avoid situations where most people are making careless decisions because of time or social pressure, or because information is hard to get.

Social Considerations

Aside from taxes, there are other important public issues with implications for consumers. Some of these issues are discussed late in some of the following chapters and late in the book. Understanding the economics involved is much easier if one theoretical principle is applied, namely, that most social policies are attempts to improve either the efficiency or the fairness of the system. Efficiency refers to the optimal use of societal resources—producing the most desired results with the least resources. Fairness refers to the distribution of the consumable benefits of the system, usually the distribution of income, although the distribution of leisure, and of nonmoney benefits of other kinds, is also involved. There is a paradox because one cannot define either fairness or efficiency without including the other, as we shall see later. But it is still extremely useful to interpret actual or proposed laws or policies separately for their effects on the distribution of income and well-being, and for their effects on the optimal and efficient use of resources. Low-interest loans to college students from low- and middle-income families, for example, attempt to ensure that society keeps its supply of skilled workers (efficiency) while increasing their total income (fairness).

A Note on Jargon

We shall try to minimize the use of jargon and technical terms, and to define them when we do use them. But, in the immortal words of Humpty Dumpty in *Through the Looking Glass*, "When I use a word, . . . it means just what I choose it to mean—neither more nor less." Words like *income, depreciation, capital*, and *interest* may sound like things we all understand, but they have precise meanings in economics. Testing whether someone knows principles is commonly done by asking what technical terms mean and why they are important. There is a glossary of terms at the back of this book.

An Encouraging Word

The economic thinking explained in this book actually simplifies decision making in a number of ways. At any one time, consumers need to consider only a few competing choices. Translations of costs and benefits into dollars use only our five simple conversion principles, which in turn use a principle that the cost of anything is often indicated by the foregone benefit of using its next-best alternative. These principles will serve you well even through changes in personal preferences, laws, and institutions.

More Information?

The elemental economic insights essential to thinking about one's affairs are not well spelled out in most economics texts or in books on consumer economics or personal finance. The bibliography which follows includes some of the best examples of consumer economics books, and range from sprightly (Maynes) to scholastic (Cohen) to value laden (Troelstrup). Economics texts are not listed, but any recent, popular one will have sections on capital and interest, risk and insurance, and prices and resource allocation. The best book for general background reading on consumer behavior is probably George Katona's capstone summary, *Psychological Economics*. Books on the current situation for consumers are revised frequently, and new authors appear, so check references like *Books in Print* for titles starting with phrases like *Consumer Economics, Personal Finance, Household . . . , Money Management*, or *How to . . . .*

Allentuck, Andrew J., and Bivens, Gordon. *Consumer Choice: The Economics of Personal Living*. New York: Harcourt Brace Jovanovich, 1977.
Bailard, Thomas E.; Biehl, David L.; and Kaiser, Ronald W. *Personal Money Management*. 2d ed. Palo Alto, Calif.: Science Research Associates, 1977.
Behr, Michael R., and Nelson, Dennis L. *Economics: A Personal Consumer Approach*. Reston, Va.: Reston Publishing Company, 1975.
Caroom, Hiram C. *Managing Consumer Dollars*. Encino, Calif.: Glencoe Publishing, 1979.
Cohen, Jerome B. *Personal Finances: Principles and Case Problems*. 5th ed. Homewood, Ill.: Richard D. Irwin, 1975.
Dorries, W. L.; Smith, Arthur A.; and Young, James R. *Personal Finance: Consuming, Saving, and Investing*. Columbus, Ohio: Charles E. Merrill, 1974.
George, Richard. *The New Consumer Survival Kit*. Boston: Little, Brown, 1978. (Television script for Maryland Center for Public Broadcasting)
Hastings, Paul, and Mietus, Norbert. *Personal Finance*. 2d ed. New York: McGraw-Hill, 1977.
Katona, George. *Psychological Economics*. New York: Elsevier Press, 1975.
Lang, Larry R., and Gillespie, Thomas H. *Strategy for Personal Finance*. New York: McGraw-Hill, 1977.
Maynes, E. Scott. *Decision-Making for Consumers*. New York: Macmillan, 1976.
McGowan, Daniel A. *Consumer Economics*. Chicago: Rand McNally, 1978.
Miller, Roger LeRoy. *Personal Finance Today*. St. Paul, Minn.: West Publishing, 1979.
Phillips, E. Bryant, and Lane, Sylvia. *Personal Finance*. 3d ed. New York: John Wiley and Sons, 1974.
Porter, Sylvia. *Sylvia Porter's Money Book*. Garden City, N.Y.: Doubleday, Avon, 1976.
Rosefsky, Robert S., and Ivener, Martin H. *Personal Finance and Money Management*. New York: John Wiley and Sons, 1978.
Troelstrup, Arch, and Hall, E. Carl. *The Consumer in American Society: Personal and Family Finance*. 6th ed. New York: McGraw-Hill, 1978.
West, David A., and Wood, Glenn L. *Personal Financial Management*. Boston: Houghton Mifflin, 1972.
Wolf, Harold A. *Personal Economics and Consumerism*. 5th ed. Boston: Allyn and Bacon, 1978.

Some Projects to Learn More

1. Secure from the library a collection of books on personal finance, economics of the household, consumer economics, and similar titles, ranging back as far in history as you can. Has the quantity of value-laden advice diminished? Is there useful information that has disappeared from them?
2. Look at the title index of *Books in Print* and the *Reader's Guide to Current Periodicals* for "How to . . ." titles and other indicators of consumer information, e.g., nutrition, budgeting, insurance, buying a . . . , and so on. Examine a sample group of titles on one such subject and see whether they agree and whether they tell you anything new and useful.

CHAPTER TWO
INVESTMENT IN YOURSELF

A character in Greek mythology named Procrustes chopped or stretched his visitors to make them fit his bed. In a similar if less dramatic pursuit of logic and order, the discussion of economic choices in this book will follow the sequence in which they are made in most people's lives. The first important economic decisions most people make are about how much and what kind of education to get. Parents, society, and friends put on pressure and bribe with subsidies, but since people are not slaves and cannot be forced to learn, the final decision is up to the individual, at least from age sixteen on. Time and money are invested in improving personal skills throughout life, of course, but the early choices are the most crucial, since they provide beginnings and open up various opportunities for later learning. This chapter will discuss investing in the acquisition of skills and knowledge, either to increase earning power directly, or to improve the capacity to enjoy what is earned.

Capital Theory

Education is partly an investment activity because it involves spending time and money now for some kind of future return we expect over a period of years. The theory of capital is involved because capital is the machinery (in this case, the skills) that results from investment and provides such future benefits as higher income in return. Houses and cars are "physical" capital, and they are easier to analyze than the "human capital" of this chapter. With human capital it is more difficult to quantify all benefits and costs, and there are more noneconomic considerations as well.

Investment in yourself means using time and spending money not for current consumption but to acquire skills and credentials that will provide future benefits. It is analogous to a household buying or building a piece of physical capital like a house that provides housing while it gradually depreciates or becomes obsolete. With learning, the benefits may be in future earning power, but they can also appear in enhanced aesthetic skills. If learning increases your ability to appreciate good music, the payoff is enhanced enjoyment every time you hear music in the future. Some human capital never seems to wear out or get obsolete the way physical capital does; it provides benefits over a lifetime.

The main self-investment decision involves formal education, which will be discussed in some detail, but the same principles apply to on-the-job training, learning through experience, and even to the costs of searching—trying out various fields of learning, types of jobs, and geographic locations in order to improve the final choice of job, location, or even hobby.

The basic economic problem is how to compare investment costs incurred now with benefits scattered into the distant future. It is compounded because the future is also uncertain (including the length of one's life). Surely a distant uncertain benefit is not as good as a current and certain one. In addition, the availability of several alternative future possibilities may hinge upon a decision to invest now in more education. We shall want to take account of the options without double-counting.

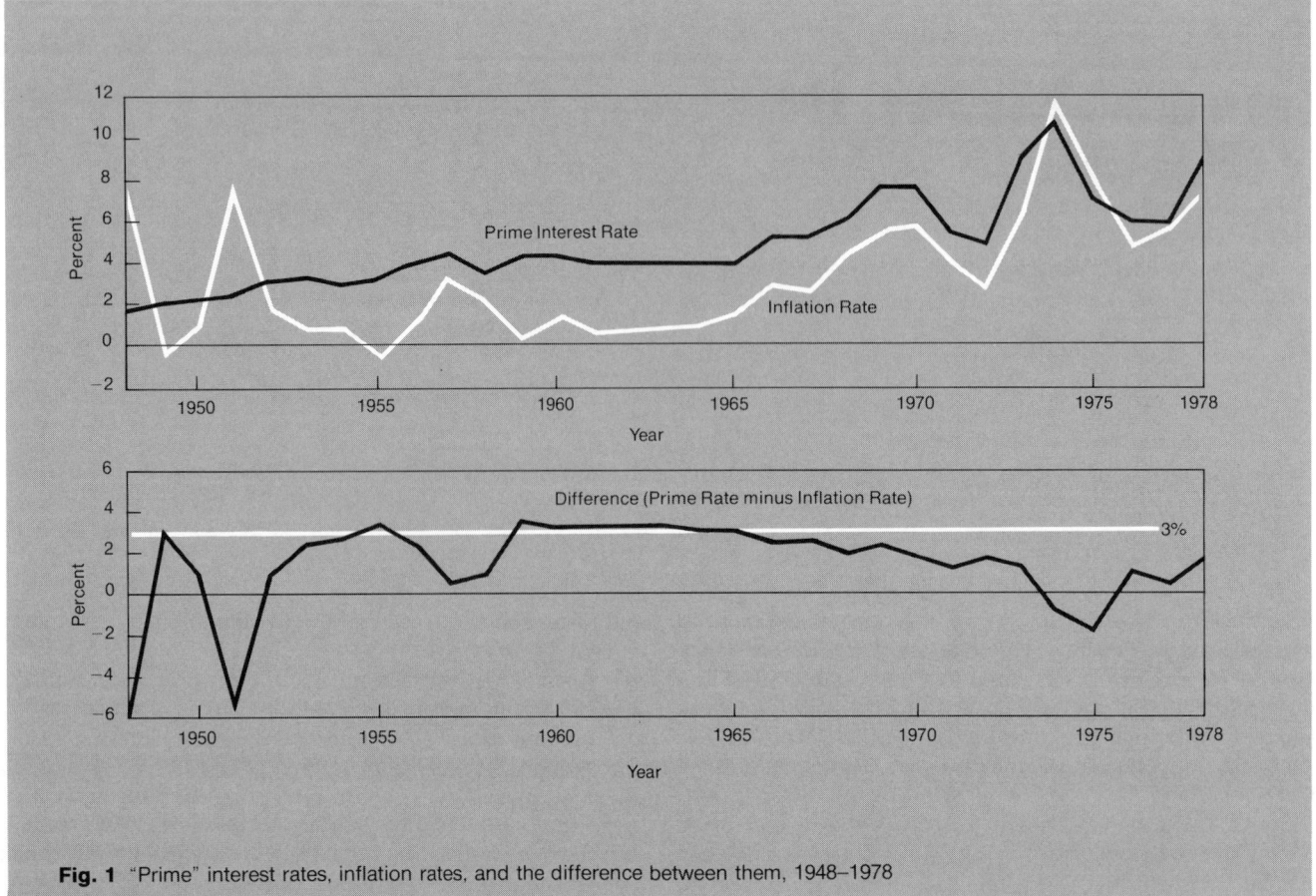

Fig. 1 "Prime" interest rates, inflation rates, and the difference between them, 1948–1978

Present Values

Since investment decisions must be made now, the sensible thing to do is to convert all costs and benefits into their equivalent present values. A dollar ten years from now is worth less than a dollar in hand now, for two reasons. First, by waiting ten years to receive it, I forego the interest I could otherwise earn for ten years if I obtained the dollar now and invested it. Second, if prices continue to rise as they always seem to, then a dollar will not buy as much in ten years as it will now. There is a way to simplify these calculations by taking account of both interest and inflation, relying on a historic tendency for market interest rates to average about 3 percent more than the rate of price inflation. (See fig. 1 for the recent time path of the "prime" interest rate charged by banks to their best corporate customers, the inflation rate, and the difference between these two rates.) The 3 percent rate also represents the fact that complex, roundabout methods of production that require tying up funds (in capital or inventory) increase output sufficiently to pay 3 percent per year on the funds. Hence, anyone who lends resources to others can expect a 3 percent return in real terms (today's prices). If the market pays more, inflation tends to wipe it out. To see this, suppose that the market interest rate is 5 percent and the rate of inflation is 2 percent. This means that lenders are increasing their real (inflation-adjusted) wealth by 3 percent per year. If the inflation rate should rise unexpectedly to 6 percent, then the real rate of interest falls to 5 percent minus 6 percent, or −1 percent. Since borrowers can use "cheaper" inflated dollars to more than pay back their loans, the demand for loans will increase. Since lenders are better off keeping their money to themselves, the supply of loans will decrease. Both of these actions will drive up the nominal interest rate, and this will continue until the inflation-adjusted interest rate rises from −1 percent to 3 percent. With an inflation rate of 6 percent, this process will drive the nominal interest rates up to about 9 percent. (It is not always possible to obtain the free market rate of interest on savings in an inflationary economy, because the interest rates paid on savings accounts in banks or in savings and loan associations are artificially held down by law and lack of competition. You will also pay more than the "market rate" when you borrow because of risk and the costs to the lender of making and collecting small loans.)

All of this means that future benefits measured in future (inflated) dollars should be converted to present values at a market interest rate. However, dollars measured in real terms—or measured in today's prices, as payoffs in earnings usually are—should be discounted at 3 percent, which is all one could earn net of inflation if the funds were kept and put into financial investments instead of being used for investment in education. This also means, as we shall see later, that in working out programs of saving for retirement or future needs, we assume we can earn only 3 percent because any higher interest rates reflect, and are wiped out by, inflation. To do that, of course, requires trying to earn free competitive market interest rates, even if the government allows banks to refuse to pay that much.

In thinking about the present value of an amount of money D, which is available n years in the future at an interest rate r, it is useful to ask the question: What amount of money today will give me D dollars in n years? If $D = \$1,000$ and $n = 1$, then I need an amount y, which, when added to the interest it will earn (r times y), will sum to \$1,000. In other words, $y + ry = \$1,000$. Rewriting, $y(1 + r) = \$1,000$, or $y = \$1,000/(1 + r)$. If $r = 3$ percent, then $y = \$971$. If the amount is available two years from now, then the amount y will earn r times y in interest in the first year but will earn more than r times y in the second year. This is because the amount that will earn interest during the second year is not just y, but $y + ry$. The "future value" of y in two years is thus $y + ry + r(y + ry) = D$. With some algebraic manipulation, it can be shown that this is equivalent to $D = y \times (1 + r)^2$. Thus the present value (y) of \$1 available two years from now is $\$1/(1 + r)^2$, and the present value of an amount, D, which is available two years from now, is $D/(1 + r)^2$.

Similarly, it can be shown that if $n = 3$, then the present value is $D/(1 + r)^3$, and, in general, the present value of D which is available n years in the future at an interest rate of r is $D/(1 + r)^n$. If the amounts D are available each year for a number of years, $D_0, D_1, D_2, \ldots D_n$, where the subscript indicates the year in which it is available, then the present value of that stream of amounts is $D_0 + D_1/(1 + r) + D_2/(1 + r)^2 + \ldots + D_n/(1 + r)^n$.[1]

To evaluate the profitability of an investment with costs as well as benefits extending into the future, it is necessary to calculate the present value of the *net* benefits, which are calculated by subtracting costs from benefits in each time period. An investment which costs \$1,000 now and pays \$600 next year and the year after will have a stream of net benefits as follows:

	Now	1 Year from Now	2 Years from Now
Benefit	$ 0	$600	$600
Cost	1,000	0	0
Net Benefit	−$1,000	$600	$600

The present value of this stream of net benefits is $-1,000 + 600/(1 + r) + 600/(1 + r)^2$. If $r = 3$ percent, then this equals $-1,000 + 583 + 566 = \$149$. That the present value is positive indicates that the investment is more profitable than investing your money elsewhere at a 3 percent interest rate. This procedure generalizes to any stream of cost and benefits.

Compound interest tables for amounts available at a single future time and amounts available every year for a number of years are given in appendix 2.1, with explanations and examples.

An alternative way of evaluating the profitability of an investment is to calculate the interest rate that causes the present value to equal zero. This interest rate is called the *internal rate of return*. In the example of the \$1,000 investment which pays \$600 in years one and two, the internal rate of return is the interest rate, r, such that $-1,000 + 600/(1 + r) + 600/(1 + r)^2 = 0$. In this case, $r = 13.07$ percent.[2] If this stream of costs and benefits is evaluated at an interest rate that is higher than 13.07, then the present value will be found to be negative. If the

---

1. Converting a future value to a present one is called "discounting," from the old banking practice of lending, say, \$94 and asking for \$100 back a year later. The interest rate implied by this is 6/94 = 6.4 percent.
2. It takes a special hand calculator or computer, or successive approximations, to estimate internal rates of return in complex cases.

rate used is lower than 13.07, then the present value is positive. Investments can be ranked according to their internal rates of return or present values. In this case, an alternative investment project would have to pay a return of more than 13 percent to be more attractive. This is useful in comparing investments of different sizes where the present values at a fixed interest rate would not be comparable, but the internal rates of return are.

We can use these principles to evaluate the profitability of a college education. As a first approximation, the costs of college to an individual can be taken to include the direct costs of tuition and, more important, the indirect costs of the earnings foregone by attending college rather than working full time. Scholarship money and part-time work will reduce these costs. The benefits of college can be taken as the difference between the earnings of college graduates and those of high school graduates during their working lives. Studies which have performed these calculations (Freeman) show that the internal rate of return to college education was between 10 percent and 12 percent during the 1960s and early 1970s, but fell to 8.5 percent in 1974. This simple calculation, however, ignores uncertainty about finishing college, the value of the option of being able to continue on to graduate work, numerous nonmoney benefits of a college education, and the possibility that the increased earnings of college graduates may be due to other factors such as motivation or ability.

Alternative Futures and Uncertainty Corrections

The decision to go to college should be based on the costs and benefits of college relative to the best alternative way of spending that time. The appropriate alternative for most people is to go to work right out of high school, so the base of comparison is the present value of an expected lifetime of earnings as a high school graduate. What can I expect from going to college? Clearly, it depends on whether I finish, and, if so, whether I go on to graduate work, and, if so, whether I finish an advanced degree.

In order to calculate some combined value for these uncertain alternative outcomes, we use our principle that the value of an uncertain gain is its amount times the probability that it will be realized. These products, which are called "expected values," can be calculated for each educational outcome and then added together. As long as the outcomes are mutually exclusive (I cannot both fail to finish college *and* go to graduate school), the products will sum to the proper expected value.

All this will be clearer with an example, even though the probabilities of future outcomes and the expected future earnings connected with each in this example are purely hypothetical. The earnings figures in table 2 are roughly reasonable, but rounded. Since they are not adjusted for future inflation, a 3 percent discount factor is used to get present values.

Columns 1–5 of table 2 are expected annual earnings at different ages, or age spans, depending on amount of education. Assume that there is a 20 percent chance that I will drop out of college after two years if I start, a 60 percent chance of finishing college and going to work, a 10 percent chance of starting but not finishing graduate work, and a 10 percent chance of getting a graduate degree. (The last two possible outcomes, with the expected earnings patterns given in columns 4 and 5 of the table, represent the basis for the "option value" of a college degree. They are also part of the "option value" of finishing high school.)

Let us begin by asking whether it is worth starting college. If I start college, each of the four possible outcomes has a value, and I can calculate the "expected value" of my earnings in each future year as the sum of four expected values. For example, if I start college, the expected value of my earnings at age twenty-three will be $8,300, which is the sum of 0.20 times the $8,000 I would be making by then if I had dropped out of college and gone to work, 0.60 times my $10,000 earnings if I finished college and went to work, 0.10 times the starting $9,000 if I had just dropped out of graduate school, plus 0.10 times the −$2,000 tuition if I were still in graduate school finishing up.

Column 1 represents expected earnings in each future year or span of five years if I do not start college, and column 6, the expected earnings if I do start. Values for the single years can be converted to present values by the single multipliers of column 7, which are from appendix 2.1 tables. Those for five-year periods can be converted to

Table 2. Hypothetical Future Earnings Converted to Expected Values and Then to Present Values

	Expected Earnings from Alternative Courses of Conduct						
Age	Go to Work After High School (1)	Drop Out of College [.20][a] (2)	Finish College and Go to Work [.60] (3)	Start Graduate Work but Drop Out [.10] (4)	Get Advanced Degree [.10] (5)	Sum of Expected Values, Cols. 2–5 (6)	Factor Used to Convert to Present Values[b] (7)
17	$ 5,000	$ −2,000	$ −2,000	$ −2,000	$ −2,000	$ −2,000	.971
18	5,000	−2,000	−2,000	−2,000	−2,000	−2,000	.943
19	6,000	5,000	−2,000	−2,000	−2,000	− 600	.915
20	6,000	6,000	−2,000	−2,000	−2,000	− 400	.888
21	7,000	7,000	8,000	−2,000	−2,000	5,800	.863
22	7,000	7,500	9,000	−2,000	−2,000	6,500	.837
23	8,000	8,000	10,000	9,000	−2,000	8,300[c]	.813
24	8,000	8,500	11,000	10,000	−1,000[d]	9,200	.789
25–29	8,500	9,000	12,000	12,000	14,000	11,600	2.508 = 4.58 × .700
30–34	9,000	9,500	15,000	14,000	20,000	14,300	3.023 = 4.58 × .661
35–39	9,500	10,000	20,000	20,000	25,000	18,500	2.611 = 4.58 × .570
40–44	10,000	11,000	25,000	27,000	30,000	22,900	2.253 = 4.58 × .492
45–49	10,000	11,000	30,000	33,000	35,000	27,000	1.942 = 4.58 × .424
50–54	10,000	12,000	33,000	37,000	40,000	29,900	1.649 = 4.58 × .360
55–59	10,000	12,000	35,000	39,000	45,000	31,800	1.447 = 4.58 × .316
60–64	10,000	21,000	35,000	39,000	45,000	31,800	1.250 = 4.58 × .273
65–69	0	0	35,000	39,000	45,000	29,400	1.076 = 4.58 × .235
Undiscounted Sum (thousands)	$ 437	$ 471	$ 1,090	$ 1,157	$ 1,300	$ 1,111	
Present Expected Value (thousands)	$ 212[e]	$ 194	$ 465	$ 474	$ 533	$ 420[f]	

[a] Bracketed numbers are hypothetical probability factors which are applied to each alternative. Thus, it is assumed that if I start college, there is a 20 percent chance of dropping out after two years, a 60 percent chance of finishing college and going to work, etc.
[b] Single years require only application of table 4, found in appendix 2.1. Five-year segments are converted to value at beginning of five years at 3 percent (4.58 not 5.0) then converted from then to present values.
[c] By way of example, this figure represents .20($8,000) + .60($10,000) + .10($9,000) + .10(−$2,000), which is what starting college would lead to on the average.
[d] This figure is −$1,000 rather than −$2,000 on the assumption that some people get their degrees prior to age 24.
[e] Sum of products of items in column 1 and column 7, i.e., $5,000 × .971 + $5,000 × .943 + ... + $10,000 × 1.25.
[f] Sum of products of items in column 6 and column 7, i.e., −$2,000 × .971 + ... + $29,400 × 1.076.

present values by first getting the initial value of each five-year set (by multiplying by 4.58), then getting its value now by continuing the process of discounting to the present. (The 4.58 means that if I had $4.58 to put in a savings account at 3 percent interest, I could withdraw $1 a year for five years.) The results, summed over the whole future, come to $420,000, not the $1,111,000 undiscounted sum. This is larger than the high-school-only present value of $212,000—larger by $208,000, which represents the value of *starting* college, if one believes our hypothesized probabilities of outcomes and their expected results in future earnings.

Popular discussions of the value of education often use undiscounted numbers. They look at the difference between $437,000 and $1,111,000 and infer that starting college is worth $674,000 more in lifetime earnings. They also usually take note only of the column 3 situation, ignoring the possibility of dropping out and the option resulting from a college degree of going on to further study. But most deceptive is their ignoring the fact that the increased earnings are far into the future and thus should be converted to present dollars.

There is no need for any additional adjustments for interest earned on savings made possible by starting to work and earn earlier (getting less education). That is already accounted for by taking present values, and so are the earnings foregone while in college. But if I must borrow money at market interest rates to go to college, the extra interest (beyond 3 percent) should be included like tuition costs.

The value of starting graduate work could be calculated in a similar way, combining the expected values for finishing and not finishing graduate work, and then comparing the discounted present value of that with the present value of my expected earnings as a college graduate, i.e., $465,000.

One of the advantages of finishing high school, in addition to the increased expected earnings, would be the value of all the various college options. In this case, however, we would multiply the expected earnings in column 1 by the probability of not going on, and the expected earnings in columns 2–5 by the (lower) probabilities of each outcome. If there were a fifty-fifty chance of starting college, then I should take half of column 1, 0.10 of column 2, 0.30 of column 3, 0.05 of column 4, and 0.05 of column 5 (or more simply, 0.50 of column 1 plus 0.50 of column 6) and compare the present value sum of that with the present value of what I could expect to earn as a high school dropout.

All this has ignored the credibility of the estimated gain in future earnings, as well as all other economic and noneconomic considerations. We turn first to credibility—the evidence on payoff in pure earnings.

Factual Evidence on the Payoff

Estimating a payoff to education in terms of future earnings requires forecasting the future, on which we have no data. What we do have is earnings of people of different ages and educations (see, for example, Cooper and Brody), and even some earnings histories of people with different amounts of education. The latter are scarce, and are difficult to use because of the vast changes in overall earnings levels that result from inflation and rising overall productivity. But we can use current age-earnings profiles for those with different amounts of education now to produce hypothetical lifetime earnings, if we can assume that the same patterns will persist. Indeed, such data are better for examining potential differences by education than for predicting lifetime actual earnings, since a combination of inflation and increased real income per person tends to raise everyone's earnings historically in a way not reflected in one-time, cross-section earnings data. As mentioned before, Freeman used this approach and estimated that the rate of return to a college education in 1974 was about 8.5 percent.

There are two reasons to think that these data exaggerate the payoff to education:

1. It may be that those who go to college are brighter, more motivated, more ambitious, and have richer parents who can help them or bright parents who have taught them. Indeed, the more efficient the college process of selecting promising students for admission, the more likely it is that their higher later earnings reflected their own individual promise rather than their investment of years of learning to increase their "human capital."

2. The available data reflect earnings of people who got their education some time ago, and entered the labor market at periods of history with less or more unemployment. With the vast increase in the numbers and proportions of people going to college and graduate school, perhaps the increased supply will drive down the price of college graduates. The recent historical experience, when the demand for highly trained people increased faster than the supply, may not continue. Or the demand may be for some kinds of training, not others. Surely the demand for teachers has been reduced by the bust that followed the "baby boom." Will we also have a continued shortage of highly paid craftsmen and some unemployed college graduates?

What these criticisms mean is that many things other than investment in human capital and skills could account for differences in earnings between those with different amounts of formal education. Complex statistical procedures can reduce the advantages erroneously attributed to education but can never eliminate them entirely.

There is some evidence, even after adjustments, that those who go to elite colleges earn more in later life than those who go to others with lesser reputations, but the same self-selection bias or spurious correlation remains possible. The advantages also seem to be associated more with the higher average test scores of students in the elite colleges than with the reputations of the colleges or their relative cost (Duncan and Morgan). Perhaps fellow students set the standards, or we learn mainly from them, or they help us to make better "contacts" later?

It is likely, of course, that there is actually some acquisition of skills or knowledge in college that pays off in later earning power. We just do not know how it happens, nor how much the statistics exaggerate it. We do know that well-educated people are more likely to plan ahead and to do more things for themselves, even things that save money.

The exercise of estimating benefits makes it clear, even in the limited economic payoff considerations, that the less certainty there is about future payoffs and the further they are into the future, the smaller their present value. And the shorter the stream of future benefits, the smaller its present value. For a person fifty years old, investment in training for a new career can produce benefits for only fifteen years or so, while investing in learning to paint or enjoy music might produce benefits (not in money but just as real) that might go on for twenty-five years or more.

All of this may seem like a lot of calculation focused only on the economic results, but it is useful, even with rough approximate calculations, as a base to which other important considerations can be added. These include the possibility that college attendance may result in increased capacity to enjoy life, provide prestige and interesting friends, allow more time to decide among career options, provide exposure to a wide assortment of potential living partners, reduce the likelihood of unemployment, and increase capacity for informed voting and participation in civic affairs. Of course, college might also be boring and require suffering through examinations!

On-the-Job Training

The acquisition of job-related skills is not restricted to the classroom. Indeed, many economists suspect that the skill investments made on the job are more important in dollar terms than investments in formal education. The costs and benefits of on-the-job training are not so obvious as those of formal education, but the principles are the same. Jobs available to someone with a given level of education vary with respect to the wages paid and the opportunities for future promotion. Some jobs pay well initially but do not provide the possibilities for advancement that other jobs do. Frequently, the jobs with the greatest possibilities for advancement will pay less initially than those without, and the wage difference can be thought of as the cost of taking the job with the greater potential for promotion. The higher future wages, of course, are the benefits. The profitability of an investment in on-the-job training can be calculated with these costs and benefits just like the investment in formal education.

The implications of these investments in on-the-job training on occupational choice should be obvious. Careful consideration ought to be given to the choice between occupations which appear attractive at first but offer little chance of advancement and those which pay less now but promise more in the future. Those who do not expect to remain in a given occupation or who do not expect to be in the labor force continuously may find the on-the-job investments unprofitable.

Other Investments

There are ways of investing in the acquisition of skills and knowledge other than formal education or on-the-job training, such as adult education and learning by doing. Even changing jobs, or moving to a new area, is a kind of investment in changing the environment in which skills are marketed. In each case, the same analysis is feasible—a stream of future benefits and costs, or of net earnings, can be converted to a present value for each alternative, and then converted to a present expected value by discounting for uncertainty.[3] If there is a fifty-fifty chance of never using a particular skill, then we should take half the present value of the stream of benefits that would result from using it, and compare that with the cost in time and tuition of the lessons.

A great many decisions about investing in yourself, in learning skills, or securing the right to something, or changing jobs or job locations, involve only a single de-

---

3. Some people, including businessmen, suggest using a higher than normal interest rate to discount to the present. They sometimes do this implicitly by insisting that an investment "pay for itself" in five years or ten years, which is the equivalent of a very high combination interest and risk-adjustment rate. This can lead to confusion by mixing up uncertainty adjustments and interest adjustments. A more straightforward method is to make the two adjustments separately, as we did in our example, or to calculate present values and then to multiply by a probability of the particular future events actually happening.

sired outcome; the main problem, then, is estimating the extent of the benefit and how many years it will last. Learning to play football might, with a low probability, provide a large stream of earnings as a professional, but for relatively few years. Learning how to use a library, or to whittle, might produce a smaller but surer and longer-lasting stream of benefits. Investing in skills is often combined with investment in related equipment—skis, a sewing machine, tools—so that in addition to the present cost there may be some future costs for maintenance and supplies.

Private and Social Considerations in Education and Similar Investments

You have no doubt noticed that some of the benefits of education accrue to the individual, and some to society in general. Even more dramatically, some of the costs are borne by others—parents, government, private philanthropy. What does this do to the private or social appropriateness of an individual's decision about how much education to get? Here the distinction between private costs and benefits versus social costs and benefits becomes important. Up to this point, our discussion of costs (tuition, foregone earnings) and benefits (increased after-tax earnings) have taken the individual's point of view. Since tuition does not cover the complete resource costs of a college education, society incurs a large part of the cost of each individual's education. But society is increasing its output (gross national product) with its investment in college education, since an educated worker is likely to be more productive than an uneducated one. If this increased output shows up as higher wages to the individual, then the benefits of college for society ought to be based on the (pretax) earning advantages accruing to college graduates. Recent estimates of the social rate of return to an investment in college based on these social costs and benefits are slightly smaller than the private return—7.5 percent versus 8.5 percent in 1974 (see Freeman).[4]

[4]. If the higher earnings of college graduates reflect "credentialism"—access to better jobs regardless of skills, or help from college classmates—then there may be no social benefit of the education to match the private benefit.

Society has never left it up to its young people to decide how much education to get, and certainly has not expected them to pay for it. Parents have always subsidized much of the cost, governments and private philanthropy most of the rest. The reason is obvious: young people do not have the resources to pay for their own education, or even to maintain themselves without a job while they get it; nor can they easily borrow to do it. Short of selling themselves into slavery to pay it back, students can provide no real security for an educational loan, and for that reason are not attractive risks. The graduate can always escape payment by not working, and even if there are earnings, legally attaching, or garnisheeing, wages is a most impractical way of collecting a debt, for reasons we shall see later (chap. 6). What loans there are for higher education come mostly from the government.

The government might, of course, pay for the education and reimburse itself through differential income taxes later, based on how much education each taxpayer had received. It is often argued that with the progressive income tax something similar happens now, since those with more education earn more and pay a larger fraction of it in taxes. Nevertheless, it remains true that most of the benefits, particularly for higher education, go to the individual, while the costs are borne both by others and by individuals through foregone earnings.

The benefits also go in part to people other than the educated individual. Parents presumably receive some kind of psychic benefit, and in rare cases some later economic reimbursement. Presumably philanthropists, including contributing alumni, also get some psychic satisfaction out of helping others get educated. As we saw earlier, society as a whole benefits from the higher productivity of better-trained individuals, and from their greater capacity to vote in an informed way and to take an active part in civic affairs.

These differences between the private and social benefits and costs of education raise questions about whether optimal decisions are likely to be made about the amount of education an individual should get, and about whether the distribution of its costs is fair or efficient. There are further complications as well. Well-educated people can earn more per hour, but they may take some of the benefit in the form of more leisure, or less overtime, so that greater productivity does not all go into an increase in national output (unless we counted recreation in that output). Furthermore, while more education means less unemployment for, and hence more production by, the *individual*, it is doubtful that this reduces *total* unemployment. Unemployment is merely pushed off onto the less educated. Society does not benefit from this concentration of unemployment; rather, the educated benefit at the expense of the uneducated.

In summary, there are a number of reasons why I might be likely to invest more, or less, in my own education than would be optimal for society as a whole:

☐ I don't pay for all of it.
☐ I get some benefits at the expense of other people—better jobs, less unemployment.
☐ I take some of the benefits as leisure, not as extra earnings, so more of my benefits escape taxation.
☐ I may not take the long view, may use a heavy discount for uncertainty, not believe in the averages, or not even know the facts.
☐ I may not be able to borrow money to finance the education, or only at a rate higher than 3 percent plus the inflation rate.

The last two considerations have led to suggestions of free or subsidized higher education on the grounds of efficiency—to assure that individuals become as well educated as they should for society's benefit. But the methods of subsidizing education have effects on income distribution (fairness) as well.

In the case of elementary and secondary education, there is a relatively even and widespread burden, which depends on the mix of property taxes, state income and sales taxes, and federal aid, mostly from federal income taxes. The benefits are also quite widespread, even though they seem to be going only to those with children in school, because most people either have had, now have, or will have children in school. If anything, more benefits go to the larger families which would otherwise have the hardest time of it and might not otherwise be able to provide proper education for their children.

Indeed, it can be argued that free public education is one of our society's greatest and most effective income-redistributive mechanisms, particularly over long periods. It even spreads the family's cost over a lifetime of taxes instead of concentrating it during the years when the children are in school. On the other hand, there are characteristics of the property tax, a main source of support for schools, that make society likely to underinvest. Property taxes are believed, often erroneously, to be inequitably assessed. They are often payable in lumps just after summer vacation season and at Christmastime.

Other problems of securing optimal amounts of education in a society arise because of state and local funding of education. An area that provides very little or inferior education may export its problems (uneducated adults) to other areas, while an area that produces well-educated people sees some of its educated youth migrate, at the peak of their human capital value, to other areas. Such migration means a movement of real wealth. Although a migration of well-educated youth (or well-educated refugees from a political regime) may temporarily depress the average earnings in the area they enter and cause them to rise in the area they leave, in the long run the transfer of benefits is to the place they go. That is why some countries feel justified in imposing heavy emigration taxes, particularly on young, well-educated people. An underdeveloped country may also have to decide between the relative benefits to society of 1,000 more college graduates, or 100,000 more people who can read and write. If they want to educate those most likely to benefit from it, they may want to select by ability and to provide not only free education but a subsistence allowance to make up for part of the foregone earnings.

How does a country decide how much to invest in the education of its citizens? Education cannot be sold for what it is worth, like potatoes, since education conveys information and ideas which are not exclusive. I can give away information and still have it. If I try to charge for it, someone else may give it away. The national decision of how much education a country should aim for, by compulsion or subsidy or both, is a difficult one. One clue, of course, is the payoff to the individuals in terms of their earnings;[5] and society benefits from the well-educated people's better capacity to solve problems, their greater propensity to plan ahead, and the greater likelihood of their engaging in community and philanthropic activities.

It is critical to the future of any society that it be willing

---

5. Insofar as the well-educated earn more per year because of less unemployment, someone else suffers. Society as a whole does not benefit, so we should use hourly rather than annual earnings in estimating social benefits. But insofar as those with higher wages take part of the benefit in leisure, annual differentials indicate social benefits better.

to invest in the education and health of each new generation, even though the current taxpayers may seem to reap little or no personal return. It would be all too easy to allow the stock of human capital in society to depreciate by failing to replace it. And the quantity of knowledge that must be passed on from each generation to the next is getting larger and larger.

Summary

It is not really very difficult to apply the logic and principles of the theory of capital to decisions about investing in skills, credentials, knowledge, or options. The longer the stream of benefits, and the greater the certainty that they will actually appear, the more it may be worth investing the money and time now. Such analysis provides a base to which all other considerations can be added, and a method to compare alternative present uses of time and money. The same logic can be applied with fewer measurement problems to decisions about investing in a house, a car, a clothes dryer, or an outboard motor, as we shall see in later chapters.

In the case of education, more than in most other investment decisions, other people are involved in the decisions, because there are social benefits and social costs that differ from those that the individual incurs, and also limits on the individual's capacity to borrow money to invest in education at a reasonable interest rate or even at all. Evaluation of public policies for education requires thinking about the differences in private and public net benefits, about ways of inducing educational investments closer to social optimum, and about the income-redistributive effects of the whole system.

More Information?
The two best-known names in the recent development of economic interest in human beings, and in education and other investments in human capital, are Theodore Schultz and Gary Becker. Extremely sophisticated attempts have been made to estimate the rate of return to such investments; these appear in professional economic journals. New data and analyses, the changing job market, and the fact that spurious correlation can never be avoided, suggest a critical view and a lookout for newer articles and books with such phrases in their titles as "payoff to education," "value of human life," "lifetime earnings." Better data and analysis may change and improve our notions about what education is worth.

Becker, Gary S. *Human Capital, a Theoretical and Empirical Analysis with Special Reference to Education.* 2d ed. New York: Columbia University Press, 1975.
Campbell, Angus, and Eckerman, William. *Public Concepts of the Values and Costs of Higher Education.* Survey Research Center Monographs, no. 37. Ann Arbor: Institute for Social Research, 1964.
Cass, James, and Birnbaum, Max. *Comparative Guide to American Colleges.* New York: Harper and Row, 1975.
Duncan, Greg, and Morgan, James. "College Quality and Earnings." In *Research in Human Capital and Development,* edited by Ismail Sirageldin. Greenwich, Conn.: Jai Press, 1977.
Duncan, Greg, and Morgan, James. "Work Roles and Earnings." In *Five Thousand American Families—Patterns of Economic Progress,* vol. 5, edited by Greg J. Duncan and James N. Morgan. Ann Arbor: Institute for Social Research, 1977.
Freeman, Richard B. *The Market for College-Trained Manpower.* Cambridge, Mass.: Harvard University Press, 1971.
Freeman, Richard B. "Overinvestment in College Training?" *Journal of Human Resources* 10 (Summer 1975): 287–311.
Nam, Charles B., and Cowhig, James D. "Factors Related to College Attendance of Farm and Nonfarm High School Graduates, 1960." In *Farm Population.* U.S. Department of Commerce, Bureau of the Census, ERS (P-27) No. 32. Washington, D.C.: Government Printing Office, 1962.
Schultz, Theodore W. *Investment in Human Capital: The Role of Education and Research.* New York: Free Press, 1971.
Schultz, Theodore W. *Economics of the Family, Marriage, Children, and Human Capital.* Chicago: University of Chicago Press, 1975.
U.S. Department of Health, Education, and Welfare, Social Security Administration, Office of Research and Statistics. *1972 Lifetime Earnings by Age, Sex, Race, and Education Level.* Research and Statistics Note No. 12, by Barbara S. Cooper and Wendyce Brody. Washington, D.C.: U.S. Department of Health, Education, and Welfare, 1976.

Some Projects to Learn More

1. Assemble a collection of books and articles that rate colleges. Do their ratings agree? How highly are they correlated with tuition and other costs; that is, are there any bargains?

2. Try to get information on the expenditure per pupil, school district by school district, in your state. Can you find how much of their funds come from local property taxes, state funds, federal funds? Can you combine the districts in each county and compare the educational expenditures with what you can learn about economic levels of the county from federal census data? Is there much redistribution? Are there more outside funds going to the poorer school districts? Do the data seem to bear out the popular notions about good and poor school districts? Is there anything in the data that would help you decide where to live if you could choose any one of several school districts?

3. If you were in charge of a small country attempting to reduce its "brain drain," how would you assess the costs to be recaptured by repayment from those who wanted to emigrate? How would you decide whether to put more resources into literacy of the whole population as against increasing the cadre of highly trained specialists?

4. Write a proposal for free college education, including a living allowance, for students with adequate academic performance, to be paid for by a surtax on their earnings for the rest of their lives. Using some rough estimates of costs and 3 percent interest, would a 5 percent surtax be enough? What would the aggregate payouts and tax collections look like until the system got in balance?

5. Find some articles on the payoff to education, or education as related to earnings. What interest rate do the authors use? How well do they handle the spurious correlation problem? Do they discuss the future persistence of the same payoffs? Do they discuss option values of the right to go on to still more education?

6. Can you get information from one college on its sources of revenue and the value of its plant and equipment? Can you allocate the costs, including the imputed rent on the plant and equipment, between teaching, research, and athletics and recreation? If you include an estimate of foregone earnings of the students, what fraction of the total costs is covered by students, government support, research income, private philanthropy (alumni, gifts), athletic tickets? Can you find out who really pays the tuition—parents, government, private scholarships?

Appendix 2.1

Consumer Decisions Involving Costs and Benefits at Different Times

No man acquires property without acquiring with it a little arithmetic also.
  Ralph Waldo Emerson

Decisions involving the future require comparing costs and benefits that happen at different times. If one can settle on some reasonable interest rate, the simplest way to compare alternatives is to calculate their "present value." On the other hand, particularly when widely different amounts of money are involved, estimating the internal rate of return on each alternative investment makes it easier to compare them.

The present value of a future stream of benefits is calculated by adding up the "discounted" present value of each future sum. At an interest or discount rate r, the present value of an amount D, n years in the future, is $D/(1 + r)^n$. When the annual cost or benefit is the same for many years, tables can be set up which allow you to calculate the present value of an annual stream without doing it for each year separately. The present value of $100 a year for ten years at 3 percent, for instance, is 8.53 × $100, or $853. In other words, if you put $853 in the bank, you could withdraw $100 a year for ten years; the difference between what you put in and what you withdrew ($147) is interest earned on the remaining balance.

The numbers in tables 3–5, plus a few useful rules of thumb, provide the basis for calculating present values in a variety of situations. The simplest situation is that in which a sum, D, is available in x years. The second column of numbers in table 3 shows how to discount D back to the present. At a 3 percent interest rate, the present value of $10,000 to be received twenty years from now is $10,000 × 0.554 = $5,540. Table 4 gives this same information in greater detail for interest rates of 3, 6, 9, and 12 percent.

The "future value" of an amount can be calculated from the numbers shown in the third column on table 3. For example, in twenty years $1 will grow to $1.806; during the same period, $5,540 will grow to $5,540 × 1.806 = $10,000.

A constant stream of costs or benefits over time can be converted into a present or future value by using the final two columns of numbers in table 3. The present value of $1 per year for twenty years at 3 percent is $14.877; the present value of $10,000 per year for twenty years is $148,770. Since an annuity is nothing more than a stream of annual payments, the fourth column shows, in effect, the cost of an annuity of $1 per year for x years. Table 5 gives a more detailed listing of these conversion numbers and also shows what they are if the interest rate is 6, 9, and 12 percent. The general formula at the bottom of the fourth column in table 3 can also be used to show that the present value of $1 per year forever is simply $1/0.03 = $33.33 or, more generally, the present value of a stream of D dollars per year at an interest rate, r, is D/r. This is helpful in chapter 4 when we convert certain constant costs or benefits of owning a home into an increased house price. A $100 per year lower property tax payment, for example, ought to increase the house price by $100/0.03 = $3,333.

The final column of numbers in table 3 shows the future value of a stream, rather than its present value. Thus, a $100 annual deposit will grow, at a 3 percent interest rate, to $2,687 in twenty years.

Several useful rules of thumb can be generated from the numbers in this table.

Table 3. Now and Then at 3 Percent

X (Years)	Present Value of $1 if Only Available After X Years	Future Value of $1 in X Years if Invested Now	Present Value (Cost of an Annuity) $1/Year for X Years[a]	Value at End of Period of Accumulation Plus Interest (Value of an Annuity) $1/Year for X Years
1	$.971	$1.030	$ .971	$ 1.030
5	.863	1.159	4.580	5.309
10	.744	1.344	8.530	11.464
15	.642	1.558	11.938	18.599
20	.554	1.806	14.877	26.870
25	.478	2.094	17.413	36.459
30	.411	2.427	19.600	47.575
35	.355	2.814	21.487	60.462
40	.307	3.262	23.115	75.401
45	.264	3.782	24.519	92.720
50	.228	4.384	25.730	112.797
n	$\dfrac{1}{(1 + .03)^n}$	$(1 + .03)^n$	$\dfrac{[1 - (1 + .03)^{-n}]}{.03}$	$\dfrac{[(1 + .03)^n - 1]}{.03}$
			$\dfrac{\text{Amount Now}}{\text{Amount Per Year}}$	$\dfrac{\text{Amount Then (at end)}}{\text{Amount Per Year}}$

[a] For a mortgage, this column gives (Amount of Mortgage)/(Yearly Payment).

Table 4. Present Value of $1 in *n* Years at *r* Percent

n	r = 3	r = 6	r = 9	r = 12	n	r = 3	r = 6	r = 9	r = 12
1	$.971	$.943	$.917	$.893	41	$.298	$.092	$.029	$.010
2	.943	.890	.842	.797	42	.289	.087	.027	.009
3	.915	.840	.772	.711	43	.281	.082	.025	.008
4	.888	.792	.708	.636	44	.272	.077	.023	.007
5	.863	.747	.649	.567	45	.264	.073	.021	.006
6	.837	.705	.596	.507	46	.257	.069	.019	.005
7	.813	.665	.547	.452	47	.249	.065	.017	.005
8	.789	.627	.502	.404	48	.242	.061	.018	.004
9	.766	.592	.460	.361	49	.235	.058	.015	.004
10	.744	.558	.422	.322	50	.228	.054	.013	.003
11	.722	.527	.388	.287	51	.221	.051	.012	.003
12	.701	.497	.358	.257	52	.215	.048	.011	.003
13	.681	.469	.326	.229	53	.209	.046	.010	.002
14	.661	.442	.299	.205	54	.203	.043	.010	.002
15	.642	.417	.275	.183	55	.197	.041	.009	.002
16	.623	.394	.252	.163	56	.191	.038	.008	.002
17	.605	.371	.231	.146	57	.185	.036	.007	.002
18	.587	.350	.212	.130	58	.180	.034	.007	.001
19	.570	.331	.194	.118	59	.175	.032	.006	.001
20[a]	.554	.312	.178	.104	60	.170	.030	.006	.001
21	.538	.294	.164	.093	61	.165	.029	.005	.001
22	.522	.278	.150	.083	62	.160	.027	.005	.001
23	.507	.262	.138	.074	63	.155	.025	.004	.001
24	.492	.247	.128	.066	64	.151	.024	.004	.001
25	.478	.233	.118	.059	65	.146	.023	.004	.001
26	.464	.220	.108	.053					
27	.450	.207	.098	.047					
28	.437	.196	.090	.042					
29	.424	.185	.082	.037					
30	.412	.174	.075	.033	70	.126	.017	.002	.000
31	.400	.164	.069	.030					
32	.388	.155	.063	.027					
33	.477	.146	.058	.024					
34	.366	.138	.053	.021					
35	.355	.130	.049	.019	75	.109	.013	.002	.000
36	.345	.123	.045	.017					
37	.335	.116	.041	.015					
38	.325	.109	.038	.013					
39	.316	.103	.035	.012					
40	.307	.097	.032	.011	80	.094	.009	.001	.000

[a] Using this line as an example of how the table works, we see that $1 available 20 years hence is now worth only $.55 if the interest rate is 3 percent or $.31 if the rate is 6 percent. (At 6 percent $.31 now will increase to $1.00 in 20 years.)

First, since the second column of table 3 shows that the present value of $1 in twenty-five years at a 3 percent interest rate is approximately $.50, this means that *any sum available twenty-five years in the future is worth about half that much today.*. Equivalently, *any amount of money will double in value in twenty-five years at a 3 percent interest rate.*

A more general rule of the same kind, at any interest rate, is called the *Rule of 72*. It links the length of time it takes to double your money *(t)* with the interest rate *(r)* by the following simple formula: $r \times t \cong 72$. Thus, an investment scheme that promises to double your money in ten years is really only providing a $72/10 \cong 7$ percent interest rate. A population growth rate of 4 percent per year, on the other hand, will double a nation's population in about $72/4 = 18$ years.

The time it takes for a *stream* of benefits to accumulate to twice its sum through interest added is fifty years: *At 3 percent, any fifty-year stream of costs or benefits has a present value equal to half its total amount* (table 3, col. 4). This means that $100 saved each year for fifty years has a present value of about $2,500. Similarly, *at 3 percent any fifty-year stream has a future value equal to twice its total amount.*

The tables and rules can be applied to a variety of situations, as seen in the following examples.

Example 1.
Assuming that the interest rate is 3 percent, choose the most profitable sum from each of the following pairs:
(1) $1,000 today versus $1,700 fifteen years from now.
(2) $1,000 today versus $100 per year for the next eleven years.
(3) $1,000 for the next five years versus investment opportunity that costs $5,000 today and has a 25 percent chance of paying you $50,000 immediately and a 75 percent chance of paying you nothing.

20 | CHAPTER TWO

Table 5. Present Value of $1 per Year at r Percent Compound Interest per Year for n Years

n	Value at r%				n	Value at r%			
	r = 3	r = 6	r = 9	r = 12		r = 3	r = 6	r = 9	r = 12
1	$ .971	$ .943	$ .917	$ .893	21	$15.415	$11.764	$ 9.292	$7.562
2	1.913	1.853	1.759	1.690	22	15.937	12.042	9.442	7.645
3	2.829	2.673	2.531	2.402	23	16.444	12.303	9.580	7.718
4	3.717	3.465	3.240	3.037	24	16.936	12.550	9.707	7.784
5	4.580	4.212	3.890	3.605	25	17.413	12.783	9.823	7.843
6	5.417	4.917	4.486	4.111	26	17.877	13.003	9.929	7.896
7	6.230	5.582	5.033	4.564	27	18.327	13.210	10.027	7.943
8	7.020	6.210	5.535	4.968	28	18.764	13.406	10.116	7.984
9	7.786	6.802	5.995	5.328	29	19.188	13.591	10.198	8.022
10	8.530	7.360	6.418	5.650	30	19.600	13.765	10.274	8.055
11	9.253	7.887	6.805	5.938	31	20.000	13.929	10.343	8.085
12	9.954	8.383	7.161	6.194	32	20.389	14.084	10.406	8.112
13	10.635	8.853	7.487	6.424	33	20.766	14.230	10.464	8.135
14	11.296	9.295	7.786	6.628	34	21.132	14.368	10.518	8.157
15	11.938	9.712	8.061	6.811	35	21.487	14.498	10.567	8.176
16	12.561	10.106	8.313	6.974					
17	13.166	10.477	8.544	7.120					
18	13.754	10.828	8.756	7.250					
19	14.324	11.158	8.950	7.366					
20[a]	14.877	11.470	9.129	7.469	40	23.115	15.006	10.757	8.344

[a] Using this line as an example of how the table works, we see that $14,877 now will provide $1,000 per year for 20 years if the interest rate is 3 percent.

Answer:
(1) From the second column of table 3, $1 fifteen years from now is worth $.642 today. So $1,700 fifteen years from now is worth $1,091 today, which is preferred to $1,000 today.
(2) Using the information in the second column of table 5, $100 for the next eleven years is worth $100 × 9.253 = $925. Thus, the $1,000 is preferred.
(3) $1,000 for the next five years is worth $1,000 × 4.580 = $4,580 today (table 3). The investment opportunity has an expected benefit of (0.25 × $50,000) + 0.75 × 0 = $12,500; its cost is $5,000, so its expected net benefit is $7,500 and it is to be preferred.

Example 2.
Suppose that you own a home, and an insulating contractor (truthfully) tells you that he will charge you $1,000 to insulate your house and that the insulation will save you $100 per year in fuel bills. If the insulation adds nothing to the sale price of the home and you expect to live there for twelve years, should you insulate?
Answer:
The present value of $100 per year for twelve years is $100 × 9.954 = $995, so it doesn't quite pay to insulate. (Would this decision change since Congress has passed a bill that allows you to deduct 15 percent of the insulation costs from your income tax bill?)

Example 3.
Use the Rule of 72 to decide between a riskless real estate investment deal which will double your money in eighteen years and a passbook savings account that pays 5 percent interest.
Answer:
Doubling your money in eighteen years implies that the interest rate is 72/18 = 4 percent, which is less than the passbook interest.

Example 4.
Suppose I earn nothing for five years while I am completing my education, then earn $15,000 per year for twenty years and $25,000 per year for the twenty years after that. What is the present value of this income stream discounted at 3 percent?
Answer:
The present value of $15,000 per year for twenty years is $15,000 × 14.877 = $223,155, while the present value of $25,000 per year for twenty years is $25,000 × 14.877 = $371,925. But the first $15,000 stream won't be available until five years from now, so we have to discount it back to the present by multiplying by 0.863: $223,155 × 0.863 = $192,583. Similarly, the $371,925 won't be available until twenty-five years from now, so it must be discounted by 0.478: $371,925 × 0.478 = $177,780. The sum of these two present values is $370,363.

Example 5.
Compare the earnings of the college graduate from example 4 with the earnings of a high school graduate who makes $10,000 per year for twenty-five years and then $20,000 per year for the next twenty years. Is the college investment worthwhile at a 3 percent interest rate?
Answer:
$10,000 per year for twenty-five years is worth $10,000 × 17.413 = $174,130 today. $20,000 per year for twenty years is worth $20,000 × 14.877 = $297,540. The value of that latter sum today is $297,540 × 0.478 = $142,224. The two earnings streams sum to $316,354, which is less than the present value of the earnings stream received by the college graduate.

Example 6.
Suppose I pay 5 percent of my salary as a Social Security contribution (tax) over the next forty years and that the govern-

ment earns a real return of 3 percent on it by "investing" it in aid to education and other social projects. Suppose further that there is no inflation and I earn $20,000 a year.

(1) What would my accumulated rights be worth at the end of that time? If the remaining balance continued to earn 3 percent, how much could the government afford to pay me per year over an expected life of fifteen years? How much of what I get back represents interest?

(2) How much difference would it make in my accumulated rights if I got a raise late in life and made $30,000 for the last five years of the forty? (Value the added $10,000 separately.)

(3) What if I made $10,000 extra on a second job the *first* five years? How much would that add to my accumulated rights at the end of forty years?

Answer:
(1) Five percent of $20,000 is $1,000 a year, which accumulates over forty years to $1,000 × 75.401, or $75,401, rather than $40,000. The $75,401 sum will provide more than $75,401 in benefits over a fifteen-year period, because the remaining balance will earn interest during that time. Each $1 per year for fifteen years has a present cost at retirement of $11.938, so $75,401/$11.938 = $6,316 per year times 15 = $94,740, which is the total payment I will get back over the fifteen years. $94,740 exceeds the $40,000 by $54,740, so $54,740 of what I get back is interest (table 3, col. 5, row 9; col. 4, row 4).

(2) Five percent of $10,000 = $500; the present value of $500 per year for five years is $500 × 5.309 = $2,654.50.

(3) But the same amount contributed in the first five years has another thirty-five years to earn interest, which multiplies its value by 2.814 to add $7,470 to my pension rights at age sixty-five.

Since the free market interest rate tends to be about three percentage points higher than the rate of inflation, a 3 percent interest rate is appropriate for discounting streams of costs and benefits that can be expected to increase with inflation. Notice, however, that the expected *market* interest rate must be used to discount streams of costs and benefits that won't increase with inflation. Suppose, for example, that the inflation rate is 6 percent and is expected to remain at that level for some time, and that the market interest rate is 9 percent. If I win a lottery and must choose between receiving $100,000 now or $15,000 per year for the next ten years, then I must discount the stream of $15,000 payments at 9 percent rather than 3. (If the payments were automatically increased to keep up with inflation, then the 3 percent rate is appropriate.) From table 5 the present value of $1 per year for ten years at 9 percent is $6.42, so the present value of the payment stream is $15,000 × 6.42 = $96,300, and the $100,000 is preferred. Most of the future costs and benefits relevant to consumer decisions (e.g., income, house value, operating costs) can be expected to increase with inflation. A 3 percent interest rate can be used to discount these future amounts without having to predict future rates of inflation. Occasionally, however, the costs or benefits are fixed in value (e.g., a fixed pension payment) and must be discounted with expected *market* interest rates.

Sometimes some costs and benefits are not measurable. Then the best one can do is to calculate the present values of the measurable parts of two alternatives and ask oneself whether the nonmeasurable differences justify the measurable ones or more than offset them.

When one is purchasing an impermanent, or wasting, asset such as a car, or appliance, it is not necessary to calculate the present value of the stream of depreciation costs and the stream of foregone interest on the money invested in the thing. It turns out that *whatever the interest rate and whatever the length of life of the asset, the present value of the stream of "capital costs" is exactly equal to the present price of the asset*. (More on this in chap. 8.) There may be other costs, of course, such as repairs, taxes, or operating expenses, which would have to be "discounted" to present values.

If the present value of the capital costs of a $1,000 wasting asset does not depend on the length of its life, the present value of the benefits clearly does. Consequently, the longer a durable lasts, per dollar of cost, the more likely it is to be a preferred alternative. Another way to think of it is that the annual costs are less.

The most important use of the basic tables of annuity value is in understanding saving for retirement. If one starts working and saving at age twenty-five, then for each possible retirement age there is a relationship between the amount saved per year and the fund available at retirement. Then, given a life expectancy, there is a relationship between the fund available at retirement and the annual retirement annuity purchasable with that fund. Finally, by specifying the fraction of the preretirement consumption level desired after retirement, we can estimate the fraction of income that needs to be saved to meet the goal (see chap. 5).

Finally, life insurance needs can also be calculated using the same basic table, this time discounting back to the present the future streams of income needed. A varied pattern can be converted into block of years, and the "present value" of the stream at the beginning of each block estimated and converted to a value now (see chap. 9).

The most important compromise or assumption in this whole analysis is that the real rate of interest is 3 percent so that if there is an inflation rate of 4 percent, there will be a market rate of 7 percent. We must assume that it is possible to earn the market interest rate if we are saving rather than borrowing.

CHAPTER THREE
EARNING, SHARING, HAVING CHILDREN, AND THE ECONOMIC STATUS OF THE HOUSEHOLD

Having determined the state of my human capital stock of knowledge, credentials, skills, and seniority, I now have a series of interrelated decisions to make about how much to work, at what kind of job, with whom to live and pool incomes and responsibilities, where to live, and how many children to have. If I want a traditional marriage, in which one partner stays home and takes care of children, then one of us must expect to earn enough to support a whole family. If I desire a more modern partnership, where housework and child care are shared, then both of us will need careers that allow something less than total devotion to work. If I expect to have no children, and a working partner, then we can work a lot less, or consume a lot more, or retire earlier with a comfortable income, or several of these. Each of the choices influences and is influenced by the others, regardless of the precise order in which they are made.

Most people will have selected an occupation, a partner, and at least a potentially permanent location and job, within ten years after leaving school. The statistics on occupational, geographic, and marital (marriage, divorce, and remarriage) mobility show a rapid dropoff after the age of thirty. Furthermore, the consequences of these choices are with us for a long time, and it becomes increasingly difficult and expensive to change them. For our purposes, we will start with the choice of a career as a logical next step after getting an education.

Selecting a Job

Finding the right job, like any other shopping and selection exercise, requires an expenditure of time and money for the purpose of securing information. Knowledge about some jobs may require actually working at them to find out what they are like. But simply finding out what jobs are available and what they require and pay takes effort, particularly since job openings are soon filled, nearly half of them by someone known personally to the employer or to other employees. Informal hiring methods are not necessarily unfair, dishonest, or even inefficient; the employer also has a problem of information about potential employees, and personal recommendation by a friend or trusted employee is an efficient and often successful shortcut. But since such informal methods have also allowed discrimination against women and minorities, we can look forward to more formal posting of and applying for jobs.

I must still invest some effort in learning about jobs and in figuring out whether a particular job provides options for advancement or transfer into other jobs. Some jobs are "dead end," while others open up new opportunities by providing on-the-job training. The latter may pay less at first for that reason.

The general interpretation of "investing in future promotion opportunities" is straightforward enough. Suppose that I must choose between two jobs, one with promotion opportunities and the other without. Suppose further that, relative to the job without promotions, the job with the future opportunities paid $1,000 more per year starting ten years from now but paid $1,000 less per year for the next ten years. The cost of taking $1,000 less for ten years at a 3 percent interest rate is the present value of that stream, or $8,530, according to table 3. The present value today of the extra earnings to start in ten years is 0.744 of its "present value" ten years from now. If that stream of extra earnings will last thirty years, it would be worth $19,600 at its start—if for twenty years, $14,877.

Converting these two streams that start ten years from now to today's values, I have $14,582 for the thirty-year stream and $11,068 for the twenty-year stream. Because the future benefits are discounted more heavily than the more immediate costs, I must expect to work for nearly twenty years at the $1,000 higher salary to make it worth the ten years of the $1,000 lower salary while learning: At twenty years the net gain is $11,068 − $8,530, or $2,538.[1]

Can one learn about the future earnings and advancement possibilities of occupations, if not specific jobs, from history, or from the forecasts of experts? The United States Department of Labor issues at intervals publications on the prospects for jobs within different occupational groups. But these have often had to be reversed within a few years. There have been rather dramatic shifts in the advantages of different occupations, with periods of oversupply and unemployment for construction workers, then engineers, now schoolteachers. What is worse, there are no longer the clear set of occupations and career lines we once thought there were. There seems to be a proliferation of specialties with no clear prerequisites of academic background and no unambiguous way of getting trained for them. Experts are fond of saying that the half-life of nearly any training (i.e., the time when it is half obsolete) is getting shorter.

A successful farmer used to say that whenever a particular crop seemed to be in great demand at a good price, he had not planted it. The same problem may apply to choice of occupations. The period when teaching was popular as a profession and attracted many people was just at the beginning of the "baby bust," the precipitous decline in the birth rate and then in school enrollment and the demand for teachers. On the other hand, the current popularity of schools of law and medicine may not prove mistaken, since there are still serious limits on the enrollment, and both professions to some extent create their own demand.

One comforting consideration is that training in one area can often be used in another, and skills are rarely related to one specific job. Hence, mastery of almost any difficult subject is likely to be of some use somewhere, sometime. Developing the discipline and skills to master one subject can make it easier to master another, too.

How Much Work?

The job I select will limit my choices about how many hours to work. Most jobs require some minimum number of hours, often forty a week, and many do not allow, or do not pay for, time beyond forty hours. Some jobs I can forget about except when I'm actually working; others expect total devotion to thinking about the job. If I want more work than my job allows, I can change jobs, look for a second job, or find ways to do work around the house that I would otherwise have to pay for. Part-time second jobs are frequently poorly paid, and do-it-yourself direct production is difficult or unprofitable for many, so roughly one-fifth of the workforce say they want more work than they can find (Morgan). This inability to find enough work is most common among those with the least education. The official government unemployment figures neglect this underemployment by defining as unemployed only those who did not work at all in a given week, were available and looking for work, were not between jobs, or were about to start work. This excludes those who wanted more work and also those so discouraged that they stopped looking.

Insofar as we have some freedom of choice about how hard to work, we have another important economic decision worthy of some systematic analysis. Working on a job involves time and some money costs as well—commuting costs, union dues, equipment and supplies (particularly for those who are self-employed), and perhaps outlays for child care for working parents. But the amounts of money are usually small compared with the value of the time spent. Income taxes also complicate our analysis somewhat, but we can handle the money costs and taxes by thinking of the money we earn net of the costs of earning it and of taxes. These net earnings are not equivalent to take-home pay, since take-home pay does not deduct some of the costs of earning the money, and does deduct some of the earnings which are "spent" for consumption costs

---

1. It may seem incorrect to calculate the present value of a stream of costs, since I incur the costs plus the interest on them, thus giving up more than $10,000 by the end of year ten. (Including interest, it would be $11,464.) If I make my comparisons as of ten years from now, the value of the twenty years of $1,000 extra is $14,877, or $3,413 larger than the $11,464 cost. But the present value of that difference is the same ($2,538).

(as when an insurance premium is automatically deducted) or "saved" (as with retirement deductions). It is inappropriate to subtract such consumption or investment (savings) from earnings, since if I paid the insurance premiums myself or managed my own retirement plan, my take-home pay would be that much higher. My income is also higher by the value of the other fringe benefits my employer provides (chap. 5). In calculating the "earnings" from unpaid production, like growing food or painting one's house, we can ask how much we saved by doing the work ourselves, rather than hiring someone else to do it.

The main choice, then, is between work and its rewards, and leisure. The phrase "work and its rewards" is used because there is often some direct satisfaction from the work itself, apart from the money earned. Hours devoted to work produce money, valued output, or direct satisfaction, but hours left free for leisure also produce satisfaction net of the money costs of the recreation. Economists deduce that the amount of work that will maximize overall satisfaction is the point where the added satisfaction from the added earnings, net of the dissatisfaction (or plus the joy) of that added work, just equals the satisfaction given up if I am deprived of that last hour of leisure. If the hour of leisure given up by increasing work hours from forty hours per week to forty-one hours is less enjoyable than the money made from that forty-first work hour, then I would be better off working more. If I am not allowed to work as much as I would like, and can find no extra jobs or special part-time arrangements to get around the limits, then I may well feel my time is worth considerably less than my net hourly earnings. If I really would like to work less than the required forty hours a week, or am forced to work overtime, I may well feel the time is worth more than the pay. This will affect any calculations about other decisions which require that I value my time. One implication of these constraints is that for a person who really wants more work and does not value leisure much, then recreation that takes more time than money makes sense.

Even without overtime pay, many people are working more than full time (usually defined as fifty forty-hour weeks per year), many mothers are working, and many people say they want still more work. Apparently most of us do not value our leisure very highly. Philosophers may spend years trying to show that we all work too much, but the evidence from our actual choices of what to do with our time suggests the opposite (deGrazia, Linder).

Similar decisions "at the margin" must be made about working at unpaid jobs. Is the benefit of an additional hour of housework, child care, or gardening worth the cost of one less hour of leisure? Some of that work hardly seems discretionary, since most people do their own housework and take care of their own children. But there are choices even here, as indicated by the fact that some working mothers are reducing their double-job burden by paying to have some of the housework and extra child care done, and that we are all reducing housework hours by eating in restaurants more often. There is also some voluntary "home production" of food, repairs to car or house or clothes, and creation of new clothes. When we contribute to charity, we can choose to volunteer time and give money in whatever proportions we choose. In fact, most people who give one also give some of the other.

The tax implications of choices are important in nonmarket unpaid production. I may have to earn $1,500 in order to have $1,000 after taxes to pay a housepainter to paint my house, leaving him with $750 after his taxes. Even with this double tax on the division of labor and specialization, there is still relatively little do-it-yourself work done, indicating that the specialist must be far more efficient or able than the amateur. Indeed, the trend is the other way, with people earning more money at their main jobs and then paying—by eating out more and more—others to do even their cooking.

The opportunities for reaching a better balance between work and leisure, and the constraints on free choices, depend not only on the kind of jobs one takes, but also on the partner one chooses to live with, if any. We now turn to the economic aspects of a decision once thought to be purely romantic.

Marriage and Other Partnerships

Although two cannot really live as cheaply as one, it doesn't cost twice as much either. Economists term such savings "economies of scale," and they are present when two choose to live together and share some overhead expenses. Overhead means not just the cost of a roof over one's head, but any living costs which can be shared, such as those associated with cars or other durable goods. It may sound absurd, if not dismal, to talk about selecting someone with whom to share income and expenses. Assortative mating has been the concern of the anthropologist and sociologist, and marriage the concern of the church and the novelist. We cannot explain why many men marry women several years younger than themselves when they should know that even a woman of the same age will outlive them by six years or more—a gap which seems to be growing, not narrowing. Nor can we explain why in some cultures brides have a positive market value (brideprice) and in others a negative one (dowry). But since it is true that alternatives to formal marriage are becoming more common and that more people are choosing to have no children at all, it makes sense to discuss the economic arrangements people make when they live together.

Sharing an apartment or house may mean merely sharing the rent, or may extend to sharing the costs and preparation of food, maintenance, and even the investment in owning the place. But it is sharing income and sharing responsibility for children that makes marriage or its equivalent a major and crucial economic choice. Particularly when it is assumed that both partners will have jobs working for money, the choice of partner is crucial. If two people are establishing careers, frequently by moving to different areas, or at least considering jobs in different locations, then sharing may involve some compromises in job choice by both partners.

The dominant pattern—women following their husbands, staying home with the children, and taking what jobs they can fit in with those prior commitments—is giving way to more balanced but more complicated joint career decisions. Some may even be postponing a final decision about a lifetime partner until both potential partners have some notion about their careers. Couples' decisions about how much work to do for money will vary depending on whether children are desired and expected, and on how much parental time each parent is expected to invest in those children.

It seems likely that new kinds of legal agreements, different from those in or implied by the standard marriage contract, will appear. It is important to make explicit and binding some otherwise vague agreements, which may be subject to mutual misperception or second interpretations or outdated law. When one partner compromises career decisions in the interest of the partnership, some longer-term commitment by the other partner to future cooperation and responsibility would seem proper. This is true for both sexes but, given past history, is probably more important for the woman. The commitment should involve life insurance on each partner, and a similar financial commitment if either partner decides to leave. We will come back to this after discussing insurance in chapter 9.

With views toward marriage changing, it has been suggested that some contractual arrangements be made and regularly remade between partners, spelling out what each is supposed to contribute to the partnership in tasks performed. Any economist will agree that this is inefficient and unduly rigid, and that it would be far better to agree on a pricing scheme that values both tasks and time contributions in dollar terms. Then negotiations could easily raise the "wage" for tasks that no one was willing to do at the old rate, and lower it for more pleasant tasks. Such an implicit price system and some rules for adjusting it allow flexibility, alternation of jobs, and adaptation to new situations. It might even be possible to combine time and money contributions in achieving a balance, at least in those cases where the woman holds a market job.

Having Children

Everyone does not first get educated, then find a job, then get married, then decide how many children to have, then decide about housing and residential location; but we can discuss the decisions in that order, coming next to the decisions about having children. Again, while this is not primarily an economic decision, it has crucial implications—costs and benefits—which need to be sorted out if only as a background for the noneconomic costs and benefits.

Over the years, the costs of children have been increasingly borne by society in a variety of ways: free elementary and secondary education, heavily subsidized higher education, public services focused on the family (parks, playgrounds, libraries), income tax allowances for dependents, and income maintenance systems like Social Security and Aid to Families with Dependent Children. But a child is still a very expensive "investment" for the parents, requiring large amounts of money and time during the very years when most parents need to concentrate on careers and to invest in cars, a house, and furnishings. Most published estimates of the costs of children seem to exaggerate the need for high-quality child care and the money costs of college, while ignoring the nonmoney costs of time demands. The cost of any added person in a family is the marginal cost of extra space, somewhat more wear and tear, and more food—overall a less than proportionate addition to costs. A first child might add one-sixth or one-fifth to the living costs of two parents (more when the child is adolescent and eating more). A second child might add a slightly smaller proportion. They may be cheaper by the dozen, but a dozen is still more expensive than eleven.

The present system of public education subsidizes large families, but overall, children are a poor investment, in crass economic terms, and the decline in the birth rate might indicate that the satisfactions from raising children do not appear sufficient to justify the investment. On the other hand, it may be the desires of women for careers, and the possibilities of luxurious living for a married couple without dependents now that good jobs for women are possible, that are influencing many couples to postpone or cancel plans to have children. One difficulty with postponing having children until careers are well along and household capital accumulated is the increasing probability of physical difficulties for mothers past thirty. It is worth noting, however, that an increase in the average age of parents at birth slows up the rate of population increase, even at the same net reproduction rate (total children born per woman), because each generational cycle takes longer.

Proposals that the government contribute a larger share of the costs of children—by family allowances, or subsidized day care, or further tax allowances—run up against some problems. First, there is the issue of fairness. For example, a family with children and one wage earner would be paying taxes to subsidize the child care for a family with two wage-earning parents when that second family might be earning a substantially higher money income. And those with no children would be paying for benefits to those with children. Second, there is the issue of the efficiency of allocating resources to these families. Most countries have decided they do not want to increase the birth rate and the pressure of population on resources. Given these decisions, why provide economic incentives to have more children?

Most policies affecting children face this same problem, namely, that concern for the children may suggest one policy, while equity for adults suggests another, and concern about the population explosion still another. Any attempt to use economic disincentives to reduce the birth rate may punish new children for the decisions of their parents!

There is a way out, similar to the one suggested for financing education, but it requires a willingness to tax at different rates individuals with equivalent ability to pay. A society could provide substantial payments to everyone raising children, but fund these payments through a surtax on the earnings of the parents for each child produced. The surtax could be collected over a long period, say forty years, and longer if there were some years of no income. The system would not need to be perfectly balanced between child care allowances and parents' taxes, but fairness to those with no children or different numbers of children would require an approximate balance. The payments would reflect a national policy of investment in children, and the taxes would reflect a national policy of reducing or encouraging the birth rate. It is now possible to identify fathers quite precisely with a little help from mothers who would want them to share the surtax. And mothers (or fathers) would have a free choice whether to work in a regular job or be paid for taking care of children. Society tends to impose on women most of the child-care duties, but under this plan they would be paid for it.

For traditionally structured families this would be a way of spreading the cost of children over forty years instead of the first twenty when there are so many other pressures. For broken families it would give the mother and father real freedom to choose between paid work and child care, and it would force fathers who now largely escape alimony and child support demands to pay while eliminating some of the hostility now connected with payments to an estranged spouse. Since parents in general would be paying through the fund for child care, it might be easier to insist that that care be adequate. If natural parents did not provide good care, foster parents would be well enough paid that it should be easier to find alternative care. But the main impact would be increased freedom of choice for women and less pressure on them to handle two full-time jobs, one of them unpaid.

Measuring Family Well-Being

Economic status is a complex result of decisions about education, job work hours, with whom to share, and how many children to have. It is useful to attempt to construct a composite measure of economic well-being that takes account of money, family composition, and leisure. Developing such a measure will help us to see how all of these decisions fit together, but such a measure is also important because so many public policies affect the level of family well-being, and the inequality inherent in the distribution of well-being.

The most common measure of family economic well-being is total annual family income, i.e., the total dollar income received by all family members from work, from dividends and interest, and from "transfers" (e.g., Social Security, unemployment compensation, welfare, etc.). But family income is clearly an inadequate measure of well-being because of vast differences in nonmoney income, family sizes (needs), and leisure time. Worse still, the money income used in most such discussions is neither what the family earns, nor what it has available for consumption, but something in between. It includes some transfer income such as Social Security benefits, welfare payments, and pensions, but leaves out nonmoney income from unpaid work and from living in one's own home (imputed free rent). It also leaves out nonmoney income from employer contributions to Social Security, private pensions, and insurance, and does not deduct taxes, costs of earning income, compulsory saving for old age, or alimony and child-care payments.

If money income is inadequate, even as a measure of current control over resources, ignoring wealth and other sources of security, a better measure is needed to help evaluate decisions about careers, marriage, and children. To determine how well off I am compared with ten years ago, or before I got married, or with my friends and neighbors, first I need a measure of income. I may start with money income—wages, interest, rent, dividends, and regular transfer income like pensions—but adjust it:

1. Deduct income taxes, commuting costs, union dues, and compulsory payments like alimony and child support.
2. Add the amount of money saved in do-it-yourself projects and the value of the child care and housework done by the family.
3. Add other nonmoney income—employer contributions to retirement and insurance and imputed rental income from living in my own home. This rental income to homeowners amounts to roughly 6 percent of house equity per year and comes about because homeowners, in effect, rent to themselves and pay themselves a profit on their investment (more on this in chap. 4).
4. Add nonmoney transfer incomes such as subsidies for meals or rent.

Divide the result—call it net real income—by some standard of needs. The official federal poverty line, which shows the minimal income level needed to provide for families of different sizes, can be used for this (the official poverty line is explained in the next section). The ratio of net real income to needs shows what fraction or multiple of the poverty standard that income provides.

Before making further adjustments for leisure time, let us examine the implications of our measure of net real income relative to needs by comparing the economic status of two single-parent households—one with a female head and two children, the other a single male head living alone—before and after they marry. Suppose that the female head works full time and earns $8,000, while the male head works full time and earns $13,000. (That women earn about three-fifths of what men do is a well-documented fact.) If taxes reduce the man's income by $2,000 and the woman's by $1,000, and if the monetary value of housework adds $1,000 to the man's income and the value of housework and child care adds $2,000 to the woman's, then, barring other adjustments, the man's net income is $12,000 while the woman's is $9,000.

In 1979, the federal poverty needs standard was approximately $2,000 plus $1,000 per person in the household, so the needs standard of the man is $3,000 while the needs standard for the woman and her family is $5,000. The *ratio* of income to needs for these two families is $12,000/$3,000 = 4.00 for the man, and 1.80 for the woman and her children. If they were to marry and continue to work as before, then their combined income would equal $21,000, their combined needs standard would be $6,000, and the income/needs ratio of the combined family would be 3.50—a vast improvement for the woman and her children and a moderate fall in the income/needs ratio for the man.

The above example shows that if family economic status is measured by net income relative to needs, then changes in status can come about from changes in family composition as well as changes in the sources and amounts of income. A recent study of such changes in status found that they were not completely dominated by decisions about work hours and earnings. Rather, changing family composition accounted for substantial fractions of the overall change in family economic well-being (Duncan and Morgan). A dramatic illustration of this is the disastrous drop in well-being of women and children after a divorce. Changes in economic status were far more favorable for women who remained married as compared to those who divorced. That the children usually go with their mother after a divorce, that women, especially those who have raised children, are unable to earn and work as much as men, and that alimony and child-support payments are inadequate if paid at all, contribute to this situation. Large changes in economic status were also found to accompany births and deaths of family members and the timing of the departure of children from the parental home. Indeed, a major conclusion of the study was that "decisions about marriage, bearing children, and encouraging older children and other adults to stay in the household or leave it may be the main decisions that affect one's economic status" (Morgan et al., p. 337).

A final adjustment to our measure of economic status is to make some allowance for the amount of work required to produce that income, and hence the amount of free time left to enjoy it. This requires combining a ratio of two dollar amounts (income and needs) with a measure in hours, or using a ratio of hours to a standard of leisure.

Other improvements to the measure of well-being can also be made. We took care of different family sizes by using the federal family needs standard, but there are still some families living "doubled up" in order to make ends meet. There is plenty of empirical evidence that most people do not prefer living with relatives other than their spouses (or equivalent) or dependent children, both from what people say and from the speed with which they "undouble" when they can afford it. (Social Security has allowed many more old people to avoid living with their children.) Our measure does not take account of doubling up.

Even the simplest adjustments for nonmoney income, different family composition, and different leisure left to enjoy the income make not only a more realistic measure of well-being, but would make a difference in public policies:

1. Many older homeowners are well housed, but have a low cash income relative to their property taxes. Failure to include the imputed net rental income of homeowners makes their income look low and makes property taxes look unfairly burdensome on the poor (chap. 5).

2. Income maintenance programs that ignore work hours produce inequities between the working poor and the nonworking poor. A maintenance standard based on a measure which combines income, needs, and leisure hours would provide a higher maintenance level for workers than nonworkers, preserving incentives to work. A bigger task is to design a system with minimal distortions of choices about work and choices about family composition and about having more children.

3. Tax and income maintenance programs that are not neutral with respect to family composition can distort people's choices about living with and taking care of others. If the needs standard assumes too great economies of scale, a support standard based on it would encourage families to split up in order to get more support. Ignoring economies of scale in the support system would encourage doubling up, with real economies but higher guarantee payments.

Family Needs Standards and the Official Poverty Line

We have used a standard of needs simply to adjust for different family size and composition, but such standards are also used to count the poor and to determine the eligibility of individual families for assistance programs. It is worth taking a look at how they are constructed. There is a long history of attempts to take account of family size and composition, through developing "equivalent-adult" scales in various ways. With the official "war on poverty" in the United States in the 1960s, it became crucial to define standards, not only for qualification of individual families, but to allocate the funds to local areas in proportion to an estimate of the number of "poor" in each area.

The base data are estimates of weekly food costs for individuals of each age and sex, produced by the United States Department of Agriculture and published for current prices regularly in *Family Economics Review*. For Fall, 1979, for example, those estimated costs were as shown in table 6. These costs are very closely related to the age-sex pattern of calorie requirements, to which we turn in chapter 5 (on budgeting), chapter 10 (on medical care and nutrition), and chapter 11 (on food buying).

To obtain a family needs standard, the food costs for each family member are summed and then adjusted for the economies of scale involved in feeding more than one—raising the total by 20 percent for single persons, by 10 percent for two, and by 5 percent for three, and lowering the total by 5 percent for five- or six-person families, and by 10 percent for families of seven or more. For families of three or more, this total of food costs is then multiplied by 3 to cover all the other costs of living. That multiplier is based on the fact that low-income families spend about one-third of their income on food. Assuming again some diseconomies in maintaining a separate household for one or two people, the multiplier is not 3 but 3.7 for two-person families, and 4.89 for single-person families. There is also a downward adjustment for farmers on the assumption that food and housing cost less for them, and there is also a special adjustment upward for single individuals over

Table 6. Estimates of Weekly Food Cost

Individuals	Thrifty[a]	Lowest	Moderate	Liberal
Child:				
7 months to 1 year	5.60	6.90	8.40	10.00
1–2 years	6.40	8.20	10.10	12.10
3–5 years	7.70	9.70	12.10	14.60
6–8 years	9.80	12.70	16.00	19.10
9–11 years	12.40	15.90	20.00	24.00
Male:				
12–14 years	13.20	16.90	21.20	25.40
15–19 years	14.60	18.80	23.60	28.40
20–54 years	14.20	18.60	23.60	28.40
55 years and over	12.60	16.40	20.50	24.60
Female:				
12–19 years	11.80	15.10	18.80	22.50
20–54 years	11.60	15.10	18.80	22.40
55 years and over	10.50	13.50	16.80	19.90
Pregnant	14.50	18.60	22.90	27.30
Nursing	15.40	19.70	24.60	29.30

Source: *Family Economics Review*, Fall 1979, p. 23.
[a] Food stamp allotment is based on this. It assumes no eating outside the home.

sixty-five. The official poverty standard is based on the "thrifty" food costs and turns out to be roughly $2,000 plus $1,000 per person per year in 1979. It is periodically adjusted for inflation to keep it from becoming unrealistically low.

The assumptions about economies of scale in living together may be appropriate for estimating levels of well-being, but if they are used to determine levels of income maintenance or other aid, they would allow the government to capture all the economies and thus remove the incentive for families to combine and capture the economies for themselves.

To see this, let us return to our example of the unmarried female household head with two children and the unmarried male household head. The needs standards of these two families are $5,000 and $3,000, respectively, and $6,000 if they combined. The total needs of the two separate families is $5,000 + $3,000 = $8,000. That the needs of the combined family is $2,000 less than the $8,000 figure illustrates the incentives for remarriage provided by economies of scale. But suppose that the government instituted an income-maintenance program which gave benefits to all families equal to needs. The payment to the combined family would be $2,000 less than the sum of the payments to the two separate families. Thus, by capturing the economies of scale for itself, the government removes the economic incentive for remarriage. These issues are important but have been given much less attention than the effects of support programs on incentives to work.

Measuring Inequality

Whatever the measure of well-being. or whatever the unit (family, individual), there has always been a need for a single, understandable measure of inequality in the distribution of well-being among units. We may want to use an inequality measure to compare different countries, different years, or the equalizing effects of taxes, income-maintenance (transfer) programs, or subsidies. And, as we shall see in more detail in chapter 12, the amounts people are willing and able to pay for each product in the marketplace is only a good measure of the social need for that product if incomes are sufficiently equitable in their distribution so that individuals' purchasing power represents those individuals' needs.

Common measures of inequality are the share of aggregate income going to the top 10 percent of the families (arrayed by income), or to the bottom 20 percent. In 1973, 4.6 percent of the income and 5.8 percent of the income/needs went to the bottom 20 percent of families in the United States, while 26.1 percent and 26.4 percent of these two measures of well-being, respectively, went to the top 10 percent (Hoffman and Podder). These simple statistics, however, ignore the shape of the distribution except at two spots. Most economists now use the Lorenz curve and the Gini coefficient as the best ways of picturing and measuring inequality. The Lorenz curve (fig. 2) plots the cumulative proportion of aggregate income against the cumulative proportion of all families receiving that much or less when families are in order by the size of their income. If every family had the same income, then the "curve" would be a straight line at a 45° angle, reaching half the aggregate income (vertically) when it covered the bottom half of the families (horizontally) arrayed according to income. If one family had all the income and the rest had nothing, then the "curve" would be a horizontal line to the right edge and a vertical line up.

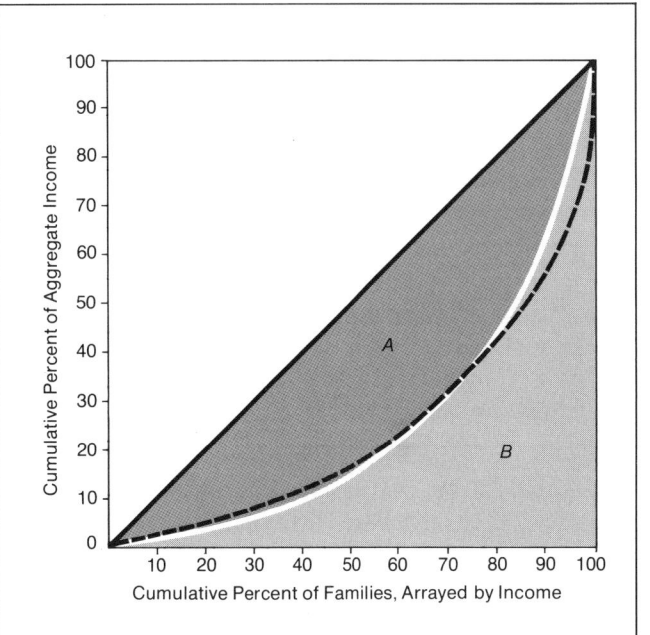

Fig. 2 Lorenz curve of inequality. The Gini measure of inequality is the ratio of area A to area A plus B. Zero inequality exists when the distribution is along the diagonal straight line, and x percent of families have x percent of the income.

Corrado Gini suggested that a good overall numerical measure of inequality would be the ratio of the area A, between the actual curve and the perfect-equality diagonal, to the entire area below the diagonal, $A + B$. Such a measure would vary from 0 (no inequality) to 1.0 (total inequality). The Gini coefficients for the 1973 income and income/needs distributions in the United States were .379 and .361, respectively (Hoffman and Podder). It is possible to have changes in the distribution—such as better income support programs at the bottom plus big increases in earnings of a few at the top resulting from inflation—with no change in the overall inequality measure. The dotted line in figure 2 illustrates this. It takes rather substantial changes in distribution to produce much change at all in the Gini coefficient, but it is the best measure we have that is also understandable.

There can be wide differences in estimates of inequality, depending on the measure and the unit used. We have already noted that if we adjust income for needs (family size and composition) there is less inequality. The reason is that it is generally the larger middle-aged families that have the larger incomes. Other improvements in the measure of well-being also change the impression of inequality. For example, work hours are longer and leisure less for high-income families in the United States, so a measure of well-being that includes a leisure component shows less inequality overall. On the other hand, hours of housework and child care and other unpaid work do not vary much with the economic status of the family, so adjusting for it does not change the distribution of well-being significantly.

Some people feel that income over longer periods, even a lifetime, is a better base for measuring inequality than yearly income. But there are no good data on lifetime incomes, and for many purposes they would be unacceptable. For example, you could not convince a poor, older family that things were really fine because their income had been adequate when they were younger. At any rate, the distribution of income and income/needs averaged over a longer time period (seven years) is somewhat more equal than is the one-year distribution (Hoffman and Podder).

A much more important distinction is that between one-year and multi-year poverty. Those who are poor persistently are quite different from those who are poor one year and not the next (Coe). Hence, formulas for distributing federal funds to local areas on the basis of the number of poor in any one year provide inadequate help to areas where most of the poor are persistently so, and too much to areas with mostly temporarily poor.

The Redistribution of Income

The measure of well-being proposed on the preceding pages embodies the income redistribution that takes place through income taxes and transfer payments. But still more redistribution takes place in more subtle ways, through the differential impact of other taxes and the differential benefits from government services, and from some government interference with free market prices. A well-informed citizen needs to have a view of the way this happens, since many issues of public policy are involved. We can classify the redistributive mechanisms from those most directly intended to redistribute income to those that have other purposes but result in redistribution, largely as an unintended consequence:

1. Noncontributory transfer systems (pure transfer of funds to those in need, without reciprocal obligation)—Aid to Families with Dependent Children and Unemployed Fathers (AFDC and variants); general assistance; Supplemental Security Income; food stamps; private philanthropy; interfamily aid (i.e., helping relatives or friends. This may in fact be reciprocal, but there is no legal requirement that it be so.)
2. Contributory transfer systems (each in some sense self-financing, but not a burden on others)—unemployment compensation; worker's compensation; other insurance; Social Security (OASDHI); private pensions
3. Taxes—federal and state income taxes; property taxes; sales and other taxes
4. Public services, subsidies, price supports—education and information (research); public health, parks, etc.; tariffs, marketing arrangements, and other price supports (a kind of tax on consumers)

There are secondary effects of any tax, transfer, or subsidy, so that it is impossible to say what its final effect is. Economists distinguish *impact*—the effect on the person who pays the **tax** or feels the first effect—from *incidence*—the more diffuse effects after things settle into a new equilibrium. Economists do not agree about incidence anyway, so here we shall look briefly at the initial impacts of the various mechanisms and some related issues.

Noncontributory Transfers

Welfare and AFDC by their very rules benefit those who would otherwise be very badly off. It was thought originally that Social Security plus unemployment compensation would eliminate most of the old welfare system, replacing it with a contributory system. While it is true that Social Security drastically reduced the number of old people on welfare, a rapid obsolescence of some job skills and an exploding number of fatherless families more than took their place. What is frightening to some observers is that if responsibilities for their children continue to be shed as most divorced fathers have shed them, there is a vast potential demand for more taxes-plus-transfers. Even when alimony and child support payments are legally awarded, the fathers responsible seldom pay them for very long. No one wants the children to suffer from the irresponsibility of parents, so there are recurrent attempts to make the fathers pay, and to provide relatively low levels of support when they do not, so as not to encourage more to leave home. Most people are "judgment proof," in the sense that courts cannot make them pay. This is because they have little in attachable assets, and are subject to dismissal from their jobs if their wages are garnisheed. Mothers bear most of the burden. If neither parent took responsibility, the cost of the necessary public child support system would be colossal.

Public income-maintenance programs have replaced most private alms-giving, but some part of the twenty to thirty billion dollars of charitable contributions, and some of the billions of dollars worth of time given in volunteer work, reduces inequality because it benefits people of lower income than the donors. No one has actually been able to determine just what the redistributional effects of private philanthropy are. For one thing, the legal definition of a charitable organization for tax purposes is broad, even allowing for some political activity. For another, since the tax incentives for giving, as well as the ability to afford it, are much greater at high income levels, substantial amounts are given to institutions appreciated by the wealthy—museums, symphony orchestras, universities.

Since charitable contributions are deductible from income for federal income tax and some state income tax purposes, the government is really paying for some fraction of private philanthropy with what would otherwise be tax money. The fraction, as we pointed out earlier, depends on the giver's marginal tax rate—that is, the fraction of additional income that is taken in taxes. The justification for this private spending of tax dollars is that it facilitates the separation of church and state and promotes diversity and initiative.

The disproportionate subsidy given to the charitable contributions of the affluent, however, has led to proposals for replacing the deductibility with a tax credit, or a matching contribution by government. With a tax credit, any taxpayer's taxes would be reduced by some fixed fraction of the amount given to charity. This would give the poor the same advantage as the affluent, so long as they paid any tax at all. With a matching grant, the government, upon proof that $100 had been given to some charity, would give some fixed fraction of that amount to the same charity. This would have the same equity results as the tax credit, but would involve the government more directly. It is the deductions allowed in the income tax that are the source of many of the loopholes we all deplore, but since we do want to encourage private philanthropy (and the affluent do much of it), policymakers are caught between a desire to encourage private philanthropy and a desire to make the tax system simpler and more equitable (Commission on Private Philanthropy and Public Needs).

There is very little aggregate interfamily aid (help for relatives), except when it takes the form of providing housing for relatives. Actual money support to relatives living elsewhere is small, apart from children in college. The redistributive effects of interfamily aid are small.

Contributory Transfers

Contributory transfer systems do not redistribute money between the covered group and the rest of society, but they do redistribute within the group, mostly by reducing short-term inequalities that result from unemployment, or accidents, or failure to save for old age. Not only is the covered group often relatively well off—they are employed, to begin with—but the compensation is also related to income level. Indeed, unemployment compensation in most states is not only related to earnings level, but it also ignores family size or other indicators of need.

Similarly, insurance redistributes income from the lucky to the unlucky, reducing disparities that would otherwise be created by chance occurrences. Veterans' benefits presumably make up in a small way for the inequitable burdens placed on some, but their current redistributional effect is not great.

Social Security is a more complicated redistributive system. It has been called social insurance, which it is only in part. It has been called a contract between generations, each generation taking care of a preceding generation in return for a promise of being taken care of in turn, which it really is not. It has some elements of redistribution in it, mostly between the least fortunate and everyone else. We will look more closely at Social Security and private pensions in chapter 5.

Taxes and Redistribution

The federal personal income tax is considered to be one of the major redistributive mechanisms in the United States. Since it has profound and differential effects on many consumer decisions, a summary of its main features is needed. It is a progressive tax, taking somewhat larger proportions of higher incomes by first totally exempting some income from taxation, and then by applying increasing tax rates to each successive block of income. The higher rate on each succeeding block of income does not apply to the earlier blocks, so you never end up with less after-tax income when you earn more. The fraction taken in taxes of an additional dollar you earn—your marginal income tax rate—is the crucial feature for many purposes. That rate varies from 14 percent to 70 percent, although it cannot get above 50 percent for earned income from work. (Your marginal rate can be higher than 50 percent even for work income, however, if you also have some nonwork income like dividends, interest, or rent.)

A second crucial feature is the possibility of deducting certain items from income before it is taxed. Deductible if itemized are specified expenses like interest on debts (e.g., home mortgages), state and local taxes, uninsured casualty losses, charitable contributions, and (when they exceed some fraction of income) medical expenses. Itemizing deductions will lower your tax bill if the sum of what you can deduct that way is larger than the "standard deduction"; for most people this happens only when their income approaches $20,000 a year.

A third feature of the federal income tax is that it does not tax some sources of income. Income from Social Security, unemployment compensation, and tax-exempt (mostly state, city, and school district) bonds is not taxed. Neither is the income that you "earn" from do-it-yourself work or from shopping around and paying a lower price for something as a result. The imputed rental income that you earn from owning your own home (and thus paying yourself a return on your investment) is not taxed either.

A fourth feature is that income from the sale of something you own that has appreciated in value (long-term capital gains) is taxed at only forty percent of the rate of other income. Capital losses, on the other hand, are fully deductible. These two facets produce a kind of subsidy to risk-taking.

Further discussion of some of the tax implications of deductibility of housing costs will be found in chapter 4, of casualty losses in chapter 9, and of special treatment of capital gains and tax-exempt bonds in chapter 8. Chapter 5 notes the need for records of tax-deductible outlays.

The importance of the income tax on consumer decisions warrants some illustrations. Suppose that you are in the 33 percent tax bracket—i.e., that the government would tax an additional dollar you earn at a 33 percent rate. The amount of charitable contributions you make can be deducted from taxable income, so each dollar contributed to charity lowers your taxable income by $1 and your tax bill by $.33. Thus, the government really "pays" one-third of that contribution because it can't collect as much in taxes, and the effective cost of that $1 contribution to you is really only $.67. By the same token, a savings account that pays a 6 percent interest rate before taxes is really giving you a return of 4 percent after taxes if your marginal tax rate is 33 percent. Since the interest payments on mortgages can be deducted from taxable income, a 10 percent nominal mortgage interest rate is really 6.67 percent. Income that you "earn" through do-it-yourself work is not taxed, so each dollar of it is equivalent to $1.50 of earned income that is subject to a 33 percent tax rate.

Your own marginal tax rate and whether you are itemizing affect the real (after-tax) cost of different things differently. But also, that other people with different tax rates are buying some of the same things you are means that you are competing with people who actually pay different prices than you do. For example, most tax-exempt bonds are bought by very high-income people whose 50 percent marginal tax rate makes the 6 percent bond yield as good as a 12 percent yield on something that is taxable. The market interest rate on tax-exempt bonds is driven down because of this. But if you have a 20 percent marginal tax rate, a taxable investment that yielded 8 percent before taxes (and 6.4 percent after) would be better than a 6 percent tax-exempt bond.

A more important example is owning a home, where the untaxed free rent and the deductibility of interest and tax payments saves high-tax people more than low-tax people and thus lowers the cost of owning for them. The same principle applies to purchases in hotels and restaurants where people on expense accounts are spending someone else's money. That someone, the employer, faces a 46 percent corporate profit tax rate itself so that each $1 of business account expense reduces its before-tax profits by $1 and its profits tax by about $.46. The price of the hotel and restaurant expenses to the company, then, is cut in half.

Over the years a substantial number of special provisions, or "loopholes," have been written into the income tax law. They were usually justified for the case or cases that precipitated their acceptance, but for other people, particularly in combination with other special provisions, they lead to unfair if legal tax avoidance. There is a continuing process of closing these loopholes and a parallel process of opening new ones, so that it is difficult to see who is winning except the tax lawyers and the companies that have sprung up to help people with the complications of filling out their income tax forms. Indeed, recent revisions of the law dealing with charitable foundations were so complicated that even the lawyers claimed not to understand them, telling their clients not to start any more foundations nor to add to their present ones.

It is important for you as a taxpayer to know ways to reduce your taxes legally. Most ways involve changing income to a different recipient, a different year, or a different form. Although specifics are discussed throughout this book, a few general comments are in order here.

Almost all income now has to have a taxpayer number (usually the Social Security number of its recipient) attached, and this is transmitted to the Internal Revenue Service by the source (e.g., the employer, or the bank paying interest). But under the states' Uniform Gift to Minors Act, assets can be put in the names of minor children with an adult as trustee. Their yield is the child's income and hence not taxed while the child remains a legal dependent for the parents' tax return. When the assets are sold, say for the child's education, the capital gain is again the child's income and subject to little or no tax. Of course, as soon as the child becomes eighteen, the ownership is unrestricted and the child can legally spend the money.

One of the attractions of some United States Government savings bonds is that, since no tax is payable on the interest until the bond is cashed (because no interest is actually paid until then), the owner can select a year of lower income and tax rates in which to cash the bonds. Similar freedom to choose the year exists with assets that appreciate in value. Such capital gains are taxed at less than half your regular rate anyway, and if you wait until you retire, your marginal tax rate may be still lower.

Recent (1979) federal income tax instructions facilitate calculation but not understanding. The "standard deduction" for those who do not itemize ($2,300 for single persons, $3,400 for joint returns) is built into the tax tables—you don't see it. But it is important to know that only if you can find more than the equivalent of that amount in things to itemize, is it worth doing so. The "marriage penalty" so widely publicized is also difficult to see in the tables. It is largest when the husband and wife's combined income is between $50,000 and $100,000, where they pay 6 percent more of their income in tax than if they were able to file two single-person returns.

Assets that go up in value can also be given away at their market value, escaping income tax. Hence, converting income into capital gains has advantages beyond that of being able to choose the year to realize them. Investments in real estate and some other things that permit very large depreciation allowances essentially do this (see chap. 7). At most, you pay income tax on less than half the gain, and only if and when you sell the asset and "realize" the gain.

State income taxes vary from state to state, but are generally much less progressive than the federal income tax. In fact, since they are deductible from income for purposes of federal income taxes, they are even less progressive than they seem. Indeed, this is true of all state taxes. For instance, a straight state income tax of 10 percent of income regardless of its size is really 10 percent for the (low-income) person who does not itemize deductions for the federal return. Consider the person whose marginal tax rate is 20 percent and who itemizes, and thus can deduct his state income tax payment from his taxable income. His federal income taxes are reduced by 2 percent, so the effective rate of the state income tax for him is really 8 percent. A person with a 50 percent marginal federal tax rate (income around $40,000) really pays only a 5 percent state income tax. The federal income tax progressivity is eroded by the right to deduct other taxes—or perhaps all other taxes are made more regressive.

Tax laws are periodically revised, so a person has no choice but to keep up with them. The difficulty with the complexity and change, aside from the inequities, is the cost of compliance. Many people end up paying fees to "experts" to help them sort out the complications. The quality of these tax services is not always adequate, leaving the consumer with one more shopping problem, and a decision about whether to invest instead in learning how to do it. The payoff to learning comes year after year in the saving of fees and also in increased sensitivity to ways of reducing taxes.

The two other main taxes most people face are property and sales taxes. Property taxes are the most maligned—accused of being erratically and inequitably assessed, of varying unconscionably from one area to another, and of being regressive. As explained in chapter 4, many of the accusations are simply wrong. Property taxes are a justifiable complement to other taxes, taxing the consumption of private and public services (free rent, police and fire protection, and schools) even by those who manage to hide part of their income from the income tax.

What about the sales tax? It depends on what is excluded from it. A sales tax that excludes food and medicine is roughly proportional over most income levels, at least before we consider it net of federal income tax offsets. But at high income levels, where people spend lower and lower fractions of their incomes on things subject to sales tax, the burden is lighter, even apart from the federal income tax advantages they have. Strangely enough, the lower middle income people—those hardest hit by the sales tax—often say they prefer it to an income tax.

The only other taxes with relatively clear redistributive effects of any importance are the federal estate tax and the state inheritance taxes, intended to reduce the inequality that results from inherited wealth. These taxes have never been very effective, because the wealthy have the resources, ingenuity, time, and legal help to devise ways to pass on most of their wealth to their children. Indeed, the affluent are much more concerned with avoiding estate taxes than income taxes, regarding the latter as somehow more justified because they come at a time when the money is being made. But once the money is part of the estate, the affluent feel it should be protected. The methods of protection are complex, involving trusts and special corporations and foundations, and we know very little about just how the intergenerational transmission of wealth really works. One of the purposes of the revised law on charitable foundations was to reduce their use as a method of avoiding estate taxes.

Effects of Redistribution on Behavior

Some of the taxes or transfers or government activities that affect the distribution of well-being have been intended to affect people's behavior as well, while others have had unintended and even undesirable effects on behavior.

The income tax was designed to preserve the incentives to work, and extra earnings always do increase one's after-tax income. But the tax is accused of discouraging work anyway, because there is no tax on the alternative—leisure. It is not clear what income taxes in fact do to work effort, since the tax as a whole reduces income, making the need for more dollars greater (an income effect), hence encouraging more work, while at the same time it lowers the marginal (after-tax) reward for working and thus discourages it (a substitution of cheaper leisure effect). In some sense, any tax on consumption expenditures reduces the rewards of work and earning.

Taxes can also affect decisions about with whom to live, and about whether to support needy relatives. The federal income tax rates were changed after complaints by single people that they were being discriminated against; this led to dramatic examples of married couples, each one earning a substantial income, who found it profitable to get divorced in December and remarried in January in order to file separate tax returns! Clearly it is difficult to write a tax law that is reasonably neutral with respect to decisions about marriage and family.

The federal income tax currently includes a $1,000 allowance (deduction from taxable income) for each dependent, so long as more than half the support of that person is provided by the taxpayer. This allowance saves anywhere from $700 down to nothing, depending on marginal tax rate. The higher the income and the less the support of that dependent hurts, the more it is subsidized by the federal government. Half the support of an aged parent living rent-free in her or his own home may cost very little, even before taxes, relative to the cost of a child away at college. This erratic and relatively minor encouragement of family responsibility is in contrast with the major, if also income-related, encouragement of organized philanthropy, which allows deductions for charitable contributions, up to a substantial fraction of income. Yet individual responsibility for members of the extended family might be more efficient administratively and in preserving motivation while reducing inequality and taking a potential burden off society.

It is the transfer system (income-maintenance payments) that has been the focus of most of the concern about the distorting effects of redistribution on behavior. Society wants to maintain at least a minimal income for people without discouraging them from working, without discouraging relatives from taking care of them, and without encouraging undue fertility. There is also concern that the money be wisely spent and the children properly cared for. The result of such concerns has been a tendency to keep the level of income supports low and to surround them with a whole set of behavioral requirements:

1. *Employment or employability tests*. To get unemployment compensation I must appear regularly, allege that I have looked for work, and accept any reasonable job. Checks on my employability are also made if I am collecting workers' compensation for a work injury or welfare payments of any kind.

2. *Relative responsibility requirements*. These are on the way out as a result of court cases and were never very well enforced, but they are still on the statute books in most states. If I apply for help, my relatives may be asked to provide for my support, unless they are very poor.

3. *A means test*. Noncontributory transfer programs like welfare, Medicaid, and Aid to Families with Dependent Children also require that I have almost no assets. I am expected to use up all my savings before I can get help. The amounts allowed in savings vary from state to state. If I run out of unemployment compensation, I may have to use up my savings before I can get on welfare. It is easy to guess what such an experience might do to my incentives to save when I do have a job.

4. *Residence requirements*. Many state-run programs have a residence requirement for eligibility, and also make it difficult for a recipient to leave the state while getting aid. Recent court decisions have eroded the residence requirements, but they are justifiable when state levels of support vary and at least part of the cost is borne by state tax funds.

5. *Categorical assistance*. Concerns about the wise use of support money by recipients have led to its being given in the form of medical care, rent payments, food stamps, and clothing vouchers. It is often accompanied by social workers who have the double task of providing counseling and guidance on the one hand, and determining eligibility for and amount of benefits on the other. Attempts to separate these functions within the same welfare office have only increased the confusion.

Since the fifty states individually administer and partly pay for these categorical assistance programs, there are huge disparities in the levels of benefits and the rules for eligibility. Federal funds given to states are accompanied by regulations and requirements intended to reduce these disparities, but the amount of support available is still substantially larger, even relative to the cost of living, in some places than others.

6. *Income test*. Of course, all income maintenance programs have an income test, reducing the support as the individual's other income rises. The difficulty is that there are overlapping programs and taxes, each with an income test, so that if I start to earn more income, I may find that my total support drops by more than my income increases as, for example:

☐ I lose my welfare or unemployment compensation.
☐ I receive fewer food stamps, or cannot get them at all.
☐ I lose the right to subsidized child care.
☐ My subsidized rent is raised, or I have to leave the housing project.
☐ My children no longer qualify for scholarships for school, summer camp, etc.
☐ My income taxes go up.

There is a federal requirement for state welfare systems that people be allowed to keep at least a third of what they earn, in addition to some allowable expenses of earning (commuting, child care). But that does not eliminate the problems of overlapping programs. Indeed, almost every time any new program is proposed, an income test is proposed for it. The result adds one more "income tax" and places another disincentive on working and earning.

Proposed Reforms

All this confusion and the explosion of the welfare rolls have led to various reform proposals, many calling for a more uniform income-maintenance system. Both liberals and conservatives have supported a simpler system, perhaps for different reasons. One version of a cash benefit system with a single income test, sometimes called a "negative income tax" because it effectively reversed the process below the incomes at which taxes became zero, has the government paying some fraction of the amount by which income falls below some break-even income level. The attempt to eliminate the other tests—employability, assets—and the restrictions on how the aid was used—categorized help like food stamps, medical care, and subsidized housing—ran up against strong public feelings that society had a right to make sure that recipients were using their aid wisely, and were working if they could. The public was not so much opposed to helping the poor as to dependency, and wanted to make people independent and self-supporting, to preserve people's "self-respect" and not just their health, education, and welfare. Others thought it important to let people make their own decisions and choices, and to eliminate inequities arising from overlapping programs and complex rules.

What most of the reform proposals have in common is:

☐ Uniform standards and rules of eligibility nationally.
☐ Separation of the social work and counseling system from the income-maintenance system.
☐ Abolition of the asset means test, perhaps with some imputed income from nonmoney-earning assets like homes included in income for the income test.
☐ Payment of benefits in cash, leaving it to independent counseling to encourage its wise use, and to authorities to prevent child neglect or abuse.
☐ Understandable rules for reduction in benefits as earned income rises, and a reasonable tax rate to preserve work incentives.

Even when massive social experiments indicated very little reduction in work under such an income-maintenance system, and no significant increase in the birth rate, the only actual move toward such a system was a small cash payment in the federal income tax for some working poor who had exemptions and deductions more than enough to drive their tax to zero.

The problem remains how to design a tax and income-maintenance system that is fair and efficient and reasonably neutral with respect to people's decisions about working for money, living with and helping one another, and having children. The importance of the second and third of these decisions in accounting for changes in the well-being of people is very large; yet most of the government attention has gone to the first—work effort. One possible way of facing the problems of designing a fair system of redistribution—taxing high incomes and supplementing low ones—is to start with a more adequate criterion of economic well-being than family income, and base the taxes or income supplements on that. Even the income/needs ratio is inadequate because it fails to take account of the leisure left after working to get that income. How could we devise a single measure of well-being that incorporated hours of free time per person with family income/family needs, when one measure is in hours and the other is a ratio of dollar amounts? If we can assume they are partly substitutes for one another, at least for small changes, we can simply take the product of the two as our measure. Or, if we believe people do not value leisure as much as income, we can weight the income/needs ratio more heavily in the measure.

If the estimate of leisure allows for the time-cost of child care, and the needs standard allows for the extra money cost of added family members, then using the well-being index as a basis for taxes or supplements should not unduly affect people's choices about having children or doubling up to economize. A needs standard should not assume full economies of scale from living together, because that would attempt to recapture all those economies for the government and thus discourage people from seeking them. It would at the same time mean the government would be subsidizing the diseconomies that come from splitting up.

No tax or subsidy program now takes account of work effort, or the leisure people have left to enjoy their income. One that did, by basing taxes or supplements on a measure of well-being, would encourage work, benefit the working poor more than the nonworking poor, and probably make everyone feel better about the fairness of the system.

Summary

We have seen that individuals have to make a set of interrelated decisions about jobs, how hard to work, with whom to share one's economic fates, and how many children to "invest in." Since the result of all these private decisions is often an unacceptable amount of inequality of income or well-being, various redistributional mechanisms are at work. These taxes, transfers, and other programs in turn often have unwanted effects on decisions about work, sharing, and having children. Important questions remain about how to achieve a combination of fairness and neutrality (proper incentives) at the same time in a complex overlapping set of programs and taxes.

More Information?

There is a sociological-demographic literature on assortative mating, some psychological and sociological literature on occupational choice and mobility, and some political science work on political socialization, but almost nothing on economic socialization—the process of finding an acceptable job, residence, and partner. Decisions about having children have been extensively studied by demographers, sociologists, and psychologists, and more recently by economists with their particular cost-benefit analysis interpretations. No one has done very well at explaining the baby boom of the midcentury and the baby bust that followed, not even the economists (see Strumpel et al.); nor is much known about joint decision making in the family, although family sociologists and market researchers have worked at it.

Tax reform really is going on, so published studies must be supplemented with summaries of recent changes.

ACTION. *Americans Volunteer, 1974*. Washington, D.C.: ACTION, 1975.

Coe, Richard D. "Dependency and Poverty in the Short and Long Run." In *Five Thousand American Families—Patterns of Economic Progress*, vol. 4, edited by Greg J. Duncan and James N. Morgan. Ann Arbor: Institute for Social Research, 1978.

Commission on Private Philanthropy and Public Needs. "Attitudes Toward Social Security." In *Research Papers*. Washington, D.C.: Government Printing Office, 1977.

Duncan, Greg J., and Morgan, James N., eds. *Five Thousand American Families—Patterns of Economic Progress*, vol. 4. Ann Arbor: Institute for Social Research, 1976.

de Grazia, Sebastian. *Of Time, Work, and Leisure*. New York: Twentieth Century Fund, 1962.

Goode, Richard. *The Individual Income Tax*. Washington, D.C.: Brookings Institution, 1964.

Hellerstein, Jerome. *Taxes, Loopholes, and Morals*. New York: McGraw-Hill, 1963.

Hill, C. Russell, and Stafford, Frank. "Allocation of Time to Preschool Children and Educational Opportunity." *Journal of Human Resources* 9 (Summer 1974): 323–42.

Hoffman, Saul D., and Podder, Nripesh. "Income Inequality." In *Five Thousand American Families—Patterns of Economic Progress*, vol. 4, edited by Greg J. Duncan and James N. Morgan. Ann Arbor: Institute for Social Research, 1976.

Johnson, Evelyn. "Canning and Freezing, What is the Payoff?" *Family Economics Review*, Spring 1976, pp. 6–13.

Kahn, Robert L. "The Meaning of Work." In *The Human Meaning of Social Change*, edited by A. Campbell and P. E. Converse. New York: Russell Sage Foundation, 1972.

Katz, Sanford N., and Inker, Monroe L. *Fathers, Husbands, and Lovers, Legal Rights and Responsibilities*. Chicago: American Bar Association Section of Family Law, 1979.

Lansing, John B., and Morgan, James N. "The Effect of Geographic Mobility on Earning." *Journal of Human Resources* 2 (Fall 1967): 449–60.

Linder, Staffan Burenstam. *The Harried Leisure Class*. New York: Columbia University Press, 1970.

Morgan, James N. *A Panel Study of Income Dynamics*, vols. 1 and 2. Ann Arbor: Institute for Social Research, 1973.

Morgan, James N.; David, Martin; Cohen, Wilbur; and Brazer, Harvey. *Income and Welfare in the United States*. New York: McGraw-Hill, 1962.

Morgan, James N.; Dye, Richard; and Hybels, Judith. "Results from Two National Studies of Private Philanthropy." In *Research Reports for the Commision on Private Philanthropy and Public Needs*, vol. 1. Washington, D.C.: U.S. Treasury, 1977.

Morgan, James N.; Sirageldin, Ismail; and Baerwaldt, Nancy. *Productive Americans*. Ann Arbor: Institute for Social Research, 1966.

Morgan, James N., et al. *Five Thousand American Families—Patterns of Economic Progress*, vol. 1. Ann Arbor: Institute for Social Research, 1974.

Orshansky, Mollie. "Counting the Poor, Another Look at the Poverty Profile." *Social Security Bulletin* 28 (1965): 3–29. (See also subsequent articles in the *Social Security Bulletin*.)

Roe, Anne. *The Psychology of Occupation*. New York: John Wiley and Sons, 1956. (Chapter 21 summarizes studies of occupational choice.)

Ruskay, Joseph A., and Osserman, Richard A. *Halfway to Tax Reform*. Bloomington: Indiana University Press, 1970.

Strumpel, Burkhard; Thornton, Arland; and Curtin, Richard. *Fertility Change after the Baby Boom: The Role of Economic Stress, Female Employment, and Education*. Final Report to the National Institute for Child Health and Development, Center for Population Research, Behavioral Sciences Branch, from Survey Research Center, Institute for Social Research, The University of Michigan. Ann Arbor: 1976.

Szalai, Alexander, ed. *The Use of Time: Daily Activities of Urban and Suburban Populations in Twelve Countries*. The Hague: Mouton, 1972.

U.S. Department of Labor, Manpower Administration. *Americans Volunteer*. Manpower-Automation Research Monographs, no. 10. Washington, D.C.: Government Printing Office, 1969.

Walker, Kathryn, and Woods, Margaret. *Time Use: A Measure of Household Production of Family Goods and Services*. Washington, D.C.: American Home Economics Association, 1976.

Wishnetsky, T., and Cash, J. *Cost of Home Gardening and Canning Green Beans and Tomatoes*. East Lansing: Michigan State University, 1975.

Some Projects to Learn More

1. See what you can find about the prospects for different occupations, particularly things that have appeared at different times in the last twenty years. How much consistency is there, and do the forecasts of years ago hold up in the light of today's labor market?

2. What subsidized job training programs still exist? Can you find any studies of their benefit-cost experience? Do they have waiting lists? How do they select among the applicants?

3. See what you can find in the literature about modern marriage contracts and commitments less or more comprehensive than marriage. Analyze them. Could you write a better one?

4. Summarize the recent writings on the effects of the baby boom and baby bust on the economy, particularly on school systems and the job market. Check particularly in the *Monthly Labor Review*, the *Social Security Bulletin, Demography*, and the index in the *Monthly Catalogue of United States Government Publications*.

5. See if you can find data on the distribution of incomes within occupations as well as average earnings. If there are differences in the variability of earnings, would you use that information in selecting an occupation? (Try United States Census current population surveys or the *Monthly Labor Review*.)

CHAPTER FOUR
HOUSING AND RESIDENTIAL LOCATION

The decision about where to live includes not only location but whether to own or to rent. Decisions about jobs, living partner, and the number and timing of children all affect decisions about location and home ownership, and they affect each other—if you want to live in some areas, you have to own your home, whereas in others you may have to rent.

A residence is more than just something likely to account for a fourth of a family's expenses. It is a package deal which includes a neighborhood, commuting and other costs for all the workers in the family, a level of available public services and of property and income taxes, and probably some local styles and standards of living which may exert some pressure to conform. And because moving is expensive in money, time, and emotional turmoil, plans which include children may necessitate a house large enough to accommodate a kind of "peak load," even if it means some extra cost before and afterward.

Considering the difficulties and costs of moving, the decision concerning housing is worth careful thought before it is made. I have to decide how much housing I need and the true costs of that housing, whether I want to own or rent my housing, and where I want to live. Each of these depends on the others, but let's take them in order.

How Much Housing?

Rules of thumb for consumers are often misleading or just plain wrong, but in the case of home ownership, the following two rules about how much a family can afford to spend on housing without undue stress on the rest of the budget may help:

1. Your annual housing cost should not be more than one-fourth of your gross annual income.
2. Do not buy a house that costs more than two or three times your gross annual income.

Equating these two rules gives a relationship between the purchase price of a house and the rental cost of a similar place. If buying a house that costs twice your income is the same as renting a place that costs a fourth of your income, then the *annual* cost of owning a house is about an eighth of its price, and its monthly cost is about one-hundredth of its price (a $30,000 house would rent for $300 a month).[1] If a house costs three times your income to buy, then it costs one-twelfth of its price each year in rental equivalent. The relationship between rent and house value comes about from competitive pressures in the housing market. If rents are much higher than they ought to be, based on house values, then some renters will become owners, and other investors will convert previously owner-occupied homes into rental property. If rents are not high enough to pay a reasonable return on the landlord's investment, then the reverse ought to occur. Both of these actions will tend to restore the relationship between rent and house value.

These rules are often misused, however, because of a misunderstanding about what constitutes the true "costs"

---

1. If a house costs twice your income, then (1) house value = 2 × income. If annual housing cost equals one-fourth of income, then (2) annual cost = 0.25 × income. Solving (1) for income and substituting into (2) gives (3) annual cost = 0.25 × (0.5 × house value) = 0.125 × house value. Thus, annual costs equal one-eighth of the house price.

of housing. Most homeowners, for example, consider that the mortgage payment is the principal cost of homeowning. But the mortgage payments are partly savings because they increase the equity in the house, and such saving is not a cost. On the other hand, the usual lists of housing costs exclude depreciation and the foregone interest on the money already invested in the house. Only by accident would the cash outlays of the homeowner reflect the real cost of a house.

It is crucial to know what housing alternatives really cost. The cost of rental is clear—rent payments plus utilities. But what is the comparable cost of a house for which only its price and the utility costs are known?

The True Costs of Owning

An economically sound estimate of the annual or monthly cost of owning a home can be made by estimating each of the components of cost. It turns out to be relatively easy, because almost all costs are roughly proportional to the price of the house. Let's look at those costs:

Depreciation is a major cost of any piece of capital equipment—the wearing out, using up, or gradual obsolescence that will ultimately require replacement. Depreciation can be offset by maintenance, but the sum of maintenance expenses and residual depreciation will amount to a roughly constant fraction of house value each year. In the case of houses, maintenance expenses include roofing and painting as well as periodic service to the plumbing, heating, and electrical systems. The sum of depreciation and maintenance costs of owning a home might be 1.5 percent of the current price per year. A 1.5 percent depreciation rate per year implies that an unrepaired house would self-destruct in $1/0.015 = 67$ years.

Repairs and maintenance to make certain the house lasts the sixty-seven years are implied in the 1.5 percent depreciation rate, but not the major alterations to make it last forever, which might be an additional 2 percent of house value per year. Experts claim that while repairs are less frequent on brick or stone houses, they are somewhat more expensive, and that the remaining difference is offset by the increased initial cost of the house. Total depreciation and maintenance costs, then, amount to roughly 3.5 percent of house value per year.

Inflation (appreciation) of house prices causes many people to say that one can ignore depreciation. This is a dangerous confusion. Capital gains—whether merely the result of inflation, or actually exceeding the general rise in prices—are important, but they differ from depreciation. One way to look at this is to think of alternative investments to a house. If inflation is driving up the prices of houses, it should also be driving up the prices of financial investments such as stocks and rental real estate, and some of these investments do not wear out or become obsolete: there is no depreciation to reduce the effect of inflation. You can point to houses in good locations that have had increases in value apart from general inflation, but there are also wise financial investments that have paid off. On the average, over the long run, most investments pay a real 3 percent plus the rate of inflation and plus enough to offset depreciation, if any. Hence, it is useful to take account separately of real depreciation and possible market appreciation of a house. Certainly if one moves to another or a larger house, that same inflation makes the new house more costly too. So holding capital gains aside as a possible benefit, rather than a deduction from cost, what other costs are there besides depreciation?

Interest costs must be considered. While most homeowners are painfully aware of the interest portion of their mortgage payments, few realize that a house with no mortgage has an interest cost which is almost as high. This is because the money tied up in a home could be earning interest if it were put in a savings account or in stocks, and this foregone interest is a very real cost of owning. Foregone and mortgage interest rates differ, since one must always pay more to borrow money than one could have earned by lending it (investing). But at a minimum, the foregone interest costs amount to at least what the money could earn elsewhere, which is 3 percent plus the rate of inflation. To this is added the extra cost of borrowing money, which will decrease to zero as the mortgage is paid off. Because inflation affects both the market value of a house and the interest costs (foregone or paid), it may seem that one offsets the other. But rather than count appreciation as a cost offset, and market interest rates as a cost, 3 percent of the house value can be taken as the annual interest cost in real terms, without having to predict future inflation rates. To this 3 percent are still added the extra real costs of borrowing money (above rates paid on savings).

So far I have a 3.5 percent depreciation cost, a 3 percent interest cost, and some differential interest cost if I must borrow. What else?

Property taxes will run between 1.5 and 2 percent per year of the current house value.

Utilities will cost 3 to 4 percent.

Insurance premiums will be 0.5 percent.

Summing these costs shows that living in a house costs somewhere between 9.5 and 14 percent of its value (i.e., current selling price) each year. Hence, the two rules about how much housing a family can afford really are equivalent. At a 12 percent cost rate, a $40,000 house costs $400 a month in equivalent rent-plus-utilities. If annual housing costs should be about one-fourth of income, and total purchase price should be about twice income, then the annual cost of housing should be about one-eighth of the total purchase price (12.5 percent).

That does not mean that the rules of thumb are right for everyone, however. Many people spend far more than 25 percent of their income on housing, and many spend far less, happily. It may make sense to own a larger house than needed right now because the extra space will be used later, or was needed earlier. It would not make sense to rent a place of the wrong size, since the costs of moving are so much less when renting and the risks so much smaller.

Tax laws make it advantageous to own and possibly to hold a house larger than present needs call for. Homeowners can deduct their property tax and mortgage interest from taxable income. They are also exempted from paying tax on the capital gains income brought about by increases in the market price of the house as long as they buy another house of equal or greater value within eighteen months after selling the old one, or are fifty-five years of age or older and elect a once-in-a-lifetime exemption from the capital gains on the house. In addition, the imputed rental income they receive by owning is untaxed. Imputed rental income is best thought of as the profit or return on his investment that a homeowner pays to himself rather than to a landlord if he were renting. To see this, suppose I sell my house, switch to renting, and invest

Table 7. Annual Before- and After-Tax Costs of Owning a $50,000 House

	Costs at Inflation Rate I		
	$I = 0$	$I = 5\%$	$I = 10\%$
Property tax at 2% of house value	$1,000	$1,000	$1,000
Interest costs at $(3 + I)\%$ of house value	1,500	4,000	6,500
Depreciation and maintenance at 3.5% of house value	1,750	1,750	1,750
Other costs (utilities, insurance) at 3.5% of house value	1,750	1,750	1,750
Total annual cost	6,000	8,500	11,000
Appreciation at $I\%$ of house value	0	2,500	5,000
Net before-tax cost (= total cost minus appreciation)	6,000	6,000	6,000
Tax savings if no mortgage			
With 20% marginal tax rate	200	200	200
With 50% marginal tax rate	500	500	500
Net after-tax cost (20% rate)	5,800	5,800	5,800
Net after-tax cost (50% rate)	5,500	5,500	5,500
Tax savings if fully mortgaged			
With 20% marginal tax rate	500	1,000	1,500
With 50% marginal tax rate	1,250	2,500	3,750
Net after-tax cost (20% rate)	5,500	5,000	4,500
Net after-tax cost (50% rate)	4,750	3,500	2,250

the proceeds. Before I can use the investment yield to pay my rent, there is income tax on it. But as a homeowner, my investment "yield" was untaxed.

The interplay of depreciation, interest costs, inflation, and tax considerations is illustrated in the set of calculations shown in table 7. House value is assumed to be

$50,000; inflation rates (I) take on values of zero, 5 percent, and 10 percent, while marginal tax rates are set equal to 20 percent and 50 percent. The assumptions about housing costs as a fraction of house value follow the previous discussion and are also shown in the table. Interest costs paid on the mortgage or foregone by having money tied up in the house are assumed to amount to 3 percent plus the rate of inflation. Here we ignore the fact that current mortgage interest rates are generally higher than interest rates paid on savings accounts. Some homeowners with older mortgages fixed at lower rates will do better than these calculations would indicate, while new homeowners may do worse.

The first seven rows of the table show that before-tax annual housing costs increase with the inflation rate but that net housing costs (after appreciation is subtracted) remain a constant $6,000 per year. Inflation increases interest costs and appreciation by identical amounts; the net housing costs remain the same.

Income tax laws benefit homeowners, particularly if they hold mortgages. The deductibility of property tax payments saves the homeowners in our example either $200 or $500 in taxes, depending on the marginal tax rate. A fully-mortgaged $50,000 house will save its owner an additional $500 to $3,750 in taxes, however, depending on the inflation rate and the marginal tax rate. The large tax savings results because homeowners can deduct all of the mortgage interest payments from taxable income but do not usually have to pay taxes on the capital gains they receive on the house. In the most extreme case in the table, a fully-mortgaged homeowner with a 50 percent marginal tax rate and facing a 10 percent inflation rate incurs housing costs that are less than half as large as either an otherwise similar homeowner living in an inflation-free world ($2,250 per year versus $4,750 per year) or an otherwise similar homeowner with no mortgage ($2,250 per year versus $5,500 per year). The cost differences for the homeowner in the 20 percent tax bracket are much less. Thus, higher inflation rates produce large financial benefits to high-income homeowners with mortgages.

These differential tax savings lead to some important market considerations. In buying a house, you compete with those whose tax subsidies may be greater than yours, if their marginal tax rate is higher and they itemize deductions. On a given house, they may face an after-tax housing cost that is less than half the cost to you, and they may bid up the price of that house as a result.

Own or Rent?

The question of home ownership is filled with emotion, and there are strongly worded arguments on both sides. Some claim it is unsound, more expensive, and foolish to own. Others insist that it makes the owner a pillar of the community, establishes credit rating, forces saving for old age, promises larger capital gains, and has tax advantages. It has already been pointed out that the question of which is cheaper—if two roughly equal houses are available, one for rent and the other for sale—can be answered by making correct economic calculations of the current costs of each. The renter's cost is rent plus utilities; the owner's costs are the various percentages of house value listed earlier.

A common source of confusion in comparing the costs of owning and renting is that after paying off the mortgage, an owner ends up with a house worth tens of thousands of dollars while a renter ends up with nothing of comparable value. The key to this problem is that most of the owner's mortgage payment is really savings and has nothing to do with the economic costs of owning.

Compare the situation of someone who has just purchased a $50,000 house, and has a twenty-year mortgage at 3 percent, with a renter of an equivalent house. Assume initially that the rate of inflation is zero and the owner pays no excess interest costs on his mortgage. From the fourth column of table 3 (p. 18) we see that for a twenty-year mortgage at 3 percent on a $50,000 house, the ratio (Amount of Mortgage)/(Yearly Payment) = 14.877, so the yearly mortgage payment is $3,361, and the monthly mortgage payment is $280. Most of the costs of owning involve payments unrelated to this mortgage payment: property tax payments of 2 percent of house value will cost an additional $83 per month, repairs and alterations at 3.5 percent will costs $146 per month, utilities at 3 percent will cost $125 per month, and insurance payments at 0.5 percent of the house price will cost $21 per month. These costs, which are unrelated to the mortgage payment (and will continue even when the mortgage is paid off), amount to $375 per month.

To see that most of the mortgage is savings, suppose that the renter pays his rent (which ought to amount to about $375 per month plus a normal return on the landlord's investment) and deposits $280 per month into a savings account that pays 3 percent. Both owner and renter consume identical housing services for twenty years. The sum of housing costs plus savings are higher for the renter than the owner by the amount of profit paid to the landlord. The owner ends up with a $50,000 house, but the renter ends up with a savings account balance of $90,283. (This is the value at the end of twenty years of the accumulated savings plus interest. From the fifth column of table 3, $280 × 12 months × 26.870 = $90,283.) The renter accumulates more than the owner because he keeps the interest on his savings, while the owner pays the interest costs to the bank. Indeed, this is exactly the foregone interest cost that the owner incurs. To convert this cost to present value terms, it is useful to calculate the amount per month that the renter would have to add to his savings account to end up with a $50,000 balance after twenty years. Using the fifth column of table 3, we see that $50,000/(Amount per Year) = 26.870, so that the monthly amount is $155. So if both owner and renter want to end up with something worth $50,000, the owner must pay $280 per month for it, while the renter pays only $155. The difference, $125 per month, is the foregone interest cost incurred by the owner. But if the landlord receives a 3 percent return on his investment, then the renter will pay the extra $125 per month as profit to the landlord. Consideration of tax effects will change these results somewhat in favor of the owner, while the excess interest costs of a mortgage will do the reverse. A potentially more important modification, however, is to allow for inflation. Inflation will drive up the house price, but it should also drive up the interest rate paid on the renter's savings. If the inflation rate is 3 percent per year, then the house price will inflate to $50,000 × 1.806 = $90,300 in twenty years. But a 3 percent inflation rate will also drive up the interest rate on nondepreciating financial investments, if not always on savings accounts. If that interest rate is 6 percent, then the renter will accumulate $123,487 on his $280 monthly savings account deposits.

The other issues involved with the decision to own or rent are more difficult to quantify. Renting leaves one flexible, able to move with less cost—no broker's fees, no difficulty finding a buyer or seller. A renter can also adjust his or her housing to changing family needs, and thus economize. In addition, time need not be spent on activities that are the landlord's responsibility and that are less productive economically than sticking to one's own occupation.

Owning, however, provides a defense against inflation in the form of an asset whose value increases and a housing cost that—unlike rent—does not shoot up in tight housing markets.[2] Owning also allows more freedom in how to use the dwelling, and provides opportunities for tax-exempt do-it-yourself activities such as painting and repairing. Remember, there are those two income tax bites: on the money I earn to pay rent and on the money the landlord, or the painter he employs, earns. The income tax is a double tax on the division of labor. In my own house, I can be relatively inefficient at do-it-yourself activities and still find them economically worthwhile. The house also remains an asset, providing security even in bankruptcy. And there are tax advantages, property taxes and interest payments being deductible from income for federal income taxes, and the imputed rent and capital gains being untaxed.

Decisions about whether to own or rent, and about how much housing to buy, are also affected by liquidity considerations, and a healthy respect for the interest charges associated with most mortgages. The amortized mortgage is a relatively recent invention and one of the first of many devices to help people manage their own finances. The villain in the old melodramas was always about to take over the farmstead because the mortgage had come due—not just a payment or the interest, but the whole thing. In those days, only the interest was payable regularly; the principal came due on the last day. An amortized mortgage, like ordinary installment credit, sets up a regular and constant monthly payment which returns both interest and principal, so that some fixed interest rate is paid

2. Also, a large house can be owned with a small investment—an example of "leverage" (see chap. 7).

Table 8. Annual Payments to Amortize a $10,000 Mortgage over *n* Years at Several Interest Rates[a]

n	r = 4%	r = 6%	r = 8%	r = 10%	r = 12%	r = 14%
5	$2,246	$2,374	$2,505	$2,638	$2,774	$2,913
10	1,232	1,359	1,490	1,627	1,770	1,917
15	899	1,030	1,168	1,315	1,468	1,628
20	736	872	1,019	1,175	1,339	1,510
25	640	782	937	1,102	1,275	1,455
30	578	726	888	1,061	1,241	1,428
35	536	690	858	1,037	1,223	1,414
40	505	664	839	1,022	1,213	1,407
45	483	647	826	1,014	1,207	1,403
50	466	634	817	1,009	1,204	1,402

[a]Divide by 12 to get monthly payments.

on the remaining balance. The first payment is, of course, largely interest, since the remaining principal is large, while the last payment is largely on the principal, there being little principal left to demand interest. Table 8 shows the amount of annual payment per $10,000 borrowed at several interest rates and for several different repayment periods. (Divide by 12 to get approximate monthly payments.) Figure 3 shows that the remaining amount owed on principal declines slowly at first. Figure 4 shows how the early payments are mostly interest and the later ones largely principal.

Lenders do not allow indefinitely long mortgage payment periods, so the amount of housing may be limited by how much I can assemble for a down payment and the monthly payments. As we saw earlier, compound interest amounts to a great deal over long periods. A useful rule of thumb here is that if the interest rate times the number of years is close to 150, e.g., 10 percent for 15 years, or 5 percent for 30 years, then the total payments add up to about twice the price of the house. At 5 percent, a $30,000 house will cost $2,000 a year for 30 years in mortgage payments, or $60,000. Monthly payments can be cut only by paying for a longer period, and hence paying more total interest, or by making a larger down payment, which hides some interest cost in the form of the foregone interest that would otherwise have been earned on the down payment money. It is important, however, to examine the common notion that extending the period over which the mortgage is repaid makes a house easier to afford. Suppose you want to borrow $100,000 to buy a house, and the going interest rate is 6 percent. A ten-year mortgage will pay it off at $13,590 a year, or $1,132.50 per month.[3] By quadrupling the period, you can cut the monthly payments in half: a forty-year mortgage would be $6,640 per year, or $553.33 per month. The total payments on the ten-year mortgage are $135,900, the total interest cost $35,900. But the total payments on the forty-year mortgage are $265,000, and the total interest cost $165,600. You have cut the current payments in half, but pay four times as long and more than five times as much in interest! The higher the interest rate, the more dramatic the interest cost differences. The difference in the present value of the costs is less, since most of the lower payments are far into the future. But you do incur more real cost by having more dollar-years of debt on which you pay interest.

In addition to the sale price of the house, the buyer often must pay many additional costs such as title insurance, title search, mortgage insurance, and closing costs. Since most of them are associated with getting a mortgage, they can be thought of as extra interest cost. There is considerable variability in the costs, and it often pays to shop around among banks for the best "deal." Buyers must trade off differences in mortgage interest rates, and it is helpful to know how to convert one-time costs into implied additional interest charges.

To convert any or all such one-time charges, closing costs, or points into an addition to the interest rate requires a calculator that handles mortgage values, but table 9 will provide some examples. It tells you how much to add to the stated interest on a mortgage to allow for charges paid at the beginning. Charges are computed as a fraction of the amount of the mortgage. Thus, if the lump-sum costs on a $50,000, thirty-year, 10 percent mortgage amount to $2,500, then $2,500/$50,000, or 5 percent of the mortgage, will add 5 × 0.12 = 0.60 percent

3. This is calculated from table 8, second row, 6 percent column.

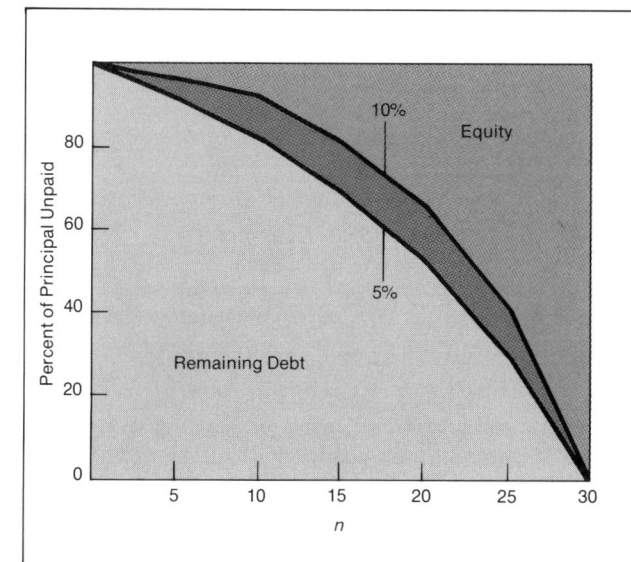

Fig. 3 Percent of principal unpaid after *n* years on thirty-year mortgages at 5 percent and 10 percent interest. For example, halfway through the thirty years, you still owe 68 percent of the original loan at 5 percent, or 82 percent of the original loan at 10 percent.

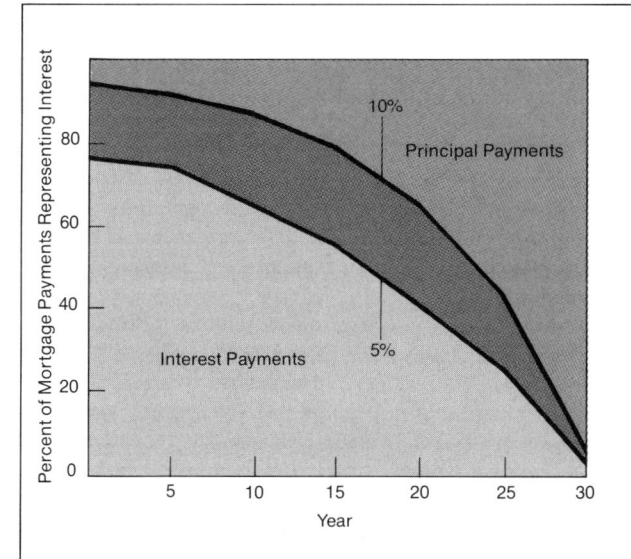

Fig. 4 Percent of annual mortgage payments representing interest on thirty-year mortgages at 5 percent and 10 percent rates. For example, in the fifteenth year of a thirty-year, 5 percent loan, 54 percent of your payments are interest and 46 percent are repayment of principal. At 10 percent, 79 percent of the payments in year 15 are still interest.

Table 9. Lump-Sum House Purchase Costs Converted to Additions to Interest Rate[a]

Stated Interest Rate	Amounts Added to Interest Rate on *n*-Year Mortgage			
	n = 5	n = 10	n = 20	n = 30
6%	.37%	.21%	.12%	.09%
8	.38	.22	.14	.11
10	.39	.23	.15	.12
12	.41[b]	.25	.16	.14[b]
14	.42	.26	.17	.15

[a]Assuming lump-sum costs equal 1 percent of the total mortgage. Thus, if lump-sum costs actually equal 10 percent of the total mortgage, multiply the figures listed by 10 to get the amount added to the effective interest rate. (This will underestimate a little.)

[b]For example, on a thirty-year, 12 percent mortgage, points, mortgage insurance, closing costs, title insurance, and other mandated charges amounting to 1 percent of the amount loaned to you add .14 percent to the interest rate. If you pay off the mortgage after five years, the interest rate cost has really been 12.4 percent for that period.

to the mortgage interest rate, where the 0.12 figure comes from the third row, fifth column of table 9. Since you are spreading the cost over the life of the mortgage, the added interest rate is higher if you pay off the mortgage sooner.

The federal Real Estate Settlement Procedures Act helps to protect the buyer even with the wide variety of customs as to how buyer and seller split closing costs. You can secure from the United States Department of Housing and Urban Development a guide to settlement costs that spells out your rights and obligations. For instance, you have a right to see an itemized list of services and fees the day before the closing. But even before that, you should have negotiated with the seller as to who pays what.

When a seller is asked to accept a purchase involving a Federal Housing Administration (FHA)- or Veterans Administration (VA)-insured mortgage, he should know that if the ceiling interest rate on such mortgages is below the going market interest rate for mortgages, he will be asked to pay "points." (Points represent added interest paid to the lender in one lump sum at the outset. They cannot by law be paid by the buyer, because that would openly raise the interest rate.) Any intelligent seller will, of course, raise the price of the house to cover this one-time charge, so just as with closing costs, the buyer ends up paying the equivalent of a higher interest rate anyway. How can one interpret points in terms of differential interest rates? One way is to take as a standard a 6 percent mortgage, and ask what the stream of payments such a mortgage promises is worth if the stream is discounted at higher interest rates of 8, 10, 12, or 14 percent. The difference in the value of these streams as a percent of the initial amount of the loan is called "points" (see table 10).

To bring the value of a mortgage up to 100 percent at the proper market interest rate, one must make someone pay the difference in cash. Using table 10 we see that, for example, a twenty-year, 6 percent mortgage worth $100,000 when the market interest rate is 8 percent would be worth $86,000, and the seller would be asked for $14,000 in "points."

You can think of this as changing either the price of the house or the interest rate, but it is really the latter, since you wouldn't pay it if you had cash to buy the house, and would pay it as interest if you bought with a conventional mortgage at market interest rates. It is important to keep in mind, however, that added interest charges from points (or closing costs) are not tax deductible like conventional mortgage charges.

There are emotional considerations favoring home ownership. Many people feel it is a symbol of having arrived, of being a good stable family, of responsible citizenship. The desire to own real property probably varies from country to country and from subculture to subculture, but it exists almost everywhere. And the notion that home ownership is usually a sign of other things is true. Research suggests that homeowners *are* better off, *do* plan ahead, *are* more responsible. They had to be that way in order to acquire a home, and they continue to be because human behavior patterns persist. At equivalent incomes and ages, they tend to save more and to accumulate more liquid assets.

Because they are more stable and more responsible, and usually have lived longer in the same community, homeowners also engage in more community activities and do more volunteer work. Buying a house, then, becomes a symbol which may have a value of its own to some people. Indeed, the data show that, other things being equal,

Table 10. Value of 6 Percent Mortgage Repayment Obligation at Different Market Interest Rates (in percent of amount of loan)

Years the Mortgage Runs	Present Value of Payments if Discounted at:				
	6%	8%	10%	12%	14%
15	100	88	78	70	63
20	100	86	74	65	58
25	100	83	71	61	54
30	100	82	68	59	51

homeowners actually spend more for housing than other people. This may be partly the result of the difficulty in moving and adjusting one's housing to current needs, so that a home sometimes reflects future or past maximum family size and need. But in part it reflects people's willingness to put more into their own homes than they would put into rent, or greater interest in their housing on the part of those who own a home.

There is a long-term speculative aspect to the question whether renting or owning is cheaper. It has to do with rents and house prices in the future, relative to one another. In the past, at times when renting seemed cheaper than buying (just before World War II, for example, after years of depression), it proved unwise to rent; housing rapidly got tighter, and as rents rose, so did house prices, closing the escape of shifting to ownership. On the other hand, during boom times when building lags behind, rents may climb to the point where it seems cheaper to buy or build a new house, but this too may be temporary; as rents fall, the market value of houses may also fall. If the market values houses at only five times annual rent instead of the eight to ten times implied in our rules of thumb, there must be some temporary surplus of houses or shortage of rental places.

Most economists would argue that we are in for decades more of inflation and that owning a home is one of the few ways an ordinary consumer can hedge himself against it—one of the few places he can put his money where its value will increase at least as fast as the overall rate of inflation. Since a person can own more house than he has actually paid for yet, he has "leverage." The colloquial translation is that it will be easy to pay off the mortgage later with cheaper dollars, while the whole house is going up in price.

At times, when it may be otherwise advantageous to purchase a house because of rising prices, there may also be credit stringencies ("tight money") so banks tend to raise not only interest rates but "standards" as well; sometimes they refuse to make mortgage loans at all. They are more interested in keeping their business borrowers, who are repeat customers, than their one-time mortgage borrowers.

It is possible to own and rent at the same time by buying a condominium, or to own with limits in a cooperative. Cooperatives and condominiums offer some advantages of scale and some control over a neighborhood. The cooperation can vary from group acquistion of land to extensive and continuing cooperation and development of community facilities.[4] The more cooperation there is, the more management skills are required, of course, and there is a tendency to rely on the voluntary work of members to provide those skills. The old adage that everybody's business is nobody's business often applies. But a cooperative can develop a fine community efficiently, and provide the kind of services the members really want at a cost level they prefer.

In practice, it seems that the successful cooperatives (a) have had individuals of high ability willing to put a lot of managerial effort into the initial development, and (b) have restricted the demands for member participation to the minimum. After the first enthusiasm is gone, most members would rather pay for the community work than rake leaves or mow the community baseball field, which adds to cost. The number of cooperatives that have failed, with financial losses to members, is substantial; even some successful ones nearly failed in the process of developing. Yet there are obvious economies of scale and advantages in bargaining to get public services. So long as the member obligations are clear and the rules set early to meet most contingencies, there is a chance of success. It helps to have members or friends who know law, real estate, building, engineering, and organizational procedures. The community spirit and mutual help that may exist in a cooperative are also added benefits.

Condominiums, on the other hand, seem to have most of the disadvantages of cooperatives without the advantages. There are complexities about exactly what you own, difficulties in getting out, and the necessity of living with group decisions. In fact, a condominium usually involves a management company over which the "owners" have little or no control and which charges monthly fees for outside maintenance, club facilities, and management. The management company can raise charges and decide what facilities to add (and charge for). The company can develop many different properties, get most of its capital back by selling the condominium apartments or houses, and still be in a position to take most of the profits in monthly charges if the place develops well. If it doesn't, the owners are left with the losses when they try to sell. (U.S. Department of Housing and Urban Development, 1976)

Why do people buy condominiums? Some like the facilities and the freedom from responsibility for outside maintenance, the ease of leaving the place empty for periods of travel, and the possibility of renting it through the management company. Others like the income tax advantages, which are the same as for home ownership. And there are possible capital gains, tax-deferred if another place is purchased that costs at least as much. Many condominiums have been purchased as vacation or future retirement homes, with the understanding that the management company will attempt to rent them when they are not needed by the owner. There is always the chance that no tenant will be found, but the costs of holding idle property are mostly hidden (opportunity) costs, and the possible difficulties in getting their money out do not seem apparent to many buyers.

In the wake of some scandals, laws are being improved to deal with varieties of ownership and semi-ownership arrangements, but it is probably unwise to get into complicated arrangements that can be difficult to get out of.

Legal Traps and Tax Issues

Not only is a house a big investment for an individual, but there are some technical and legal pitfalls to be avoided when buying or building one. Clear title to the land can be a problem; legally, if you build a house on someone else's land, that person owns the house without any compensation to you. This fear is prevalent enough to support a profitable business in title insurance to cover the risk.

In building a house, one indirectly engages various artisans, who are protected by "mechanic's lien laws." These laws state that any "mechanic" not paid for his work on

---
4. A cooperative may form a corporation to own the land or the buildings, or both. Or members may agree to sell back to the cooperative when they leave.

the property can place a lien on it. As the home buyer, you may have paid the contractor or the speculative builder, but if he fails to pay the workmen, you are responsible for paying them. Some people end up paying for their house twice. The "how-to" books urge you to secure a signed "waiver of lien" statement for each step in the building process before paying that installment on the house. Sometimes the banks will secure it for you, but it is a difficult process and still may not avoid trouble. The number of builders who go through bankruptcy should be enough to give one pause. When a builder gets behind, it is only too easy for him to use the money from one buyer to pay the workers for their work on a *previous* house.

Similarly, builders are sometimes careless about restrictions, such as minimum setbacks of buildings from lot lines. Buyers then find it necessary to go through complex and expensive negotiations to purchase a few feet of land from a neighbor in order to be legal. Some builders are also careless about drainage, and owners can find themselves with major engineering problems. But as we shall see later, the biggest risk comes from buying or building a house in a neighborhood not yet stabilized, i.e., one only partly built up. The value of a house depends heavily upon the neighborhood and can be diminished by persisting empty lots, or badly designed houses, or large apartment buildings, or various noxious commercial uses. Legal protection against such deterioration is weak.

Another legal detail about housing that everyone should know is the doctrine of easement. If someone wants to do something which infringes on another's property, such as using half of a joint driveway, the owner may be asked to agree to a formal easement. More important, if someone infringes on property for many years without objection, that person acquires the right to do so indefinitely; this is called a "prescriptive easement." To avoid this, people with private roads shut them off once a year with a "private property" sign, thereby retaining the right to close them in the future.

Legal details of leases or sales contracts are varied enough from state to state and complex enough that a lawyer is often needed. On the other hand, there are standard lease forms and local traditions about such matters as damage deposits which may help the unassisted buyer or tenant.

Spreading from the Midwest to other parts of the country is a different way of purchasing homes, where the title does not pass to the buyer until the last payment is made. These arrangements are called "land contracts." In ordinary times, land contracts are often used when the buyer has little or no down payment or even a poor credit rating, and hence carry an interest rate higher than on conventional mortgages. A major advantage of a land contract is that its terms are negotiated by the buyer and seller and not by a bank. The seller's risk is small, since he or she can reclaim the property without elaborate, costly, and time-consuming foreclosure proceedings. A land contract usually says that if any payment is missed, all previous payments are considered rent, and the owner can reclaim the property. But in fact, the courts have decided that a person cannot sign away such rights (accumulated equity in the house) that way, so the buyer does accumulate an investment in the property. Legally, the seller owes the property taxes until the deal is transferred, but the contract may call for the buyer to pay them.

An additional consideration in the decision whether to rent or own is the curious legal position of the tenant relative to the landlord. There are situations, more common in other countries, where the land is only rented to those who build on it. However long the lease, there are problems when it ends, and problems in the interim about adjusting for inflation or market changes. The "tenants" may do very well on fixed ground rents, as in Hawaii, until the lease runs out and the landowner escalates the rent.

Under the law of most states, the relation between landlord and tenant is not considered a contractual one, but a lease agreement.

Therefore, no matter how badly the landlord fails in his obligation to the tenant, unless there is an existing statutory exception, the tenant must continue to pay his full rent, at the proper time, or face eviction. (Lipsky and Neuman)

Some attempts at reform have been made, particularly in New York City, with systems for putting rents into escrow to be used for repairs.

A worse problem for the poor is that they often have no leases at all, but rent from month to month. This means that the landlord can evict them, or raise the rent suddenly, in retaliation for any complaints about unsatisfactory conditions. If the situation is bad enough, the tenant may move out, claiming "constructive eviction," and be free from any obligation to continue rent, but it is often difficult to move and find another place.

Finally, where there is high turnover, landlords may demand a damage deposit, and sometimes keep it whether or not there has been damage. Various reforms have been suggested or instituted, including a public fund into which damage deposits can be placed, with independent determination of their disposition, and into which rents or parts of rent can be placed when needed repairs are not being done by the landlord. All this would increase the total cost of renting slightly, but would also treat tenants more equitably. It might eliminate a marginal supply of rental housing where the rents had been low because of bad maintenance or an implied obligation of the tenants to do any maintenance that becomes necessary. The damage deposit works a particular hardship on low-income renters, who are usually at a disadvantage in bargaining position and legal sophistication. The legal situation is changing, however, with many states providing new protections for tenants.

Buying and Selling

At any one time, only a limited number of places to live are available, and a buyer does not know what else may become available before a choice has to be made. Neither is there any very adequate or easy-to-secure information to help in the search. Realtors can be one source of information. They often keep records of past sales prices, know the reputation of areas and neighborhoods, and should offer good guesses as to the market values of the available houses. Direct inspection of a neighborhood late in the afternoon should reveal the age distribution (school children), traffic patterns, and general appearance. The assessor's office (city or county) can provide assessed values for specific properties, and the (county) registrar of deeds has data on the last few transfers of title. The sales price can usually be inferred from the federal tax stamps on property transfers. The city assessor can provide the average assessment ratio, for each area if it varies, which can then be used to estimate the market value for an individual house. Mortgage lenders also have notions about good places to live, often rather conservative, of course, and the office of the school system has information about school districts.

Besides the difficulty of getting information, and the need to wait until something suitable comes on the market, there are other substantial costs of moving. Even from rented place to rented place there are the costs of moving furniture and possessions. In selling a house and buying another, each transaction costs both buyer and seller various amounts. The realtor takes 5 to 7 percent, title insurance 1 to 4 percent, and statutory fees up to 2 percent. The overall difference between what the buyer pays and what the seller gets ranges from a few percentage points to ten or fifteen (Payne). Technically, the seller pays the realtor, and pays any "mortgage points," though he probably raised the sale price of the house to cover the latter.

The buyer pays the closing costs (transfer tax and title insurance, totaling usually 2 to 3 percent) and sometimes prepaid property taxes, insurance, and special tax assessments, although these last three are not really transaction costs.

The realtor's fee will be divided between the realtor who arranged the sale and the one who got the house listed. This means that a realtor is rarely a disinterested source of advice, since the realtor gets the full commission on houses that he has put on the list, partial commission on those that other realtors have listed, and nothing on houses sold without listing at all. It is often difficult to sell or buy a house without a realtor, however, since the market is so unorganized and the "product" so heterogeneous. A realtor can provide a screening function for those who consider their time too costly to do much searching on their own.

There is frequently a kickback, from the title insurance company to both lawyers in the transaction, of part of what a buyer must pay for title insurance. Indeed, there are even lawyer-run title insurance arrangements, usually called "attorney's funds," with the profits going to the lawyers. This clearly deceives the consumer as to who is being paid for what—entirely apart from the conflict of interest on the part of the lawyers—in cases where there is a choice about title insurance companies, procedures, or need. In fact, there are communities where almost no one gets title insurance or lawyers' title guarantee, and other areas where almost everyone does. We do not know whether this reflects real differences in the risk and need for insurance, or merely the organized sale of a service in some areas. But the buyer has little choice if a mortgage is necessary and the mortgage lenders insist on title insurance.

Selling a house involves some additional decisions, the most important being how much to ask for it. The ideal way might be to set no price, but to try to get buyers to make offers and compete with one another, for instance by promising to take the best offer above some minimum by some deadline. This is a difficult tactic, but without it one of two mistakes is likely. The price can be set too low, and the first lucky person to discover it will buy the house at less than its market value. Or the price can be too high, wasting time and energy, and perhaps causing the house to be left empty for a while, in which case people may figure there is something wrong with it besides the price. It is difficult to believe that the houses that are sold before they ever get on the market could not have been sold for a higher price. However, it is often true that a particular house has only one person really interested in it and that a buyer often sees only one house that seems right. In such cases, there may be a wide range of prices within which both would be satisfied.

Where—The Question of Neighborhood

Conventional wisdom says that the value of a house depends on three things: location, location, and location. Selecting a residence is a package deal which includes a neighborhood and a community, commuting opportunities, different public services and taxes and other costs, and a different prospect for future development.

Selecting a location with an eye on the differential costs of living in different places may be misleading. A glance at any table showing comparative living costs will reveal that only the shelter costs really vary much from place to place. This is understandable; most other things are sold on a national market—you can even get your prescriptions filled by mail. The apparent differences in shelter costs may not reflect different costs of living, but rather different standards of living or different ways of paying for certain basic services. Some communities provide more services than others, and charge higher taxes. Some economists think that differential consumer preferences are best served when various neighboring communities provide alternative levels and combinations of services, each one attracting people who prefer that particular mix. This may be a slow process, however; people have to live somewhere near their work, and moving is difficult and expensive. That tax increases for specific services have to be voted on locally probably helps local communities better serve their residents' needs.

How does this affect the apparent cost of housing in a community? Suppose a community decided to increase recreational facilities and to tax houses in the area $200 a year more to pay for it. The value of owning a house or living in that area is presumably reduced by $200 a year, the extra cost. At 3 percent, $200 a year forever is worth $200/0.03 = $6,667 today. But if people value the recreational facilities at more than $200 a year—as most must since they voted for them—the net value of living in the area may go up a little. More important, if *most* people value the services more highly than they dislike the taxes, house values and rents will go *up*, not down. Note, however, that the cost of housing will look high in this community, simply because it includes more public services. Rents will be higher too, covering the landlords' higher taxes, and justified by the recreational facilities for which the taxes pay.

There might be differences in the efficiency with which different communities use their tax money, but that would be impossible to sort out. It is not even easy to find out what the community spends its money on, because there are both capital and operating costs, and federal revenue-sharing funds to help offset them. It makes more sense simply to select a community with the mix of services you want, if you can afford it. One warning—cost of living data by area are often price indexes, all with 1967 costs as base, so that they are relative differences in price increases since 1967 rather than actual cost of living differences. (Brackett and Lamale provides genuine comparisons.)

So the community with more services may not have higher taxes relative to house prices, and the community with higher rents and house prices may even give more per dollar in the form of libraries, parks, fluoride in the water, community centers, recreational facilities, police and fire protection. The real cost of living might be higher in a town where residents have to join a club to go swimming, buy all their own books, and generally cannot share many expenses with others.

Aside from costs and services, what makes a good neighborhood? No longer quite so important are issues of commuting costs and location with respect to schools, shops, and services. With the difficulty of forecasting the future location of jobs and schools, such considerations take second place to forecasts about the future of the neighborhood. Public transportation availability may take on new importance with high fuel prices.

Since the forecasts of experts have a self-justifying quality, coming true because people believe them, bankers and realtors are a good source of information about the future of neighborhoods. They tend to like homogeneous neighborhoods with uniform house and lot sizes, similar architectural styles, uniform land use, and similar types of people. In spite of democratic egalitarian opposition to the idea, most people prefer voluntary segregation by social class at least. No matter how much space one can afford around the house, there are still neighbors, and wide differences in living styles and standards of upkeep can be irritating all around.

There is vast literature on neighborhood and community design and beauty, most of it expressing the tastes of the writers and often ignoring the economic costs of what is proposed. What most people are concerned with, however, is not architecture or trees, but the simple neatness, cleanliness, and orderliness of an area. A study comparing the attitudes of architects and planners with those of ordinary residents found startling discrepancies in their ideas about what made a good neighborhood. The "experts" reflected the tastes of only the highly educated minority of residents (Lansing and Hendricks). The rest of the people focused on cleanliness and neatness.

Homeowner's Protection

If the value of a house and the owners' satisfaction in living in it depend on what goes on around it, what defenses have they against changes that will ruin the neighborhood?

First, there are zoning laws restricting the uses of property and the kinds of dwellings allowed. Their efficacy has been reduced in the past because zoning boards have often capitulated to pressures to alter things, or have zoned too much land for more intensive uses in the first place. It is clearly safest to own a home in an area zoned entirely for single family houses. However, zoning almost never specifies the number of occupants per house or per square foot, and the definition of "single family" can be stretched. Furthermore, it is difficult to administer regulations against renting out rooms and particularly difficult to enforce regulations that have been ignored for years.

Property owners often form associations, either to press the zoning boards or the city administration for better safeguards, or to act in other ways. While they sometimes oppose things which would not really do much harm, such associations have in some cases managed to preserve a delightful neighborhood in the midst of decay and ugliness. The classic example is Beacon Hill in Boston, the Louisburg Square area in particular (Firey).

A third way of protecting a neighborhood is to introduce into the deed of sale a restrictive covenant requiring each buyer to abide by certain restrictions. Old racial restrictive covenants have been declared unconstitutional and therefore unenforceable. Others become obsolete, because they specify architectural styles, minimum dollar values per dwelling, or other standards of the moment. Still, they remain a possible way of specifying standard densities (minimum square feet per occupant, for instance) or other basic requirements.

Given the weaknesses of regulations or standards and the difficulties of enforcing them, the household choosing a neighborhood is really faced with a problem of predicting what may happen, assuming they will not have much power to affect the trend of events. There is some pattern to the way cities develop, and there are some rules of thumb used by realtors and city planners in making predictions. Old, small houses tend either to become the homes of lower-income or transitional families or to give way to apartments, even though a society with more and more well-financed older people might expect to develop such residential areas for them. New areas with much empty land can develop rapidly in good or bad ways depending on what the owners of the empty lots do. The sizes of lots often dictate the kind of uses, and it is very difficult to change that. Standards of lot size have risen as people's incomes have risen, and better transportation has allowed them the space, until single family homes on less than 10,000 square feet seem to be considered deficient and might have lower resale value. Developers often attempt to hide the smallness of lots just as they try to hide the lack of adequate space inside, partly by selling houses while there are still empty lots next door or behind.

Good standards for community services require both the willingness and the ability to pay for them. The former may be revealed by recent history. The latter is affected by the tax base relative to the potential needs. Some business or industry is often essential to help pay for things.

Design, Style, and Site

Choice of a residence also involves decisions about design and style, and about site or position of one house in relation to others. If you are buying, there are two sometimes competing criteria to be used—your own preferences and needs, and the resale value. One way to separate matters of taste from generally applicable principles is to ask what affects most people's satisfaction with their residences. The answer appears to be space, so the number of square feet of livable floor space in a house is crucial.

Builders commonly make houses seem larger than they are by using open planning with fewer halls but larger rooms. This results in the need to use rooms for halls—to walk through the middle of the living room in order to get from the front door to anywhere else in the house, for example. Occasionally, to get more rooms in a house, builders make all the rooms slightly undersized, which is hardly noticeable until the buyer tries to install furniture.

Basements and second floors allow the use of smaller lots, and apparently most people prefer the traditional two-story house with basement. Some people believe the one-floor house is far more efficient to live in, but in areas where people prefer more traditional places, resale of a one-floor house could be a problem.

The positioning of a house can affect the privacy it affords as well as its energy demands. The sun is a powerful oxidizing agent that can destroy a set of drapes in a few years. Rooms that face north and east can have good light without the heat of the midday sun. Because the prevailing wind direction is usually from the southwest, a southeast outside area can have the morning sun plus protection from the wind. Access to the house is important too, particularly from cars. It is also useful to be able to get into the house without letting in too much rain or snow or wind.

The Social Approach to Housing and Community

Because of heavy interdependence among the use of land, the importance of housing, and the way people's activities affect their neighbors, governments have always been involved in the problems of housing and community. Leaders have commonly felt that some people did not have adequate housing and could not (or would not) get it for themselves. They have tried to improve the housing through various approaches, which can be classified as either bribery or coercion.

Coercion includes building codes and ordinances, or the use of police powers to insist on minimum standards of sanitation and safety. The difficulty is that such powers cannot force a landlord or owner to improve the dwelling, but can only threaten to prohibit occupancy. That leaves the occupants without housing, and the empty building to breed rats and be an eyesore. Furthermore, a landlord can "bleed" a dwelling, by not paying taxes or doing any maintenance for some years, and then simply abandon it at the point where its present value (expected stream of rents net of obligations) is zero or negative. Hence, the powers of government to enforce standards, particularly in rental housing, are limited.

Bribery means subsidizing housing in a variety of ways,

trying to insure that the benefits go largely to the poor and to those who would not otherwise have adequate housing. Laissez faire economists can point to many instances where the subsidy goes to the wrong people or creates inefficiencies or misallocation of resources. Sometimes it is partly converted from a subsidy in housing to a subsidy in cash (as when recipients illegally rent out rooms to others).

Many subsidy programs end up helping the lower-middle-income group rather than the really poor, because the manager of a housing project tends to screen out "undesirables" who might give the place a bad name. Since any new housing is expensive, the more recent programs attempt to provide rent subsidies that allow the poor to live in older dwellings with the government paying some of the rent, usually some fraction of the amount by which the rent exceeds 25 percent of income.[5]

Housing Costs Too Much?

Social policies have also attempted to reduce the costs of housing in ways which interfered less with the free play of market forces. The original purpose of FHA mortgage guarantees was to reduce the apparent risk to lenders and get them to offer lower interest rates. The insurance reduced the risk, thus the interest, and hence the cost. As we have seen, over a long period the rate of interest has a substantial effect on the total cost of a house. The FHA rate ceilings were an attempt to keep interest rates down (below market rates), but of course they failed. What happened was that private lenders started the practice of charging "points," which merely converts the extra interest into a cash payment at the beginning. The law prohibited the buyer from paying more interest, but it did not prevent the lender from making someone pay a lump-sum premium for the loan. Indeed, in some low-income areas, the very complexity of the point system led to the development of "mortgage brokers" who handled the details and took a commission for themselves, ultimately costing the borrower more than if the whole system had

---

5. These programs change so rapidly that there is little point in providing a detailed description of them. You might like to take any one of the current ones and analyze it (a) in terms of its redistributive aspects: how much subsidy to people at what income levels, and (b) in terms of its effects on resource allocation: would the housing not exist, or these people not have such good housing, without the program?

not existed. As it is, FHA mortgages, with the 0.5 percent charge for the insurance, end up costing what a conventional mortgage costs in many cases. Their main advantage to the individual may well be the FHA inspection and procedures requiring minimum standards of quality.

How else might one reduce the cost of housing? Many commentators point to the various restrictive rules of the building trades, others to the welter of building codes which inhibit innovation. The basic structure of the housing industry, however, probably accounts for much of the problem. It consists of a relatively inelastic demand (unresponsive to price) for houses, supplied by a large number of small competitive builders, each purchasing materials and services from a large number of independent trades or material suppliers. The derived demand seen by each of those suppliers is extremely inelastic. If the plumbers' wages amount to only 5 percent of the cost of the house, then a 20 percent increase in the salaries of plumbers will raise the price of the house by only 1 percent, and the builders find it hard to resist such demands from the plumbers. Whenever there are more buyers than sellers, the sellers have the upper hand, but this is particularly true where the demand is inelastic. When this is combined with the restrictive rules in the building trades, particularly restrictions on entry into the trades, and inadequate competition among the limited number of producers of, say, plumbing equipment, it is not hard to see why housing is expensive to build.

Why didn't this happen to automobiles? A few manufacturers took over and drove hard bargains with the suppliers, producing their own parts if and when necessary. They also managed to convince customers to choose from a limited number of styles and designs. Henry Ford used to say his customers could have any color vehicle they liked, as long as it was black. An elastic demand helped. With increasing volume, more variety was possible, but nothing like the fantastic variety implied by building each house to a specific design to please one customer or one speculative builder. Large-volume speculative builders of houses saved money, not just by volume buying, but also by building the same basic house over and over again.

Aside from construction costs and interest costs, the other major component of the cost of housing is the property taxes that must be paid on the house. They amount to between 1 and 3 percent of the value of the house each year, depending on the services provided and the cost of those services. The literature is full of charges that property taxes are badly assessed, inequitable, and regressive, falling more heavily on the poor. Actually, these complaints are badly overstated.

Property taxes combine an official tax rate (often made up of a city school district and a county rate) and an "assessed valuation" which is usually some fraction of the market value of the house. So:

$$\frac{\text{Property taxes}}{\text{Market value of house}} = \frac{\text{Taxes paid}}{\text{Assessed value}} \times \frac{\text{Assessed value}}{\text{Market value}}$$

which means that:

$$\text{Real tax rate} = \text{Official tax rate} \times \text{Assessment ratio}.$$

A comparison of assessment ratios shows them often higher in rural areas (mostly because property values have gone up less there than in cities), and some people conclude that this means the tax in rural areas is unfairly high. But, in fact, the tax rates are generally much lower in the rural areas, more than offsetting the reverse differences in assessment ratios. There can be wide variability in tax rates or in assessment ratios, but these factors can tend to offset one another so that the effective tax rate does not vary much. So it is misleading to focus only on rates of assessments while overlooking the effective taxes relative to property values. Finally, when tax rates relative to market values of houses are high, it usually means that more services are being provided, and the houses are consequently worth more than they would otherwise be.

The property tax has several additional strikes against it in the popular mind. It is payable in lumps, during summer vacation season and right after Christmas in most places. It is seen as mostly financing the public school system (which it does), a public service that at any one time seems to benefit only those with children in the public schools, although almost everyone has had or will have some similar benefit. Indeed, what many people do not realize is that even if they will not personally benefit from or use some proposed new community facility or service, enough others will, so that everyone will "get his taxes back" in the form of increased value of his property.

Finally, the property tax is claimed to be regressive, falling more heavily on low-income people, as personified by the retired couple on a fixed income who have trouble eating and also paying their rising property taxes. In fact, the statistics used to prove this point are misleading. They usually consist of property taxes paid (by homeowners only) as a fraction of the income of families in different income groups. But:

1. Income alone is not a good measure of ability to pay. The addition of nonmoney income, including the imputed rent on the owner's equity, reduces the amount of regressivity. That homeowners can deduct property taxes and mortgage interest from their taxable income also reduces regressivity.[6] On the other hand, if we adjust income for family size, larger families have less income per equivalent adult and somewhat larger houses, so the impression of regressivity is increased.

2. Renters also pay property taxes, since (at least in the long run) the price of any product must include all its costs. But most renters have lower incomes and smaller quarters. If one estimates their indirect property taxes and combines them with the taxes of homeowners, most of the regressivity disappears (Morgan, David, Cohen, and Brazer).

3. The data often cut across tax districts, ignoring differences in services received.

We are left with some older people with currently low incomes living in houses too large for their real needs and paying heavy property taxes relative to their current income. Property tax relief is provided for them in many states, but usually not for older renters who may actually be in worse shape.

When house prices and, hence, assessed values and taxes rise faster than incomes or other prices, an already disliked tax becomes "intolerable," particularly since few state or local governments have the sense to reduce tax rates in such a situation. Solutions such as California's Proposition 13 which restrict property tax increases unless the property is sold produce inequity of a new sort.

As another example of the importance of understanding capital theory, let us interpret the recent trend to get rid

---

6. The tax advantages become obvious if you rent your home to someone and spend a year in a rental house in another town. You have to pay income tax on the rental income you receive and so does your landlord. Exchanging houses rather than renting has clear tax advantages.

of the property tax in favor of local income taxes. Since the level of services is presumably unaffected, what will this do to the market values of houses? They should go up, of course, by an amount equal to the present value of the stream of tax reductions. A property tax cut of $100 per year should add about $100/0.03 = $3,333 to the price of a house. This does not cut the cost of housing to anyone thinking of buying a house after the change—he will in fact have to pay more. It is doubtful that it will reduce rents in the short run, providing instead an immediate benefit to landlords. The change largely benefits homeowners who may want to leave the community and can now sell at a price that includes their capital gain. Those who stay can get theirs only as a dribble over the years. So what seemed like a nice liberal idea—to get rid of the noxious regressive property tax in favor of a fairer, even progressive, income tax—turns out to provide capital gains to homeowners who sell, some tax relief in proportion to house value (and income) for other owners, and a bonanza for landlords.

Another of the real costs of housing is the cost of the land and the services required. As the quality of sewer, water, and other services provided rises, the costs of installing and providing these services also rise. These costs can be reduced by more systematic development, using all the land in one area before extending services to new areas, and also by reducing lot sizes, although that reduces people's satisfaction too. Delay or restrictiveness in extending such services can produce a rise in the market values of those building lots that have basic services available, simply because of their scarcity; this rise in market value provides monopoly profits for the developers who "got in on the ground floor," and keeps the price of houses up. It is hard to escape the feeling that a kind of conspiracy exists in many areas between the bankers, realtors, and developers to keep the extension of services and the amount of building down to a level that will "preserve property values" (and profit levels, and speculative gains). That many people with interests in property serve on official bodies making such decisions is an unstudied example of conflict of interest.

Renters who are angered by rising rents traditionally go after landlords, who are often merely charging market prices, instead of seeking to increase the local supply of housing and reduce the local restrictions that create monopoly profits.

Various restrictive practices and regulations have proven very difficult to eliminate, and these work to keep the prices of houses high. The production of several key building materials is so concentrated as to allow market restriction. The craft unions, with their apprenticeship systems and licensing rules (administered by members of the craft), have managed to drive their wages higher than would be possible with "free entry." But perhaps the major obstacle to efficiency and competition in building has been the myriad of state and local building codes and regulations, and their varied enforcement (sometimes arbitrary and even corrupt). With no ability to standardize, to manufacture components efficiently that will be legally usable everywhere, it is difficult for mass production methods to be applied to the housing industry. In the face of this, it seems ludicrous for those interested in housing to focus continually on design innovations which are likely to introduce more complexities and still higher costs. To give an example of local codes: In many places the use of plastic pipe is still prohibited or restricted. Or, even after the development of the flexible pipe-cleaning devices that could clean out sewer pipes under the house as well as down to the street, local codes may dictate that the opening be in front of the house instead of in back of it, requiring entering the pipes from a vent on the roof. Insulated sandwiches of plywood make stronger panels than the usual two-by-fours with plaster, yet are illegal where local codes specify minimum wall thicknesses.

The attempt to maintain the quality of housing by legal restrictions has focused on the inputs (materials and methods) of construction rather than the outputs (accessibility of the plumbing, safety of the structure), perhaps because it is easier. But this focus on acceptable materials and methods is much more rigid and resistant to innovation than standards of fire resistance, stress bearing, damp-proofness, and other aspects of construction would be.

Urban Development

On a broader scale, governments have been concerned with the general direction of urban development, with coordination in expansion and in the provision of services, and with longer-term planning. The large number of administrative bodies and private parties making irreversible decisions about the uses of land and investments in land make coordination a real problem. School boards, which are separate bodies, decide where to put schools, but it is the cities and counties that have to provide the roads and face up to the housing development bound to occur around each school. And the public utilities will have to allow for changing service needs. It is the basic capital investment programs that most need coordination: the provision of water and sewer services, which are expensive and geographically rigidly fixed. Since they tend to be provided by branching off from main conduits, expansion on the whole circumference of the circle around a central city is costly and inefficient. The area to be covered goes up with the square of the radius, or distance to downtown. All this affects the cost and quality of housing.

Many cities and counties have planning departments and commissions to improve coordination. However, these planning commissions generally have power only to recommend or to stop projects from getting some federal funds. At best they can develop maps and other displays of alternative future developments, publicizing the problems of the basic decisions being made. Since anything that is done may well affect property values and possible development, speculators and builders watch the planning carefully. On the other hand, any open discussion of new plans can lead to resistance by property owners, since almost any change at all will arouse the fears (often unjustified) of some group.

Indeed, the private ownership of property, in a situation where things are so interdependent, leads to many difficulties. Any action to change a city can create capital gains and losses. Since there is no way to collect the gains in taxes (though the British tried for years, calling it a "betterment" tax), nor to convince the public to compensate the losses (though the British also do this), the net result is resistance to change, and a distribution of gains and losses if the change takes place.

With enough public money, everyone can be "bought off"; most of the land is bought by the government, its uses are changed, and it is then resold. (The old term for this process was "excess condemnation." It has never worked very well, economically speaking, entirely apart from some legal problems.) The nature of the problem of private land ownership was dramatically illustrated when the British decided, in the Town and Country Planning Act of 1947, to "nationalize" the right to change the use of land. An expert commission had argued that compensation requirements made planning impossible, because private owners demanded compensation for the loss of possible future increases in land values. These increases constituted a "floating value" much greater than the total real increases, because people on every side of the city expected the expansion to move their way (Great Britain Ministry of Works and Planning).

The act allocated 300 million pounds sterling to compensate for the loss of these speculative "development rights." But emotional resistance, and an unwillingness to assess development charges or to insist on buying land at its existing use value, led to a breakdown in practice.

The problem remains. If one compensates losers, change becomes expensive, particularly if the total claims are more than the total losses (because of uncertainty as to who would actually have developed his land). If one refuses to compensate losers, then people who expect their land to lose value will resist change. Private property ownership makes both planning and major development projects difficult and expensive. The problem is intensified because most people exaggerate the possible effects of change on their property values, particularly downward effects. A system of guarantees against losses in market value, relative to some index to account for inflation, might calm these fears and be much less costly. (It might also make public authorities genuinely more concerned with what their developments do to property values.)

One potential answer is longer-term future planning, to avoid the development of private vested interests or to buy them out earlier and more cheaply. The difficulty with any planning is that the planners have great economic power and knowledge, which they are expected to employ in the public interest and not for private gain. By the time a man is wealthy and respected enough to be entrusted with such responsibility, he is also often a property owner or a friend of property owners, and the old problem of conflict of interest arises once more. The reader who does not believe this is invited to start an inquiry as to the property holdings of members of the local zoning board, assessment board, housing commission, building permits office, school board, and city council.

Slums—Cause or Effect?

The obvious problems associated with concentrated areas of deteriorated housing (slums) has led many people to assume that the slums somehow caused the problems. Yet it is more a matter of the concentration of people with problems in a single area. It is not clear that the incidence of illness, or of crime, can be attributed to poor housing, or crowding, rather than to such causes as low incomes and poor diet (Schorr). Indeed, one dramatic study of people moved from slums to a housing project showed a deterioration in their health, attributed by the researchers to the fact that the people had to pay higher rents and so had less left for adequate food (M'Gonigle and Kirby).

If the problem is really a combination of social pathologies—low incomes, mental illness, various forms of antisocial or illegal behavior, and most recently racial prejudice—then improving the housing seems unlikely to help very much. If the improved housing is not subsidized, the people cannot pay the rents and are simply driven elsewhere; the result is the spread of slums. If it is subsidized, a few people get an income subsidy tied to housing (which may not even be what they need most) at substantial cost.

It used to be a common notion that slums are owned by a few rich slumlords, or by churches, or banks. The only systematic study of slum-clearance areas was done many years ago during the Depression, by the National Housing Agency (predecessor to the Federal Housing Administration). They found that slum properties were owned by a very large number of not very affluent people, themselves only a generation or less out of the slums (U.S. National Housing Agency). Indeed, part of the problem was that these people did not have the resources to care for or improve their properties. Whether, since then, there has been a concentration of slum properties in the hands of a few is not known, but the massive abandonment of deteriorated properties in major cities makes it seem unlikely. Lending institutions have been charged with creating slums, or preventing their rehabilitation, by "redlining," refusing to lend in certain areas or charging higher rates. The institutions claim that experience justifies this discrimination, which merely reflects different risks, but the evidence is unclear.

Another issue still unsettled is whether the government should encourage new housing where there *is* a market—at upper income levels—and let the series of transactions free poorer and poorer houses in a kind of trickle-down process until older, cheaper housing becomes available for low-income people. The main counterargument has been that old housing is usually in the wrong place or needs to be scrapped anyway.

It is difficult to document the trickle-down effects on a single house as it gets older and older. What can be studied is the chain of moves precipitated by the opening up of a new dwelling unit. The occupants of the new unit came from somewhere, and perhaps vacated another dwelling. One can ask who occupied that vacated dwelling, and where they came from. By following such a chain through its links, one can see how many people are able to change (usually improve) their housing before the chain ends (someone moved out of a previous dwelling but left someone, perhaps parents, still there, or a dwelling was demolished). It turns out that the trickle-down process works, except for minority groups, where neighborhood segregation makes it difficult (Lansing, Clifton, and Morgan). This suggests that housing for minority groups would best be improved by stimulating new housing for them.

Property Values and Race

We have seen that all kinds of things can affect the value of a house, many of them outside the owner's control. Anything that affects a whole community may leave homeowners able to escape only by selling at a loss. Homeowners in small, one-company towns may find, for example, that if the company fails, they can neither earn a living in the town nor find anyone to buy their houses.

A major source of fear has been of a mass movement into a neighborhood of a distinctively different or lower-income group, or one with different living habits. If a neighborhood consists largely of rather old and out-of-date houses, or has been in transition to other uses anyway, the possibility of a mass exodus, faster than new immigrants can take up the slack, leads to the possibility of a substantial fall in house values, at least temporarily.

In some neighborhoods people failed to realize that a history of discrimination had so restricted the housing opportunities of blacks that they were able and willing to pay *more* for equivalent houses than whites. What happens to property values then depends on the extent of white panic, the speed with which they move out. Values might end up higher than before any nonwhites moved in. Luigi Laurenti's classic 1960 study which showed this is worth reading even today. The process contains an element of self-fulfilling prophecy, since if enough people believe their properties will depreciate, and act on that belief, the depreciation is likely to happen. Indeed, the greater the panic, the greater the opportunities for speculative gains, through buying at panic prices and selling to minority group members later at inflated prices. Many realtors' associations have set up rules against such "block busting," and expel members caught doing it, but these rules are difficult to enforce.

The Role of Government

Sometimes it pays to back off from a question and take a more distant look. Why should subsidies and other large expenditures be required in the housing and urban development fields at all? What is there about housing that makes it impossible for market forces and private enterprise to work? Are we merely using housing as a device to improve the lot of the poor, or do we believe that even if we solved the poverty problem we should still have a housing problem?

If we were to select some item to provide to low-income families free or at some subsidized price, is housing a better choice than bread, or medical care, or transportation? For example, would free public transportation, by increasing the range of choices, open up enough extra housing possibilities to improve housing more than housing subsidies would?

Could the need for more resources going into housing be tackled by encouraging competition, rather than by governments taking up large areas of expensive land suitable for high-density, high-yield use and devoting it to low-rent housing?

The answers are not simple, nor clear, because there are many constraints in the world, and much interconnectedness. It does not pay one person to upgrade property in an area where the rest of the properties are deteriorating. How to get coordination without bureaucratic control or government ownership remains a problem.

Summary

Deciding where to live, whether to own or rent, and how much space to buy are tied in with decisions about jobs, living partners, and children. This chapter has discussed the pros and cons of owning a home and has shown that it is possible to compare the alternative costs, even if most of the benefits are intangible. The costs of renting (rent plus utilities) are straightforward enough, but the tendency to equate mortgage payments with costs of owning is very misleading. Mortgage payments are partly interest costs and partly savings. The true costs of owning consist of interest costs (paid in the mortgage or foregone), utility payments, taxes, depreciation, and insurance costs. These costs amount to about 1 percent of house value per month and increase about as fast as house prices. Houses appreciate and depreciate at the same time, and the appreciation of housing should be compared with the appreciation of alternative investment opportunities when making choices.

Housing costs seem to differ a great deal from one location to another, but many of these differences can be explained by differential public services, taxes, or distances to jobs.

There are a number of important legal aspects of housing, including zoning, mechanic's lien laws, prescriptive easements, and problems of legal title.

Public policies about local planning, local services, transportation, and the like often have dramatic effects on neighborhoods and house values. While it is possible to tax the winners and compensate the losers where these decisions are made, this is rarely done. It is important to understand and perhaps even try to influence the decisions made by local authorities and the rules of state and federal programs.

More Information?

Libraries or bookstores have tables of mortgage payments and sample lease forms.

The assessor's office in a city or county has information about the history of assessed values of properties. They may also have information on sale prices, and they know roughly the ratio of assessed to market valuation for each small area, and the property tax rates in each area.

Registrars of deeds have records for each property of the last deed transfer and the amount of federal transfer tax paid, from which one can usually infer the price.

School offices have maps of school district boundaries and information about future plans for school building.

Savings and loan association mortgage departments and other lenders have staff with knowledge of the local area and the usual prejudices about different communities and ethnic purity.

Realtors have information about past sale prices of many properties in town, their own evaluations of neighborhoods, and their own vested interests.

Long-time residents with tastes and standards of living similar to yours provide an already-adjusted and screened view that may be the most efficient way of getting the general picture.

There may be a city or county planning commission with projections of future developments, maps, and information about areas with problems of water, sewers, drainage.

For more general information, not focused on one community, there is an overwhelming outpouring of published material about housing and community, written from many points of view and scientific perspectives, often with great passion. The list which follows unashamedly combines "how-to" books, a few general discussions, and most of the best empirical studies.

American Bar Association. *Home Buyer's Guide*. Chicago: The American Bar Association, 1967.

Anderson, Martin. *The Federal Bulldozer, a Critical Analysis of Urban Renewal, 1949–1962*. Cambridge, Mass.: M.I.T. Press, 1964.

Beyer, Glenn H. *Housing and Society*. New York: Macmillan, 1965.

Blumberg, Richard E., and Grow, James R. *The Rights of Tenants: The Basic ACLU Guide to a Tenant's Rights*. New York: Avon Books, 1978.

Brackett, Jean B., and Lamale, Helen M. "Area Differences in Living Costs." In *Proceedings of the Social Statistics Section*. Washington, D.C.: American Statistical Association, 1967.

Branch, Melville C. *Urban Planning and Public Opinion*. Princeton, New Jersey: Princeton University Press, 1942.

Brooks, Patricia, and Brooks, Lester. *How to Buy a Condominium*. New York: Stein and Day, 1975.

Brown, Robert Kevin. *Real Estate Economics*. Boston: Houghton Mifflin, 1965.

Butcher, Lee. *The Condominium Book: A Guide to Getting the Most for Your Money*. New York: Dow-Jones Books, 1975.

Center for Auto Safety. *Mobile Homes, Low-Cost Housing Hoax*. New York: Grossman King, 1975.

Cherlow, Jay, and Morgan, James N. "Commuting Time and Speed." In *Five Thousand American Families—Patterns of Economic Progress*, vol. 4, edited by Greg J. Duncan and James N. Morgan. Ann Arbor: Institute for Social Research, 1976.

Davis, Joseph C., and Walker, Clayton. *Buying Your House: A Complete Guide to Inspection and Evaluation*. Buchanan, N.Y.: Emerson Books, 1975.

Dean, John P. *Home Ownership, Is It Sound?* New York: Harper and Brothers, 1945.

Firey, Walter. *Land Use in Central Boston*. Cambridge, Mass.: Harvard University Press, 1947.

Frieden, Bernard J. *The Future of Old Neighborhoods*. Cambridge, Mass.: M.I.T. Press, 1964.

Galbraith, John K. *The Affluent Society*. Boston: Houghton Mifflin, 1958.

Goodman, Emily Jane. *The Tenant Survival Book*. New York: Signet, 1972.

Great Britain Ministry of Works and Planning. *Final Report of the Expert Committee on Compensation and Betterment* (The "Uthwatt Report"). London: Her Majesty's Stationery Office, 1947.

Grebler, Leo. *Housing Behavior in a Declining Area* (Long-Term Changes in Inventory and Utilization of Housing on New York's Lower East Side). New York: Columbia University Press, 1952.

Griffin, Al. *So You Want to Buy a Mobile Home*. Chicago: Henry Regnery, 1970.

Hebard, Clumman. *Condominiums and Co-ops*. New York: John Wiley and Sons, 1975.

Hoyt, Homer. *One Hundred Years of Land Values in Chicago*. Chicago: University of Chicago Press, 1933.

Keats, John. *The Crack in the Picture Window*. Boston: Houghton Mifflin, 1957.

Klein, Woody. *Let in the Sun*. New York: Macmillan, 1964.

Kosnar, Carl J. *How to Sell Your Home Without a Real Estate Broker*. New York: McGraw-Hill, 1975.

Lansing, John B.; Clifton, Charles Wade; and Morgan, James N. *New Homes and Poor People* (A Study of Chains of Moves). Ann Arbor: Institute for Social Research, 1969.

Lansing, John B., and Hendricks, Gary. *Automobile Ownership and Residential Density*. Ann Arbor: Institute for Social Research, 1967.

Lansing, John B., and Hendricks, Gary. *Living Patterns and Attitudes in the Detroit Region*. Detroit: Detroit Regional Transportation and Land Use Study, 1967.

Lansing, John B.; Marans, Robert W.; and Zehner, Robert D. *Planned Residential Neighborhoods*. Ann Arbor: Institute for Social Research, 1970.

Laurenti, Luigi. *Property Values and Race (Studies in Seven Cities)*. Berkeley, Calif.: University of California Press, 1960.

Lipsky, Michael, and Neuman, Carl A. "Landlord-Tenant Law in the United States and West Germany—A Comparison of Legal Approaches." *Tulane Law Review* 44 (1969): 33–66.

M'Gonigle, C. C. M., and Kirby, J. *Poverty and Public Health*. London: V. Gollancz, 1936.

Mass-Observation. *People's Homes*. London: John Murray, 1943.

Maynes, E. S., and Morgan, James N. "The Effective Rate of Real Estate Taxation: An Empirical Investigation." *Review of Economics and Statistics* 39 (1957): 14–22.

Mencher, Melvin. *The Fannie Mae Guide to Buying, Financing, and Selling Your Home*. New York: Doubleday, 1973.

Morgan, James N. "Housing and Ability to Pay." *Econometrica* 33 (1965): 289–306.

Morgan, James N. "A Note on the Time Spent on the Journey to Work." *Demography* 4 (1967): 360–62.

Morgan, James N.; David, Martin; Cohen, Wilbur; and Brazer, Harvey. *Income and Welfare in the United States*. New York: McGraw-Hill, 1962. (Chapter 19, "Property Taxes and the Benefits of Public Education")

Morton, Walter. *Housing Taxation*. Madison, Wis.: University of Wisconsin Press, 1955.

Murray, Robert W., Jr. *How to Buy the Right House at the Right Price*. New York: Macmillan, 1968.

National Association of Home Builders. *Condominium Buyer's Guide*. Washington, D.C.; National Association of Home Builders, 1975.

Netzer, Richard. *The Economics of the Property Tax*. Washington, D.C.: Brookings Institution, 1966.

New York Temporary Housing Rent Commission. *High Rent Housing and Rent Control in New York City*. Albany, N.Y.: State of New York, 1958.

Newman, Sandra. *The Residential Environment and the Desire to Move*. Ann Arbor: Institute for Social Research, 1974.

Paxton, Edward T. *What People Want When They Buy a Home*. Washington, D.C.: Government Printing Office, 1955. (A study by the Survey Research Center, University of Michigan, for the Housing and Home Finance Agency)

Payne, John C. "Ancillary Costs in the Purchase of Homes." *Missouri Law Review* 35 (1970): 455–516.

Reid, Margaret. *Housing and Income*. Chicago: University of Chicago Press, 1962.

Rejms, Ruth. *Everything Tenants Need to Know to Get Their Money's Worth*. New York: Doubleday, Dolphin, 1975.

Rose, Albert. *Regent Park, A Study in Slum Clearance*. Toronto: University of Toronto Press, 1958.

Rose, Jerome G. *Landlords and Tenants, a Complete Guide to the Residential Rental Relationship*. New Brunswick, N.J.: Transaction Press (Rutgers), 1973.

Rossi, Peter H. *Why Families Move*. Glencoe, Ill.: Free Press, 1955.

Rothenberg, Jerome. *Economic Evaluation of Urban Renewal*. Washington, D.C.: Brookings Institution, 1967.

St. Louis Metropolitan Survey. *Background for Action*. University City, Mo.: Metropolitan St. Louis Survey, 1957. (Taxes and services in city and suburbs)

Schelling, Thomas C. *Models of Segregation*. Santa Monica, Calif.: The Rand Corporation, 1969. (Mild preferences can lead to extreme segregation.)

Schiltz, Michael E. *Public Attitudes Toward Social Security, 1935–1965*. Research Report no. 33, Office of Research and Statistics, Social Security Administration, U.S. Department of Health, Education, and Welfare. Washington, D.C.: Government Printing Office, 1970.

Schorr, Alvin. *Slums and Social Insecurity*. Washington, D.C.: Government Printing Office, 1963.

Sokolski, A. M. *The Great American Land Bubble*. New York: Harper and Brothers, 1932. (History of speculation and peculation from colonial times to the present)

Stone, P. A. "The Economics of Housing and Urban Development." *Journal of the Royal Statistical Society, Series A* 122 (1959): 417–83.

Straus, Nathan. *Two-Thirds of a Nation*. New York: Alfred A. Knopf, 1952.

Thompson, Wilbur R. *A Preface to Urban Economics*. Baltimore, Md.: Johns Hopkins University Press, 1965.

U.S. Department of Commerce. *Price Index of New One-Family Houses Sold*. Washington, D.C.: Government Printing Office, quarterly.

U.S. Department of Commerce. *Annual Housing Survey*. Washington, D.C.: Government Printing Office, 1975 and subsequent years.

U.S. Department of Housing and Urban Development. *Your Housing Rights*. Washington, D.C.: Government Printing Office, 1970.

U.S. Department of Housing and Urban Development. *Wise Home Buying*. Washington, D.C.: Government Printing Office, 1975.

U.S. Department of Housing and Urban Development. *Settlement Costs*. Washington, D.C.: Government Printing Office, 1976.

U.S. Department of Housing and Urban Development. *Questions About Condominiums*. Washington, D.C.: Government Printing Office, 1976.

U.S. Department of Housing and Urban Development. *Housing Surveys, Parts I and III: Occupants of New Housing Units, Mobile Homes and the Housing Supply*. Washington, D.C.: Government Printing Office, 1969. (Two studies done by U.S. Census)

U.S. Department of Labor, Bureau of Labor Statistics. *Rent or Buy? Evaluating Alternatives in the Shelter Market*. Bulletin 1823. Washington, D.C.: Government Printing Office, 1974. (Useful tables)

U.S. National Housing Agency. *Who Owns the Slums?* National Housing Bulletin no. 8. Washington, D.C.: U.S. National Housing Agency, Office of the Administrator, March 1946.

Walker, Mabel, et al. *Urban Blight and Slums, Economic and Legal Factors in Their Origin, Reclamation, and Prevention*. Cambridge, Mass.: Harvard University Press, 1938.

Watkins, Arthur M. *How Much House Can You Afford?* New York: New York Life Insurance Company, 1963. (Free)

Watkins, Arthur M. *The Home Owner's Survival Kit: How to Beat the High Cost of Owning and Operating Your Home*. New York: Hawthorn Books, 1971.

Wilner, Daniel M.; Walkley, Rosabelle Price; and Cook, Stuart W. *Human Relations in Interracial Housing* (A Study of the Contact Hypothesis). Minneapolis: University of Minnesota Press, 1955.

Winnick, Louis. *American Housing and Its Use, the Demand for Shelter Space*. New York: John Wiley and Sons, 1957. (Based on the 1950 Census of Housing)

Wood, Robert C. *Metropolis Against Itself*. New York: Committee for Economic Development, 1959.

Wren, Jack. *Home Buyer's Guide*. New York: Barnes and Noble, 1970.

Some Projects to Learn More

1. Select a county, and map the various jurisdictions in it—school districts, city boundaries for property taxes, water, and sewer districts. Can you find the tax rates and map them as the tax districts overlap? Are there also income taxes in part of the county? Are there areas of low tax rates but high services? Are high tax rates on property offset by lower ratios of assessed-to-market values? (This may require getting a sample of recent sales from realtors or the registrar of deeds.)

2. Visit some new houses and condominiums for sale, getting floor area, prices, other financial details. Are prices per square foot about the same? What do basements, garages, and one-floor construction do to costs? Do older houses cost less? How many use the living room as a passageway? What do the condominium salespeople tell you about the monthly charges and their future trend?

3. If there are any housing projects in the area, see if you can find out what fraction of the total real cost is collected in rents, and who subsidizes the rest. (It may be hidden in the capital costs, but you could still assume that gross rent plus utilities should be at least 10 percent per year of the total investment.) What income test is applied for lowering rents, and how much does a tenant's rent rise if the family income goes up by $100?

4. Find out about existing programs for federally assisted housing, and analyze the amount and kind of subsidy involved. How redistributive is it in terms of aiding low-income families?

5. Select ten or twenty addresses in different parts of town. If a five-year-old telephone directory is available, locate names and addresses where the same name and address did not appear five years ago, to get recent movers. Visit the tax assessor's office and the county registrar of deeds to get the assessed value and the amount of federal tax paid on the last few transfers. Estimate the market value from the assessed value and the assessor's statement about the ratio of market to assessed value in the areas, from the recent title transfers, from looking at the houses, or even asking a realtor. If you find startling discrepancies, you might even call on the occupants and ask them whether they know why, and what they think the place is worth. Is there anything about the neighborhoods that can explain differences in the house prices?

6. Talk with mortgage lenders, realtors, and lawyers about closing costs and other transaction costs in houses in the area. What fraction have title insurance, and are there payments from the title insurance company to lawyers or realtors?

7. Find out all you can about leases, damage-deposit procedures, and tenant's rights in the area. Are there any escrow arrangements to hold the rent when maintenance is inadequate?

8. Study the local zoning board and any other agencies with power—building inspector, housing commission. What local property do their officers and members have besides their own homes? What do they say about the kinds of pressures they have on them?

9. Sample the directory of students at your college, or employees in your company; make a small telephone survey to ask their rents or house values, amount of living space, and distance from school or work. Is there any evidence that those who live closer pay more for their housing? (Ask them how long it takes to get to school or work as well as how far it is.)

10. Make a map showing locations of low-cost housing, housing projects, and trailer parks. What property taxes are they paying? Does it look as if they get more public services than they pay for?

11. Find out what has happened to the 1947 Town and Country Planning Act in Great Britain, and whether new legislation has altered it.

CHAPTER FIVE
LONG-TERM FINANCIAL PLANNING AND DAY-TO-DAY BUDGETING

If your outgo exceeds your income, your upkeep will be your downfall.
    Ben Franklin

For most people, the term "budgeting" conjures up visions of hours spent recording and manipulating the receipt and expenditure of money. They agree that the goals of budgeting—keeping outgo in line with income, and accumulating sufficient savings for retirement or other future needs—are worthy enough; but they consider the procedure so tedious and time-consuming that few families budget effectively.

Budgeting is really an exercise in accounting, but we can keep it from being too difficult if we keep our language precise and use some convenient shortcuts. The basic trick to accounting is to bridge the gap between the flows of money (in and out) that are easy to see and record, and the more comprehensive *real* flows of consumption, income, and accumulation of wealth. Depreciation of a car, employer contributions to pension funds, and increases in the prices of common stocks are examples of expenses or income that do not show up as cash expenditures or receipts. Yet these are as important as the cash expended on groceries or the income from a paycheck. Further complications arise because some of the cash we receive (as from the sale of a house or common stock) is not income.

Note the ways in which such terms as *expenditures*, *expenses*, *receipts*, and *income* are used in the preceding paragraph. Expenditures and receipts are the visible flows of money that we spend or receive. Unfortunately, these cash flows often differ from the more important *real* flows of expenses (consumption) and income. Some expenses (such as depreciation of a car) do not show up as expenditures, while some income (such as an employer's contribution to a pension fund) is not received in the form of cash. Much of the exercise of accounting is getting from the easily visible receipts and expenditures to the crucial flow of income and expenses.

The comprehensive treatment of all income and expenses, and the details on how to monitor both precisely, will be saved for the last half of this chapter. Few people will find it worthwhile to keep detailed records of every income and expense item. Realistically, financial planning calls for two things: first, a simple way of keeping consumption in line with income; second, a way of setting savings goals that will allow one to meet such future needs as retirement, children's education, and bequests.

A Simple Budgeting Scheme

The simplest way to start watching financial affairs is to apply the bathtub theorem, which says that if it came in the faucet and isn't in the tub, then it went down the drain. If I choose a monthly accounting period, then I can measure the water in the tub at the beginning and end of each month by adding up cash, checking, and savings account balances, and measure the faucet flow by keeping track of the money received. Such receipts usually consist of some taxable income that must be recorded anyway. Monthly expenditures are the water down the drain, and instead of keeping track of every cent spent, I can calculate total monthly expenditures by subtracting the increase (or adding the decrease) in cash and bank accounts from monthly income. Monitoring these monthly expenditure totals is an easy way of ensuring that spending is consistent with income. (An even simpler, although ill-advised, method is to control expenditures by running out of money each month so that expenditures automatically equal receipts!)

Budgeting is not quite as simple as this, however. I soon discover that expenditures fluctuate from month to month and, more important, that these expenditures are an inadequate guide to consumption. Some of the variations in expenditures are due to the months with five Saturdays (if I shop on Saturday), or vacation months, or the months that the property tax bill or annual insurance premium comes due, but these variations tend to average out and can be handled by some "rubber budgeting" method of averaging expenditures over several months or watching a cumulative expenditure total. The biggest expenditure variations arise from "capital transactions": buying a car or an appliance, investing in common stocks, bonds, or real estate, or paying off debts. These expenditures are obviously quite different from the monthly expenditures for goods or services consumed during the month. A common stock purchase is not consumption at all, while the purchase of a car represents a little present consumption (i.e., the use of the car's services during that month), but is mostly consumption that will take place well into the future. It is crucial to distinguish current consumption from current expenditures because current consumption must be kept below income in order to avoid bankruptcy—or, more optimistically, in order to build up wealth.

I could take care of financial transactions like investing in common stock, bonds, or real estate by simply subtracting the value of any such new investments from the estimate of monthly expenditures. (Note that I do not have to add the money received from the sale of investments to monthly expenditures because that money also came through the faucet and, if not in any bank account or cash at the end of the month, must have been spent.) Can transactions involving physical capital like a house, car, or appliances be handled with a similar subtraction? Unfortunately, not completely. Although capital transactions do have an investment component which ought to be subtracted from expenditures, they also have a consumption component which ought to be counted as expenditures. Not only will a small piece of each item of physical capital bought in a particular month be consumed, but a small piece of *all* physical capital will be consumed—regardless of when it was purchased. This consumption consists of the depreciation and the foregone interest costs of money tied up in owning the household capital; this is an important consumption item which does not show up in monthly expenditure estimates. Fortunately, the consumption costs of household physical capital are relatively stable from month to month (or can be spread in a stable pattern),[1] so they don't have to be recalculated and added to expenditure totals every month. It is usually easier to set a monthly expenditure goal that takes account of the average depreciation costs being incurred. Alternatively, I could set a monthly goal for increases in cash and bank account balances to offset these depreciation costs. I could even keep these additional savings in a separate account and then use the money in that account to purchase new items of household capital when the old ones need to be replaced.

Our "simple" scheme has become complicated, but only a little. In essence, it applies the bathtub theorem to estimate monthly expenditures and then converts expenditures to total consumption by adding to the expenditure estimate the depreciation costs of household physical capital and by subtracting any purchase of financial or physical assets.

A final adjustment is advisable because cash receipts are an imperfect measure of income. Employers frequently deduct from a paycheck some consumption costs (e.g., union dues, life or medical insurance, income tax) and some savings items (Social Security, pension accruals). Employers may also make contributions for current consumption (medical and life insurance) and for savings (Social Security, pension accruals).[2] The final adjustment needed to convert expenditures to consumption is to add (1) employer deductions for consumption items, and (2) employer contributions for consumption. To compare this comprehensive consumption measure with the

---

1. The simplest way to estimate the monthly depreciation costs of most durables is to estimate the expected life of the piece of capital and its resale value at the end of its life, and then divide the difference between initial cost and resale value by the number of months of life. See chapters 4 and 8 for ways of estimating depreciation costs for houses and cars.

2. It may seem strange to classify insurance and income tax as consumption. Monthly insurance premiums buy "protection" for that month, and that protection is the service being consumed. Income taxes are consumption in the sense that they pay for the services provided by government.

total income received, I must add the value of all employer deductions and contributions to income.

We have used the bathtub theorem to manipulate receipts and cash-plus-bank balances to arrive at a comprehensive measure of monthly consumption (expenses). This consumption can then be monitored and compared with income to ensure that the consumption is less than income by an amount consistent with savings goals.[3]

Would it be easier to go from a monthly estimate of changes in cash-plus-bank-account-balances to an estimate of net savings (and then compare that actual savings with the savings goal)? Not really, because the changes in those account balances have to be adjusted by adding: (1) any net purchases of assets, physical or financial, since the cash expended for these purchases went down the drain but was really saved rather than being consumed; (2) employer deductions for savings programs (Social Security, pensions, or any other nonconsumption benefit); (3) employer contributions for such savings programs; and (4) interest earned on pensions or on the savings component of any life insurance policies, and by subtracting: (5) depreciation of household capital.

At this point you might wonder about the purpose of keeping all of these records without any idea about how much should be saved each month. One reason is that this simple scheme will indicate whether consumption and savings patterns are changing and drifting into trouble. Another is that the total expense estimate can be used to check up on the detailed expenditure records. But the ultimate reason for any such records is to keep saving (and thus consumption) within some target saving goals. Setting such goals requires a long-range plan. It is to the details of that plan that we now turn.

Long-Range Planning

There are two main aspects of long-range planning. One is the accumulation of savings for retirement and more immediate goals like children's education or the down payment on a house. The other is the pacing of the acquisition of a house, car, and appliances (and their replacements) so as to avoid the excessive interest charges associated with undue debt and to lessen the effects of the large depreciation and foregone interest costs of those investments. Indeed, the proper timing and monitoring of these lumpy and attractive expenditures may be the most crucial part of all household financial management and the potential source of most of the trouble.

Planning for an orderly acquisition of household durables is fairly simple if you maintain a separate savings or checking account for such expenditures. You may think that you could spend a considerable amount of money initially to build up a stock of housing, cars, and appliances, and then cut back drastically, spending only when replacements are necessary. In fact, most American families spend about 15 percent of their yearly income on such equipment. Perhaps it is the persuasion of advertising or planned product obsolescence, or perhaps it is real improvements in quality that encourage perpetual replacement and upgrading. Whatever the reason, some substantial fraction of income should probably be allocated each year to household capital. In terms of budgeting, a fixed proportion of income (15 percent) might be allocated to a savings account and the money in that account then used to repair the house or the other repairable items of household capital, or to buy new items.[4] In addition to that allocation, an amount to save toward longer-range goals should be determined.

Setting Saving Goals

All families constantly make decisions about saving, sometimes explicitly with saving goals, sometimes implicitly with expenditure decisions. How to decide how much to save and set aside for future use? For what purposes will these savings be used?

---

3. For simply watching and controlling monthly consumption, I can use take-home pay as income and ignore the steady and semi-voluntary consumption handled by the employer.

4. Note that this account is used for the maintenance and repair expenses of a house (e.g., new roof, paint), but not for additions that increase its permanent value. Building the equity in a house is part of the savings program. The capital account suggested here takes care of expenditures on cars and appliances, and lumpy intermittent repairs on them or the house.

☐ A reserve fund for emergencies and to avoid using expensive short-run credit
☐ Providing for children's education (or the continuing education of adults)
☐ Accumulation of a down payment for a house
☐ Bequeathing of something
☐ Providing for retirement

The first needs are relatively small and are usually accomplished within the first few years after completing an education. How much to invest in the children is a highly individual decision. It would not be difficult, with the tables in the appendix to chapter 2, to figure the present value of four years of future college costs, and thus the amount to be paid into a savings account each year for, say, fifteen years that would accumulate to that goal at a 3 percent interest rate (e.g., $1,075 per year for fifteen years produces $20,000). Inflation will affect both college costs and the amount that must be saved each year to meet those inflated costs. If the rate of inflation is 3 percent and the market interest rate is 3 percent + 3 percent = 6 percent, then the $20,000 college costs will inflate to $31,160 in fifteen years. (This is calculated from table 3, p. 18.) Even at a 6 percent interest rate, an annual savings of $1,075 will provide a sum of only $25,048, which falls short of the goal. However, if savings are increased each year by the inflation rate, then the savings goal will be met. Indeed, increasing an annual savings amount by the rate of inflation will always ensure that the inflated savings goal is met, provided those savings can earn market interest rates.

The need for a large down payment for one's first home depends on how tight mortgage money is and on house prices. In recent years, larger and larger amounts have been required on both counts.

The next purpose on our list, bequests, hardly ever becomes important until late in life, and then only for those who find that by luck or ability or oversaving they have more than they need for their children and their own old age. We return to bequests, gifts, and estate taxes when we discuss life insurance in chapter 9.

This leaves savings for retirement. Social Security and the rapid growth of company pension plans complicate the process of designing this savings goal. It is easier to work out a total retirement-savings goal, and then to estimate

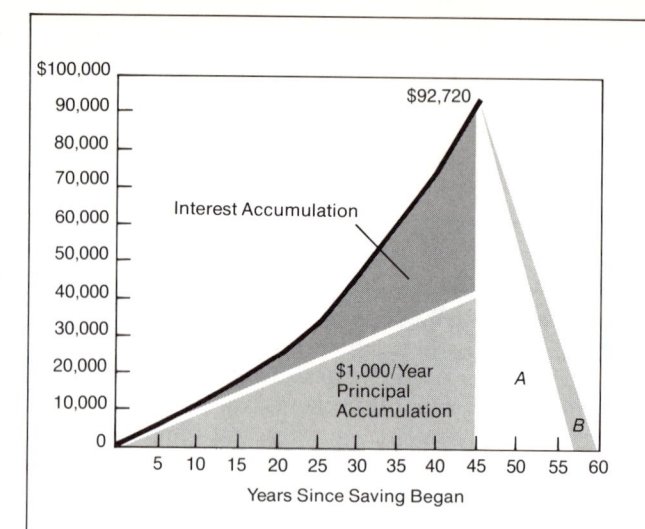

Fig. 5 How an annuity works. This figure shows the value of an annuity with forty-five years of accumulation and fifteen years of payback. Area A represents a $6,181 annuity payment without interest on the remaining balance for twelve years; area B represents the increase from obtaining interest on the remaining balance. Interest accumulations during input years total $47,720; during output years, $23,782; overall, $71,502. So $45,000 in saving produces $116,502 in pension payments at 3 percent interest.

the fraction of the goal that Social Security and private pensions will provide for; the remaining fraction must come from private savings.

The Algebra of Annuities

The process of saving for retirement and then living on the stream of payments provided by that savings fund involves the algebra of annuities. As detailed in the appendix to chapter 2, the compound interest on savings accumulated over a long period of time produces a fund that is much larger than the sum of the savings payments. Even with a 3 percent interest rate, a forty-five-year accumulation period (e.g., from age twenty to age sixty-five) produces a fund that is more than *twice* as large as the payments into it. Figure 5 shows how savings of $1,000 per year for forty-five years accumulates to $92,720, rather than $45,000, at a 3 percent interest rate.

Compound interest also has important implications for the size of the stream of payments provided by the savings fund after retirement. If I want to use up the $92,720 fund over the fifteen years I expect to live after retirement, I will have more than $92,720/15 = $6,181 per year, because of the interest earned on the fund during those fifteen years. In fact, I would have $7,767 per year in the fifteen years after retirement. In this example, the compound interest provides a stream of payments which is 25 percent larger than the stream of payments which did not include the interest. Overall, the $7,767 for fifteen years is more than 2.5 times the $45,000 I would have accumulated without interest ($7,767 × 15 = $116,502).

Retirement planning may seem complicated by the uncertainty regarding the date of death. If I die sooner than expected, then I will not have used up all of my savings. A more serious risk is to outlive my savings by living longer than expected. Such complications are simplified by companies (usually insurance companies) that will sell me a lifetime annuity upon retirement, based on my life expectancy. The annuity is really just the stream of payments (which include interest) provided by the cash used to purchase the annuity. The companies eliminate the risk to them of my living too long by selling many such annuities. The funds from those who die sooner than expected provide for those who live longer than expected.[5] For a couple, the most sensible kind of annuity gives one-third of the total annuity payment to each partner and one-third to "joint or survivor." Thus, as long as both partners are living, the payments are one-third to each, plus one-third to "joint," so the couple receives the full payment. When one partner dies, the survivor receives his or her own one-third share plus the one-third "survivor" share. The smaller total needs of the surviving partner can probably be met with an annuity payment which is two-thirds as large as the payment when both were alive. The price of this annuity is obviously less than the price of one that gives the full payment until both partners die.

We will proceed with our analysis of retirement planning using the assumption that life expectancy at age sixty-five is fifteen years. This is too optimistic for the average man and about right for women. But it is also roughly correct for the "joint-or-survivor" annuity scheme just discussed.

We now have two rules of thumb to simplify our calculations—that the real interest rate will be 3 percent regardless of inflation, and that the average life expectancy is eighty. If I can fix three more things, then the fraction of my income I need to save for retirement can be calculated or looked up in the tables to follow. The three are: (1) my desires about my post-retirement standard of living relative to my pre-retirement standard, (2) the age I start accumulating, and (3) my expected retirement age.

Starting with the first of these, it is crucial to understand that I do not need a retirement income as great as my pre-retirement income. When I retire:

1. my income taxes go down, because neither Social Security payments nor the portion of my pension that was paid for with after-tax income are taxed, because I receive double income tax exemptions at age sixty-five, and because tax rates are lower on smaller incomes;
2. my Social Security tax stops;
3. some expenses, like commuting and union dues, stop;
4. *I no longer have to save for my retirement*.[6]

That I no longer have to save for my retirement means that I should rephrase the issue of pre- and post-retirement income, and ask instead what fraction of pre-retirement *consumption* (income minus saving) I need after I retire. Calling this ratio F, we can proceed with some simple algebra.

First, I need to know how many dollars I must save per year for each dollar per year in retirement benefits. By fixing the dates when I start accumulating and when I expect to retire, I have also determined the number of years of accumulating savings for retirement (the difference between retirement age and starting age), and the number of years of retirement (eighty minus age of retirement).

Knowing the number of years of savings accumulation allows me to calculate the ratio of savings per year to the sum I will have accumulated at retirement. Call this ratio K_1.[7]

---

5. Many kinds of annuities are available, including those that refund to the survivors of those who do not live long enough to "get their money back" the difference between the purchase price and the total payments made. Needless to say, these annuities are much more expensive than those without such refunds.

6. I could also list the fact that I start *receiving* Social Security income and a pension, but it may be simpler to ignore them, then count the contributions to those programs as part of the required saving. I could also take the changed taxes out of the picture by using income after income taxes and Social Security taxes as the base for calculations.

7. The values of K_1 at different years of savings payments and a 3 percent interest rate can be calculated from column 5, table 3, $K_1 = 1/$(value of sum/yearly payment).

Knowledge of the number of retirement years allows me to calculate the ratio of the accumulated sum at retirement to the annual pension that sum will purchase. Call that ratio K_2.[8]

The amount I must save per year relative to my pension per year is:

$$\frac{\text{Yearly saving}}{\text{Yearly pension}} = \frac{\text{Yearly saving}}{\text{Sum accumulated at retirement}} \times \frac{\text{Sum accumulated at retirement}}{\text{Yearly pension}} \quad (1)$$
$$= K_1 \times K_2.$$

Now if I want a pension equal to some fraction, F, of my pre-retirement consumption (income minus saving), I have:

$$\text{Yearly pension} = F \times (\text{Income} - \text{Saving}). \quad (2)$$

But from (1), Yearly saving $= (K_1 \times K_2)$ (Yearly pension) and substituting this into (2) gives:

$$\text{Yearly saving} = K_1 \times K_2 \times F \times (\text{Income} - \text{Saving}). \quad (3)$$

Rearranging (3) gives:

$$\text{Yearly saving} = (K_1 \times K_2 \times F \times \text{Income}) - (K_1 \times K_2 \times F \times \text{Saving}). \quad (4)$$

The crucial number I want is the *ratio* of yearly savings to yearly income so I know what total fraction of income I must save each year in the form of Social Security, pension contribution, and my own private saving. Rearranging (4), I have:

$$\text{Saving}[1 + (K_1 \times K_2 \times F)] = (K_1 \times K_2 \times F \times \text{Income}), \quad (5)$$

which implies:

$$\text{Saving/Income} = \frac{K_1 \times K_2 \times F}{1 + (K_1 \times K_2 \times F)} \quad (6)$$

Thus, I can calculate the savings/income fraction if I make some assumption about my desired ratio of pre- to post-retirement consumption. Tables 11 and 12 hold F constant at 100 percent (no reduction in consumption at retirement) and show the consequences for required saving (as percent of income) of varying the accumulation period or the length of retirement. Table 12 also assumes a constant

8. The values of K_2 at different years of post-retirement life expectancy and a 3 percent interest rate can be calculated directly from column 4, table 3, chapter 2 (p. 18).

Table 11. Savings Goals if Post-Retirement Consumption Equals Pre-Retirement Consumption[a]

Years of Saving	Percent of Income to be Saved for n Years of Retirement					
	$n=5$	$n=10$	$n=15$	$n=20$	$n=25$	$n=30$
5	46%	62%	69%	74%	77%	79%
10	28	43	51	56	60	63
15	20	31	39	44	48	51
20	14	24	31	36	39	42
25	11	19	25	29	32	35
30	9	15	20	24	27	29
35	7	12	17	20	22	24
40	6	10	14	17	19	21
45	5	8	11	14	16	17

[a] This also can be interpreted as showing the fraction of an increase in income that must be saved if the extra yearly annuity is to equal the extra yearly income minus the extra savings.

Table 12. Savings Goals if Post-Retirement Consumption Equals Pre-Retirement Consumption[a]

Age When Saving Starts	Percent of Income to be Saved for Retirement Age x				
	$x=50$	$x=55$	$x=60$	$x=65$	$x=70$
20	29%	22%	17%	11%	7%
25	35	27	20	14	8
30	42	32	24	17	10
35	51	39	24	20	12
40	63	48	36	25	15
45	79	60	44	31	19
50		77	56	39	24
55			74	51	31
60				69	43
65					62

[a] This is identical to table 11, with the categories rearranged to make it easier to see the consequences of retiring earlier, or starting payments later. An expected life of eighty years is assumed in these calculations.

expected duration of life (eighty years) and shows the effects of changing retirement ages. Table 13 then shows the effect of varying F for the fraction of pre-retirement consumption needed after retirement, various combinations of years of accumulation, and years of retirement. All of these tables assume a 3 percent real rate of interest.

Suppose I start working at age twenty-five and work

Table 13. Savings Goals for Different Post-Retirement Consumption Standards

	Percent of Income to be Saved[a]			
Retirement Age	F^b = 1.00	F = .90	F = .80	F = .70
70	8%	8%	7%	6%
65	14	13	11	10
60	20	18	16	15
55	27	25	23	21
50	35	32	30	21

	Percent of Income to be Saved[c]			
Starting Age	F = 1.00	F = .90	F = .80	F = .70
30	17%	15%	14%	12%
35	20	18	17	15
40	25	23	21	19
45	31	29	26	24
50	39	37	34	31
55	51	48	45	42
60	69	65	62	59

[a] Assuming constant starting age (25) and expected life (80).
[b] F = desired ratio of post-retirement consumption to pre-retirement consumption.
[c] Assuming constant retirement age (65) and expected life (80).

until I am sixty-five. Then table 12, second row, fifth column, indicates that I must save 14 percent of my income to maintain my pre-retirement consumption after I retire. If I want to retire earlier, I have fewer years of saving, more years of retirement, and fewer years of interest accumulation on the saving. Moving to the left along the row in table 12 rapidly increases my required saving ratio to 20 percent, to 27 percent, and to 35 percent of my income. On the other hand, starting the savings later in life (and going down the same column of the table) only increases the required savings rate to 17 percent, or 20 percent, or 25 percent for five-year changes in starting age.

A common problem that arises with these calculations is that they all assume a constant pre-retirement real income when, in fact, the real incomes of most workers rise over the years of earning. One way I can handle this problem is to estimate my most likely permanent or average real income level, find what fraction of it I should be saving, and then try to save that real dollar amount regardless of the year-to-year fluctuations in my actual income. That dollar amount will, of course, change by the inflation rate each year. Alternatively, I can treat each major change in real income separately. I cannot simply save the same fraction of any income increase as of the pre-increase income level. To see why this is true, consider an increase that comes just a few years before retirement.

If I want post-retirement consumption to equal the new consumption standard that the additional income provides, it is obvious that I must save a much greater percentage of that increase than the percentage of income I was saving up to that point. Fortunately, however, the same tables can also be applied to any increases in pre-retirement income. *Any increase in pre-retirement real income can be thought of as a separate income stream*. If one substitutes "increase in income" and "increase in saving" for "income" and "savings" in equation (6), the formula is unchanged:

$$\frac{\text{Increase in savings}}{\text{Increase in income}} = \frac{K_1 \times K_2 \times F}{1 + (K_1 \times K_2 \times F)}.$$

As an example, consider an income increase that occurs at age sixty, five years before retirement. Table 12, fifth column, shows that I must save 69 percent of such an increase.

The reason that I don't have to save all of any increase in income that occurs only a few years before retirement is that saving for retirement helps me in two ways: it provides funds for retirement, but it also reduces my current consumption level. It is that consumption level that determines my retirement income needs and goals.

The converse of this is that in a retirement plan that guarantees a pension that is some fraction of the income just before retirement, any salary increase late in life is very costly to the employer in terms of pension fund contributions. What seems like the same proportional salary increase to all employees really gives much more to the older employees through added pension benefits. For personal planning it means that if I have a company pension that puts a constant fraction of my salary into a fund and I have salary increases late in life, then I should supplement these pension payments with private savings of my own. Or if I have an individual retirement account, I should contribute to it larger and larger fractions of increments of income, the later they begin. For women who start working late in life, or get most of their promotions then, this is particularly important. This inflexibility in pension plans in adjusting to income increases later in life is true of Social Security and largely true of private pensions under the federal Employee Retirement and Income Security Act. In the latter, the only two allowable plans are "guaranteed contribution," which must be the same percent of salary for all employees, or "guaranteed benefit," where the last years' earnings cannot be weighted very much more heavily than earlier years.

Table 13 shows that the later the increase in income, the greater the percentage that needs to be saved, varying according to ratios of pension to pre-retirement consumption levels. Note, however, that the reasons for partial replacement—because some expenses drop on retirement—are less applicable to *increments* in income; required saving does not fall proportionately.

Social Security, Private Pensions, and Saving Goals

Now that we have the logic of determining the total saving required for a retirement program, we need to consider that some of the saving is already being done by Social Security taxes and perhaps a company pension. One way to handle the problem is to calculate the amounts going *into* these plans and deduct them from the savings goal, assuming that they will provide a 3 percent interest accumulation after taxes. With Social Security, this is relatively easy, although it is important to keep in mind that some of the Social Security tax pays for current benefits (the cost of what amounts to substantial disability insurance and life insurance), so only six-tenths of the Social Security tax ought to be treated as saving for retirement benefits. For most workers, Social Security saves roughly 5 to 8 percent of income for retirement benefits. Most companies have estimated the cost of their pension plans as a percentage of payroll. This has the advantage of making it unnecessary for the employee to predict either future income or future inflation.

The alternative way of accounting for these automatic savings is to estimate the actual amounts, presumably in current prices, that will be available upon retirement from Social Security and any company pension. You can count on Social Security, in spite of the alarmists. Such societal obligations are seldom defaulted. They were met in Germany even through defeat in two wars and a disastrous inflation or two. With the passage of recent laws, company pensions are reasonably safe, although they are always subject to change or cancellation of future accruals.

Estimating what your Social Security retirement check will look like can be done as follows: Ask your local Social Security office to give or mail you the latest version of their leaflet, *Estimating Your Social Security Check*, and a postcard you can mail in to the Social Security Administration in Washington requesting your "covered earnings" history. The process starts with averaging, for the best X years, the incomes on which Social Security taxes were paid. These incomes, or so-called "covered earnings," started with a yearly maximum of $3,600 in 1936 to 1951, are expected to hit $29,700 for 1981, and will continue to rise. For someone born in 1918, X is twenty-four years; each succeeding age group has to average covered earnings from a larger number of years. Earnings from early years are now increased to allow for inflation. The leaflet contains a table by which you can go from average yearly covered earnings to the amount of your monthly retirement benefits at sixty-five, or at earlier retirement ages. It also tells what other benefits there would be for dependents. The maximum possible benefits for a single person retiring at age sixty-five in 1978 were $489.70 per month; the table goes up to higher average covered earnings which will be impossible to reach until future years of higher limits are averaged in.

This method requires predicting earnings for the years until retirement, and averaging them in, up to the maximum for each year. Thus, retiring at sixty-five instead of sixty-two not only provides higher benefits at the same average earnings but also allows an increase in average earnings—substantially if early years of low earnings can be dropped and later years of high earnings added. Benefits are adjusted for inflation automatically by law now. Ten years of covered employment are required in order to receive any retirement benefits at all. In any case, it is unlikely that Social Security alone will be enough to take care of retirement.

Private pensions are now easier for the individual to evaluate because reforms (1974) require clear information about the amounts you can expect, fairly rapid "vesting" so you do not lose the pension if you change jobs, and insurance in case the pension fund becomes insolvent.

For those without a private company pension plan to supplement Social Security, it is possible to achieve some of the same deferral of income taxes by setting up an Individual Retirement Account (provided for by the same 1974 Employee Retirement Income Security Act). However, this requires finding an institution, such as a bank, mutual fund, or insurance company, to handle the account, paying them for managing your savings, and hoping that the account will be properly supervised and regulated. The history of mutual funds (chap. 7)—with excessive turnover of investments, relatively poor yield records, and large payments to brokers—might well be repeated with these retirement accounts. Their tax-deferral benefits may not prove advantageous enough to make it worth giving up control of your savings.

One additional rule of thumb is to assume that Social Security takes care of replacement for income under about $8,000 a year and that company pensions and private savings plans should be organized to cover the rest. The simplest and best method, however, is to estimate current contributions to all kinds of retirement programs as a percent of current income, and to deduct this amount from the total saving goal. This requires the least forecasting of, or correction for, inflation.

For couples, the exercise can be done with pooled incomes, achieving savings enough to purchase three annuities, one-third on each life and one-third "joint or survivor," so that either survivor has two-thirds of the amount thought necessary for two. Such a long-term plan and commitment, in a world where the marriage law does not cover such issues, needs an explicit contract between partners, married or not, as to the ownership of the accumulations should their relationship change. With children, there is even greater need to assure that the accumulated assets will be available for their proper care until they are all grown. The estate-tax law does not recognize nonmoney work, assuming that the major dollar earner was solely responsible for the asset accumulation. In fact, one could argue that the saving would have been impossible without cooperation, so that either partner could claim it all. As we shall see (chap. 7), there may be other tax considerations influencing the choice of who should hold title to the assets, so the need for explicit contract cannot be avoided simply by having separate ownership of individual assets.

Summary of Budgeting Steps

This introductory discussion of savings goals and budgeting can be summarized in the following set of guidelines:

1. Determine the fraction of your income (and of increases in your income) which must be saved each year to meet your post-retirement consumption goals.

2. Estimate whether your Social Security and private pension plans are forcing you to save enough to meet these goals. If they are not, develop a savings or investment program which saves enough to meet the goals. Thus, if you must save 15 percent of your income each year to meet your goals and find that Social Security "saves" 5 percent of your income for you and a company pension plan saves 5 percent, then set up a system that saves an additional 5 percent. Many banks will automatically deposit specified fractions of paychecks into savings accounts. A whole-life insurance policy also forces you to save, although it does not pay as high a return on your savings as most other investments you could make. Paying off a house mortgage is an additional method of forced saving, but you should count such savings for retirement only if you plan to "consume" the equity in the house upon retirement (e.g., by selling it or mortgaging it to purchase an annuity). Try to earn market interest rates on these retirement savings. As a general principle, a mix of investments in stocks, mutual funds, and money market funds (chap. 9) will provide a long-run market rate of return.

3. Define your other savings goals (e.g., children's education) and commit enough of your income each month to meet them.

4. Commit an additional fraction of your income (15 percent, on average) to a "household capital" savings account. Use this money to purchase or repair cars, appliances, and other items of household capital. Try to delay new purchases until this savings account balance is high enough to pay for them. If you deplete this account and must borrow from your other accounts (e.g., your retire-

ment savings account, checking account, credit cards) or through a conventional bank loan, borrow as little as possible and delay further purchases or repairs until your "household capital" account is solvent.

5. Deposit the remainder of your income into a checking account or an interest-bearing combined savings and checking account. Fund all remaining expenditures from this account. If possible, restrict these expenditures so that this checking account remains solvent. If you must borrow from your other accounts, do so on a short-term basis only. If you consistently run out of funds in this account, keep detailed track of your expenditures and discover ways in which they can be cut back.

For many readers, these simple steps will be sufficient to meet and keep goals for savings, durables, and other budget items. If this applies to you, you can rejoin us at our discussion of behavior and policy on page 82. For the rest, a more detailed discussion may be necessary.

Detailed Financial Analysis

A proper financial analysis of the household rests on accounting principles which, in turn, rely on the careful use of such terms as *income*, *expenses*, *assets*, and *liabilities*. As stated earlier, the tricky part of financial accounting is to convert the visible flows of receipts and expenditures to the more basic real flows of income and expenses. *Income* is the accrual of rights over resources and includes such "invisible" items as an employer's contribution to a pension fund or the interest earned on such funds. Converting household physical capital to financial capital (e.g., selling a car for cash) produces cash but no income. *Expenses* are consumption, including losses of rights over resources. They too can be invisible (as with depreciation). Converting household financial capital to physical capital (e.g., using cash to invest in a car) is an expenditure but not an expense.

There are three basic accounting identities, all of which use *real* flows:

1. The income account: income minus expenses equals profit (change in net worth or equity).
2. The balance sheet: assets minus liabilities equals net worth (or equity).
3. The capital account: new investment minus depreciation equals increase in the value of the capital equipment.

Each of these is more complicated for a household than for a business firm, not just because the household has different goals, but because there are so many nonmoney flows to be counted, some without a market measure of their value. A full accounting could require inclusion of the value of human capital in assets and obligations to others (relatives mostly) in liabilities. The motives differ from those of a business firm, since the goal is not to maximize profit but rather to spread consumption evenly over a lifetime. The income account for a household is really "income minus consumption equals savings," and a major purpose of household financial management is to assure the proper rate of saving, not to maximize it.

The capital account is complex because it involves investment in three different kinds of capital: human, financial, and physical or household capital, the last being things to be used in the future, like a house or car.

Accounting procedures normally begin with a balance sheet, showing assets and liabilities at a point in time. Assets and activities produce income and expenses during a given period of time (typically a year). At the end of the time period, there is a new balance sheet. The three different kinds of capital on the household balance sheet complicate the process sufficiently to call for a picture, figure 6. It starts at the beginning of the year with the following assets and liabilities:

1. Stocks of "human capital" and time (twenty-four hours per day per person) which can produce both money income from a job and household goods and services, including housework and child care.
2. A stock of financial capital (e.g., savings accounts, common stocks, property) which produces money interest, dividends, rents, and capital gains or losses. The "unrealized" capital gains or losses will not be visible receipts or expenditures.
3. A stock of household physical capital, most of which produces a stream of services which the household consumes. Some capital also helps to make money on a job or produce household services (e.g., driving a car to work and using a washing machine to do the laundry).

By allocating time between working for money, producing at home without pay, and everything else—leisure, recreation, and maintenance (sleeping)—two kinds of income

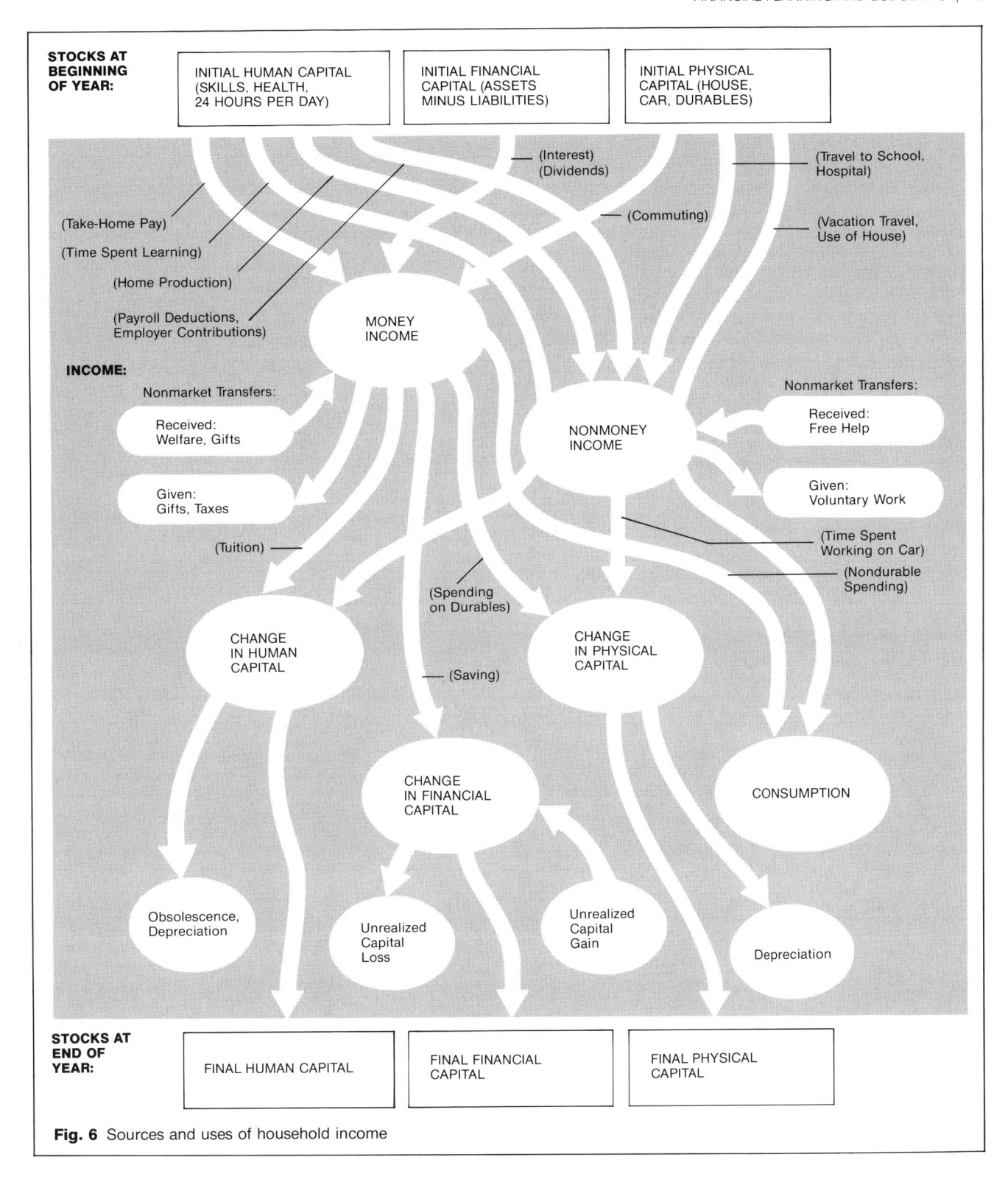

FINANCIAL PLANNING AND BUDGETING | 75

Fig. 6 Sources and uses of household income

are produced (money and nonmoney) which are allocated four ways (consumption and changes in human, financial, and physical capital). It is worth the time to work through figure 6 systematically so we can understand this process.

Money income is produced by effort on a job (human capital) and by financial assets or investments. Nonmoney income is produced by effort around the home (housework) and by household capital in the form of imputed rental income (the return on my investment if I own my own home), transportation (if I own a car or bicycle), and so on. In the household production process, of course, household capital depreciates. This is shown in the lower right corner of figure 6. Whether human capital depreciates is more difficult to say, although some of it may become obsolete. The acquired skill of knowing how to thread pipe, for example, is not worth much if everyone is now using copper tubing with sweated solder joints, or plastic with glued joints.

Two nonmarket mechanisms come into play to alter the amount of income (money and nonmoney) that is actually available for allocation to consumption and change in capital stocks. These have been picturesquely labeled (by Kenneth Boulding) the "economy of love" and the "economy of fear."

The "economy of love" refers to the giving and receiving of money or time without any reciprocal obligation: philanthropy by the giver, charity to the recipient. Some of it is to or from family members living elsewhere, although this is relatively small. There is a substantial amount of time and money spent helping religious or charitable organizations. Actually, if valued at what the time would be worth working for money, the value of volunteer work in the United States is about as large as the amount of money given to church and charity (Morgan, Dye, and Hybels).

The "economy of fear" includes war and robbery, but mostly it refers to government taxes and "transfers." Income taxes and Social Security taxes are deductions from income, while unemployment compensation, welfare, and other such benefits are additions to disposable income. There are also nonmoney aspects of this (military conscription, and free or subsidized public services), but we ignore them.

What happens to the income, money or not, left to dispose of? Some may be invested in education and skills (human capital) in the form of tuition and time spent learning. Some is invested in financial capital, a process commonly called "saving." Some is invested in the purchases of physical capital (car, house) or in repayment of debt on them, which is really purchasing them in pieces. The remainder is consumed. The term "remainder" is well chosen, because financial planning largely consists of decisions of how much to invest in the three forms of capital. The allocation of the remaining income to various forms of consumption is a relatively trivial problem by comparison.

Some of the disposition of income is automatic and constrained. Compulsory insurance (the survivor and disability insurance component of Social Security, worker's compensation, and unemployment compensation) probably belongs in the "economy of fear," but voluntary insurance premiums could be considered as part of consumption (since the insurance premiums purchase "protection" for a period of time). Insurance benefits can be considered as part of income. Time invested in learning is nonmoney income automatically invested in human capital. The housing and transportation services of a house and car are nonmoney income that are automatically consumed. Some employer's contributions and payroll deductions are automatically either a financial investment (as in a pension right) or consumption of nonmoney income (e.g., medical insurance or subsidized lunches).

The task, with what is left, is to allocate income (money and time) satisfactorily among consumption and the three investment categories: (1) investment in human capital (job skills and education); (2) investment in financial capital (stocks, bonds, bank accounts, real estate, etc.); and (3) investment in household (physical) capital for future consumption (house, car, appliances, skis). The allocation among investment categories is more difficult to do systematically and sensibly than the division of consumption expenditures, and it has more serious long-term implications. Consumption patterns can be rearranged with relative ease, but investing too much in household equipment may leave too little for saving and consumption, and with a need to borrow at high interest rates. Since there is a poor resale market for most consumer durables, and sometimes a sticky, slow one for houses, readjustment is difficult once the investments are made. The three capital accounts require more thought and planning than consumption, which really should be considered a residual.

A major first purpose of financial analysis is to figure out how much to save and invest each year, so we know how much we can consume each year. We have already discussed the process of setting savings goals and controlling expenditures on household capital. What remains is a detailed discussion of monitoring the processes.

Sources of Income

If I want to account for all of my income from last year, I should examine each of the following categories. Income that is automatically saved is marked with an asterisk.

1. Some income is in cash receipts: take-home pay, rent, interest, dividends, realized capital gains, and transfer incomes like pensions.
2. Some income is in cash, but not actually received: *employer contributions to Social Security, *employer contributions to a pension fund, employer-paid insurance and other fringe benefits. The first two of these are income that automatically becomes savings; the third is income that is involuntarily consumed.
3. Some income is in the form of payroll deductions, for: *Social Security, *pension plan, income taxes, insurance, and other things. Again, the first two of these are income *and* saving; the latter two are income that is automatically consumed.
4. Finally, there are some even less visible forms of income: *interest accruals in pension fund; *increased cash value of life insurance (chap. 9); *unrealized capital gains or losses in the value of human capital or financial capital; imputed income reflecting a return on my investment in house, car, and durables, which provide a stream of services that are consumed. (An estimate of this income might be 6 percent of the net equity in these investments.) I might even want to value my home production of food, repairs, etc., and add it to my income. The first three items are income that is saved, although the second is only an approximation of the interest earned on the life insurance saving reserve (see chap. 9). The third looms large if you have used the year getting educated, since increases in human capital are a capital gain. The fourth is income from the house or car that was consumed. If imputed rental income seems much too theoretical, consider the alternative of investing the same money in stocks and using the returns to pay rent. Each rental payment includes profit to the landlord, so it is only fair to give homeowners a profit on their investments also.

That completes an accounting of all income and some saving for last year.[9]

Estimating Savings

What about savings; how do I estimate that? I have already uncovered seven savings components. Two of these appear on my pay statement; I have to estimate the others. In addition, I must add the following five savings items:

1. Net reduction in debts (repayments on principal less new debt incurred); this can be negative if my debt increased.
2. Net purchases of financial investments like stocks, net of sales.
3. Net purchases of physical assets (house, car, durables), net of trade-ins or sales.
4. Contractual savings flows, if any, and accruals of interest in them (bond-a-month club, dividend reinvestment plans).
5. Increase in liquid assets (cash, bank accounts).

Not only is my income much more than my take-home pay plus some other receipts, but my savings is much more than the increase in my liquid assets that most people think of as savings. People who say they are "going broke" are often saving a great deal, but are periodically out of cash.

There is one final, crucial savings item: depreciation of my house, car, and other household assets. Depreciation is negative saving in the form of consumption with no matching income.

To recapitulate, I can estimate my savings for the year as follows:
1. increase in liquid assets,
2. net purchases of physical assets,

---

9. I could also include expense account reimbursements and gift money in income and consumption, but they should probably be excluded from both, since they are not taxable, not wholly discretionary, and lumpy in amounts and timing.

3. net investments (stock, etc.),
4. net reduction in debts,
5. Social Security contributions (employer and withheld) or some fraction of them,
6. increase in pension rights (employer contributions withheld, but not the interest accruals),
7. increase in cash value of life insurance, or any contractual saving balances,
8. *minus* depreciation.

My saving goals assumed a 3 percent return on the accumulation, so I should not include the interest on savings as part of the saving to meet those goals. It is just as well, because the interest accruals in pension plans and Social Security are impossible to estimate anyway. If my estimated saving last year was not adequate relative to my income, then I may want to try to increase it next year. At the same time, I can ask whether my net purchases of physical assets were on target, because my estimate includes both the saving for retirement and other purposes and the saving invested in physical assets. If I take 15 percent of income as an expected average investment in physical assets, first to build up a stock and then to replace and upgrade it, then in a year when I invest more than usual in physical assets, my total saving may look all right when my other, longer-term saving is really too small. I cannot merely monitor my total saving-plus-investment-in-durables, but must watch both against standards for each.

We now have some estimates of savings to compare with a savings goal or goals. It is instructive to ask what would happen both to savings and to the goals if I made certain large capital transactions.

Suppose I buy a car. This means that I shall have depreciation on it each year, and my other saving will have to be larger to offset the depreciation and to build up a fund which will enable me to buy a new car when the old one needs to be replaced. If I buy on credit, the repayment of principal will automatically reduce my debt and thus increase my savings. Indeed, some people seem to buy on credit as an automatic if expensive way of assuring that they will save enough of their income to offset the depreciation.

If I buy a house, I am likely to have a big, new contractual saving item—repayment of the principal of the mortgage—and, of course, a new depreciation item. They are unlikely to cancel out, because in the early years very little of the mortgage payment is applied to principal (chap. 4).

Before we proceed to discuss methods of watching monthly performance to make certain saving is adequate, it is useful to keep in mind that while real accounting for real flows is important, liquidity may also be important. There are periods in the family life-cycle where liquid assets are scarce and pressure to borrow is strong. Some extra saving, or slowing of the pace of acquisition of durables, may well avoid high interest costs and possible harassment.

There are also some tax considerations. These influence who "owns" the assets, and the kind of records that are kept about expenditures and about sources of funds for acquisition of assets. Where more than one person is involved, management and recordkeeping also require some collaboration. If some of the saving is for children's education, the funds can be put into their names with an adult as custodian so the interest or dividends are the children's income (escaping taxes) even though they can still be claimed as dependents.

Monitoring Current Expenditures to Achieve Saving Goals

Suppose that I have now set a goal for saving and a subgoal for investment in physical capital, partly by building up component needs for old age, children's education, and physical capital, and partly by asking how much I can expect to improve on last year's performance. There are always special situations that justify departures from norms.

First, I simplify things by deducting from my saving goal, and my recording, the unseen saving items and those that come out before I get my paycheck. They are reasonably stable and largely compulsory anyway.

This leaves four positive saving items that must take care of the rest of my saving goal and depreciation. So I have a new short-run saving goal: the total saving goal, minus Social Security and pension contributions, plus depreciation, equals a goal for the total of:

1. increase in liquid assets;
2. net investment in physical assets;
3. net investment (purchases) of financial assets; and
4. net reduction in debts.

I might even take out the repayments on principal of my mortgage both from the goal and from the "net reduction in debt" since it is contractual, varies continually, and is a nuisance to put in every month.

Each month, then, I want to see that the sum of those four items is sufficiently large to assure me that I am meeting my total saving goals. Actually, there are very few of the second and third (capital transaction) items in any one month, and if I took out the mortgage, there may be no other debt-change items. So I am really focusing on monthly changes in liquid assets, corrected for any debt change or other capital transactions. The only record-keeping required for this is a monthly adding up of my cash and bank accounts, and a check to see whether they need "adjusting" for any capital transactions. I may also want to adjust for the receipt and expenditure of gift or expense account money. I don't want to think I undersaved the month I spend such money, or saved the month I received it and put it in the bank. So I adjust my monthly saving estimate by deducting such nonincome receipts, and adding back nonconsumption expenditures.

Monitoring Consumption to Achieve Saving Goals

I can eliminate the results of irregular income flows by monitoring monthly consumption rather than saving, since consumption is distorted only by erratic and unusual expenditures like vacations. To do this, I can rely once again on the "bathtub theorem" as it applies to the household: monthly receipts minus increases in liquid assets equals monthly expenditures. I need to add up my liquid assets every month anyway, and my monthly receipts are easily accessible, usually only a few items that are already recorded for income tax purposes.

My monthly saving goal implies a monthly consumption goal, from which I can derive a target for monthly consumption expenditures by deducting depreciation and expenses paid by my employer or deducted from my paycheck. I can estimate the relevant monthly consumption expenditures, first simply, then with corrections: expenditures equal receipts minus increase (plus decrease) in liquid assets minus the following corrections:

1. Purchases of physical assets (car, etc.)
2. Purchases of financial investments (stock)
3. Reduction in debts
4. Expenditures of gift or expense money

Note that a consumption estimate has to be corrected only for the use of gift or expense money. When such money is received, it affects both receipts and the increase in liquid assets, and one cancels the other. The same is true for *selling* an asset for cash.

There is also an advantage in a monitoring system that focuses on consumption maximums rather than saving minimums, in that it is easy to go on to a monitoring of some of the major *components* of consumption. I may want to see just where the major changes are occuring, or what it is that is drifting upward.

What has been proposed here is a very simple beginning that adds up liquid assets around the first of each month (a few days off will not matter), deducts the increase in assets from the previous month's receipts to estimate total expenditures for last month, and then makes whatever important corrections are needed to convert this to an estimate of consumption expenditures. If one is then motivated to know more, it is relatively easy to keep some track of major components of expenditures.

A summary way of thinking about keeping track of one's finances is to start with the simplest situation and note how one can handle the various complications that are likely to come along:

1. If I have no capital account or debts, my increase in cash is saving, and the rest is consumption.
2. The minute I own anything that depreciates, I must deduct that depreciation from the estimate of my saving and add it to consumption.
3. My employer may pay for things, or deduct certain items from my pay; at least once a year I need to look at these as part of my income and of my consumption or saving.
4. If I incur or pay off any debts, these are, respectively, negative and positive saving.

5. If I have life insurance with a cash surrender value, it is probably also accruing an increased cash value, which is both interest income and saving (chap. 9).

6. If I buy (invest in) financial or household assets, that is saving and investment, not consumption; the subsequent depreciation of the household assets is consumption.

7. Realized capital gains increase my assets, so I have to count them as income too.

8. Loans to others and repayments of such loans can be treated like (risky) investments and disinvestment.

9. I can probably ignore unrealized capital gains—increases in the value of assets I own—since they are always potentially illusory until realized by a sale.

10. Finally, if I want to be precise in my analysis of finances, I should count as part of my income, *and of consumption*, the imputed income from my home and other depreciating assets, instead of counting only the depreciation as a correction to saving (see chaps. 4 and 8).

Detailed Expenditure Monitoring

Once you have an easy and revealing record of total monthly expenditures, you may want to keep track of some of its major components like food or clothing because they are more interesting or controllable than others. There are many guidebooks with expenditure standards by categories for different income levels and some even for different family sizes. The United States Department of Labor regularly issues revised estimates of hypothetical budgets for a family of four at three levels of affluence, for each of the major urban areas. Expenditures are estimated for seven broad categories. Such standards are not really very useful, however, especially for the nonfood categories. People's tastes are highly variable, and their expenditure patterns also depend heavily on their stocks of household capital. (Expenditure studies do not show those housing and transportation expenses that are not cash expenditures.) Furthermore, most of the budget studies on which the standards are based do not properly handle the distinction between homeowners and renters, or the nonmoney aspects of the budget, or the differences according to age, income, and family composition. Personal experience, rather than some arbitrary outside average, is a better guide and a better base from which to try to make changes.

Food may be the one exception, since there has been a lot of study on diets and food costs, and there is still a wide range of cost within which one could have an adequate diet. There is another reason for wanting to watch food expenditures: needs depend heavily on the ages and sexes of the family members. Since the sexes of family members do not change and the ages increase by one year per year, family food needs can be estimated far into the future as soon as a family is completed. If one assumes that the family style of living and eating habits will not change, one can multiply the percentage increase or decrease in family calorie requirements by current expenditures on food to estimate future food expenditures.

If a family composition is such that the standard is 7,000 calories a day and the family now spends $250 a month on food, then ten years from now when the teenage children have driven the requirements to 14,000 calories, it might cost $500 a month to feed that family, plus an inflation adjustment. Or one could actually calculate the United States Department of Agriculture food needs in dollars (with its built-in adjustment for economies of scale in feeding larger families) and use expected percentage changes in that dollar food need to extrapolate one's own family food expenditures (see table 6 in chap. 3, p. 30). Either of these is better than using average expenditures on food by family income groups, even separately by family size, since they do not allow for varying age-sex mixes in the family, or for differences in preferences.

Still More Detail

If still further expenditure detail is to be recorded, the principle still applies of step-by-step elaboration to see whether the benefits justify the effort. Some expenditures are deductible for income tax purposes, or may be when they get large enough; others are relatively easy to keep track of. Some may call for control.

Some people keep track of all large outlays and set up a "sundries" category for the rest. Some allocate money to envelopes or bank accounts, and devote each to a special purpose. Some try to write checks for as many things as possible, which also avoids the need to carry much cash. However one does it, the problem of categories and definitions must be solved early. One principle is that items which are close substitutes for one another belong in the same category. So the telephone bill belongs in "transportation and communication" along with postage stamps and gasoline. On the other hand, gifts to friends and those to church may need to be separate, since only the latter are tax-deductible philanthropy.

The worst problems are the kinds of expenditures that fall partly in one category, partly in another. A vacation trip involves unusual food and car expenditures which are really recreation, and gasoline that is for recreation rather than transportation of the usual sort. How much of the depreciation on the car is for recreation and how much for commuting or regular transportation? It would make a difference whether you charged it by the day or by the mile!

Similar problems arise when there are children. If their clothing expenditures are lumped into "clothing," you won't know how much it costs to have children or what to plan for when they leave home. But separating expenditures for each child, or for all the children, gets cumbersome if it extends to medical costs or books, and is difficult for food.

So, before writing down a lot of numbers, it is essential to decide just what the purposes of the detail are and what categories will meet those purposes. Will they be broad enough to minimize complicated or arbitrary classification or allocations, and yet narrow enough to be meaningful? The interpretation and use of many of the categories of expenditure will require combining the current expenditures with some similar expenses for which there was no actual outlay, because they were deducted from payroll, or were nonmoney costs. The total cost of housing, for example, includes depreciation, interest on the mortgage, property taxes and insurance, utilities, repairs, maintenance, and foregone interest on the money invested in it. Even transportation costs should include depreciation, insurance, parking fees deducted from your paycheck, gasoline, and foregone interest on the investment. Medical costs often include payroll deductions for group insurance, or even an employer payment for such insurance.

It may still be useful and interesting to keep track of some of the large monthly expenditures, particularly food and clothing. Even if many people count soap, toilet paper, cigarettes, and beer in their supermarket bills for "food," the trends and month-to-month fluctuations are still interesting and instructive. It is up to you whether you want to keep some rough trends in view, or meticulously allocate your liquor expenditures between "Recreation" and "Gifts and Entertainment," depending on how much of it you drink yourself!

When any major expenditure is made, a question arises whether it should be treated as an investment and depreciated (by raising current saving goals to offset the depreciation), or whether it is current consumption. Generally, the longer something will last, the more it qualifies as an investment, but in practice it would be a nuisance to treat a lot of small things like electric razors and ballpoint pens that way. On the other hand, a household investment account which monitors the total stream of such new investments may let you avoid continually adjusting a depreciation estimate.

Clothing is a special case, since expenditures on it tend to come in bunches. What seems called for is some annual clothing budget, perhaps figured separately for each family member, and a check of cumulative expenditures to see whether they are in line. For instance, if a family allows $50 a month for clothing, and their monthly expenditures are $20, $15, $100, $40, $5, $120, their running average is right on target and all is well; but if they are $45, $60, $55, $75, $50, $75, things are drifting out of control and need reexamination.

In general, keeping track of expenditures is most rewarding when records are needed for tax purposes, or where expenditures are lumpy or irregular, or where there is some need for controlling consumption. Personal expenditures of individual family members may need recording if only to avoid disputes. Charitable contributions may need to be tracked in order to keep them up to some goal and properly allocated.

Outside the Budget

It has been suggested that reimbursable business expenses, and perhaps gift money, might well be kept outside the budget, not counted as income or consumption and removed from estimates of monthly saving or consumption in short-range budgeting. But it is generally not good to have many different kinds of money because the temptation arises to violate the principle of never spending money on one thing if spending it elsewhere, or saving it, would provide more satisfaction. This applies whether the money is separated by use or by source of income. If there are several income receivers in a family, and they make their own decisions what to do with their money, the results are likely to be less total family satisfaction than if at least some of the income were pooled and allocated on the basis of family priorities.

Consumer Saving Behavior

Household saving behavior varies widely in an affluent country like the United States, with some people saving nothing out of high incomes and others building up substantial amounts out of very small incomes. The vast bulk of private saving in the United States is contractual or even involuntary, because it is in contributions to Social Security and private pensions, repayment of mortgage and other debts, and increased cash surrender values of life insurance. In other words, much of consumer saving is not discretionary and does not vary much from year to year. But consumer expenditures vary, because of variations in investments in houses and cars and other consumer durables. The published data on aggregate national "individual saving" do not include these investment-saving items, but do show the changes in liquid assets or debts that commonly accompany them. The aggregate "individual saving" data also include the volatile saving of farmers and unincorporated businesses, whose losses in bad years are "dissaving" and whose profits may well be "saved" (invested in more inventories and equipment). The main reason the aggregate "individual saving" numbers seem to respond to income is that they include farmers and small businessmen and ignore the investment aspects of consumer durables. Households do not vary their consumption much, only their rate of expenditures on cars and durables and houses.

Another misconception has to do with the effects of income inequality on saving. Since, in general, people with higher incomes save more than people with low incomes, it might seem that redistributing income from the affluent savers to low-income spenders might decrease total saving. In fact, this would be true only if the marginal changes in saving were different, that is, if low-income people would save only 10 percent of any income increase, but high-income people would cut their saving by only 20 percent of any decrease in income. Such data as are available are not sufficient to show such a curvature of the relation of consumption to income. Indeed, what the data do show is that there are wide differences in the propensity to save between rich and poor. Psychologically and logically, this is easy to understand. The thrifty have accumulated wealth and will continue to do so, having found it satisfying and their aspirations for further saving having been raised by their own past success in saving. The poor, meaning those with no savings whatever their income, have given up trying to save and have short time horizons. So a redistribution of money from rich to poor, not from high-income people to low-income, might well decrease aggregate saving (Kosobud and Morgan; Klein).

A longer-run result of these differences between people is that families tend to become either increasingly successful over their lives at accumulating assets, or increasingly discouraged. This is accentuated because some have the right to accumulate private pensions at work, while others do not. A private pension plus Social Security makes an adequate retirement income a possible goal and encourages people to save still more (Katona). The overall result tends to be a polarization into two groups: those who are well prepared for retirement and who may even retire early on purpose, and those who have only Social Security, cannot plan to retire, and retire when they must, usually in difficult financial circumstances. Even the most optimistic extrapolations of future increased Social Security benefits conclude that they will not be adequate to overcome these differences (Barfield and Morgan; Schulz).

Those theories about household saving that assume long time horizons and rationality fail to recognize that most people have only the vaguest notion of what their income will be even five years hence, with the possible exception of graduate students going into professions. We have seen how to adjust saving to changes in income, and so adapt to changes in situations and expectations. Recent inflation and gyrating asset values have made planning seem even more difficult. Most households go through a continuous process of readjusting their expectations, goals, and standards of living. Experience changes their subjective probabilities about the future and about what kinds of actions will lead to what kinds of results, and even their tastes and preferences.

In summary, it is mostly consumer investments in houses, cars, and durables that vary from year to year, not consumption expenditures. Long-term changes in saving result from contractual commitments which reflect revised expectations of the future and revised aspiration levels and retirement plans. Indeed, when economists analyze consumer spending for national policy purposes, they include both current consumption and investment in durables, even though the latter is not current consumption but a commitment to levels of future consumption. The investment in homes is left out of consumer spending altogether and put into business investment along with business plant and equipment expenditures. The household consumption aggregate includes all the expenditures on durables and imputed rent on owner-occupied houses, but all the value of housework and child care and home care of the ill, aged, or disabled is left out of both income and consumption.

The inclusion of imputed rent on owned houses in household income and consumption leads to a common misinterpretation of trends in aggregate consumption patterns. It is commonly said that over the years a larger and larger fraction of consumption is of "services." One thinks of hairdressers and houseworkers, but the "service" category includes imputed rent and actual interest payments, which go up as people change from renting to owning a home and as interest charges increase on mortgages and installment credit. On the other hand, the aggregate consumption estimates do attempt to separate durables from other things, whereas most budget study data bury expenditures on cars and appliances in the categories "transportation" and "housing" along with gasoline and the electric bill.

Aggregate Implication of Spending-Saving Decisions

Modern economic policy pays a lot of attention to the way people use their incomes, because consumer expenditures are the largest component of the flow of purchasing that keeps the economy going or produces inflation if it is excessive. The basic analysis of the President's Council of Economic Advisors and of the Joint Economic Committee of Congress and of the Congressional Budget Office consists of asking whether the likely expenditures of consumers, governments, business firms (for new investment), and the rest of the world (buying more from us than they sell to us) will be sufficient at current prices to buy the total national output at full employment. If less, there will be unemployment and, more rarely, deflation of prices. If the total is too much, inflation threatens, unless output capacity can be expanded. In recent years we have had inflation and unemployment at the same time, and economists have argued that although there is still a trade-off, there is no possibility of getting zero unemployment and no inflation at the same time. The need for forecasting the expenditures of business and of consumers remains.

Given this concern about national balance, it is crucial to know how much consumers can be expected to spend. For this purpose, it does not matter whether the spending is for current consumption or reflects investment in houses, cars, and other durable goods. In other words, those concerned with national economic policy are interested in expenditures, not consumption, and with "hoarding," not saving. Consumers may feel equally well off whether they put more in the bank or spend more improving their homes, but the economy is depressed by the former and stimulated by the latter.

Since it takes time for the various fiscal and monetary stabilizing policies to work, it is important to predict consumer expenditures. In an affluent society, consumers have wide discretion in those expenditures, particularly such expenditures as vacations and replacement or upgrading of durables. If consumers are not confident and optimistic about the future, it makes sense mostly to cut investment expenditures that commit them to future consumption and debt repayments. Instead of stimulating consumers to buy more before the prices rise again, rapidly rising prices may discourage the commitments involved in buying more durables, for fear the money will be needed to pay for higher priced goods and clothing.

In other words, the major fluctuations in consumer expenditures reflect not so much changes in current consumption as changed willingness to make commitments.

There is substitution between liquid saving and investment in durables. In that choice, the consumers' outlook for their own and their country's financial future is crucial. The same confident outlook might also encourage other discretionary expenditure, of course, such as travel, recreation, entertainment. So prediction of consumer expenditures, as distinct from consumption, requires measurement not only of incomes, of prices, and of the state of household inventories, but also—crucially—of consumer attitudes and expectations. Such measurements have been conducted for many years on a succession of representative national samples by the Survey Research Center of the University of Michigan, and in recent years also by the United States Census Bureau and some private firms (Katona).

National Fiscal and Monetary Policy and the Consumer

When the forecasts of business investment, net exports, consumer expenditures, and the government deficit (net spending) indicate a problem, there are economic policies to deal with it. Our concern here is how these policies affect households. There are two major classes of government economic policies, fiscal and monetary.

Fiscal policy refers to changes in taxes and government spending, and hence the size of the government deficit. One can increase total spending, and hence employment, either by increasing government spending, or by cutting taxes to let people spend more out of their greater after-tax income. It is believed, for good theoretical reasons, that a deficit produced by increasing government spending stimulates the economy more than an equivalent deficit produced by cutting taxes. What is more important, the relative role of the federal government becomes larger or smaller in the economy depending on which way the deficit is altered. When inflation threatens, one can cut back government expenditures, or increase taxes, or a combination of the two. The former reduces the size and role of government; the latter increases it.

The impact on consumers depends not only on whether the fiscal policies increase or decrease the role of government, but which government taxes or expenditures are affected. The tax cut of 1964 was regarded as a triumph of the new fiscal policy because increasing the potential government deficit eliminated a recession, but it was largely a reduction in the taxes of the affluent. The same amount of stimulus could have been provided by a program of income supplements (negative taxes) at the bottom, abolishing poverty in one stroke. Instead, we relied on the benefits to "trickle down," which did very little for the poor.

The alternative to fiscal policy (or its partner, if you prefer) is monetary policy, which makes it more or less expensive for those who need to borrow money to get it. We shall not explain the techniques, but they result in raising interest rates, which makes it difficult to borrow, when the government wants to restrict total spending. The impact is rather uneven. Those who are most likely to be forced to restrict their activity are young people trying to buy their first house, or school districts trying to float bond issues, and not large corporations, which have growing profits to invest at such times and regular lines of credit with institutions that want to keep their business. Nor are older families affected much, since they have accumulated savings and are thus free from such heavy dependence on borrowing. The use of monetary policy tends to force a relatively small number of people to cut back their spending in the national interest.

Social Security

The Social Security system has been much in the news recently. A number of plausible sounding statements are repeatedly made about it:

☐ It is going broke because payments are exceeding receipts, and the trust fund is heading for zero, leaving trillions of dollars in unfunded liability.
☐ We must stick with the "pay as you go" system, and dare not pay for any of the benefits out of general tax revenues, or we will violate the insurance principle that makes benefits a matter of right rather than charity.
☐ Social Security taxes are regressive, taking a larger share of income from those earning less than $15,000 than from those earning more.
☐ The Social Security system discourages saving, and hence, the investment we need for economic progress.

Actually, the first two of these are absolutely false, the third is true but irrelevant and misleading, and the fourth is of doubtful truth and in any case more relevant to problems of general economic management than to an analysis of social insurance policy. Misunderstandings of the system are so serious and so pervasive that any discussion of the realities involved must start with a look at the basic economic facts on which a social insurance system rests.

The Importance of Interest

In a society without any social security system, individuals by themselves or through their employer can save during an average of forty years of working life and buy a lifetime annuity on an expected lifespan at sixty-five of about fifteen years.

That forty years' accumulation of savings will earn interest in a properly functioning market economy. The productivity of real capital, made possible by the willingness of the savers to forego current consumption, produces a yield of 2 to 3 percent annually in constant-value dollars. In the world as we know it, there is also inflation, and market interest rates tend to be higher than the true interest rate by the rate of inflation. To be sure, savers cannot always recover the full amount added by inflation, and short-run inflations can occur without compensatingly high interest rates, but for simplicity we will assume that the real annual interest rate is about 3 percent.

Compounding of interest over such long periods as the average working life makes a startling difference in the amounts accumulated. With a 3 percent annual rate, forty years of saving $1,000 a year will accumulate $35,401 in interest in addition to the $40,000 principal. Further, additional interest earned while this sum is being used up as periodic retirement benefit payments will add another $19,303, so that nearly *58 percent* of total retirement benefits are *interest*. Given that inflation has been and is likely to remain with us, the assumption of (at least) a 6 percent market interest rate is more realistic; at that rate, our $40,000 in savings will provide a total of $238,950 in retirement benefits, more than 82 percent of it being interest! (See table 14.)

The Trust Fund Issue

The question now arises, where is the interest paid or accumulated in our Social Security system? Nowhere. The so-called "trust fund" is a small balancing account. No real (that is, fully funded) trust account was ever created, for good and sufficient reasons.

Recall that Social Security began in the depths of the Great Depression, when arguments arose over whether there were 10 or 20 million unemployed. It is easy to imagine the problem of taxing payrolls to raise the billions of dollars necessary to fund the system fully—not to mention the difficulties of trying to invest such amounts. There were really only two investment alternatives: buying government bonds or buying common stock. In the former case, the interest would have come out of taxes anyway, and in the latter case, the government would have ended up owning much of American industry. We have a word not much honored in this society for government ownership; while socialism probably seemed more attractive in the thirties than at any other time, it is unlikely to have been favored by a majority even then.

Beyond these philosophical considerations are the fiscal consequences of fully funding Social Security from its beginning. Those people or firms who might have sold bonds or stock to the trust fund would almost certainly not have spent the proceeds, given the economic conditions of the times. The result of such removal of spending from consumption without its being offset by additional investment would have been a completely unacceptable deepening of the Depression.

When the system began, there were many older people on state or county welfare, or eligible for it but too proud or unknowledgeable to get it. The first great act of federal revenue sharing was to make some of them eligible for Social Security benefits without having "earned" them by a lifetime of saving via payroll taxes.

Table 14. Percent of Total Retirement Benefits from Interest Rather Than from Original Contributions, at Various Interest Rates

Years of Contribution	Years of Retirement	$r = 3\%$	$r = 4\%$	$r = 5\%$	$r = 6\%$
35	20	57	68	76	82
40	15	58	69	77	83
45	15	61	72	81	86
40[a]	18[a]	59[a]	70[a]	78[a]	84[a]

[a] Early retirement assumption (contribution ages 22–62, benefits ages 62–80).

Thus began the fictional explanation of the system: that Social Security was financed on a pay as you go basis (though in any real sense it was not), with each generation taking care of a preceding one in return for a promise of being cared for themselves. It would have been more accurate and honest, and might have avoided much of the current nonsense, to have explained that each generation pays its own way—except those first people who could not afford it—and that each generation's saving earns them the right to interest as well as principal return later on. The consumption foregone by each generation in its paying of Social Security taxes makes possible additional capital accumulation, which makes possible a higher future living standard for themselves and succeeding generations—a higher living standard in which they should continue to share during retirement. Of course, the organization of the economy may be such that the savings provided are not transformed into productive investment, but this is not the fault of those doing the saving; they should not be penalized. In fact, the first great use of deficit spending to stimulate a depressed economy occurred when the government "borrowed" the Social Security contributions, and spent them rather than building a trust fund. It was the only wise thing to do.

Benefits to which each generation is entitled can be ascertained. Actuaries can make calculations of the benefits resulting from whatever levels of payroll taxes are democratically agreed upon, assuming market interest rates earned on the cumulative amounts paid in. That done, the inflation adjustment of benefits would be justified as payable out of the higher (because of inflation) interest rates "paid" on the funds which have been accumulated (in theory). Additional desired payments, such as disability or survivor benefits, can be priced into current payroll taxes, since they involve an expected value of total benefits times a known probability in a given year (of becoming disabled or dying, for example). There might still be some desire to increase benefits to those who had not fully earned them in the economic (insurance plus annuity) sense, but such intergenerational transfers would then be open and above board.

If we then start with the moral imperative that people who contribute to a social insurance system deserve a return that includes interest accumulation, we have a way of keeping the system basically a contributory one, without arguing about where the current benefit payments are "coming from." There will still be a kind of redistribution within each generation, of course, between the lucky and the unlucky. That kind of insurance redistribution, in the form of disability benefits, survivor benefits, and the implicit subsidy to those who live a long time from those who die early, is generally regarded as equitable and deserves the term "social insurance."

Suppose we agree to rationalize the system (in both the American and British senses of that term) so that it is fully equitable, each generation paying its own way and earning interest on its own accumulated "savings." What then?

On behalf of the generation that has contributed during all or most of its working life to Social Security, there must be the general understanding that their savings have facilitated some of the increase in living standards now enjoyed by all of society. To be sure, that saving may have seemed to have been done by others, who in turn thought and think they own its fruits (interest and dividends); and those currently working undoubtedly feel that they are "entitled" to the higher real wages which they are now receiving. But equity demands that those who have been paying into the Social Security system have the right, upon retirement, to receive some of that higher "earned" income, namely, the amounts necessary to pay them back with realistic interest.

Some are currently rewriting history, arguing that Social Security has discouraged and is discouraging saving rather than providing it, but this confuses total saving with Social Security contributions. It is true that having such a system requires national levels of investment sufficient to provide the productivity (and thus increased output) from which the implied interest on savings generated by payroll taxes can be taken. Indeed, economists should have been working out the implications of the system for optimal goals for aggregate investment, rather than concentrating entirely on its implications for short-run fiscal policy. The differences between cash payments (of working generations) and cash benefits (mostly of other generations) do affect fiscal and monetary balance, but so do many other things like wars and shifting international trade balances. That some such effects occur is no excuse now for fiscal-policy tinkering with the equity of the Social Security system. In fact, during most of the period since Social Security started, we have had ample investment and low interest rates. And even now, it is difficult to believe that we cannot afford to make good our obligations to past contributors of Social Security taxes, when we still have unemployed resources and manpower.

What does this imply for the future? For one thing, that the so-called trust fund, always a fiction, has outlived whatever usefulness it may have had and should be replaced by reasonable actuarial calculations. Payroll taxes should be set on the basis of desired benefits assuming a 3 percent real return on people's contributions. And, for the already retired, benefits should be adjusted on the basis of crediting market interest rates to their (imaginary) reserves—this as a matter of right, not as an "adjustment" to rising price levels or as a "gift" from those currently working.

To avoid such an honest solution by simply raising payroll taxes on current workers will surely create a cumulative and massive problem for the future. When those generations get to retirement age, they can appropriately ask why—since they paid much higher payroll taxes—they should not get proportionately higher retirement benefits. We could postpone the showdown for a time by raising payroll taxes again, but the problem would recur with the next generation. People are already arguing that with the increased taxes, Social Security does not promise to give you your money's worth. It is difficult to see how people can at the same time argue that the Social Security benefits are an undue burden on society and that the system is not a good buy for the individual if he or she could opt out of it. Perhaps they mean that older generations do too well, later generations poorly, but the relation of contributions now of workers to benefits now of the retired prove nothing. Benefits should always be larger because they include interest!

Where should the money "come from," if not entirely from payroll taxes? It really would only confuse the issue to pretend that some of the Social Security benefits "come out of" current Social Security taxes, and the rest out of general revenue. They *all* come out of general revenue, which includes contributions from payroll taxes. The choice of which particular tax source should depend on considerations of the taxes' effects on incentives and their general fairness.

There are some noninsurance redistributions within the system, of course, produced largely by the floors under benefits, and by the fact that not everyone has dependents who may survive to receive benefits. The system in that sense is more "unfair" to those who never marry or never have children than it is (for example) to women in general. Further, considering both benefits and taxes, it is not regressive, but in fact progressive, for a substantial proportion of lower-income beneficiaries. High-income people pay a smaller proportion of their income in payroll taxes because of the ceiling on covered earnings, but there is a ceiling on benefits as well.

Finally, let us put to rest that size-of-generations bugaboo. While relatively larger cohorts of retirees will require larger proportions of the national income, it is in substantial part their savings (including their Social Security savings) which have made possible the larger gross national product from which their retirement benefits will legitimately be drawn. It is not the changing sizes of the generations that will cause us trouble, but our refusal to make the Social Security system a true social insurance with honest actuarial calculations.

The system is not going broke, the balance in the trust fund is irrelevant, the differing sizes of generations means nothing in terms of the intergenerational equity of the system, and most of all, seeking "pay as you go" balance by raising payroll taxes simply sets us up for bigger problems in the future. It might help clarify the issue to remove what little noninsurance redistribution still exists within the system, given the potential improvement in our noncontributory income-maintenance programs. Then the system, which is after all predominantly a social insurance scheme, could be defended strictly on that ground.

Sex and Policy

The changing roles of women force us to reexamine many policies and ideas, but we cannot ignore the genuine and persisting sex differences in life expectancy. A female at birth can expect to live eight years longer than a male, and five or six years longer at age sixty. So far, the gap has been getting wider rather than narrower, in spite of the fact that more women are working, smoking, drinking, and undergoing tension. These sex differences in life span are worldwide, unexplained by environmental, occupational, or economic differences. They apparently reflect innate biological or genetic advantages of the female.

In addition, for physiological reasons, the age pattern and types of medical care needed differ between the sexes. In view of these differences, genuinely equal treatment is not the same as identical treatment. If an employer puts the same amount into a retirement fund for a man and for a woman, the woman will get fewer dollars per year because she will live longer. To give her the same yearly pension would be discrimination in reverse. The difference in required funds is less than the relative difference in life expectancy, because the extra years come at the end, allowing more years for interest to be earned on the remaining balance. But for the same yearly pension, a woman needs a larger retirement fund.

In the case of life insurance (or Social Security survivor benefits), women should be charged less, because they are less likely to die and "win" the benefits. Some working wives who never need the insurance or disability benefits, and qualify for more retirement benefits as a dependent than from their own earnings, feel their own taxes got them little. Gradual changes are reducing this discrepancy, and there are other ways in which women benefit more.

The longer life expectancy of women, plus the fact that they are less likely than men to work after age sixty-five and more likely to have lower earnings and thus to benefit from the redistributional aspects of the system, mean that in general women are not being shortchanged by the Social Security system (U.S. Senate). There are some changes needed, particularly for working women, but a systematic application of the logic many critics have applied (getting out what you put in) would benefit mostly single working people without dependents, both men and women, but mostly men. They now get the least because they have no dependents to benefit from the system. It is beyond the scope of this book to go into the details, and rapid change can be expected to bring the system up to date anyway. But the ordinary consumer must beware of simplistic criticisms that ask for more benefits for some people without asking whether those who would pay for them would also feel the change was fair. Many changes that seem "fair" also are regressive in their impact.

Summary

A basic understanding of accounting and of the algebra of annuities allows the household to analyze its financial state and recent performance, and to set some goals for saving, for investment in household capital, and hence for consumption. It also makes it clear why retiring early hurts three ways, and why the later in life an income increase comes along, the larger the proportion of it that should be saved.

Some simple methods are suggested for using current receipts and cash balances plus some capital-transaction adjustments to monitor the basic processes of earning, consuming, and saving. More elaborate financial records and recordkeeping are suggested only after successful application of more simple and primitive procedures, and are used for selected purposes such as tax records, family harmony, holding down certain types of expenditures, or holding up savings.

Social Security arose out of the unwillingness or inability of many families to provide adequately for their own retirement. But it is only a floor, inadequate by itself, and supplementary private pensions cover only part of the nation's households. The result may well be a split between discouraged households with only Social Security who give up trying to save, and advantaged households with two or more pensions who may even choose to retire early.

The current affluence, and the substantial fraction of consumer expenditures that can be postponed or expanded, make it difficult to predict the consumer spending so crucial to national stabilization policy. Consumers' confidence in their own and their country's financial future so affects their willingness to make expenditures, particularly expenditures that commit them to a pattern of future consumption and payments, that regular measurement of consumer attitudes is essential.

Consumers will be affected by the mix of monetary and fiscal policies used to stabilize the economy, and by the mix of "socialism" (Social Security) and private enterprise (the big insurance companies) used to handle retirement, illness, and the needs of survivors.

More Information?

Most of the "how to" publications on financial planning are written from the special points of view of those with something to sell—lawyers, trust experts, stockbrokers. They tend to sell complex solutions which require expert help, seldom providing frank details on the cost of that expert help. The budgeting guides tend to focus on trivia such as detailed record-keeping rather than the analysis and planning that tells what records are essential and how to interpret and act on them. The analysis requires a combination of economic analysis and accounting, but accounting books are written for business accounting, and economic analyses of life-cycle saving are not written for the layperson.

Ashley, Paul P. *You and Your Will.* New York: McGraw-Hill, 1975.

Barfield, Richard, and Morgan, James N. *Early Retirement: The Decision and Experience and a Second Look.* Ann Arbor: Institute for Social Research, 1975.

Barlow, Robin; Brazer, Harvey; and Morgan, James N. *Economic Behavior of the Affluent.* Washington, D.C.: Brookings Institution, 1966.

Boulding, Kenneth. *The Economy of Love and Fear.* Belmont, Calif.: Wadsworth Publishing Company, 1973.

Brosterman, Robert. *The Complete Estate Planning Guide.* New York: Mentor, 1964.

Dacey, Norman. *How to Avoid Probate.* New York: Crown, 1965.

Greenough, William E., and King, Francis P. *Pension Plans and Public Policy.* New York: Columbia University Press, 1976.

Katona, George. *Private Pensions and Individual Saving.* Ann Arbor: Institute for Social Research, 1965.

Klein, Laurence R., ed. *Contributions of Survey Methods to Economics.* New York: Columbia University Press, 1954.

Kosobud, Richard F., and Morgan, James N., eds. *Consumer Behavior of Individual Families over Two and Three Years.* Ann Arbor: Institute for Social Research, 1964.

Morgan, James N.; Dye, Richard; and Hybels, Judith. "Results from Two National Surveys of Philanthropic Activity." In *Research Paper,* vol. 1, prepared by the Commission on Private Philanthropy and Public Needs. Washington, D.C.: U.S. Treasury, 1977.

Nader, Ralph, and Blackwell, Kate. *You and Your Pension.* New York: Crossman, 1975.

Pension Benefit Guaranty Corporation. *Individual Retirement Account: Plan for Your Retirement.* Washington, D.C.: Government Printing Office, revised at intervals.

Schulz, James H. *The Economics of Aging.* Belmont, Calif.: Wadsworth Publishing Company, 1976.

U.S. Department of Agriculture. *A Guide to Budgeting for the Young Couple.* USDA Home and Garden Bulletin. Washington, D.C.: Government Printing Office, 1967.

U.S. Department of Agriculture. *A Guide to Budgeting for the Family.* USDA Home and Garden Bulletin. Washington, D.C.: Government Printing Office, 1968.

U.S. Department of Health, Education, and Welfare. *Estimating Your Social Security Retirement Check.* Washington, D.C.: Government Printing Office, August 1978 (or latest edition).

U.S. Department of Health, Education, and Welfare, Social Security Administration. *Social Security Handbook.* Washington, D.C.: Government Printing Office, latest edition.

U.S. Department of Labor, Labor Management Services Administration, Pension and Welfare Benefit Programs. *What You Should Know About the Pension and Welfare Law, A Guide to the Employee Retirement Income Security Act of 1974.* Washington, D.C.: Government Printing Office, 1978.

U.S. Department of the Treasury, Internal Revenue Service. *A Guide to Federal Estate and Gift Taxation.* Publication No. 448. Washington, D.C.: Government Printing Office, 1975. (Check for later version.)

U.S. Department of the Treasury, Internal Revenue Service. *Federal Tax Guide for Survivors, Executors, and Administrators.* Publication No. 559. Washington, D.C.: Government Printing Office, 1977.

U.S. Senate, Special Committee on Aging, Task Force on Women and Social Security. *Women and Social Security: Adapting to a New Era.* Washington, D.C.: Government Printing Office, 1975.

Some Projects to Learn More

1. Construct a balance sheet and income statement for yourself, putting in as many nonmoney items as you can. What difference do nonmoney items make?

2. Use the bathtub theorem to measure your expenditures weekly for ten weeks. What would adjustments do to account for fluctuations? What else explains the week-to-week instability?

3. Read some current discussions of the Social Security system. Are the criticisms valid? What is the author trying to suggest or prove? Is the system unfair to women?

4. Calculate the present value of the survivor benefits in Social Security for a family with two children, from the time of the second birth every five years until the wife is sixty-five.

5. Read some of the recent writings on economic forecasting or on national stabilization policy (inflation and unemployment). Write a critical appraisal of the way in which consumer expenditures and consumer investments and home purchases are handled.

6. Find out about some local banks or other institutions that will handle Independent Retirement Accounts. Do they have any records of their earned yields on such accounts? What kind of regulation is there on such accounts?

CHAPTER SIX
BORROWING AND CONSUMER DEBT

In the usual sequence of things, even with the best financial planning, the need to borrow may well arise. A liquidity crisis is particularly likely if you have children, because pressures to accumulate household durables combine with family earnings which may be lower if only one parent works full time. Proper financial planning may allow you to avoid borrowing for the small durables and even for the car, but buying a house is sure to call for a loan.

Wherever you borrow and for whatever period, the loan will almost certainly call for repayment in regular amounts during the period. The old melodramatic villain demanding the full repayment on the due date is no more. Instead we have amortized loans.

Amortization Algebra

The characteristics of an amortized loan are simply enough. A regular monthly or weekly payment is calculated which over a stated period will return to the lender his principal plus interest at some fixed rate on the remaining balance owed. Calculating the monthly charge is a bit of work, so there are tables which can be used, similar to those at the end of chapter 2 but for monthly or weekly payments. There are also inexpensive pocket calculators that will give payments, or interest rate, or present value if you enter values for the other two.

What confuses borrowers is that if they compare the two most available numbers, the amount borrowed and the total financing charges (extra amount paid back), they think the interest rate is just the charges divided by the initial amount borrowed. In fact, such a calculation gives an interest rate which is half as large as it should be. The reason is that the interest rate ought to be calculated as the ratio of finance charges to the average remaining balance. The initial amount borrowed is about twice as large as the average amount borrowed. After the first month, since each payment is partly a repayment of principal, the amount on which interest should be calculated is smaller. On a twelve-month loan, the amount on loan varies from the full amount the first month to slightly more than one-twelfth of it for the last month.

Figure 7 depicts the pattern of remaining debt, using the high 36 percent annual rate of the small-loan company to dramatize a point. That the average amount owed is about half the initial amount is obvious from noting that the triangle A is about equal in size to the triangle B. It is not exactly half, because the early payments are largely interest, and because the first payment is at the *end* of the first period.

The important point is that since on the average only a little over half of the initial amount of the loan is unpaid, the interest rate is really nearly twice what it seems. Another way to see this is to put yourself in the lending business with a portfolio of loans, a new one starting each month, and figure out how much capital you would have to have to stay in business. Slightly over $600 would support twelve $100 yearly loans!

Under the 1969 Truth in Lending law, the true annual interest rate on the remaining balance must be given on the loan contract, but it is still important to know how to estimate the rate of interest when you know the facts of a loan, or to estimate the monthly payments when you know the amount, period, and interest rate.

Suppose I borrow an amount, A, and agree to pay back P per period for N periods.

I have to repay NP in all, which includes $NP - A$ in interest charges.

But the average amount of the loan is roughly $A/2$, so the credit cost per dollar is $(NP - A)/(A/2)$.

But I want an *annual* interest rate figure to compare with the alternatives of "borrowing" from my savings account or to compare with the rates of other loans. I divide the credit cost per dollar by the number of years the loan runs, which is $N/12$ if the payments are monthly, or $N/52$ if they are weekly.

One small correction is necessary because the first repayment occurs at the end of the first period, and the early payments are mostly interest. (I really average more than half the amount borrowed.) I can do this well enough by multiplying the estimated rate by $N/(N+1)$.

So the true annual interest rate on a loan with monthly payments is

$$\frac{NP - A}{A/2} \times \frac{1}{N/12} \times \frac{N}{N+1}$$

or

$$\frac{\text{Interest charges}}{\text{Half the amount borrowed}} \times \frac{1}{\text{Number of years}} \times \frac{\text{Number of payments}}{1 + \text{Number of payments}}.$$

The first term adjusts for the amortization feature by using half the amount borrowed as the average amount of the loan.

The second converts to an *annual* rate.

The third adjusts for periodicity.

Suppose I borrow $800 and repay it in twenty-four monthly installments of $40 each. The interest rate can be calculated as follows:

$$\frac{40 \times 24 - 800}{400} \times \frac{1}{24/12} \times \frac{24}{25} =$$

$$\frac{160}{400} \times \frac{12}{25} = \frac{1{,}920}{10{,}000} = 0.192 = 19.2\%$$

An apparently small difference in the monthly payments makes a big difference in the interest. What if the same loan called for only $38 a month instead of $40? See if you can work out the interest rate and get 13.4 percent!

A few lenders claim to deduct the total interest charges at the beginning of the loan; this is commonly called "discounting." In the example above, the $800 loan would be called a $960 loan, the $160 in interest deducted before repayment begins. But that should not confuse you if you remember that the amount you really are borrowing is the amount you get. And don't divide the interest charges by the amount borrowed plus the interest charges; that's a meaningless number.

That the early payments are largely interest and the last few largely repayment of principal leads to some additional confusion when a loan is repaid early. Halfway through a loan period, I still owe more than half the loan.[1] In addition, some added prepayment penalties may be justified, because there is a fixed cost of making a loan (credit check, forms, etc.) that has to be covered out of what seem to be interest charges. The bank or lender counted on spreading those fixed costs over the whole loan period. Even without a penalty, the calculation of how much interest you save by paying off the loan early (if that is permitted) is done using the "sum of the digits method." It is really rather simple. One assumes that on a twelve-month loan, you pay interest on 1/12 of it the last month, 2/12 of it the next-to-last month, and so forth, up to 12/12 of the amount the first month. The total interest is thus made up of monthly interest of 1/12 plus 2/12 plus ...

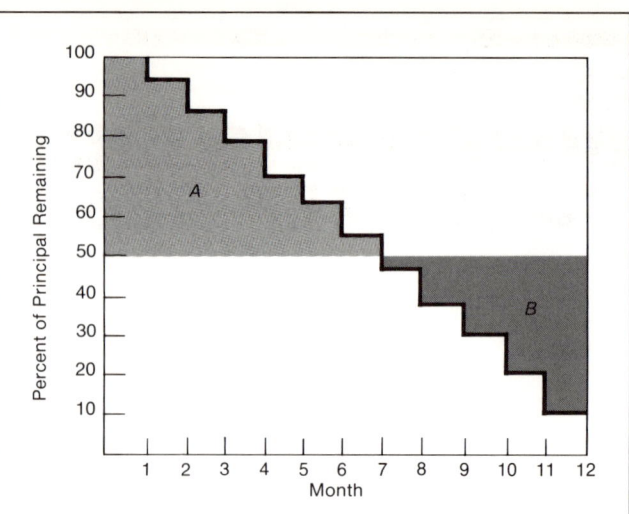

Fig. 7 Remaining principal on a twelve-month amortized loan at 36 percent annual interest. Similarity in size of triangles A and B demonstrates that the average amount owed is roughly half the initial amount borrowed.

1. See figure 3, p. 47.

plus 12/12, for a total of 78/12. For a loan of N payment periods, the interest is thus in $N(N + 1)/2$ parts.

Suppose I want to pay off a twelve-month, no-prepayment-penalty loan that has three $40 payments yet to go, and $60 in total interest charges. Using the sum of the digits method, 1 plus 2 plus 3 or 6/78 of the interest cost has not yet been incurred and should be deducted from the amount I have to pay. Instead of the last three regular $40 payments ($120), I would have to pay 6/78 times $60 less than that, or $120 − $4.62, or $115.38.

Even lenders get confused by the fact that interest is really earned and paid on the remaining balance. They occasionally worry that the market value of a car bought on credit can drop below the total installment payments still due on it. The vision of people defaulting, thinking that they could get a better car with the same money, is clearly only a nightmare, since it ignores the unearned interest included in the total "payments still due." The lender is safe so long as the market value of the car exceeds the remaining principal. Actually, even if the value falls below the principal of the debt, there is little cause for concern since borrowers would ruin their credit ratings by defaulting, and in fact the car is not the total security for the debt—the borrower's wages can be garnisheed too.

Varieties of Lenders

Loans vary in size, duration, and risk. Risk, in turn, depends partly on the property, if any, which is used as security for the loan. Home mortgages, with a house for security and FHA or VA insurance against default to boot, ordinarily carry interest rates only a little above the rates paid on savings accounts. Installment credit and credit card interest rates can be twice as high, finance company loans can be double the installment rate, and illegal backstreet lenders could double the rate again.

There are costs in making a loan, and they are generally included in what we think of as interest charges. For rather small, short-term loans, what seems like a high interest rate may actually be mostly the costs of checking on credit rating and the work of making the loan. There are also different risks of default, which are largely handled by charging more for unsecured loans, or by restricting credit to customers with certain characteristics. Not everyone can get even a credit card. The use of centralized organizations to keep track of people's credit ratings has led to concerns about the dossiers of unchecked information on individuals that can harm them unjustly. There are also problems concerning whether methods of classifying credit applicants into risk groups are proper and fair. We return to these issues later in the chapter.

An individual needing to borrow should shop for a "best buy," which means the highest class of loan for which he or she is eligible, and the best terms available in that class. Studies done in the past have indicated a wide range of different interest rates even within the same city (Jung).

We have already discussed mortgages, but not their rates. There is not much competition between mortgage lenders, but the total finance charges are so large that shopping for slightly lower interest rates may well pay off. If rates are similar, there may at least be better provisions for speeding up repayment with less penalty, and fewer restrictions against refinancing should interest rates drop.

The Truth in Lending Act has made it easier to know and compare interest rates, but the act and the printing of the rates tends to give them an air of authority and official sanction which allows one particularly confusing practice known as "packing" to continue. It is called packing since it packs part of the price of the purchase into what the buyer thinks are interest charges.

Packing involves writing the installment contract at a very high interest rate, which low-income borrowers or poor credit risks may think is what they have to pay, but then selling the actual installment contract to someone else for a sum larger than the remaining principal. The extra is really the result of rediscounting the obligated stream of repayments at a more realistic interest rate, and the difference goes to the seller. The seller thus gets more for the product than the buyer thinks he paid, and the interest is really less than the buyer thinks. To see this, consider the following simplified example: Suppose a car buyer is quoted a $5,000 car price and a three-year monthly payment installment loan contract with $1,500 in finance charges. The quoted interest rate will be

$$\frac{NP - A}{A/2} \times \frac{1}{N/12} \times \frac{N}{N+1} = \frac{1{,}500}{2{,}500} \times \frac{1}{3} \times \frac{36}{37} = 19.5\%.$$

If the car dealer immediately sells the installment contract to a bank for $5,500, then the full price of the car is $5,500, the finance charges $1,000, and the interest rate is:

$$\frac{1,000}{2,750} \times \frac{1}{3} \times \frac{36}{37} = 11.8\%.$$

The same result can be achieved if the seller sends you to a particular lender who has agreed to set up a "bad debt reserve" and refund the unused amounts in it to the seller. It is easy to set aside far more than is needed, a delayed extra payment for the buyer with higher "interest" charges. There is nothing illegal about this, but it is obviously a deceptive practice. One way to find out whether it is going on is to bargain with a car salesperson about the price of a car on the assumption that you are going to buy on credit, and then offer to pay the best price in cash. If the salesperson suddenly checks with the manager and finds they cannot offer that price after all, or adds the figures again and they total $100 more, it seems likely that they were counting on "pack"—a little something extra paid by the bank or finance company out of your "interest" charges.

Why should banks engage in such a deceptive practice, and get blamed for higher interest rates than they are really earning, and be so unwilling to make the arrangements public? Presumably they are competing for the loans, and dealers would not send them the business without the kickbacks. The 1969 Truth in Lending Act is unlikely to improve the situation. What it might have done was to include a provision that if a credit obligation is transferred from the seller or first lender to anyone else for an amount other than the remaining principal, that fact and the amounts would have to be announced to the buyer. Banks might welcome a compulsory publication of the facts, and such publication would make it easier for consumers to shop for things they buy on credit.

Sources of Loans

Loans for purchase of things which themselves serve as security for the loan are available from banks, installment finance companies, and credit unions. Loans based not on specific objects but on your general credit rating are available from banks, credit unions, stores, and with credit cards.

Credit unions are technically cooperatives, some established under the Federal Credit Union Act, and others under state laws. They are presumably organized and run by their members, although some members primarily keep their savings there, and others primarily borrow. They claim to have more of a consumer orientation and avoid some of the worst practices of other lenders. For instance, they generally place no penalties on prepayments. On the other hand, their managers sometimes start sounding like bankers wanting to increase business and profits, for example, by suggesting you buy a new car every two years, and only pay off enough to be able to refinance the new one, thus maximizing the amount of borrowing and interest charges you pay.

Lenders reduce their risks by insisting the borrower carry insurance that will pay off the debt in case of trouble. With homes this is usually limited to fire and casualty insurance, although life insurance may also be part of the deal. With cars it includes collision insurance and sometimes life insurance on the borrower. With other loans it tends to be life insurance. These insurance coverages are costly, and should be avoided if possible. Credit life insurance in particular violates the principles of how much insurance to carry (chap. 9) and is expensive in these small pieces. "How-to" books suggest avoiding these "package deals" and at least getting credit and insurance separately. As with any compulsory package deal, there may well be confusion as to just how much you are paying for what.

Charge accounts used to be the free credit of the affluent, but most have given way to store credit cards, available to more people and charging substantial interest unless each monthly bill is paid within a short period after it is received. Competing with store credit cards are bank, gasoline company, and general credit cards. From the consumer's point of view, they all have similar characteristics: a limit on the amount you can buy with them, a billing date, and an interest charge each month if you do not pay within a stated number of days after that date. Most bank credit cards (Visa, MasterCard) are either free or require a modest annual charge. This means that you can still get the low-cost credit of the charge account by paying bills within the deadlines. Most general credit cards (American Express, Carte Blanche) charge a larger annual fee.

It is easy enough to see why a store or gasoline company would issue a credit card, but what about the bank credit cards or the general credit cards which are honored wherever their signs are displayed? In addition to the interest charges on delayed repayments, these companies thrive by giving the vendors less than the amount of the sale, by about 4 to 6 percent. If I pay a hotel bill of $100 with my Master Charge card, the hotel gets $95 or so. Why should a business stand for this? Because they think it brings more business, saves them handling their own credit, and reduces cash and robbery problems. On the other hand, someone willing to pay cash could justifiably ask for a discount, and Consumers Union won a court case declaring that the vendors could not be prohibited by their credit card contracts from giving such discounts. For those who find it unpleasant to negotiate discounts, it is possible to use the credit card to save some interest even though the interest you save until you have to pay the bill is far less than what the store pays by having you pay with the card rather than with cash.

Think of paying for a $100 item:

1. If you pay cash, you pay $100 right away, and the store gets it right away. If you pay by check, there is only a slight delay.
2. If you use the store's credit card and pay before the interest charges start, you may have as much as forty-five days to pay. You save the 50¢ or so in interest if you keep your money in a savings account, and the store loses interest on its money for the same period.
3. If you use the store's credit card and take six months to pay, you pay slightly over $105 including interest, and the store nets about $102 because their interest costs are lower.
4. If you use a bank credit card (and the store may not allow this, particularly if they have their own credit cards) and pay before interest is charged, you pay $100 and save a little interest. The store gets about $95 with a little delay.
5. If you use a bank credit card and pay over six months, you pay some $105 including interest, and the store gets $95.

What all this means is that the store is subsidizing the user of bank credit cards at the expense of the cash customer. And the credit card user who delays and pays interest is helping to pay for the free credit of the credit card user who pays before interest is charged. Where a store credit card is involved, those who use the card and pay on time are subsidized by those who end up paying interest—and perhaps also by the cash customers, although most stores try to make their credit operation self-financing, i.e., no burden to the cash customers.

The customer can, of course, do a little better by keeping track of billing dates, using whichever card gives the longest time to pay on that purchase date, and paying at the last day possible. He or she may save half a percent in interest compared with paying cash.

The store does best if customers use store credit cards and pay over months with interest. They do next-best with cash, somewhat worse if their customer uses the store credit card and pays on time, and worst of all if the customer uses an outside credit card (6 percent discount to store), regardless of when the customer pays the credit card company. Some hotels now ask for a check instead of a credit card, for this reason.

Obviously, except for the confusion and possible nuisance if they are stolen, a variety of credit cards allows the consumer to get a lot of free credit, avoid carrying cash, and still have a record of expenditures without writing many checks. Unfortunately, some of the credit companies have so abbreviated their billings that it is difficult to sort them out, and proving you paid a particular bill is more difficult than if you have a canceled check.

The new combined checking and savings accounts that keep most of your funds in a savings account until they are needed to cover your checks clearly make this careful timing easier. Pay-by-phone also facilitates it. But there are costs—the opportunity cost of your time to schedule everything, and the (negative) expected value of the cost of being late with a payment and incurring financing charges (the charges times the probability of incurring them). And the savings account interest in combined checking and savings accounts is usually lower than you could get elsewhere. (See chapter 7 on money market funds.)

For some, the choice may seem to be between buying on credit or not buying at all. It is easy to get into such a situation and stay there all your life. But a small, one-time delay of a few purchases can make a permanent shift from persistent borrowing and paying interest to regular saving and earning interest.

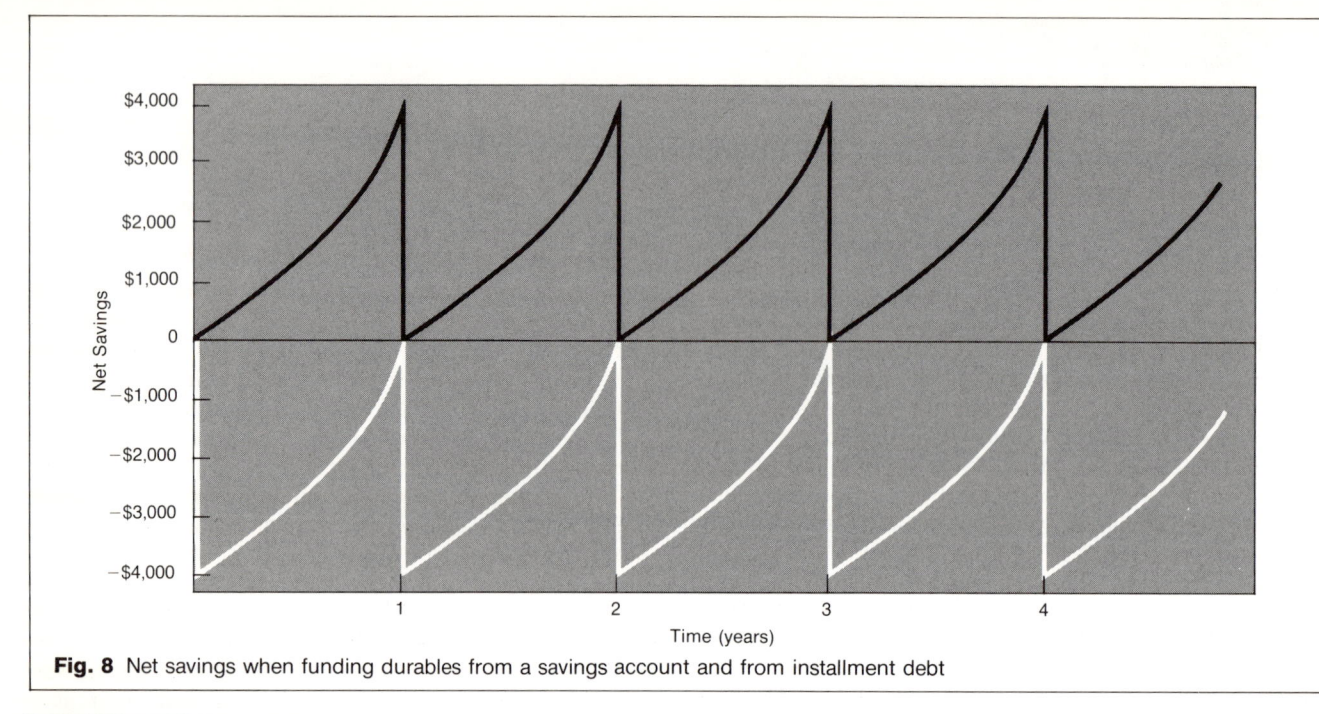

Fig. 8 Net savings when funding durables from a savings account and from installment debt

The Timing of Purchases and Debt

As explained in chapter 5, most households can expect to spend almost one-sixth of their incomes on consumer durables. There are two common ways of budgeting these expenses, with very different implications for the interest charges a household will pay. The first method is to fund purchases of durables from a (positive) savings account balance. An initial period of sacrifice with minimal expenditures can build the account balance to the point where durables can be purchased outright, rather than on credit. The advantage of this method, of course, is that this savings account earns interest. A second method is to finance the purchases by borrowing, gradually repaying the debt and then incurring new debt when the original one is mostly paid off.

These two methods are depicted in figure 8. Both assume that the household spends $4,000 per year for durables. The black line shows the pattern for the household that saves and then spends; the white line shows the pattern for purchases financed by debt.

Although the purchase patterns are identical except for the initial year, the costs of these patterns differ greatly. By funding purchases from a positive savings account balance, a household maintains a $2,000 average balance and earns interest on that balance. The average balance for the indebted household is −$2,000, and interest charges are paid on that amount. If the savings account earns 6 percent interest, then the annual interest payment will be about 0.06 × $2,000 = $120. If the indebted household is charged 18 percent interest on its $2,000 average debt, then it will pay about 0.18 × $2,000 = $360 per year in finance charges. The difference, $480 per year, is the reward to the household that postponed its purchases for the initial year. The present value of that reward over a thirty-year period at 3 percent interest amounts to nearly $10,000. Tax considerations reduce this reward by a percentage amount equal to the marginal tax rate, since the interest earned on savings is taxed and interest paid on debts can be deducted from taxable income.

Credit Ratings

Getting credit cards, like getting a loan, requires establishing your credit rating. People used to say that a person should borrow some money and pay it back, if only to establish a credit rating. Credit rating bureaus rely on more than that, but there is an argument for taking out one of the free bank credit cards and using it like a free credit charge account, partly to establish your credit rating.

What is in your record at the credit rating organizations is important, because it may affect your ability to get low-cost loans or even to get a job. The concern for privacy and the possible misuse of various public records, plus some extreme cases of unwarranted damage, led to the Fair Credit Reporting Act of 1971, provisions of which are summarized in appendix 6.1. The main concern is that unchecked erroneous information can get into such files and do a great deal of damage to an unsuspecting individual. It may have been a different Pat Jones, or Pat may have had a legitimate complaint, or the whole thing may have been amicably settled, or the charges may have been dismissed, or Pat declared not guilty; but the record may not contain the final outcome, only the report of trouble. Now, at least you have the right, if you are denied credit on the basis of a credit bureau report, to see it and have it corrected, or at least have your own version added to it. You can also find out who has been given the incorrect information and have the bureau send them corrections.

Credit ratings are also based on general characteristics of individuals as well as their personal credit ratings. This can be unfair to individuals who find themselves in a geographic area or population class that is rated high risk by lenders. Increasing demands are heard that these ratings be justified by actual experience or that they be made more discriminating and less stereotyping (prejudicial). There is justification for charging more where risks are high, but broad risk groups, such as everyone in a low-income area, are bound to be unfair to some of the people in those areas or groups.

We have said little about the small-loan companies and the illegal lenders. The latter lend to those whose credit is so bad that even the high legal maximum interest rates, varying around 36 percent, of the small-loan companies are too low to cover the risk. The obvious advice is to avoid them and to borrow only what you can borrow from lower-interest lenders.

Some people try to avoid the problem by borrowing from friends, often at no interest at all. This is very economical but sometimes loses friends. If a national sample of individuals is asked how much money they owe to other individuals, and how much money other individuals owe to them, the aggregate amounts recalled should be about equal; but in fact the average amount people remember they owe is substantially smaller than the average amount people remember as owed to them! It is clearly wise to secure a signed receipt promising some specific interest per year and repayment of the principal by some fixed date if you lend to anyone, however lovable. With the receipt, you might have a chance to recover the debt in small claims court, or be able to deduct the loss on your income tax. It is easier to wait for a long-delayed repayment if interest is accumulating. In drawing up such a loan agreement, however, make certain that the stated interest rate does not exceed the maximum legal rate dictated by state usury laws.

Trouble: Repossession, Garnishment, and Bankruptcy

If you do find difficulty keeping up with the payments on a loan, a whole new world of complications opens up, even apart from what happens to your credit rating and your chances of borrowing in the future. There may be friendly dunning letters, from a collection agency if the creditor is a small store or a doctor who doesn't want to bother personally. If a purchase was the reason for the loan and the loan involved an item as security (chattel mortgage), the item may be repossessed. Actually, the repossession rates have been quite small, generally less than 1 percent on cars, for instance, indicating that people have been handling their credit rather well or that lenders have been carefully selecting those to whom they would lend.

For small debts, there are small claims courts, set up to help individuals secure justice, but largely used by sellers to collect from customers. There are limits to the amounts that can be collected this way. When substantial amounts are involved, the process goes from warnings to repossession to garnishment to bankruptcy.

Garnishment is technically a legal action requiring an employer to turn over part of an employee debtor's salary to a creditor. The rules vary from state to state as to how sure one must be that the debtor was notified and given a chance to object that this was not a proper obligation, and as to the amount of earnings exempt from garnishment. Some states even set exemptions in dollars, unadjusted for family size or inflation. Texas does not even provide for garnishment at all.

The threat of garnishment is often enough to make people pay up, even if they have to borrow elsewhere to do so. Employers dislike the nuisance and feel that an employee cannot be working well when most of the wage is being diverted. Consequently, many companies fire anyone whose wages are garnisheed a second time. People selling shoddy merchandise or services on credit may use the threat of garnishment and loss of job to collect what might otherwise be regarded as illegitimate claims. A Federal Trade Commission study of the Washington, D.C. area indicated that most of the garnishments were secured by eleven sellers selling mostly to low-income people. The real question is whether the use of garnishment against dishonest or disorganized consumers justifies its availability to dishonest sellers. Technically the claim must be a valid one, but uninformed victims with no legal help can do little. Sometimes they are not even notified until their paycheck is cut.

Faced with the threat of garnishment, or unable to pay anyway, the debtor may find the only way out is to go bankrupt. Many people think of bankruptcy as something businessmen do, but the vast bulk of bankruptcies are personal. The number has been growing at a rate alarming to some observers. Data are easy to find because the bankruptcy law is a federal law, and the Administrative Office of the United States Courts issues annual *Tables of Bankruptcy Statistics*, personal and business, area by area. These files are accessible. To go bankrupt you must file a form giving your assets and debts and last year's income. Some experts think that people are more likely to go bankrupt in states where the exemptions from garnishment are inadequate to survive on; others think that bankruptcy is more likely where people are informed of its availability.

Some critics have felt that bankruptcy was too easy a way for a debtor to evade obligations, and have urged an alternative—court-enforced scheduled repayments. The federal bankruptcy law contains a provision, Title 13, under which the federal judge assigns a lawyer to negotiate with creditors, take over the debtor's paycheck, and make scheduled repayments to the creditors and an allowance to the debtor. The provision was put in at the urging of many liberals concerned that people be helped to learn how to handle their money, pay off their debts, and keep their self-respect and their credit rating.

The American Bar Association has been urging a change in the law allowing the judge to make Title 13 mandatory. This, it is argued, allows the judge to deal with those using bankruptcy as an easy escape and to help those who really want to pay. To other critics, Title 13 looks like an expensive use of lawyers in a court-enforced collection of private debts without adequate regard for the quality or legitimacy of the original obligations. It is quite clear from the official statistics that the use of Title 13 depends on the judge. The ratio of Title 13 cases to regular nonbusiness bankruptcy varies dramatically from one federal judicial district to another, being very high in Alabama, southern Georgia, and western Tennessee.

Once a debtor goes bankrupt, he is not allowed to do so again for six years, not even in another state, since the law is federal. In fact, some high-pressure credit sellers or lenders seek out recent bankrupts as better than average credit risks among the poor, since they can no longer escape into bankruptcy and can thus be put under the full duress of garnishment. A new Bankruptcy Act signed into law late in 1978, while failing to follow some of the recommendations of a National Commission on Bankruptcy Laws such as counselling on alternatives, did provide a few additional consumer protections. It allows the debtor to opt for the uniform federal exemptions, which are generally more favorable to the bankrupt than those allowed by many states. If a creditor tries to protect his claim from discharge by claiming that the debtor made a false financial statement, he may be subjected to liability (sued for damages) if he loses, and would have to pay the court costs and attorney's fees. On the other hand, in response to some abuses, educational loans cannot be discharged by bankruptcy until five years after the loan is due, by which time most people would have enough assets so that bankruptcy might not appear so cheap.

The Title 13 scheduled repayments, unlike bankruptcy, can be repeated whenever necessary. In both cases legal fees are about the same—several hundred dollars. One ingenious researcher decided to investigate the notion that Title 13 taught people how to handle their money and preserved their credit ratings. He investigated in Alabama and found that many of the victims were going through the scheduled repayment process for the third or fourth or fifth time! Clearly, paying lawyers to schedule their repayments was not teaching them to stay out of trouble (Haden).

But again, we really do not know whether the availability of bankruptcy aids more people to get out from under impossible or unjust obligations than it aids dishonest people to avoid repayments they could perfectly well make. There is Texas with no garnishment law, and no evidence that creditors suffer more there than elsewhere, or that there have to be more repossessions. Without expensive government procedures for collecting debts, with debtors and courts bearing the costs, perhaps lenders would be more careful to whom they lend, and how much.

We saw earlier that studies of people who go bankrupt indicate that a substantial number are recently married and have had increasing incomes in the three years prior to bankruptcy. The former implies that two people merging their finances do not always learn how to plan together and schedule purchases. The implication of the income increases might be (1) that people overcommit income increases in a spirit of enthusiasm, or (2) that they were already overburdened with debt but decided to wipe the slate clean. There are also more bankruptcies in one area than another, perhaps because people find out about it from one another. Rumor had it that in Chicago one could pay an attorney to handle one's bankruptcy on the installment plan—going bankrupt for "a dollar down and dollar a week."

The difficulty with the research on bankruptcy is that is has focused on those who go bankrupt, not on others in equally uncertain circumstances who manage to pay off their debts. The one exception found that trouble is so rare that it is hard to find enough cases to study (Hendricks et al.).

A specialized group of "credit counselors" or "debt adjusters" has arisen to help those in trouble. They range from genuinely professional counselors, sometimes in nonprofit organizations, to frauds on a par with the small-loan company offer to consolidate your debts by lending you money (at 36 percent) to pay off a lot of small debts (most of them with lower interest charges or none at all). Some of the more progressive labor unions and employers have encouraged credit unions and provided credit counseling, as do the Armed Services. Of course, what people need most is not disaster relief when they are in trouble, but advice of the kind provided in chapter 5. Perhaps an account out of which all down payments and debt payments are made, kept separate from the rest of the family money, might help by warning that one more purchase would overload the "capital account."

There are some other problems with the law relating to debt. One is the "holder in due course" doctrine, by which a third or fourth party who acquires the debtor's promise to pay can demand payments without any responsibility for the legitimacy of the original transaction or the quality of the product. The aluminum siding or storm window contractor can get your signature, sell it to the bank, and skip town, and the bank can legally collect. Many states have already abolished the doctrine. Boat sellers claim that without this doctrine no bank will finance a boat because so many customers would claim problems and stop payment.

These problems have led to attempts to establish a uniform national credit code. However, though the provisions of such a code might bring dramatic improvements to some states, in others the code might not be as good as the law that already exists. A second problem is that no one is really sure whether it is better to have stricter regulations or to encourage more competition. The latest Uniform Credit Code would do a lot to encourage more competition in the lending business, abolish the holder in due course doctrine, and make other improvements, but it was opposed by some consumer advocates because the interest ceilings were not low enough (Curran and Fand). The difficulty with interest ceilings is not only that they tend to become interest floors as well, but that the lenders are forced to refuse credit to those whose risk level requires a higher interest rate. It seems likely that more competition, allowing more people to get into the lending business, even at a variety of interest rates, would help consumers more than additional regulation.

You might think that the variety of arrangements would make it impossible for competition to work, but imagine careful car buyers shopping around for cars. If they know what they have to trade in, and how many months they will take to pay, then they look for the best car relative to the monthly payments it "costs." They will end up with the best combinations of trade-in, price, and credit terms, and so competition still works. The critical thing is whether people shop around for the best deal and not whether they understand the intricacies.

Aggregate Debt and Economic Policy

When installment credit exploded in volume after World War II, there was great concern at two levels—first, that many were getting themselves into financial trouble, and second, that the availability of credit would increase the instability of the economy by allowing wide fluctuations in total consumer spending from year to year. Both fears turned out to be groundless.

In fact, the use of installment credit was expanding in the upper-middle-income groups, so that aggregate consumer debt could expand faster than aggregate consumer income. As a matter of perspective, it is interesting to note that the use of credit moved into England and southern Europe much more recently and slowly. In England it is called buying on the "never never" or "hire purchase." In Germany credit is still frowned upon as evidence of bad household management. Americans would be astounded to see a solid German citizen plunking down a year's salary or more in cash for an automobile.

It is probably the postponable nature of most durable expenditures, rather than the availability of credit, that accounts for instability of total consumer spending. Those who buy for cash are equally able to postpone or speed up. What credit has done is to make credit users vulnerable to monetary policy when the government wants to induce people to spend less, or more. Direct regulations on the terms of installment credit—down payment and period to repay—are difficult to enforce. What is the actual down payment relative to the car price if the dealer can simultaneously change both price and trade-in value without really changing the deal? Without such regulations, merely making interest rates high or credit tight does not have much effect on the lower-quality credit markets where interest rates are mostly risk premiums anyway. It mostly affects those wanting to buy houses and, if rates get high enough, probably car buyers as well. The effect is more complex if rampant inflation is simultaneously raising the prices of houses and cars year after year, because people might buy and borrow anyway "before prices get any higher." (They realize that the *real* interest rate is not higher.)

A Cashless and Checkless Society?

Science writers are interested in the possibility that purchases could be automatically and instantly paid for by direct computer lines to the individual's bank account. Regular monthly charges could also automatically be deducted. What such a system is also likely to do, however, is to eliminate the free credit implicit in the present delays between purchase and the removal of the funds from your account. Even if you pay by check, there are a few days of "float" before it clears and is deducted from your account. On the other hand, pay-by-phone allows you to pay bills a few days before each is due, better than instant payment but not as good as checks, which take a few more days to clear.

If everyone is in the same boat and competition works, then some of the reduction in costs of credit and of paperwork might be passed on to the consumer in lower prices. Think of the time it takes for customer and clerk to complete a credit card sale, and think of another clerk entering it into a computer, a bill made out and mailed, yourself writing a check and mailing it, and the payment being entered into the computer again.

From the consumer's point of view, the advantages would be great and the possible difficulties minimized if the reporting of transactions were detailed and clear. Otherwise, illegitimate charges could easily be slipped in. The need for better information extends to paycheck stubs as well. As long as the same system deposited "take-home" pay into the account, the reporting form could also list gross pay and treat all the deductions like any other expense. Indeed, some employers are already attempting to inform employees of the estimated amounts of (nontaxable) income they are getting in the form of employer contributions to Social Security, pension fund, health insurance, subsidized lunchroom, etc.

Since computer printing is cheap, it should be possible, perhaps for a very small charge, to send a monthly list of expenditures that even had the individual items from the grocery store identified (or identified by class). The machine that reads the tag for pricing and inventory control has already done the work. This will be taken up again in the chapter on shopping (chap. 11).

Summary

A little algebra and a few simple ideas make it clear that interest rates on amortized loans are nearly twice as high as the casual observer may think, looking only at credit charges and amount borrowed.

A variety of lenders with a variety of interest charges exist, serving markets with different risk and with different capacity to shop around. Consumers obviously should shop around for credit, benefiting themselves and others in a market not known for effective competition.

Regulations to protect or help the consumer have not been very effective. They have driven some borrowers into the expensive arms of illegal lenders, and others into repayments scheduled by a hired lawyer.

More Information?

Much of the literature on debt, garnishment, and bankruptcy focuses on problems relatively few get themselves into. A comparison of systematic studies by Hendricks and Youmans and by the National Commission on Consumer Finance with passionate books by Bazelon or Sullivan is a useful exercise.

Since the adoption of the Truth in Lending Act, it is relatively easy to find out current rates on various kinds of loans, and the side conditions. You can make a list of billing and payment dates on your credit cards and other bills and find out how interest is calculated on your savings account.

Bazelon, David T. *Paper Economy*. New York: Random House, 1963.

Bonker, Dick. "The Rule of 78." *Journal of Finance* 31 (1976): 77–88.

Brunn, George. "Wage Garnishment in California: A Study and Recommendations." *California Law Review* 53 (1965): 1214–53.

Burger, Robert E., and Slavicek, Jan J. *Layman's Guide to Bankruptcy*. New York: Van Nostrand-Reinhold, 1971.

Curran, Barbara A. *Trends in Consumer Credit Legislation*. Chicago: University of Chicago Press, 1965.

Curran, Barbara A., and Fand, David J. "An Analysis of the Uniform Consumer Credit Code." *Nebraska Law Review* 49: 724–44.

Paul H. Douglas Consumer Research Center. *Credit Insurance: A Handbook for Consumers*. Washington, D.C.: Paul H. Douglas Consumer Research Center, 1977.

Dunkelberg, William C., and Stafford, Frank P. "Debt in the Consumer Portfolio: Evidence from a Panel Study." *American Economic Review* 61 (1971): 598–613.

Earl, David R. *The Bankruptians*. New York: The Exposition Press, 1966.

Haden, Harry H. "Chapter XIII Wage Earner Plans—Forgotten Man Bankruptcy." *Kentucky Law Journal* 55 (1967): 564–617.

Hall, Perry B. *Family Credit Counselling—An Emerging Community Service*. New York: Family Service Association of America, 1968. (Report of a study of nonprofit programs)

Hendricks, Gary; Youmans, Kenneth; and Keller, Janet. *Consumer Durables and Installment Debt: A Study of American Households*. Ann Arbor: Institute for Social Research, 1973.

Herrmann, Robert O. "Families in Bankruptcy—A Survey of Recent Studies." *Journal of Marriage and the Family* 28 (1966): 324–30.

Jacob, Herbert. *Debtors in Court* (Consumption of Government Services). Chicago: Rand McNally, 1959.

Jung, Allen. "Charges for Appliance and Automobile Installment Credit in Major Cities." *Journal of Business*, October 1962, pp. 386–91.

Katona, George, et al. *The 1968 Survey of Consumer Finances*. Ann Arbor: Institute for Social Research, 1969. (Chapters on debt, changes in debt, and difficulties in repayment)

Mandell, Lewis. "Consumer Perception of Incurred Interest Rates: An Empirical Test of the Efficacy of the Truth in Lending Law." *Journal of Finance* 26 (1971): 1143–53.

Mandell, Lewis. "Consumer Knowledge and Understanding of Consumer Credit." *Journal of Consumer Affairs* 7 (Summer 1973): 23–36.

Ryan, Mary E., and Maynes, E. Scott. "The Excessively Indebted: Who and Why?" *Journal of Consumer Affairs* 2 (Winter 1969): 107–120.

Shuchman, Philip. "The Fraud Exemption in Consumer Bankruptcy." *Stanford Law Review* 23 (1971): 735–73. (You cannot wait until other debts have been discharged, then collect yours claiming fraud.)

Shuchman, Philip. "Impact Analysis of the 1970 Bankruptcy Discharge Amendments." *North Carolina Law Review* 51 (1972): 233–57.

Shuchman, Philip, and Jantscher, Gerald P. "The Effects of Federal Minimum Exemption from Wage Garnishment on Nonbusiness Bankruptcy Rates." *Commercial Law Journal*, 1972, p. 360.

Stanley, David T., and Girth, Marjorie. *Bankruptcy: Problem, Process, Reform*. Washington, D.C.: Brookings Institution, 1971.

Sullivan, George. *The Boom in Going Bust*. New York: Macmillan, 1968.

Uniform Consumer Credit Code: Final Draft. Chicago: Commerce Clearing House, 1968.

U.S. Administrative Office of the U.S. Courts. *Tables of Bankruptcy Statistics*. Washington, D.C.: U.S. Administrative Office of the U.S. Courts, yearly. (Free)

U.S. Federal Trade Commission. *Economic Report on Installment Credit and Retail Sales Practices of District of Columbia Retailers*. Washington, D.C.: Government Printing Office, 1968. (Judgments were concentrated among eleven low-income retailers, rare elsewhere.)

U.S. National Commission on Consumer Credit. *Consumer Credit in the United States*. Washington, D.C.: Government Printing Office, 1973. (Also a set of volumes of technical studies, volume 1 of which has three studies on awareness and decisions by Shay and Schober, Day and Brandt, and Deutscher)

Some Projects to Learn More

1. Apply for one of the free bank credit cards. If you are turned down, ask about seeing your credit record under the Fair Credit Reporting Act. How much interest could you save if you bought just after the billing date and kept your money in a savings account until just before the payment deadline? Can you find what fraction of the billings are paid to the sellers?

2. Visit the nearest United States Bankruptcy Court. If you can, talk briefly with the judge, ask about what leads consumers into filing for bankruptcy, and the extent to which it is too easy an escape. What does the judge think of Title 13, and how often is it used in his or her court?

3. Make a list of the state law provisions for garnishment, particularly exemptions. Then compare the latest *Federal Tables of Bankruptcy Statistics* to see whether, other things considered, bankruptcy is more frequent where the garnishment laws are tougher. If you can find states that have changed their garnishment laws, has it changed their relative position in the bankruptcy statistics?

4. Ask some local banks and car dealers about dealer reserves and about sale of installment contracts for more or less than the principal still owed on them.

5. Find out where you could borrow to buy a car, and compare the terms and interest rates.

6. Check on the details, costs, and interest rates of combination checking and savings accounts and pay-by-phone. How much do they really keep in your checking account at no interest?

Appendix 6.1

FTC Buyers Guide No. 7
Fair Credit Reporting Act[1]

If you have a charge account, a mortgage on your home, life insurance, or have applied for a personal loan or job it is almost certain there is a "file" existing somewhere that shows how you pay your bills, if you have been sued, arrested, or filed for bankruptcy, etc.

And some of these files include your neighbors' and friends' views of your character, general reputation, or manner of living.

The companies that gather and sell such information to creditors, insurers, employers, and other businesses are called "Consumer Reporting Agencies," and the legal term for the report is "Consumer Report."

If, in addition to credit information, the report involves interviews with a third person about your character, reputation, or manner of living, it is referred to as an "Investigative Consumer Report."

The Fair Credit Reporting Act became law on April 25, 1971. It was passed by Congress to protect consumers against the circulation of inaccurate or obsolete information, and to insure that consumer reporting agencies exercise their responsibilities in a manner that is fair and equitable to consumers.

Under this new law you can now take steps to protect yourself if you have been denied credit, insurance, or employment, or if you believe you have had difficulties because of a consumer report on you.

Here are the steps you can take.

You have the right:

1. To be told the name and address of the consumer reporting agency responsible for preparing a consumer report that was used to deny you credit, insurance, or employment or to increase the cost of credit or insurance.

---

[1]. U.S. Federal Trade Commission, *FTC Buyers Guide No. 7, Fair Credit Reporting Act*. Washington, D.C.: U.S. Government Printing Office, 1975. Permission is granted to reprint this leaflet, in whole or in part, in a legal and nondeceptive manner.

2. To be told by a consumer reporting agency the nature, substance and sources (except investigative-type sources) of the information (except medical) collected about you.

3. To take anyone of your choice with you when you visit the consumer reporting agency to check on your file.

4. To obtain all information to which you are entitled, free of charge, when you have been denied credit, insurance, or employment within 30 days of your interview. Otherwise, the reporting agency is permitted to charge a reasonable fee for giving you the information.

5. To be told who has received a consumer report on you within the preceding six months, or within the preceding two years if the report was furnished for employment purposes.

6. To have incomplete or incorrect information re-investigated, unless the request is frivolous, and, if the information is found to be inaccurate or cannot be verified, to have such information removed from your file.

7. To have the agency notify those you name (at no cost to you) who have previously received the incorrect or incomplete information that this information has been deleted from your file.

8. When a dispute between you and the reporting agency about information in your file cannot be resolved, you have the right to have your version of such dispute placed in the file and included in future consumer reports.

9. To request the reporting agency to send your version of the dispute to certain businesses for a reasonable fee.

10. To have a consumer report withheld from anyone who under the law does not have a legitimate business need for the information.

11. To sue a reporting agency for damages if it willfully or negligently violates the law and, if you are successful, you can collect attorney's fees and court costs.

12. Not to have adverse information reported after seven years. One major exception is bankruptcy, which may be reported for fourteen years.

13. To be notified by a business that it is seeking information about you which would constitute an "Investigative Consumer Report."

14. To request from the business that ordered an investigative report, more information about the nature and scope of the investigation.

15. To discover the nature and substance (but not the sources) of the information that was collected for an "Investigative Consumer Report."

The Fair Credit Reporting Act does not:

1. Give you the right to request a report on yourself from the consumer reporting agency.

2. Give you the right, when you visit the agency, to receive a copy of or to physically handle your file.

3. Compel anyone to do business with an individual consumer.

4. Apply when you request commercial (as distinguished from consumer) credit or business insurance.

5. Authorize any Federal agency to intervene on behalf of an individual consumer.

How to deal with consumer reporting agencies

If you want to know what information a consumer reporting agency has collected about you, either arrange for a personal interview at the agency's office during normal business hours or call in advance for an interview by telephone.

The consumer reporting agencies in your community can be located by consulting the "Yellow Pages" of your telephone book under such headings as "Credit" or "Credit Rating or Reporting Agencies."

If you decide to visit a consumer reporting agency to check on your file the following checklist may be of help.

For instance, did you:

1. Learn the nature and substance of all the information in your file?

2. Find out the names of each of the businesses (or other sources) that supplied information on you to the reporting agency?

3. Learn the names of everyone who received reports on you within the past six months (or the last two years if the reports were for employment purposes)?

4. Request the agency to re-investigate and correct or delete information that was found to be inaccurate, incomplete, or obsolete?

5. Follow-up to determine the results of the re-investigation?

6. Ask the agency, at no cost to you, to notify those you name who received reports within the past six months (two years if for employment purposes) that certain information was deleted?

7. Follow-up to make sure that those named by you did in fact receive notices from the consumer agency?

8. Demand that your version of the facts be placed in your file if the re-investigation did not settle the dispute?

9. Request the agency (if you are willing to pay a reasonable fee) to send your statement of the dispute to those you name who received reports containing the disputed information within the past six months (two years if received for employment purposes)?

For more detailed information on the Fair Credit Reporting Act or to report a violation of the Act contact the FTC in Washington or the nearest regional office. The FTC offices are located in the following cities:

Atlanta, Ga.; Boston, Mass.; Buffalo, N.Y.; Charlotte, N.C.; Chicago, Ill.; Cleveland, Ohio; Dallas, Texas; Denver, Colo.; Detroit, Mich.; Honolulu, Hawaii; Kansas City, Mo.; Los Angeles, Calif.; Miami, Fla.; New Orleans, La.; New York, N.Y.; Oak Ridge, Tenn.; Phoenix, Ariz.; Portland, Ore.; St. Louis, Mo.; San Antonio, Texas; San Diego, Calif.; San Francisco, Calif.; Seattle, Wash.; Washington, D.C. area field offices; Upper Darby, Penn.

Look under "Federal Trade Commission" in the telephone directories of these cities for the addresses and telephone numbers of the field offices.

CHAPTER SEVEN
THE INVESTMENT OF SAVINGS

Most families at some time accumulate some savings which can be invested until they are needed. The financial analysis in chapter 5 indicated that most saving is contractual—payments into the Social Security system or into private pensions, paying off the mortgage or other debts, and increasing the cash surrender value of life insurance (chap. 9). Someone else decides how much those savings amount to each year and where they are invested. But when we do manage to accumulate some money that we control, the question arises where to stash it until it is needed.

Theory of Investment

Before talking about the characteristics of different kinds of financial investments, it is useful to understand the theory. Any investment is expected to produce a flow of future benefits. If the investment is in physical capital, such as a house, car, or washing machine, the benefits are streams of services: housing, transportation, clean laundry. This chapter will consider financial investments, whose benefits take the form of interest, dividends, rents, or gains in resale value (capital gains). The present (discounted) value of those future benefits, less the present value of any future costs, is what the asset is worth, i.e., its price. Physical investments have limited life and depreciation costs, but financial investments usually involve little or no future costs, and the benefits may extend into the indefinite future.

Calculating the present value of a stream of financial benefits (yields) is a straightforward application of the principles discussed in appendix 2.1 (p. 18). The present value of a finite stream of constant benefits using a 3 percent interest rate is shown in the tables there. Calculating the present value of a stream that goes on forever is actually simpler than for a limited period. As shown in appendix 2.1, the present value of $1 a year forever, discounted at 3 percent, is $1/0.03 = $33.33. More generally, the present value of x at an interest rate r is x/r.

Why base these calculations on an interest rate of 3 percent when a savings account will pay 6 percent or more? Again, because when interest rates are higher than 3 percent, the difference tends to measure the expected rate of inflation, so the rate of return in today's prices is still 3 percent. A higher interest rate can be used if the stream of benefits is risky. A 6 percent rate is appropriate, for example, for an investment with an even chance of paying nothing at all.

The relationship between the price of a financial investment and its rate of return is best seen in the case of a riskless bond which promises an interest (coupon) payment of $30 per year forever. In fact, almost all government and corporate bonds have maturity dates when the face amount of the bond is paid to the investor, but let us begin with the simplest case and then complicate it with considerations of maturity dates and risk. If this bond is traded in a competitive market, then investors will insure that its price is in line with the price of alternative investments. In an inflation-free world with a going rate of return on financial investments of 3 percent, the selling price of this bond will be set so that:

$$\frac{\text{interest payment}}{\text{price}} = \text{rate of return},$$

or

$$\text{price} = \frac{\text{interest payment}}{\text{rate of return}} = \frac{\$30}{0.03} = \$1,000.$$

In other words, the price of the bond is the present value of $30 per year forever at a 3 percent rate. If the actual price of this bond were higher than $1,000, then its rate of return would be lower than 3 percent, and no investor would be interested in the bond until its price was lower. If the price were less than $1,000, then the rate of return would be higher than that paid by alternative investments, and investors would bid up the price of the bond to $1,000.

If the rate of inflation suddenly rose from zero to 6 percent, and was expected to remain at 6 percent forever, how would this affect the price of the bond? With 6 percent inflation, market interest rates and going rates of return on financial investments should climb to about 9 percent. Since the interest payment from the bond is fixed at $30, the price will adjust so that

$$\text{price} = \frac{\$30}{0.09} = \$333,$$

which is the present value of $30 per year forever at a 9 percent interest rate. Investors who paid $1,000 for this bond will be faced with a capital loss of $667. The loss can be realized immediately if they sell the bond for $333, or gradually if they hold onto the bond and watch its fixed dollar return become worth less and less in the future.

Now suppose that the bond matures in twenty years, pays $30 per year in interest, and has a $1,000 redemption (face) value at the end of that period. In a world with stable prices and a 3 percent going rate of return, the price of this bond will equal the present value of the interest payment and the present value of the redemption value:

Present value of $30 per year for twenty years
   at 3 percent   = $30 × 14.877 = $446
Present value of $1,000 in twenty years
   at 3 percent   = $1,000 × 0.554 = $554
                                              Total $1,000

If this maturing bond is bid for by investors living with 6 percent inflation and a 9 percent interest rate, then the price will equal:

Present value of $30 per year for twenty years
   at 9 percent   = $274
Present value of $1,000 in twenty years
   at 9 percent   = $178
                                              Total $452

Investors who paid $1,000 for this bond will face a smaller capital loss than with the perpetual bond, but the loss is still substantial.

Another way of understanding the role of future prices and interest payments is to ask why investors would buy this bond for $452, since the interest payment of $30 per year amounts to a 6.6 percent return on the $452 investment, rather than a 9 percent return? The answer, of course, is that the $1,000 redemption value at maturity is closer and worth more with each passing year. The price of the bond will rise accordingly, and the capital gain from the price increase will make up the difference between the rate of return from the interest payment and 9 percent. After one year, for example, the price of the bond is:

Present value of $30 per year for nineteen years
   at 9 percent   = $269
Present value of $1,000 in nineteen years
   at 9 percent   = $194
                                              Total $463

The $463 price is $11 more than the $452 price the year before. The total return on keeping the bond for the first year is ($30 + $11)/$452 = 0.09. One year before the maturity date, the market value of the bond is:

Present value of $30 for one year at 9 percent   = $ 28
Present value of $1,000 in one year at 9 percent = $917
                                              Total $945

The 9 percent return for the last year consists of $30 in interest and $55 in capital gain. (Note that absolute size of the annual capital gains increases over time.) In fact, tax considerations lead some investors to buy long-term bonds with low interest coupons because most of their return is capital gain rather than interest, and the former is taxed at less than half the rate of the latter. This is called "riding the yield curve," although a more accurate but less catchy term would be "riding up the curve of the present value."

If a bond is risky, in the sense that its future stream of benefits is uncertain, then its price will adjust to reflect this. As an extreme example, suppose that a bond promising to pay $30 per year forever actually has a 50 percent chance of paying nothing and a 50 percent chance of meeting its promised payments. If the going rate of return is 3 percent, then the price of the bond will be bid down to the point where its *expected* yield is 3 percent. It should be obvious that a nominal yield of 6 percent, coupled with an even chance of no yield, is equivalent to a certain yield of 3 percent. The price of this risky bond, then, will be bid down to the point where:

$$\text{price} = \frac{\$30}{0.06} = \$500.$$

Actually, investors will insist upon a nominal yield which is higher than 6 percent as a premium for their risk-taking. (Everyone would prefer a sure thing.) The bond price, then, will drop to less than $500.

The same principles apply to the stock market, although there is no fixed dollar dividend comparable with bond interest, and no fixed redemption value at some maturity date. One could treat a stock as an infinite stream of dividends, but most of us intend to sell the stock and use the money at some time in the future, and find it difficult enough to think about an infinite future. Besides, a major part of the short-run return on stocks is the increase in their market value, which is why one year's dividends relative to market price of the stock is usually less than the market interest rate.

Suppose I pay $100 for a share of stock that gives me $5 in dividends and has a market value of $105 by the end of the year. My return is then 10 percent, half of it in capital gain. Ordinarily, this return should be higher than the going rate of return on safer investments. The fortunes of the company and its future earnings, dividends, and increase in stock prices are uncertain to some degree. There is a large competitive market for stocks, and their prices presumably reflect the prevailing assessments of many investors about risks, future profits, and dividends. The individual buying stock can either assume that the market is reasonably efficient in reflecting possibilities—that apparently high rates of return reflect higher risks—or can try to outguess the experts. However, the individual might also want to take a longer view of the future than many investors, and look for companies with good long-range prospects.

In the case of common stock, the investor owns a fraction of a company, and that same fraction of its annual earnings (profit), after taxes and interest costs. Part of those earnings is paid as dividends, and part (retained earnings) is reinvested—theoretically to increase earnings and dividends in the future. So the annual yield on a share of stock is the dividends plus the increase (or minus the decrease) in its market price, and the rate of return is this sum divided by the initial price.

Increases in the future market price of the stock should, other things being equal, be some function of retained earnings. Without attempting to understand the detailed process by which added investment increases total earnings, and hence future dividends, and hence the price of the stock, let us assume that the future increase in the price of the stock is some fraction, R, of retained earnings per share, i.e.,

$$\text{Increase in stock price} = R(\text{Earnings} - \text{Dividends}).$$

Then

$$\begin{aligned}\text{Yield of the stock} &= (\text{Dividends} + \text{Increase in price}) \\ &= [\text{Dividends} + R(\text{Earnings} - \text{Dividends})] \\ &= R(\text{Earnings}) + (1 - R)\text{Dividends}.\end{aligned}$$

If the present value of such a stream of yields (forever) is calculated by dividing it by 0.03, or (allowing for risk) by 0.06, then:

$$\text{Price of stock} = \frac{R(\text{Earnings}) + (1 - R)\text{Dividends}}{0.06}$$

and

$$\text{Price/Earnings} = \frac{R + (1 - R)(\text{Dividends/Earnings})}{0.06}.$$

This means that the price-earnings ratio depends upon R, i.e., the effects of reinvestment on future profits and dividends, and on the fraction of earnings paid out in dividends. It will also depend, of course, on the rate used to discount for interest and risk. But if we take 6 percent as an example, we can show the effects of R (the return on reinvestment of profits) at fixed payout ratios (dividends/earnings) on the price-earnings ratio. And we can show the effects of the payout ratio on the price-earnings ratio at fixed levels of expected profitability of additional reinvestment.

Figure 9 shows the sensible result that low payout ratios (high reinvestment) can decrease or increase the price-earnings ratio, depending on the profitability of investment. Figure 10 shows that a higher expected profitability of reinvested profits raises the price-earnings ratio more, the larger the fraction of profits reinvested.

The precise way in which reinvested profits affect expected future earnings, and hence expected future dividends, and hence the expected future price, and hence the current price, of a stock is not crucial to the analysis. What is important to remember is that earnings should affect stock prices either because they produce dividends or because they result in increases in the price of the stock. Remember also that it is *future* earnings that matter most.

The market value of a stock also depends on the interest rate used to evaluate the stream of yields. When comparing stocks with alternative investments adjusted for differences in risk, the stock price has to fall or rise to make the expected rate of return better than that of alternative investments. If market interest rates go up, and safe, liquid, short-term alternatives are available at 12 percent interest, stock prices have to fall until they are expected to yield something comparable. It used to be assumed that stocks were a good investment to protect against inflation, but when the inflation leads to a monetary policy of very high interest rates, large investors sell their stocks and take the high interest rates. For the individual counting on the dividends (which usually keep rising with inflation) and not intending to sell the stock for some time, this fall in stock prices is less of a problem—except perhaps emotionally.

Perhaps the most useful conclusions from this discussion of the various factors that affect price-earnings ratios is that whenever a stock is selling for unusually low or high multiples of earnings, it implies that most investors have some unusual expectations about the future profits of the company. Actually, of course, the expectations about future profits can change as a result of various events, not only because of reinvested profits.

A very high price-earnings ratio, say 30 or more, would seem to imply (from fig. 10) that most of the earnings were being reinvested and that the added investment was expected to be very profitable. The R of 2 (a dollar per share reinvested raising the stock price by $2) can be thought of as loosely reflecting a rate of return on new investment more than twice the rate on existing capital. A dollar per share reinvested has to increase future profits and divi-

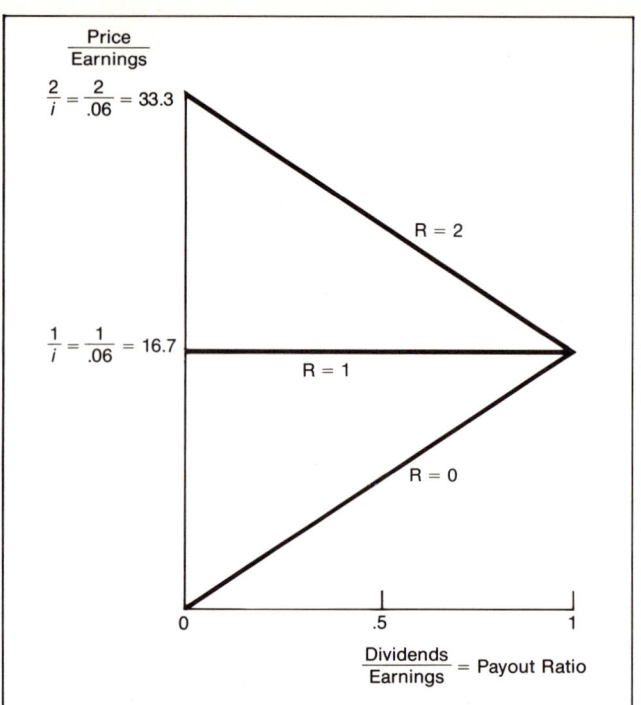

Fig. 9 Effects on price-earnings ratio of payout ratio at different expected profitability of reinvestment (R_i)

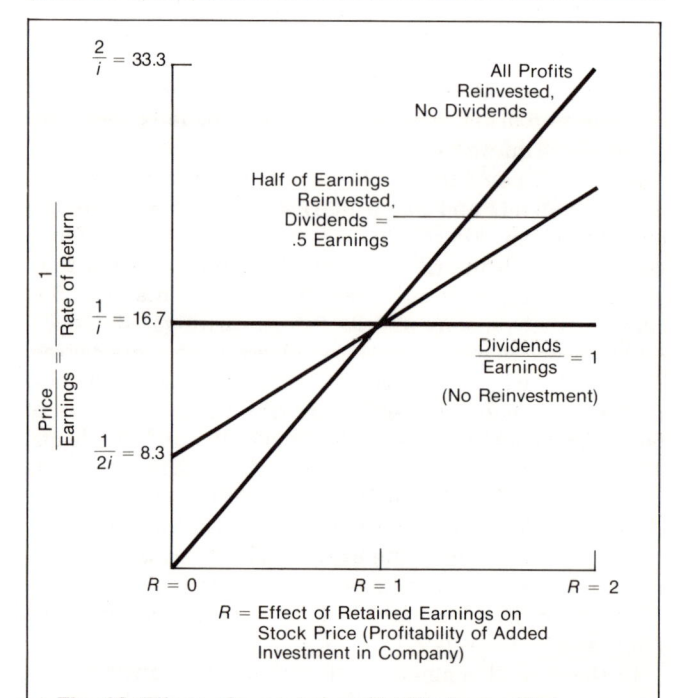

Fig. 10 Effects of expected profitability from added investment on price-earnings ratio at different payout ratios

dends sufficiently so that it adds $2 to the value of the stock even when discounted back to the present. Remember that some investors prefer reinvestments and capital gains in stock prices, because of the lower income taxes on capital gains, while others who need a flow of income may value a dollar of dividends more highly than promises of future gains. The company itself may produce high returns from reinvested profits if it combines them with borrowed funds and takes advantage of the "leverage," which will be explained shortly.

Very low published price-earnings ratios do not necessarily mean that the stock is a bargain. The expected future earnings may be very low, or the stock price may be expected to fall.

The whole stock market can respond to generalized uncertainty about the future, or generalized expectations about the future profitability of business, or the yields available in alternative investments. The ordinary individual is often unable to consider some of those alternative investments if they involve sending funds abroad, or require very large minimum purchases.

Desirable Characteristics of Investments

The general principle of valuing any financial investment by estimating the present value of an expected set of future yields, including capital gains, applies to any investment. But there are other things besides rate of return that concern us about investments. You may weigh them differently, but each has some importance. The characteristics by which to judge alternative investments, in addition to rate of return, are:

Liquidity. I may want some assurance that I can get my money back rapidly when I want it, without having to wait until the market is in better shape. Illiquidity involves both the simple time delay in finding a buyer and completing a sale, and fluctuating prices so that any particular time may be a bad time to sell. Some investments (such as some bonds) have a fixed price at which they will be redeemed—usually at some date in the future—some have fixed annual yields in dollars, some have neither or both.

Safety. I want to be reasonably sure that I can get the principal of my investment back, even if not immediately.

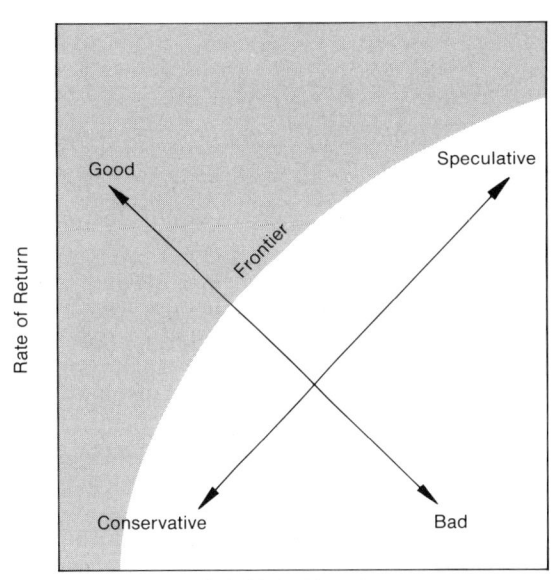

Fig. 11 Combinations of rate of return and risk in financial investments. Investments with combinations of rate of return and risk above the frontier (in shaded portion) are not to be found.

What we earlier called "risk" is a combination of low safety, low liquidity, and variability of yield.

There is a tendency for high-yield investments to be high risk as well. What I want is the best combination of high yield and low risk, something in the upper left part of figure 11.

Risk can be reduced through diversification, which means reducing the variability of my total yield by reducing the correlation between the individual yields or even by selecting investments with negatively correlated changes. For instance, some stocks suffer in inflationary periods and some benefit, so a mixture of the two reduces my risk.

Inflation Protection. A third desirable characteristic of investments is inflation protection. It is provided when yield and price go up with the rising price level. I want to "hedge" against inflation, which means I want to make a commitment that offsets the risk of some other commitment already made or inevitable. For example, a baker who makes a contract to provide bread over the next year at a given price may also "hedge" by promising to buy wheat for future delivery at a specified price. This will prevent his being caught between rising prices for wheat and a fixed price for his bread. Of course, if the market price of wheat were to *fall* below the specified future delivery price, he loses some profits he would otherwise have made.

Most people think the best inflation hedge is an asset whose yield is mostly capital gain, but an investment can be good or bad protection against inflation regardless of whether its yield is mostly in cash or in increased sale value. For instance, if I buy a bond at a discount because its interest rate is lower than market, then part of my return is the increased market value of the bond at maturity (capital gain) and part is the cash interest paid; but both of these are fixed and cannot respond to an acceleration in prices or in real national income. In fact, more inflation means a higher market interest rate, which will reduce the market price of the bond. On the other hand, a share of common stock could be in a company that paid out all its earnings in dividends, but the earnings (and thus the dividends) would rise with rising prices. In this case there is good protection against inflation but very little capital gain. So the tax advantages of capital gains, and the hedging advantages of investments whose yields rise with inflation, do not always go together. However, both do seem to be associated with somewhat more risk.

Tax Considerations

In addition to the advantage of taking my yield as capital gains rather than as currently taxable dividends or interest or rent, there are other tax advantages of those investments that allow me to postpone the legal receipt of income, or to change the timing to a year when my tax rate is lower. There are also special tax provisions that make it advantageous to invest in oil wells, or cattle raising, or reforesting land. Wherever my own management or effort increases the value of my investment, a kind of labor income is converted into a capital gain taxable at less than half the rate, and then only when the capital gain is "realized" (i.e., when the asset is sold). On the other hand, if I want to put assets in the names of minor children (for their later education, for example) so that the dividends will be *their* income and hence not taxed, even though they remain dependents on my tax return, I might want assets that require little or no management, such as a mutual fund with automatic dividend reinvestment. Stockbrokers usually know the rules for reducing taxes by putting assets in the name of minors with someone as trustee. The rules vary from state to state and can be affected by Internal Revenue Service rulings. A recent IRS ruling makes it difficult for a parent to be the trustee, and having someone else do it may raise the cost. A more complex way of tax avoidance is the setting up of a trust or even a private foundation, and some investments are more appropriate or acceptable for that purpose.

Estate taxes also engendered another legal trick: putting assets in the names of more than one person, generally by "joint tenancy with rights of survivorship and not as tenants in common." In common tenancy, both parties have to sign for everything, whereas in joint tenancy either one can. And either can run off with it all. The "survivorship" phrase makes the survivor automatically owner of the whole, escaping probate and estate taxes in at least some states. But it can later be construed as a gift of half the total value unless it can be proved that both parties contributed to the estate. Or, it may still be treated as one person's asset at death. Joint ownership used to allow playing games as to whose income the yield was, but now it is necessary to specify who is reporting the income for tax purposes.

Women have a legitimate complaint that officials, in deciding who paid for an asset that is jointly owned, ignore the contribution of unpaid work done mostly by the wife, and assume that the contributions were in proportion to dollar earnings.

It is possible to postpone taxes on retirement savings by setting up an Individual Retirement Account under the Employment Retirement Income Security Act of 1975, provided you do not already have an employer-arranged pension. For the tax postponement you give up liquidity and control over how the funds are invested, and you also must pay management fees to the institution handling the account. If you manage your own Individual Retirement Account, or similar Keogh plan if you are self-employed, you need investments that satisfy the regulations. Or you can postpone taxes on the yield of savings already taxed as income by buying a deferred annuity. You can even cash the part that is your own investment first, paying taxes on the accumulated interest or dividends as you take the last dollars out. The possibilities of trouble are great in an area so new, with so little regulation, and with customers blinded by their eagerness to postpone taxes. If you need the money before retirement, you have to pay all the taxes on it immediately.

It seems that most of the devices used to avoid or postpone income taxes require giving up some liquidity by tying up funds in various ways. If you need cash, you may even have to borrow and pay interest, even though you own assets.

Information and Management Costs

The less fixed the yield, and the more uncertainty about the quality of an investment, the more I must invest in getting information to select it and in continually acquiring information as to whether to keep it. There are also transaction costs—brokers' fees, federal transfer taxes, legal fees. In some investments, such as rental real estate, the management costs are extensive, and it may even be difficult to find individuals or firms to handle the task. On the other hand, for those who have the time and skill and desire to do the management and even maintenance work themselves, such investments are a source of income that is legally property income and does not disqualify them from receiving Social Security or other retirement benefits. Managing your own assets, whether real property or financial investments, may be an excellent post-retirement occupation.

Social and Ethical Considerations

The rate of profit in things which pander to people's vices always seems to be higher than average, so I may find myself wondering whether I have some responsibility in this respect. Should I invest in stocks of companies accused of exploiting black labor in South Africa, or selling "noxious" products like cigarettes or armaments? Unfortunately, the companies which make baby clothes or sell food never seem to make as much money.

Characteristics of Available Investments

Each of us must weigh the various characteristics of investments, or ask ourselves how much yield is to be traded for other advantages. With the various characteristics in mind, it is useful to go through a list of the main places where savings can be invested. We will consider financial investments roughly in the order of the prevalence of their use.

Savings Banks or Savings and Loan Associations

Savings accounts in either kind of institution (many people do not distinguish between the two, even though the savings and loan associations generally pay higher interest) are perfectly safe, provided that the particular institution is insured by the Federal Deposit Insurance Corporation or the Federal Savings and Loan Insurance Corporation. Although there can be a long delay in getting one's money in the case of default, this is rare. In practice, a savings account is nearly as "liquid" as cash or a checking account. The banks will even write an occasional check for you. You may be able to have the bank automatically transfer funds from your savings account to your checking account so you can maximize the amount on which you earn interest without any danger of overdraining your checking account. If combined checking and savings accounts are declared illegal, some similar arrangement is likely to replace them. Many people are using savings accounts not so much for long-term savings as for accumulating funds for large expenditures (Mueller and Lean). When interest rates rise, large differences in rates may develop between areas, between institutions, and particularly between a savings bank (subject to restrictions if it is a member of the Federal Reserve System) and a savings and loan association. Since banking can easily be done by mail, it is surprising that the movement of funds does not wipe out these differences, but many people prefer to keep their funds locally or perhaps do not trust distant institutions.

Of course, in return for their safety, simplicity, and liquidity, one accepts lower yields in savings accounts and no increase in value with inflation. But keep in mind that one of the "returns" from liquidity is avoiding the necessity of borrowing at very high rates; another is being able to take advantage of bargains.

Government Bonds

A bond must specify its interest rate in advance and cannot raise it as market rates change, the way a savings bank can. Hence, there is a risk with a bond that rising market interest rates may leave you stuck with the old lower yield and unable to sell the bond before maturity without a loss. After World War I, people who had patriotically bought government bonds suffered substantial losses when they cashed them, because market interest rates had risen. To avoid this problem, the United States government, beginning during World War II, has issued some savings bonds with a schedule of guaranteed redemption values at least as high as the purchase price. But still there is a loss in the opportunity cost sense. If you buy a fifteen-year bond at 4 percent and discover the market interest rate has risen to 6 percent, you cannot earn the 6 percent. Had you kept the money in a savings account, you could switch. The scheduled bond redemption values do not earn even the full 4 percent if you cash the bond before the end of the fifteen years.

The reverse of this picture is also true. Falling market interest rates will raise fixed-rate bond prices. That increase is technically a capital gain, taxed at less than half one's usual marginal rate; and the gain can be taken whenever it is most advantageous by timing the sale of the bond.

State and local government bonds, including school bonds, have another feature—income from their interest is exempt from federal income taxes. Of course, they have lower yields because of this, which may more than offset the tax advantage except for very high-income people. There are pressures to eliminate this exemption on the argument that the implicit subsidy to states and localities from lower interest costs could be given in other ways that do not provide a tax loophole for the wealthy.

If your marginal federal income tax rate is 30 percent, then you keep 70 percent of ordinary income including interest, 88 percent of capital gains, including increases in the value of discounted bonds, and 100 percent of interest from tax-exempt bonds. If your marginal tax rate is 50 percent, you keep 50 percent of ordinary income including interest, 80 percent of capital gains including increases in the value of discounted bonds, and 100 percent of interest from tax-exempt bonds. (Forty percent of any realized capital gain is taxable income.)

When considering tax-exempt bonds, it is useful to convert their yields into equivalent rates of return on taxable income for comparison. For example, at a 50 percent marginal tax rate, a tax-exempt bond that pays 5 percent is equivalent to a taxable bond that pays 10 percent. At a 30 percent tax rate, a 5 percent tax-exempt bond is as good as a taxable bond paying 7.14 percent (5/0.70). Similar calculations are possible for bonds bought at a discount so that part of the yield is capital gain taxed at half the rate. A bond that yields 6 percent, half in coupon interest, half in capital gains, gives the investor with a 50 percent tax rate 3.90 percent after taxes, equivalent to 7.80 percent before taxes in a fully taxable investment. At a 30 percent tax rate, it would give 4.74 percent after taxes, equivalent to 6.77 percent before taxes.

The safety of government bonds is rated by two different organizations—necessarily, because many institutional investors like insurance companies are restricted to the safer ratings. The two ratings can be interpreted as follows:

Moody's	Standard and Poor's	
Aaa	AAA	Highest quality
Aa	AA	Just off top grade
A	A	Fair to good
Baa	BBB	Medium to fair
Ba	BB	Poor to Medium

Some experts feel that the result of rating is the forcing of higher yields for those bonds with the lower ratings, out of proportion to the increase in risk. Risk of default exists even with the top-rated bonds, although it is generally assumed that safety is higher for the counties than the cities, the states than the counties, and so on. There is also the risk of loss through changing market interest rates if you have bonds with a distant maturity date, even if you do not need to cash them, because you miss the opportunity to earn more.

Real Estate

Probably nothing has been so romanticized or exaggerated as the potential profits from speculating in land, particularly empty land.

If we remember the Rule of 72—that the years it takes for an investment to double in value at a compound interest rate of r is $72/r$—then how do we interpret a story about a man who bought land for $10,000 and sold it ten years later for $20,000? Even if he had no other costs, he got only 7 percent per year on his investment—and the advantage that the return was a capital gain. But if we take account of his property taxes and any maintenance costs, he might well have done better in the stock market. Houses and rental real estate also provide a rental income, and have risen dramatically in price in some periods.

But real estate, particularly rental real estate, has some advantages as an investment. Its value goes up with inflation. Current tax laws allow deductions for accelerated depreciation on investment in rental real estate, so that for tax purposes one understates the current income and converts the rest into a capital gain. The technical aspects of "double declining balance" depreciation need not concern us, except to note that depreciation is allowed more heavily at first, as a fraction of the remaining value (net of depreciation already taken), *and* at double a reasonable rate. This means, for instance, that on an apartment house purchased for $100,000, some $4,500 can be taken in depreciation the first year. If the net income (net of interest on the mortgage, taxes, and other operating costs) is $4,500, then there is *no* taxable income and yet a $4,500 "tax-free cash flow." When the apartment house is sold, the capital gain must of course be figured on the depreciated value—$100,000 minus all the annual depreciation deductions—but that gain is taxable at only 40 percent of the usual income tax rates and can be carefully timed to take place in a year when other income is low. The boom in rental real estate, particularly small apartment buildings, is in part a result of these tax laws, which were designed originally to stimulate business investment in plant and equipment.

There are even ways in which such real estate investments can be combined with a personal corporation. Rules about the proportion of corporation income that must be paid out in order to avoid penalty taxes depend on whether the income is from active or passive investments, and rental income is considered "active." The rules are subject to change, administratively and through tax reform, so there is little point in describing the present loopholes and special provisions. It may be of interest to note that the present rules about personal corporations were designed to prevent such prior abuses as incorporating one's yacht along with some stocks or bonds and then using the yields from the latter to maintain the former, reporting no net income.

The success of investment in real estate can depend heavily on whether you have knowledge of special opportunities (from, say, having been in a community for many years, or in an occupation where you accumulate such information), and on whether you have the skills and time to put into maintaining and managing properties yourself. If you do your own investment analysis, management, etc., you save two income taxes—your own and the one that would have to be paid by the specialist you hired.

As we saw in chapter 4, there is no evidence that buying and renting out single-family houses is profitable. It may be the high and rising cost of labor for maintenance and repairs, or the way rental occupants usually treat a house, or the willingness of people to pay a great deal more for their own house than they would pay to rent one of similar quality. In any case, no one would recommend the rental of single-family homes as a good investment except in situations such as an expected escalation of house values.

A final disadvantage to renting real estate is due to common misconceptions about fair price and the belief that during inflationary periods rents should not rise. The assumption is that since the owner bought the place at an earlier time, he need not raise the rent when prices go up. That the owners would be making more if their money were elsewhere, or that they are being asked to take less than a market price to provide a benefit for their tenants, escapes the critics. Even the old notions that rent on land, that gift of God, is unjustified, and that capital gains are ill-gotten returns, contribute to making "landlord" an odious term. When people say, "Rents are too high," it might mean that there are undue restrictions on the supply of new dwellings or some conspiracy among owners of rental property. But it is more likely to mean that no one has asked, "Compared to what?"

Common Stock

It is difficult to talk about common stock briefly, since it covers such a wide range of combinations of yield, safety, and capital gains. The proportion of American families owning some common stock has risen in the years since World War II, from 10 percent to nearly 25 percent, although a large proportion of these own rather little and seldom buy or sell. The vast bulk of the trading that dominates the stock markets is done by institutional investors, mutual funds, and a small number of wealthy people.

This very fact affects the nature of stock as an investment, since no individual can keep himself so well informed about short-run prospects of individual companies as the highly paid experts responsible for the investment of huge sums of money.

Technically, owning a share of stock is owning a piece of a corporation equal to the fraction of the total number of shares one owns. But the stockholders' claims come after those of other creditors, so what they really own is the "net worth" of the corporation, the value of its assets net of all other obligations. Corporate accounting is conservative, based largely on original investment costs minus depreciation, so the "book value" of a share of stock may bear little relation to its market value. After all, it is the earnings a company can be expected to make in the future that really matter. In rare cases, the book value of a stock may be more than the discounted value of the expected future earnings of the company, in which case it may be ripe for liquidation (or may have failed to depreciate its plant and equipment adequately and be ready for bankruptcy).

One clue to past accounting is the relation of the depreciated value of plant and equipment to its original cost value in the corporate balance sheet. If there has been a regular pacing of investments, and reasonable depreciation, one would expect the accumulated depreciation allowance to be about half the value of the plant and equipment, unless the company is very new or has not had to keep expanding much in recent years.

But it is the level and stability of the earnings history and expectations that matter. One technical aspect which affects the level and stability of earnings available to the stockholders is "leverage." Leverage refers to *any technique of controlling more assets than one owns*. To illustrate, let us compare two very simple companies.

Company A has $100,000 worth of assets and no debts, so the common stockholders owning the 1,000 shares of stock benefit directly from the company's earnings. If the company makes $10,000 in a year, the stockholders may get half of their $10 per share earnings in dividends and the other half in increased stock values through reinvestment. If the company earns $5,000, the stockholders get a benefit amounting to $5 per share. If it earns only $2,500, the stockholders get $2.50 per share in cash or capital gains.

Company B also has $100,000 in assets from selling 1,000 shares of stock, but borrowed another $100,000 by issuing corporate bonds at 5 percent. Thus, they have $200,000 in assets with which to earn money, but must set aside $5,000 each year to pay the interest on the bonds. If they make 10 percent on their assets, or $20,000, there is $15,000 left for the stockholders, or $15 per share. If they make only 5 percent, or $10,000, then there is only $5,000 left for the stockholders after the bond interest is paid. And if they make 2.5 percent on the $200,000, there is barely enough to pay the bond interest and nothing for the stockholders, in either dividends or reinvestment. Hence, in the two cases the stockholders have the following:

Rate of Return on Assets	Rate of Return on Stock No Leverage (A)	Leverage of 2:1 (B)
10%	10%	15%
5%	5%	5%
2.5%	2.5%	0

Whenever the corporation can earn more on the borrowed assets than the interest on the loan, the additional earnings benefit the stockholders. But because the interest is a fixed obligation, it can also reduce the stockholders' return. Leverage applies to individual investors as well. Capital gains in the housing market imply larger rates of return to those with low-interest mortgages on their homes than to those who have completely paid off their mortgages. An individual investor can increase his leverage in the stock market by buying stocks with borrowed money or by using puts and calls (see below), as well as by buying stocks in leveraged companies.

Leverage is used more by companies whose earnings tend to be stable, such as public utilities, so it is simpler to compare past fluctuations in earnings per share, which combine the effects of leverage with the actual market fluctuations.

Over a period of years, a company may issue new stock or declare stock dividends or splits. This makes long-term comparisons difficult. If the new stock is sold at market prices and not at special prices to executives, it can be disregarded, although it may reduce the total leverage. Each share represents ownership of a smaller fraction of a larger company. But if each stockholder is issued another share of stock for each share he has (i.e., a stock split), then the assets per share and the dividends per share are cut in half, and so is the market price of the stock. The folklore about stock splits is that they raise the value of the stock, but in fact the stock price tends in most cases to reflect the split exactly, falling just to the point at which the value per share times the number of shares outstanding is the same as before the split. The market value of the expected future earnings of the company is not affected by the legal details of ownership. Often the purpose of stock splits is to cut the price per share, in order to make trading easier and less expensive (since broker fees are considerably lower if stocks are purchased in blocks of 100 shares). The stock is split *because* it is going up!

The ordinary investor is not helped by the conventional ways of expressing stock prices and earnings. We noticed earlier that the price-earnings ratio is the *reciprocal* of a kind of "rate of return" on money invested in the stock. A price-earnings ratio of 20 means the company is earning at a rate equal to 5 percent of the market value of all the stock out, so the stock may yield about 5 percent—not all of it in dividends, however. Dividends per share are not meaningful by themselves, either. The two figures that *are* relevant are earnings per share divided by price per share, and dividends per share divided by price per share, each calculation giving a cash yield in percentage terms for comparison with other stocks. Neither of these figures is available without some extra calculation. The fluctuation of these figures over a few years reveals something about the stability of a single stock. The relationship between them also reveals something, since the common practice is to pay out about half a company's earnings in dividends. A company paying out much less than that may be reinvesting a great deal in expectation of future profits, or it may be having a difficult time and need the cash. A company paying out more than half of its earnings may be doing insufficient reinvesting, may be unwilling to cut its dividend payments in the face of falling earnings, or may lack profitable uses for the funds.

The ordinary person who is thinking of investing in stock is faced with a bewildering number of choices, difficulty in getting good information about the earning prospects of companies, stockbrokers who know little and are themselves often victims of folklore, and an active rumor mill which is sometimes right in the very short run just because so many people listen to it. There are three choices: stick with large companies which already spread the risk over many products, purchase a variety of stocks, or go to mutual funds or investment trusts which invest in an assortment of stocks. Before we can discuss the merits of these choices, we must discuss mutual funds.

Mutual Funds or Investment Trusts

One way to pay someone else to select stocks for you is to purchase shares in a mutual fund or an investment trust, which then reinvests the money in the stock market. These have different stated objectives. Some put most of the money in bonds, or real estate, or preferred stock. Some invest in foreign corporations. Some specialize in new ventures, risky but potentially profitable. Hence, the investor still has a problem of selecting among investment trusts. Of course there is a fee for this service, partly a fraction of the yield, ranging up to 1 percent per year of the investment but averaging closer to 0.75 percent, and partly (at least in the case of most funds) a "load," or percentage cost paid when the shares are purchased, often around 8 percent of the price. This is the commission the agent or salesman gets.

The 0.75 to 1 percent of the investment that pays for the management fees and operating costs of the mutual fund leads to another piece of folklore, namely that a fund is a bargain because the market price of its shares is less than the market price of the shares of common stock it owns. People who say this forget that this differential has existed from the beginning and will probably continue, so when you sell the mutual fund, you will sell below the market value of the shares of common stock it owns per share of its own stock. The difference reflects the capitalized value of the management fee charged by the fund—unless that fee is offset by higher than average yields on the stocks. Indeed, the bigger this difference, the bigger the fund's charges, and perhaps the less of a bargain the fund! A reverse difference can reflect the belief that the fund managers are able to buy undervalued stocks.

In order to induce brokers to sell their funds, some have an 8 percent commission, or "load" (difference between buying and selling price), which goes to the seller. For these funds, of course, the net yield is quite low until that transaction cost has been amortized over a number of years.

There are, however, some "no load" funds. You save the load, but have to deal with the company that operates the fund directly. And there are funds whose stock is sold like any other stock. There are books in the library listing all the funds and giving their experience (Wiesenberger).

Funds are organized as open-end or closed-end funds, which means only that some continue to issue new shares and invest the proceeds in the market, while others maintain a fixed size, managing the fund already invested and the capital gains that are reinvested and not paid out. There is no particular reason to prefer one over the other. The total size and record is more important. Some of the funds are sold on the stock market like any other stock, making them easy to keep track of and easy to purchase through a stockbroker, who charges only the usual fees. For 100 share lots of moderate price, the fee falls to about 2 percent of the sale price.

Assessing the records of funds is difficult, because one must decide how fast to write off the 8 percent loading, and how to compare a new, rapidly growing fund with an older, more static one. The promotional literature of the funds themselves is often difficult to understand or even deceptive in selection of base years. It is easier for a new, rapidly growing fund to produce a good record, because it can invest in good prospects without the extra costs of getting out of some previous investment first. For this reason, many a "great" new fund becomes average after only a few years. The extrapolation of past success into the future is dangerous anyway. Supposing that there is a large random element in individual fund experience, then the very fund which has recently shown the most capital appreciation may be the one most likely to suffer reverses in the future as it regresses toward the average.

Various studies have tried to determine whether one does better buying a mutual fund or a random assortment of stocks. Does the fund's better selection pay for its management fees and for the 8 percent loading? The answer, of course, will depend on the period studied, the number of years allowed to amortize the 8 percent, and the exact random selection of stocks; but in a substantial number of studies the mutual funds appear to be no bargain. Only if the investor is as judicious in selecting a mutual fund as in selecting stocks does it seem to pay. Indeed, the risk spreading implicit in large, diversified corporations may well be as great as that in a mutual fund, particularly one that focuses on an industry such an electronics, or computers, or chemicals.

Selecting Stocks or Mutual Funds: Information and Advice. Unfortunately for the average person interested in investing rather than speculating, most of the standard sources of information on common stocks seem to be geared to short-run fluctuations and speculation. The stock market report in the newspaper gives such recent information as the high and low price for the day and perhaps for the year to date (rather than for the last twelve months), the dividends (often for the year to date rather than per year), and the number of shares traded yesterday. The information sheets distributed by stockbrokers are better, but frequently go back only a few years and provide very little information on such essential questions as the total amount of capital investment done by the company in the past few years. Anyone who wanted to know the longer-run variability in earnings or stock prices would find it difficult to estimate. Of course, extensive historical information on stocks is in the library (Standard and Poor's; Moody's Investors Service).

Stockbrokers themselves are paid according to the volume of stocks they buy or sell, except in certain special cases. Hence, they are likely to tout special deals, or mutual funds that pay them 8 percent, or anything to get you to buy something. There is little evidence that customers switch to brokers who give better advice; in any case, the "advice" is usually packaged by the main office and simply relayed by the broker. Stockbrokers tend to try to sell such short-run bargains, so unless you make clear your longer-run investment intentions, you may end up getting hot tips daily from your broker.

The extreme form of the hot tips is a fraudulent practice, largely abolished, of extensive high-pressure touting of certain stocks through offices full of people and telephones (called "boiler rooms"). This effects a kind of self-fulfilling prophecy if people believe the tips and act on them. The money is made by buying the stock before touting it and selling it afterward. Altered forms of this—trading in stocks one is advising others to buy or sell—still exist.

The Securities and Exchange Commission now requires

reports on all stock trading by officers of a corporation and on the buying or selling by anyone of more than some fraction of the total shares of a corporation.[1] They are also demanding more and more detailed accounting data from corporations. The annual reports of corporations to stockholders are also required to report the full remuneration of the officers and their ownership of stock in the corporation. And of course, there are rules about stock prospectuses and the issuing of new stock. All this tends to prevent the worst kinds of frauds, although some scandals still erupt. The issuing of stock in new ventures with many shares going to the founders free or cheaply for their "trouble" still goes on abroad. Mail is then used to sell the stock in the United States.

The market for stocks and mutual funds is well organized, with many well-informed large investors. The more nearly perfectly competitive and informed the traders in a market, the fewer the bargains. Some people believe the stock market already reflects future yield prospects and associated risks rather well. You may notice that a company has a great new product, or has been having exploding sales and earnings, but the chances are that many others noticed it earlier and have already bid up the price of the stock. So the only way to do better than average is to know something other investors don't know or interpret incorrectly, and to be willing to invest and wait while its effect shows up. Or if you believe the reason for the depressed price of a stock is temporary, you might get in while others are waiting for clearer signs. There are many books about how to make money in the stock market, but they mostly seem to be saying "buy cheap and sell dear" without explaining how to do it. Indeed, in the present world of massive unexpected events, new government regulation, disruptions of basic supplies, gyrating prices of basic materials, diversification seems crucial and optimal selection impossible.

Timing of Investments. One more piece of conventional wisdom has to do with stock price averaging. It says that if one puts a constant stream of money into the stock market without regard to short-run fluctuations, one does rather well, getting more shares when the price is low and somewhat fewer when it is higher. In one sense the advice is sound; it does pay to disregard the short-run fluctuations and keep putting money in, because over the long run the stock market has gone only up, reflecting the growth in national income, real as well as inflationary. In another sense it is not sound; one would do better if he somehow managed always to invest during periods when the stock market was depressed. In a third sense it is also good advice; it implies that it is wise to put money in, but not to speculate. The brokers' fees and costs of keeping informed are likely to wipe out any gains from speculation for most people.

There do seem to be waves in the stock market, partly reflecting changing government monetary policy. The stock market competes with other forms of financial investments, and if tight monetary policy drives up interest rates, some marginal shifts of money out of stocks to other investments can be expected. Adjusted for risks and tax advantages, the yields for different forms of investments tend to be comparable. One can even find other investments, such as "riding the yield curve" on a bond, with a similar mix of current yield and capital gain. And, of course, high interest rates depress the market prices of real estate and make it attractive again. (Remember the rule that the price of an asset is the discounted value of its expected future yields.)

It is possible to buy stocks of foreign corporations or funds which invest in foreign corporations. The usual risks are increased by the possibilities of nationalization or of changing exchange rates and by the greater susceptibility of companies in smaller countries to losses of markets when other countries impose tariffs or quotas. There are also complex and changing tax advantages and disadvantages. Remember the rule about the market interest rate being approximately 3 percent plus the expected rate of price inflation. What does this mean about the advisability of investing in stocks or bonds in some other country promising a higher percent return? It might just mean that that country was having a higher rate of inflation, but if they did have more inflation than the United States, they are likely to devalue the currency, which would mean that you would get fewer dollars back than you expected.

All in all, common stocks or mutual funds remain an ideal investment for the household's longer-run savings,

---

1. Businesses have sprung up selling summaries of what insider trading is going on, on the assumption that insiders are acting on inside information.

providing a hedge against inflation, high yields, relatively small management costs (if one sticks to the larger companies or funds), some liquidity because of the stock exchange, and the receipt of about half the yield or more in the form of capital gains, which can be taken when convenient and which are taxed at lower rates than other income.

Puts and Calls: The Options Market

It is possible instead of buying stock to buy the right to buy it at a stated price. Then if the price goes higher than the stated price, you can take the stock or sell the option for a profit, while if the price goes down you only lose the amount you paid for the right to buy it. These "call options" are sold by stockbrokers operating through the Chicago Board of Options Exchange, which works much like the stock market, and publishes closing prices in the newspapers. A call option specifies a regular listed stock, a price per share at which you can buy the stock ("striking price"), and the month the right expires (at the end of the month). The price of the option is the amount you pay now per share for that right, although you must purchase units of 100 shares. The striking price plus the option price per share will always be above the current market price, of course; otherwise you could realize an instant profit. But purchasers hope the price will rise enough to cover the purchase price of the option, the striking price, the broker's commission, and the cost of realizing the option for cash. The periods during which options can be exercised have been standardized to end on the last business day of January, April, July, or October.

So "Ford 40 April at 2⅝" means I can buy the right to purchase 100 shares of Ford stock at $40 per share any time between now and April 30 for 100 times 2⅝ or $262.50, plus commissions. If the price gets above that by more than the cost of exercising the option, I can make a profit, or wait hoping it will go still higher before the end of April.

Buying a "put" gives you the right to *sell* 100 shares of stock at a stated price, and you make money if the price falls so you can buy the stock at a lower price than you can sell it for. If you already own the stock, it is a way of being sure you can unload it on the way down. If not, you can exercise the option, for a fee, without ever buying and selling actual shares.

Obviously, this is a form of legalized gambling, where you can hope for large gains with a small investment, but can limit your losses. Brokers find handling options more profitable than selling stock. There is a $6 charge per option, plus 1 percent, plus a surcharge. If an option is exercised, the broker makes another commission. And, of course, those who write options leave a difference between put and call prices that leave them a profit. There is reason to believe that few buyers make money, but most sellers do because they are hedged, either selling both puts and calls, or selling calls on stocks they hold.

There are many complex combinations of puts and calls with and without owning the stock that allow all kinds of gambling with leverage and some hedging to cut possible losses.

Commodity Futures

Another kind of gambling, requiring somewhat larger sums and perhaps inside information on crops, weather, etc., uses commodity futures. These are essentially the rights to future delivery of some commodity like grain. The buyer of futures bets that the price will go up before he takes delivery so he can sell at a profit. The seller of futures bets that the price will fall. As the market really works, the futures themselves are sold, and the commodities are almost never actually delivered. Such markets perform a useful social function, like that of Joseph in Egypt, inducing less use and more storage today if shortages are expected in the future. Indeed, in spite of the common belief that the market is a noxious exploitation of the farmers, economic analysis shows that the gamblers either improve the allocation of resources or are penalized with heavy losses. If they compete sufficiently, they make only normal profits for their services, so that in a sense the more informed speculation, the better. A well-run grain market reduces the price fluctuations to those reflecting the costs of storage, helping to spread consumption evenly over time in the face of fluctuating supplies. When speculators expect a bad year, they drive up the current price, thereby encouraging less consumption and more storage.

For the ordinary household, commodity futures are closer to gambling; no one is likely to know as much about the expected crops and market demands as the professional traders. Even the proper regulation of these markets to prevent fraud is still far less adequate than with stocks.

Small Businesses

A person can invest in a small business without being directly involved in managing it. This often requires more capital than one person has, so that a partnership or a corporation has to be formed. In a partnership each partner is responsible for the conduct of the others, which involves risks that the other partners may be dishonest or inefficient, and presents problems if one partner leaves or dies. A corporation limits one's liability to his actual investment and allows postponement of some taxes on undistributed profits, but subjects the earnings to the corporate income tax on profits. A small business can put its resources into real estate, farms, cattle, oil wells, trees, retailing, or even manufacturing. Sometimes businesses grow out of hobbies—photography, saddlemaking, etc. The main difficulty is that any business requires time and energy, and holds considerable risk. A small business is risky for an active partner, and even riskier for a "sleeping partner." Small business failures have been numerous enough to indicate that many people go into unwise ventures or have inadequate experience in accounting and business management. The mortality rate has been highest with retailing ventures, perhaps because they are easiest to get into, relying on rented quarters and an inventory financed by suppliers. And a retail business often arouses the enmity of customers, who exaggerate the gross mark-ups and underestimate the costs.

Preferred Stock, Corporate Bonds, Debentures

There are a variety of other financial investments, generally unsuitable for the ordinary household because they serve other purposes and require substantial amounts of money. Preferred stock has a guaranteed or fixed dividend that is paid before any common stock dividends. The yield is safer for that reason, but, being fixed, it will not go up with inflation or higher profits.

Corporate bonds are elaborately rated as to quality and are most appropriate for insurance companies, which must preserve the principal of their investments because of their obligations to their policyholders. (Insurance companies are not allowed by most state laws to invest more than a fraction of their assets in stock.) The better corporate bonds are safe, and sometimes even provide capital gains when bought at a discount, but they provide fixed yields with little apparent advantage over a savings account. Interest payments on bonds have claim to the company's earnings before even the preferred stock.

The one debenture of some interest to the average investor is the "convertible" debenture often issued by utilities. It is really a bond with the right after a certain period of conversion to common stock of the company. If the price of the stock falls, the debenture can be held as a fixed-yield investment. If the price rises, the debenture can be converted to stock at a bargain. Often there are savings in the transactions costs as well (no broker's fees).

Checking Accounts and Checking-Saving Combinations

Money kept in a checking account can be a kind of investment if it avoids service charges. With combination checking and savings accounts, a relatively low interest rate is paid on the savings account, but if a sufficient balance is kept in the savings account, no charges are made for the checking account or the automatic transfers that replenish it from the savings account. Again, this is really a kind of yield on the funds "invested" in the two accounts, in addition to the interest paid. Whether the total yield is better than alternative investments may well depend on how many checks you write.

Money Market Funds

The inflation of the 1970s which produced higher interest rates, combined with legal ceilings on savings account rates, led to the creation of a new financial instrument, the money market fund. These funds pool individuals' savings and make short-term commercial loans, providing the savers with high yields, high liquidity, and reasonable security through diversification and the short duration of the loans. Some of these money market funds are offered by banks, some by stock brokerage companies, and still others directly from the companies. Minimum deposits, transaction costs, check-writing privileges, and liquidity differ substantially from one fund to another, and are likely to change in such a competitive business. Since the yields depend on what can be earned on short-term government and corporate bonds, and no legal ceilings apply, the yield to the saver is high when short-run commercial interest rates are high, as in any inflationary period. Savings are not insured in such funds, and the yield can change rapidly, but the risk of capital loss appears small, and you can always get out if rates start to drop. Remember, however, that as interest rates drop, there are large capital gains to be earned on longer term investments, including stocks. A stock, depressed so that its yield is quite high, will appreciate when that same expected future stream of yield is discounted at a lower interest rate. If you do decide to save through money market funds, an investment of time spent acquiring information about them may have a high payoff.

Odds and Ends

Beyond what we have listed, the possible places where one might invest savings tail off into antiques, paintings, precious metals, diamonds, or foreign currencies. Most of these require either special skills or inside information if one is to make any money. Many produce nothing, so any yield can come only from an increased demand facing a stable or decreasing supply—often a temporary situation. When one has both time and skills to invest, there is a variety of special investments. Some people purchase old houses, live in them while they fix them up, and then sell them. Under present tax laws there is not even a capital gains tax on such a profit provided the seller buys another house costing at least as much within a year. This means that all the effort put into such a venture would earn tax-free income. The question, then, of course, is whether one could earn still more, even after taxes, by concentrating on his main occupation, because the main return here is not so much on the financial investment as on the labor.

For those with a long time horizon and a love of nature, trees are an excellent investment, aided by a number of special subsidies (including free seedlings in some states) and some tax advantages.

It is important to remember the principles of compound interest, and at market interest rates, when comparing investments. An antique chair that doubles in price in twenty-five years earns less than 3 percent (remember the Rule of 72)!

Some Technical Details

We have already discussed some technical considerations, such as joint tenancy, the cost of trading, trusts, putting assets in the names of children, and partnerships versus corporations. Other technicalities concern state and local taxes and estate and inheritance taxes. Estate planning is discussed more fully at the end of chapter 9.

The "dividends" received from a mutual fund are not entirely current income, at least for purposes of the tax law. Part is considered a distribution of the capital gains realized when the fund sold one stock in order to purchase another. Some funds attempt to maximize the fraction of dividends that is capital gains for the tax benefit of their customers.

A curious provision of the tax law states that if an appreciated asset is given to charity, the full market value can be deducted as a charitable contribution, but no capital gains tax is payable on the difference between that value and the original cost. Anyone who has owned stock for any length of time, and who is making contributions anyway, would therefore be well advised to make contributions in stock rather than cash. It might even be an incentive to weed out stocks which seem to be going nowhere. Strangely enough, even among the affluent very few people do this (Barlow, Brazer, and Morgan). This loophole is being restricted by revisions in the law.

The tax advantages of investment in real estate without the management problems are available in real estate investment trusts. In one outstanding case, that advantage has been used to speed up racial integration in middle-class housing. One can purchase shares in a mutual real estate investment trust, called M-Reit, where the funds will be used to purchase, renovate, and maintain apartment buildings that will be operated on an open-occupancy basis. The dividends will be tax-free because of the double declining balance depreciation allowed.

In any investment program, particularly one focused on stocks or mutual funds, there are choices between investing more time or money in information or advice, on the one hand, and reducing the need for it by diversification on the other. Diversification can come through investing in large multi-product firms, or in a large number of different firms, or in mutual funds which invest in many different firms, or some combination of these. There is no best advice here. The choice may depend on whether you want to make detailed choices and follow the fates of several individual companies, or pay a commission to a mutual fund for taking that responsibility.

How does one assess the payoff to more information? If one pays for it (in management fees) by investing in a mutual fund, the payoff is in the expected higher return. If you are thinking of paying for advice from the many firms which offer it, you should ask why anyone who could really predict the stock market would sell the information rather than use it to get rich. And if a large number of investors receive advice from some service, what might happen?

First, it could be fairly obvious information already acted upon by others, so that the stock price would already have taken account of it. Large speculative operators may have gotten the information early and acted on it, only to unload on you at the higher price.

Second, the very price changes predicted might happen, but only because the subscribers to the service took the advice, in which case the long-run movements might be unaffected.

The basic problem for the small investor is that he or she is competing with large professional investors who have a great deal of information and a much wider range of alternative investments. The investors of pension funds, for example, have specialists who follow subcategories of investments.

There are schemes now in which the dividends on stocks or mutual fund shares are automatically reinvested in more stock, and with the right to purchase more stock through the same mechanism. The charges for the automatic reinvestment are not always clearly stated in advance, and the varying purchase prices require detailed records for paying capital gains taxes when the stock is sold. It can be a convenience for stock held in the names of minors for their college education because it avoids dividend checks. The right to purchase more stock for a fee smaller than the usual broker's fee can also be attractive. It might be better, if you have the time, to make fresh decisions about additional investments, but it is an automatic saving-investment device for those who feel they might otherwise spend the dividends. Indeed, making it difficult to spend savings is one way to encourage holding on to them.

We discuss estate planning in more detail in chapter 9 since it is related to life insurance, but two aspects are relevant to investment decisions: records and patterns of ownership of assets, and putting assets into trusts. With estates large enough to exceed the exemptions and the marital deduction (half the estate up to $250,000), it is useful to have assets clearly owned by one or the other marital partner, with evidence that he or she furnished the funds for purchase. If assets are in joint tenancy with rights of survivorship, it is important to have evidence that each of the two owners contributed to the acquisition. At present, the rules tend to ignore nonmoney work, mostly of wives, so that a jointly owned asset is sometimes ruled to have been a gift of the employed partner to the "nonworking" one. The marital deduction lessens this problem, and with past and expected increases in that deduction, it should be important only to the very rich.

When assets are put in trust, there is the problem of who will manage them, and sometimes the regulations seriously restrict the investment options. A trust is essentially a fictitious "person" owning some assets for the benefit of someone else. Because the trustee is responsible for proper management and can be made personally liable for the results of bad management, he tends to be quite cautious about investing the money.

Complex business deals, whether for profit or tax avoidance, often involve tricky legal and tax filing problems. These can absorb time and money, and it may prove difficult to extricate yourself from them. There is an emotional cost in such complications, particularly when one gets older and thinks about turning things over to a survivor. Indeed, any investment that is difficult to sell can prove to be a problem, perhaps more from the uncertainty and worry than from any real long-term loss. This speaks against partnerships, new businesses, real estate in undeveloped areas, and unlisted stocks not sold on the major exchanges.

What People Do

Given the reasons for investing savings and the options open to them, what do people do? Most of them put their money in fixed-yield assets like savings accounts and United States bonds. If one asks them whether that was wise in view of continuing inflation, they say that of course it was, except that they should have saved more. If one asks about common stock as an alternative, they reply that they don't know much about it or that it is risky. This means that for most people their only important hedge against inflation is their own home. Consciousness of inflation has not been accompanied by any insights about investment for most people; instead, it is seen as requiring that one economize and not make new commitments, in order to be able to meet the (higher) food and clothing bills in the future.

Among the more affluent, of course, consciousness of the importance of capital gains is quite salient. On the other hand, even the affluent are not usually actively attempting to reduce their income taxes; they are more concerned with earning money and getting a good yield on their investments than on exploiting tax loopholes (Barlow, Brazer, and Morgan). This implies, of course, that special tax provisions available only to the wealthy and used by only a fraction of them are unfair not only as between rich and poor but as between rich and rich, and could be abolished more easily than some people think.

At the same time, the affluent, and particularly the wealthy (those with high assets as well as high income), are quite concerned about passing their estates on to their heirs and eager to escape estate and inheritance taxes. So despite the traditional economist's belief that the heaviest taxes should be on inheritances, popular opinion is against more effective taxation of estates.

The pattern of asset ownership varies with the amount of assets involved, of course; the wealthy are more likely to be in stocks and in business ventures. There are also different patterns between age groups, the young people having a larger fraction of their assets in the home and savings accounts, older people in real estate and stocks.

Most people seek relatively little information or advice, and yet even among the wealthiest, the actual delegation of decisions about investing assets is quite rare.

Given that our estate and inheritance taxes can be relatively easily avoided by various devices, including trusts, one might think that the main source of the wealth of today's wealthy would be inheritances. But in fact, during the last half-century there have also been vast profits made, and vast capital gains on the profits that were reinvested. We tend to pay attention to the inheritances because they are fascinating or irritating (Lundberg).

Most economists would argue that the pattern of ownership of assets is less important than the control over their use. Vast amounts of corporate wealth are owned by widows and orphans, pension funds, etc., but their productive use is directed by managers who are rewarded mostly for their results. From a hard-headed economic point of view, it would be the wasteful consumption of assets one would object to, and not the technical ownership of them, unless that ownership were used for harmful purposes. Many an underdeveloped country pays too much attention to ownership and too little to making sure the resources are kept in the country and put to productive use.

Some Social Aspects of Private Investment

Whenever individuals do not need to consume all they currently earn, resources are available for others to use by borrowing. The procedures by which others secure the rights to use these resources vary from relatively direct ones (as when a saver invests in a friend's business or purchases a new stock issue) to quite indirect ones, as when the individual puts money in a bank and the bank lends the money to someone else. Of course, lending institutions can lend more to some than the total others are saving, by creating credit.

Many have argued that society needs more equity (risk) capital, so that businesses can expand without the threat of large fixed charges to ruin them in bad years. Some critics worry about the large amounts of savings tied up in reserves of insurance companies, whose investment was restricted to high-grade bonds and some mortgages, or in the Social Security trust fund, which invests in government bonds. Others decry the heavy use by corporations of reinvested profits, freeing them from competing for funds in the market and allowing them to buy up other companies and thereby form large conglomerates.

The concentration of stock ownership in the hands of relatively few high-income individuals and large institutional investors has raised concerns about the disparity in the extent to which rich and poor are protected against inflation and about concentration of political or economic power. Evidence of misuse of power is scanty, however, and the increasing prevalence of home ownership has provided even lower-income families with some defense against inflation. In addition, the repeated and now mandatory revisions of Social Security benefits to take account of rising prices make them less vulnerable to inflation. One could argue, however, that better information for small investors and the encouragement of more direct recourse to the stock market for industrial expansion would be a good thing.

Summary

We have multiple objectives when we have savings to invest. We want the principal to be safe but also protected against erosion by inflation. We want some liquidity or availability; yet we want to minimize taxes, and that may require sequestering funds in retirement accounts or putting them in the children's names. We want to select the best individual investments but find it hard to believe that the advice and information we can secure are unbiased or sufficient. Many of the old rules have broken down. The stock market no longer offers promise of a hedge against inflation, and real estate may well prove to be just as undependable in the coming decades as stocks were in the past. We may be tempted to do a little speculation in options or futures or individual stocks or real estate, but we realize that we are competing with well-informed experts and have no source of unbiased advice.

We are invited to try a number of new devices, many focused on reducing taxes even at the expense of taking current losses in drilling oil wells or renting property; yet we read regularly about disastrous or even fraudulent schemes that have fooled even relatively sophisticated and wealthy people.

We are particularly attracted to retirement account arrangments that allow us to postpone income taxes even on current income that we set aside. But we can also defer taxes on the yield of our savings or convert it into capital gains that are taxed at half the rate and are easier to take in the best year for us. We can shift some assets to others, like children, to reduce or avoid current taxes on the yield, and later taxes on the estate.

The crucial economic insight in all these decisions is the relation between the present value of an asset and its expected future stream of yields. These calculations must be combined with adjustments for tax implications and for inflation. In order to get 3 percent real after taxes, it may be necessary to earn more than market interest rates.

More Information?
Once again, most of the information comes from those with something to sell. Stockbrokers make their commission on sales, and their reputations on short-run gains, while the ordinary investor needs long-term investments with minimal turnover. But brokers do have mass-produced assessments of individual stocks summarizing their records and prospects.

Ansbacher, Max G. *The New Options Market*. New York: Walker and Company, 1975.

Arvia, Raymond P. *The Cost of Dying and What You Can Do About It*. New York: Harper & Row, 1974.

Ashley, Paul P. *You and Your Will*. New York: McGraw-Hill, 1975.

Barlow, Robin; Brazer, Harvey; and Morgan, James N. *The Economic Behavior of the Affluent*. Washington, D.C.: Brookings Institution, 1966.

Brosterman, Robert. *The Complete Estate Planning Guide*. New York: Mentor, 1964.

Brutus [pseud.]. *Confessions of a Stockbroker*. New York: Bantam Books, 1971.

Clendenin, John C. *Introduction to Investments*. 5th ed. New York: McGraw-Hill, 1969.

Computer Directions Advisors, Inc. *Risk-Adjusted Mutual Performance Review*. Silver Spring, Md.: Computer Directions Advisors, Inc., annually.

Dacey, Norman. *How to Avoid Probate*. New York: Crown, 1965.

deCamp, Catherine Crook. *Money Tree*. New York: Signet, 1972.

Doane, C. Russell. *Investment Trusts and Funds from the Investors' Point of View*. Great Barrington, Mass.: American Institute for Economic Research, 1971. (Later editions likely)

Engel, Louis. *How to Buy Stocks*. 6th rev. ed. New York: Bantam Books, 1969.

Fisher, Philip. *Conservative Investors Sleep Well*. New York: Harper & Row, 1975.

Frank, Robert. *Successful Investing Through Mutual Funds*. New York: Hart Publishing Company, 1969.

Friend, Irwin; Blume, Marshall; and Crockett, Jean. *Mutual Funds and Other Institutional Investors, a New Perspective*. New York: McGraw-Hill, 1970. (Undistinguished performance and conflicts of interest)

Gastinam, Gary L. *The Stock Options Manual*. New York: McGraw-Hill, 1975.

Gordon, George Byron. *You, Your Heirs, and Your Estate*. Rockville Centre, N.Y.: Farnsworth Publishing Company, 1973.

Hermin, Sidney S. *What to Do When Your Bills Exceed Your Paycheck*. Englewood Cliffs, N.J.: Prentice-Hall, 1975.

Hirsch Organization, Inc. *Mutual Funds Almanac*. Old Tappan, N.Y.: Hirsch Organization, Inc., annually.

Hoyt, Homer. *One Hundred Years of Land Values in Chicago*. Chicago: University of Chicago Press, 1933.

Irwin, Robert. *How to Buy and Sell Real Estate at a Profit*. New York: McGraw-Hill, 1975.

Kinsman, Robert. *Your Swiss Bank Book*. Homewood, Ill.: Dow Jones-Irwin, 1975.

Kinsman, Robert. *The Robert Kinsman Guide to Tax Havens*. Homewood, Ill.: Dow Jones-Irwin, 1978.

Lass, William. *Make Money in Pure-Bred Cattle*. New York: Popular Library, 1972.

Lewis, Alfred A., and Berns, Barrie. *Three Out of Four Wives—Widowhood in America*. New York: Macmillan, 1975.

Loeb, Gerald M. *Your Battle for Stock Market Profits*. New York: Simon and Schuster, 1970.

Lundberg, Ferdinand. *The Rich and the Super Rich*. New York: Lyle Stuart, 1968.

Mader, Chris. *Real Estate Investing*. Homewood, Ill.: Dow Jones-Irwin, 1975.

Markstein, David L. *How to Make Money with Mutual Funds*. New York: McGraw-Hill, 1969.

McLaughlin, David J. *The Executives Money Map*. New York: McGraw-Hill, 1975.

Miller, Jarrott T. *Options Trading*. New York: Henry Regnery, 1975.

Mintz, Morton, and Cohan, Jerry S. *America, Inc.: Who Owns and Operates the United States?* New York: Dial Press, 1971.

Moody's investment publications. New York: Moody's Investors Service, annual.

Morris, William T. *How to Get Rich Slowly But Almost Surely*. Englewood Cliffs, N.J.: Reston Publishing Company (Prentice-Hall), 1973.

Mueller, Eva, and Lean, Jane. "The Savings Account as a Source for Financing Large Expenditures." *Journal of Finance* 22 (1967): 375–93.

Munnell, Alicia H. *The Future of Social Security*. Washington, D.C.: Brookings Institution, 1977.

Neal, Charles. *How to Keep What You Have, or What Your Broker Never Told You*. New York: Doubleday, 1972.

No-Load Mutual Fund Association. *Directory of No-Load Funds Association*. New York: No-Load Mutual Fund Association, periodically.

Owen, Lewis. *How Wall Street Doubles My Money Every Three Years*. New York: Manor Books, 1969.

Projector, Dorothy, and Weiss, Gertrude. *Survey of Financial Characteristics of Consumers*. Washington, D.C.: Board of Governors of the Federal Reserve System, 1966.

Reilly, James F. *Too Good for the Rich Alone*. Englewood Cliffs, N.J.: Prentice-Hall, 1975.

Rosefsky, Robert. *The Money Book*. Chicago: Follett, 1975.

Ross, Martin J. *Handbook of Everyday Law*. Greenwich, Conn.: Fawcett, 1967.

Sargent, David R. *Stock Market Profits and Higher Income for You*. New York: Simon and Schuster, 1975.

Seldin, Maury, and Wesnik, R. W. *Real Estate Investment Strategy*. New York: John Wiley and Sons, 1975.

Siegel, Edward. *How to Avoid Lawyers*. Greenwich, Conn.: Fawcett, 1971.

Smith, Adam [pseud.]. *The Money Game*. New York: Random House, 1969.

Sokolsky, A. M. *The Great American Land Bubble*. New York: Harper & Brothers, 1932.

Standard and Poor's, Statistical Service. *Statistics*. New York: Standard and Poor's, periodical.

Stephenson, Gilbert T., and Wiggins, Norman A. *Estates and Trusts*. 5th ed. Englewood Cliffs, N.J.: Prentice-Hall, 1973.

Train, John. *Dance of the Money Bees*. New York: Harper & Row, 1975.

U.S. Department of the Treasury, Internal Revenue Service. *A Guide to Federal Estate and Gift Taxation*. Publication no. 443. Washington, D.C.: Government Printing Office, January 1975, revised.

U.S. Government Printing Office. *Official Summary of Security Transactions and Holdings*. Washington, D.C.: Government Printing Office, periodically. (Six to eight week lag between date of transactions and date of publication)

Watkins, A. M. *Buying Land*. New York: Quadrangle, 1975.

Widicus, Wilber W., and Stitzel, Thomas E. *Personal Investing*. Rev. ed. Homewood, Ill.: Irwin, 1976.

Wiesenberger Investment Services. *Investment Companies, Mutual Funds, and Other Types*. New York: Wiesenberger Investment Services, annually.

Wisemenon, Robert. *Questions and Answers on Real Estate*. 8th ed. Englewood Cliffs, N.J.: Prentice-Hall, 1975.

Wysong, Perry. *How You Can Use the Wall Street Insiders*. Fort Lauderdale, Fla.: Wilton House, 1971. (See U.S. Government Printing Office)

Some Projects to Learn More

1. Select five stocks, and using Moody's or some other manual, secure data on trends in their earnings and dividends per share, and their price per share. Adjust for stock splits and acquisitions of other companies. Calculate earnings as a percent of net worth, and explain why the percent differs from the market interest rate.

2. Select some mutual funds, with and without "loading," and compare their records. Do the funds that charge an 8 percent purchase "loading" perform better, so you get back your loading in a few years?

3. Select three alternative portfolios: three mutual funds, three large corporations, and ten diversified stocks. Follow them backward for ten years, estimating the yield (if the investment were made ten years ago) and the year to year fluctuations in yield and in price. Which is the most stable in terms of yield; of price?

4. Investigate the market for real estate investments. If possible, talk with some investors about their experience and about the relative importance of rents as against capital gains.

5. Investigate the laws of your state about (a) joint tenancy, and (b) putting assets in the names of minor children with a parent or relative as trustee.

6. See whether you can identify an area of empty land ripe for development. Then check the Registry of Deeds for transfers of ownership in recent years, estimating prices from the federal transfer tax stamps. Have the speculators been making money?

7. Write a paper on the advantages and disadvantages of putting assets in joint tenancy. (Check for recent articles in legal journals.)

8. Take any three recent paperback books on mutual funds, or how to make money on stocks or real estate, and write a critical review. What did you learn that you could not have figured out for yourself? Do they agree? Do the authors represent any special interest?

9. Write for a list of no-load funds to the No-Load Mutual Fund Association, 475 Park Avenue South, New York, New York 10016. See how many are reported in Wiesenberger, and how their records compare.

CHAPTER EIGHT
INVESTMENTS IN CONSUMER DURABLES

We have already discussed the largest consumable investment individuals make—an owned home. And we have seen that a crucial aspect of financial management and budgeting is to maintain proper levels of annual investment in human capital, physical capital, and financial capital (savings). The depreciation of consumer durables is a large and often neglected part of the cost of living. We even suggested that one method of spacing acquisitions and staying aware of costs was to allocate some annual percentage of income for the combined replacement, acquisition, and upgrading of the house and household equipment.

There are still problems in deciding how much to invest in what durables. Such investments commit the family to a pattern of consumption, costs, and even payments far into the future. The costs of buying or selling are such that we want to minimize mistakes. Having already discussed houses, we focus here on cars, other durables, and additions and repairs to homes.

Theory Again

A new element enters our capital theory with most consumer durables and cars because of their rapid market depreciation, large differences between their purchase price and their selling price as "used" items (trading costs), and the gap between their market value and use value. The first-year depreciation cost of most durables is extremely high, so we legitimately spread costs over expected years of use. Then, when we want to compare such alternatives as buying a new durable versus repairing and keeping an old one, we do it in terms of costs per year. The cost of keeping something one more year must be based on the difference in what it could be sold for now and a year from now. The cost of buying a durable must be based, in part, on the purchase price, which might easily be 50 percent higher than selling price.

The difference between market value and use value can be very large for some appliances which have almost no secondhand market, substantial for an old car ascertainably in good condition, but relatively small for a house unless there is something an individual particularly likes about it that others do not appreciate.

The benefits of most consumer durables are extremely difficult to quantify, so we need good estimates of the costs of alternatives; then we can ask whether a more costly alternative is worth it in terms of benefits.

Two of the most important costs are depreciation and foregone interest. Dealing with the present value of streams of these costs over time may appear complicated at first, but, fortunately, there is a way to shortcut the calculation of the present value of a stream of depreciation and foregone interest costs by knowing one nonintuitive fact: for a depreciating asset with no resale value at the end, *the present value of the stream of depreciation and foregone interest costs is exactly equal to its present cost-to-own, whatever its expected life and whatever the interest rate used.* Cost-to-own here means resale value if I already own an item, purchase price if I do not. Thus, the present value of the depreciation and foregone interest costs of buying an $800 used car and keeping it until it is junked is exactly $800—and that amount does not depend on whether it wears out in one year or ten. If there is a resale value—I intend to trade it in before it is junk—then the total cost is the present cost-to-own minus the (discounted) present value of the trade-in.

To see this, suppose that I buy a durable for a price P_0 and keep it for two years. Suppose further that its resale value at the end of the first year is P_1, is P_2 at the end of the second year, and that the interest rate is r. The discounted stream of depreciation costs is:

$$\frac{P_0 - P_1}{1 + r} + \frac{P_1 - P_2}{(1 + r)^2}$$

and the stream of foregone interest costs is

$$\frac{rP_0}{1 + r} + \frac{rP_1}{(1 + r)^2}.$$

Adding these two streams together and rearranging terms gives:

$$\frac{P_0}{1+r} + \frac{rP_0}{1+r} - \frac{P_1}{1+r} + \frac{P_1}{(1+r)^2} + \frac{rP_1}{(1+r)^2} - \frac{P_2}{(1+r)^2}.$$

This sum can be simplified further:

$$\frac{P_0(1+r)}{(1+r)} - \frac{P_1}{(1+r)} + \frac{P_1(1+r)}{(1+r)^2} - \frac{P_2}{(1+r)^2} = P_0 - \frac{P_2}{(1+r)^2}.$$

It is easy to generalize this to n periods and show that the sum of the depreciation and foregone interest costs equals

$$P_0 - \frac{P_n}{(1 + r)^n}.$$

Thus, if resale value at the end of the period is zero ($P_n = 0$), the depreciation and foregone interest costs are *completely* independent of the number of years of ownership and the interest rate.

An intuitive reason why this is true is that a less lasting durable has more depreciation each year, but less remaining value and fewer years to cost me in foregone interest. If I want to compare keeping an old one with buying a new one, I need only the cost-to-own now, expected life, and any differences in operating costs to get differences in yearly cost that I can compare with differences in benefits or satisfaction.

While this shortcut will prove extremely useful in comparing the costs of alternatives, the following pieces of economic insight will also help:

1. I still must discount other future costs and benefits with a 3 percent interest rate, and use present-day prices. Inflation will increase trade-in values, but it will also raise the rate of interest, so I am safe in using the 3 percent figure. If I have to borrow money, however, the difference between what I am charged on the loan and what I could receive if I invested the money myself is part of the cost of the purchase.

2. In comparing costs of an owned durable with those of a newly purchased replacement, I cannot consider only next year for the new one, because the trading costs and the pattern of market depreciation are such that it will seem prohibitively expensive. I must calculate an averaged per-year cost over the expected life of the new purchase.

3. Inflation is no excuse for ignoring depreciation, particularly since inflation simultaneously increases the cost of replacing the durable. Moreover, if I took current market prices, the apparently lower depreciation would be offset by the higher market interest rate.

4. The principle that past (sunk) costs should be ignored applies to decisions about whether to fix up and keep an old car or appliance. It works several ways. A series of high repair bills already paid does not justify keeping a car just to "amortize" the bills, if the car promises to require still more repairs. On the other hand, repairs that would not be recoverable in the trade-in value of the car may still be worth making if they allow the use of the car for another year or two. Careful maintenance usually has less effect on the resale price of a car than on its usefulness to the owner.

5. Finally and perhaps most important, in deciding about replacement, I must be honest with myself about how long I expect to keep the replacement. I cannot plan to trade in a five-year-old car and claim I will keep the new one for ten years without kidding myself. Hence, replacement choices should usually compare one more year of the old one with one-plus-the-age-of-the-old-one years on the new one. If I have a five-year-old car, the comparison must be the cost of keeping the old car one more year with a six-year-average cost of a new car. Or, if I buy a newer model used car, I compare with average cost per year on that one if it is kept until it is as old as my present one will be a year from now.

Automobiles

In applying all this to decisions whether to buy a car, or to buy an additional one, or to replace one, some additional rules of thumb are useful:

1. The costs of trading cars are substantial. Dealer's margin, sales tax, and title-transfer costs range from approximately 20 percent for a new car up to 50 percent for a low-priced used car. Trading costs also include the time and money costs of shopping. Spreading these costs over several years of use before trading again is obviously economical.

2. Cars depreciate at a rather steady 25 percent per year of their resale value at the beginning of the year. In spite of folklore about popular or durable cars like Mercedes, Volvo, Volkswagen, or Cadillac, the exceptions to this rule are few and far between.

3. If my old car could be sold for $500, but would cost $1,000 to buy from a used car dealer, it is the $500 that I should use in estimating my costs if I keep it.

We can illustrate these principles by working out the costs of the choices I face if I own a five-year-old car and must decide between keeping that car for an extra year or buying a new one. We will ignore inflation for the moment and assume that both cars cost $5,000 new and both have sale prices as shown in table 15. The sale value numbers in that table are synthetic but realistic, and are based on the fact that cars generally depreciate at about 25 percent per year. The table also shows depreciation, foregone interest, and the present value of sale value—all of which can be calculated directly from the sale value numbers.

The costs of keeping my used car for an extra year include dépreciation and foregone interest, as well as operating and repair costs and insurance premiums. As shown in table 15, the depreciation and foregone interest costs of keeping a five-year-old car for one extra year are $237 + $21 = $258. The one-year depreciation and foregone interest costs of the new car are, of course, much higher: $2,000 + $150 = $2,150. If I have to borrow money to buy the new car, then I have to also add in the excess interest charges. This is unfair to the new car, of course, charging the whole trading cost to one year, and it ignores

Table 15. Depreciation and Foregone Interest Costs on a Car Costing $5,000 New (in today's prices)

At End of Year	Sale Value	Depreciation for Year[a]	Foregone Interest for Year[b]	Present Value of Sale or Trade-in Value[c]
First	$3,000	$2,000	$150	$2,913
Second	2,250	750	90	2,122
Third	1,688	562	51	1,544
Fourth	1,266	422	38	1,124
Fifth	949	317	28	819
Sixth	712	237	21	596
Seventh	534	178	16	434
Eighth	400	134	12	316
Ninth	300	100	9	230
Tenth	225	75	7	167

[a]Depreciation is calculated as the difference between the second column amount and its value at the end of the previous year. If we allow for inflation, the numbers would be smaller, and foregone interest at market rates higher. First year also includes a $1,000 dealer's margin.
[b]Three percent of value at beginning of year.
[c]See the 3 percent interest rate column of table 4 at the end of chapter 2 (p. 19).

some differences in operating costs. On the other hand, I would be kidding myself to compare the ten-year average cost of the new car with the average yearly cost of five more years of the old one, unless I have some compelling reason to expect to keep the new one much longer than I am thinking of keeping the old one.

So, to keep myself honest, I must compare one more year's cost of the old car with the six-year average costs of a new one. The latter does not require calculating a lot of present values of depreciation and interest; I can shortcut by deducting the present value of the trade-in after six years from the original $5,000 price and dividing by six: ($5,000 − $596)/6 = $734. The question then is whether the style, safety, luxury, economy, new features, and freedom from bother of the new car are worth $734 − $258, or $476 a year.

There would, of course, be some savings in operating and maintenance costs on the newer car. But even major prospective repair and maintenance costs on the old one probably will not amount to more than one or two hundred dollars per year, on the average. In addition, insurance costs would be lower on the older, less valuable car, since collision insurance never covers more than the market value of a car (chap. 9).

All this might seem relatively simple and obvious, except that popular books on family finance tell you to trade in "when the cost of upkeep begins to outrun the cost of depreciation," which is either meaningless or wrong. It is meaningless to look only at the present car and ignore the alternative, and certainly wrong to compare part of total cost with another part. The United States government was also misleading when it wrote:

> The longer he keeps the car, the greater are his savings in depreciation. But after the first two years he begins to face a series of outlays for tire and battery replacements, repairs, and incidentals that more than offset his savings in depreciation.[1]

If the statement means that the difference in operating cost between the present car and (the average yearly cost of) a new one kept the same number of years tends to get larger than the difference in depreciation, then it might make partial sense. But the data given by the publication also include periodic replacements, ignore the cost of the money tied up in the car, ignore the trading costs, and divide by an ever-smaller number of miles driven, which makes the cost per mile look larger.

A number of credit unions, supposedly cooperatives run in consumers' interest, quote the Department of Transportation as suggesting trading for a new model at the end of two years. What is worse, some suggest financing this two-year turnover with a "balloon note" loan where the remaining loan balance owed at the end of two years is as large as the value of the car. What this does is maximize the amount on loan, maximizing the interest costs as well as the depreciation and trading costs. In the case of our $5,000 car, these latter three costs amount to a whopping $1,375 per year.

Calculations similar to those we discussed for trading in for a new car can be used to compare buying a new car with buying a used car. I must again start honestly by predicting how long I shall keep a car. If it is to be six years, then I must compare the six-year average cost of a new car with, say, the three-year average cost of a three-year-old secondhand car. And I cannot use table 15 for the *cost* of buying a three-year-old car. Although I could sell one for $1,688, I am likely to have to pay about $2,200 to buy one in equivalent condition.[2] Subtracting the present value of a $712 sale value three years hence (0.915 × $712, or $651) from the $2,200, I get $1,549, or $516 per year for the used car, compared with the $734 per year we already estimated for a new car kept six years. These calculations take account of both depreciation and interest, except that if I have to borrow, there will be extra interest charges on the new car.

Again, I must ask whether the extra repairs on the used car will more than offset that difference, or reduce it to where the joy of a new car appears cheap. And it depends on how I value my time spent fussing with a car, the cost of repairs, and whether I have another car to reduce the inconvenience of breakdowns.

Remember that the current cost of acquiring or keeping a car minus the present value of what I can get for it when I trade it in is the same as the present value of the streams of depreciation and foregone interest at 3 percent during the period. I can ignore inflation, because if depreciation is smaller in current (inflating) dollars, the market interest rates are higher. Since inflation is erratic and unpredictable, it is simpler to work in "real terms" or "constant dollars," adding only the higher interest costs of borrowing instead of using savings. Annual costs are 28 percent per year, whether that is 3 percent interest and 25 percent depreciation or 13 percent interest and 15 percent depreciation because there was a 10 percent inflation.

With older cars, the differences between buying and selling prices, and between market values and use values, lead to some unusual choices for families with more than one car. It would be good to have one fairly new, large, dependable car for trips and highway driving; but when that car gets old, trading it in for a smaller, used car to serve as the second car would save little or nothing. Yet buying another large new car leaves the family with two large cars. Even high gasoline prices do not change this situation appreciably. Indeed, a simple calculation will reveal that it is hardly ever worthwhile even to buy a new smaller economy car just to save on gasoline. The higher capital costs will swamp the savings in gasoline costs. Of

---

1. U.S. Department of Transportation, *Costs of Operating an Automobile* (Washington, D.C.: Government Printing Office, 1972).

2. See any National Auto Dealers Association *Official Used Car Guide* for wholesale and retail prices. The older the car, the wider the difference.

course, once trading is worthwhile, then selecting a smaller car saves depreciation, interest, and operating costs.

A possible alternative to a second car is public transportation. Whether public transportation will appear more advantageous in the future is hard to say. There are other costs and problems with public transportation, particularly the cost of the extra time taken in travel and waiting. It always seems that the bus arrives one minute before I get there and every fifteen minutes thereafter! A major deterrent to using public transportation is that once I own a car I need consider only the extra (marginal) cost of driving it to work. And if I pay for parking by the month or year, even that cost is not affected by one trip more or less. Only drastic measures such as a heavy tax on parking spaces and the use of the revenue to provide free, frequent public transportation would have a chance of altering our socially and economically inefficient but personally pleasurable driving habits. The air-conditioned car with automatic transmission makes the contrast with public transportation even more dismal.

When During the Year?

Almost peculiar to cars is the annual model year, with the emphasis on changing at least the exterior every year. Secondhand cars are sold largely by their model year with relatively little attention to how long they have actually been in use. This leads to some implications about the best time of year to buy a car.

A common advertising slogan is "Your old car will never bring as much on a trade-in as it does right now." What the ad does not say, of course, is that the price of a new one will also never be so high again, since it is also depreciating, and by *more* dollars per month. The actual bargained price on a new car is not constant, but falls gradually as the time of a new model's introduction approaches. The recent rapid inflation has caused car companies to raise the sticker prices of new cars several times during the model year, but the inflation-adjusted prices still fall during the year. Regardless of inflation, a car does not start wearing out until it is put in use. So should I buy late in the model year to save money, or early to get a lot of use out of the car before the new models drive down its price?

The answer depends on how long I intend to keep the car. If I keep it for ten years, its market value will be very small and will depend more on its condition than on its model year. So buying late in the model year will give me the same real service at lower initial cost. On the other hand, if I intend to trade in every few years, the model year is more important than mileage, or condition, or the length of time the car has been on the road. In that case, it pays to buy early in the model year, getting as much use as possible before new models reduce the price. To put it another way, end-of-model-year bargains reflect the market's style obsolescence, not a decline in use value. If style is what matters to an individual, those discounts are no bargain.

That the depreciation in market price reflects far more style obsolescence than physical depreciation, particularly with cars, means that those people willing to concentrate on the real services provided (transportation) can reduce their costs by keeping each car a long time, or by buying used cars after their market value has fallen well below their use value. There is always the risk of getting a bad car, and the cost of repairs is going up. Yet many of us consider the irritating and unpredictable repair expenditures to be much more important than they are. It pays to keep track of them to make sure perceptual distortion is not operating.

There are also choices as to how fancy a model to buy and with how many accessories and special features. Price differentials tend to overprice these "extras," a kind of price discrimination that allows those who have money to spend it. Comparing trade-in prices according to special features indicates that the price differential narrows; the extras depreciate faster than does the basic car. The standard remark often made is that the manufacturers make their profits on the accessories, and the dealers on the credit. (See chap. 6.)

Other Durables

Most smaller appliances and durables have little or no resale value, so their total cost is price plus operating costs; the cost per year depends on how long they last.

Benefits per year depend on how much they are used. One argument for a gas clothes dryer over an electric one is that the costs of each use are lower, so I am encouraged to use it more, so I get more benefits without affecting how long it lasts.

What can be said about a durable that costs twice as much and lasts twice as long (such as special auto mufflers)? In fact, they are roughly equivalent if you keep the durable for the longer time period. The depreciation and interest cost per year are identical and the average amount of money tied up is the same; the only difference is two trips instead of one to the muffler shop. But if I trade the car in, I may never need the second trip.

The largest potential difference in cost of appliances may well be in the differential likelihood of breakdown and the need for major repairs. In recent years, Consumers Union has been securing repair experience on cars and some major appliances from the readers of *Consumer Reports* and summarizing the results in the *Reports*. Even though the readers are above average in income, education, and probably critical acumen, the differences between brands should not be biased by that. There is the difficulty that data on two years of repair experience are available only on two-year-old models, which may differ from the current models. To reduce this problem, *Consumer Reports* also attempts to check whether major design changes have taken place.

We return in chapter 12 to problems of consumer information, and in chapter 11 to some strategies for shoppers. Of course, all such calculations may be outweighed by the lure of some new piece of equipment. A calculation of the number of likely days of use of a snowmobile per year times its expected life in years would reveal a rather expensive form of recreation for most owners. A tennis racket is likely to get more use, particularly with the explosion of indoor facilities.

Shopping around for durables is likely to pay off, particularly when combined with some watchful waiting, because dealers' margins are substantial, and there are sales. There is a tendency for the "best buys" reported in *Consumer Reports* to be difficult to find, and for the low-rated models to be available at greater discounts. What to look for is the best combination of price (low) and quality (high), assuming that "quality" can be compressed into a single dimension, as in figure 12. In really competitive markets,

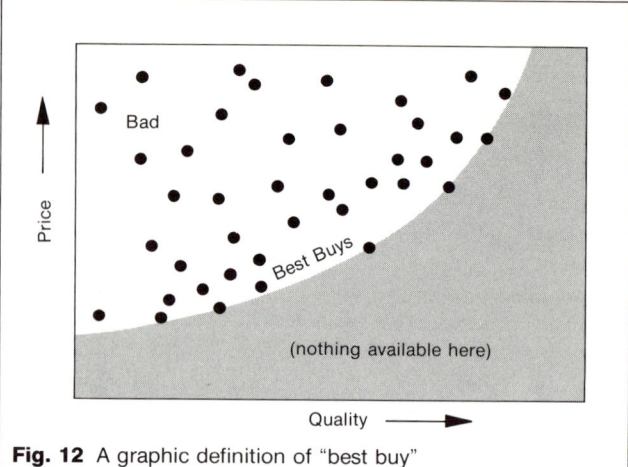

Fig. 12 A graphic definition of "best buy"

almost all the combinations of price and quality would fall along the "efficiency frontier" curve, and the consumer need only decide how much quality is worth paying for (Maynes). But in many markets there are some high-price, low-quality possibilities, which everyone wants to avoid. Once again, a few careful shoppers can improve the market for the rest of us, allowing the best buys to prosper and eliminating the bad buys.

Benefits

We have said little about estimating the benefits that durables provide, because in most cases they are so difficult to quantify that we can only set differential costs of alternatives against their differential benefits. But sometimes the benefits can be given an economic value. An appliance might save time, which can be valued at some hourly rate. It might also save money. One can evaluate a clothes dryer by computing the difference between its total costs and the present value of the savings in laundromat charges and time, and comparing that difference to the differential satisfaction and other benefits.

Some appliances or pieces of equipment require spending time as well as money for the benefits, e.g., television, recreation equipment, cars. On the other hand, some durables save time, by getting the same things done faster or more automatically, so you can do many things simultaneously. Most of the programmed appliances require little attention, so you can be cooking, washing and drying clothes, and playing with the children at the same time. Some appliances reduce planning time, increase flexibility to adapt to emergencies, or reduce necessary inventory. Pressure cookers and microwave ovens not only cut cooking time but allow last-minute changes. Clothes dryers vastly reduce the necessary inventory of clothing, towels, and sheets by cutting the time from dirty to clean to about an hour. On the other hand, a dishwasher increases the need for planning ahead to be sure that a needed item is not in the device waiting for the next load, and also increases the required inventory of dishes and cutlery if the machine is not to run half-empty. Of course, it increases the quality of the result—the dishes are sparkling and sterilized.

Sometimes the decision to own an appliance depends heavily on estimated use. A gas clothes dryer costs more to buy but less to operate than an electric clothes dryer. Obviously, the heavier the use over which the fixed (purchase) costs are spread, the greater the advantage of a gas dryer. Rising costs of energy mean that the best design for appliances like washing machines may change. In Europe, where electricity and hot water have always been much more expensive, washing machines are more complex and cost more to build and maintain, but are more economical in their use of hot water and electricity. They allow more alternation of agitation and soaking. With the United States government already requiring that consumers be given information about the energy demands of new appliances, manufacturers may well begin offering consumers a choice between the old models and newer models that cost more initially but save energy. The consumer must then calculate, on the basis of how much the machine will be used, which is the most economical, and then add other considerations such as more concern for future generations than even current high energy prices represent.

The economics of a food freezer are more complex. It reduces the number of required shopping trips, increases flexibility of planning and menus, and allows saving of leftovers. It is often touted as allowing stocking up on bargains. All these savings must be compared with the costs of the freezer—depreciation, interest, electricity costs, and possibility that a family might eat more expensive things by stocking up on luxuries. On the other hand, stocking up on bread and freezing it may reduce trips to the store and the impulse purchases that go along with them, and this might encourage greater use of staple foods. The whole issue of stocking up and of large-size economy packages depends on what it does to consumption as well as to costs (chap. 11).

A philosophical issue arises about benefits when a new appliance or piece of recreational equipment appears. If people find they cannot get along without it, are they better off than before? Or were they "brainwashed" by advertising or by their friends and neighbors? At the other end of the scale, the rapid style obsolescence and frequent upgrading of appliances leaves a supply of old, very cheap ones that are still serviceable, or could be with little work. Repairing an appliance is simpler than it once was, because whole components can be replaced. Repair people frequently suggest replacing an appliance when, with a few repairs, it will serve for many more years.

Shared Ownership or Renting of Durables

Some equipment is used only at rare intervals, and one way to reduce its cost is to share its ownership and use, particularly if the cooperators are not all likely to want to use it at the same time. Lawn mowers and sailboats are likely to be wanted by everyone on the same weekends. There can also be a problem of maintenance and repair, because "everybody's business is nobody's business." The group might well want to pay one member to be responsible for maintenance and repairs.

The organizational problems of owning things cooperatively are apparently larger than the economic and tax advantages. Commercial rental businesses have developed to take advantage of the economic efficiencies, renting power tillers, rug shampooers, power chain saws, party glassware, and hundreds of other rarely used appliances. There has always been a big rental market for such things as boats and summer homes. Some stores even lend a spreader when they sell lawn fertilizer, hiding the rent in the price of the fertilizer. This is still a bargain for the person who fertilizes his lawn once a year and does not have storage space for another piece of equipment.

Do-It-Yourself Repair and Maintenance of Appliances

Most modern appliances come with detailed parts lists and diagrams showing how they are put together. If you save these, it is often possible to locate the trouble, get at it effectively, and replace the offending parts. The cost of labor for diagnosis and repair is so high now that all the repair person generally does is replace whole components, even when only a small subcomponent is broken. In the case of cars, it is often possible to buy the component at a junkyard, or to get a rebuilt rather than a new one.

You can start to learn how to fix things and also avoid some frauds by watching the repair people and by keeping the replaced parts. Examination of the part can teach you exactly what went wrong and assure you that the repair person was not replacing parts just because it is fast and easy and because most people do not object to paying for new parts. It is easy to condemn repair services for replacing parts that were not bad, but a little thought will show that it might actually save money in wages to waste a little in parts. If it costs $16 just to get a repair truck to your house and $16 an hour for the truck and repair person, then putting in $10 worth of parts, only half of which were really needed, might be justified to save half an hour or a second trip.

An advantage of investing in your own skills in diagnosing and repairing is that since you are around when the trouble starts, you often have better information with which to diagnose the trouble and more time to experiment. Indeed, detailed knowledge of a particular appliance and why it stopped working may well allow less expensive repairs. You are less likely to replace a whole appliance when only a new pump motor is needed. Needless to say, it is possible to get in over your head, particularly with complex electronic equipment.

The surprising thing, considering the double taxation on the division of labor and the advantages of being able to fix things without waiting for a repair person, is that there is so little of this do-it-yourself activity. Division of labor and specialization apparently really do make people more efficient and productive. We return to the problem of the quality of repair work in chapter 12.

Additions and Repairs to the Home

Investing in home modernization or repairs involves the same economic calculation of a cost and comparing it with a benefit. The benefits are difficult to quantify but often last for many years and, even when discounted to a present value, can be very great. The costs are likely to involve substantial amounts of time, because there are complex problems deciding just what to do, even if you hire someone to do it, and problems of supervision. Hence, even apart from the advantages of the tax-free income from doing your own work, there is a saving of the cost of the communication and negotiation needed if you were to hire others to do the work. And some of the investment in learning how to do things, or how to get them done, can pay off in greater efficiency in later similar activities. One gets confidence in tackling new tasks, an ability to find out from library or friends or experts how to do it, and the proper balance between caution and courage in making decisions and acting. The best craftsmen are often so busy that they are happy to tell you how to do it yourself.

There are other sources of information. *Books in Print* lists well over a thousand books whose titles begin "How to . . ." and there are many more that will tell you about carpentry or electric wiring or drywall construction, and so on. They must be chosen carefully, because many such books tell you just enough to encourage you but not enough to keep you out of trouble or to allow you to do the job right. Local building codes exist, with the necessity for permits and inspections if the alteration or addition is extensive. Most inspectors are quite considerate of people who want to do things themselves; they even give advice. For very extensive work it may be wise to engage an architect on an hourly basis as a consultant to help with the original plan and even to draw some plans. Given most state laws about architects, however, it is unwise to contract with an architect for a whole job until hourly consultation has at least led to agreement on the plans and scope and a lot of confidence in a good working relationship. Otherwise, you may be obliged to pay the architect a percentage of the amount bid on the work even if it is not within your stated budget limits, the design is unacceptable, or the work is never done.

Additions to a home may or may not improve its sale value. If you intend to stay in the home for a long time, very idiosyncratic changes for your own needs may be worth it even if no buyer would appreciate them. Changes that bring a house up to modern standards—for instance, adding a second bathroom or a whole family room—may seem expensive but are the most likely to be recoverable in the sale price.

Sources of Information

Shopping is one obvious source of information on durables (chap. 11). There are various sources, discussed in chapter 12, of market information and background information on what to look for. There are manuals of used car prices, based on dealers' auctions and other information, giving retail, wholesale, and "loan value" prices on cars by make and year model, with adjustments for special equipment. Dealers do not like to share their copies of the National Automobile Dealers Association manuals of prices (which come out monthly, separately for each region of the country), but the more forthright ones will do so if pressed.

Product testing agencies like Consumers Union have also started reporting evidence on actual as against list prices for appliances, reflecting the confused nature of the market. Sometimes discounts reflect difficulty selling an item, or a manufacturer's policy in setting a published price, or the imminence of new models. For most appliances there is a range of models within each brand with different special features and different prices. It often seems to be the deluxe models that are discounted most. How is the consumer to decide whether the extra features are worth it? Some of the descriptions in the mail order catalogs are useful, but mostly it is a matter of personal judgment. If the washing machine has a way to save the wash water for a second load, will you have a tub to hold it, and is hot water supply enough of a problem so you would use it? Do you want to save on a dishwasher by omitting the feature that adds a wetting agent to the last rinse, and then have water spots on your glassware?

The price structure for smaller appliances is more complex than most people think. Besides the seasonal sales, there are "discount stores" that post "list prices" higher than they actually are, so that their "20 percent discount" is really closer to 10 percent. There are also catalog discount houses with no store costs, shipping from warehouses or even direct from the manufacturer at much larger discounts. This is common in specialties like hi-fi and camera equipment, and the ads usually appear in the specialty magazines. The guarantees are usually honored by the catalog houses, but you may have to ship a defective durable back and wait a long time for a replacement or refund. Some of what you pay for at a retail store—information, advice, and help in securing warranty repairs—may be worth it!

Information about quality and durability is harder to get than information on prices, and may be more important. A washing machine that lasts five years instead of ten and has twice as many repair bills is no bargain at half the price. The consumer may find it difficult to decide whether the fancier appliances are giving more durability and better service or merely special features and style. As mentioned earlier, *Consumer Reports* summarizes the experiences of its own readers with repairs and reports this regularly along with results of laboratory tests on cars and some major appliances.

You may wonder why there is not a detailed account here of some of the tricks used by sellers. It is not because they do not exist, but because they are endlessly varied and constantly changing. For the most part, they rely on carelessness, gullibility, or avarice on the part of the buyer. A modest amount of shopping and the knowledge that really big bargains are unlikely should go a long way. Students experimenting with the effects of shopping and bargaining report that simply standing and hesitating, or returning after visiting another dealer, often results in some recalculation of the price or special offer that lowers the price. They also report that sellers like to suggest alternative features, muddying up the price comparisons. Or they want you to believe the bargain will not remain available long enough for you to make sure it is a bargain. It is a great help to specify precisely what you want; otherwise, price comparisons get very difficult.

Two tricks, however, are so frequent that they deserve to be mentioned. "Bait advertising" means advertising a huge bargain that the store doesn't have, immediately runs out of, or resists selling, and then switching the customer to something "better." The classic example used to be the $29 used sewing machine. "Low balling" refers to offering a low price which is turned down by "the manager" after the customer is committed emotionally; it assumes that once committed you will stand still for another $100.

Whenever you run into the more extreme forms of "bait advertising" or "low balling" it pays to leave immediately and report it to the nearest Better Business Bureau.

There are special problems of low-income families in buying durable goods (Caplovitz). This is partly because of the combination of a need for credit and a poor credit rating, and partly because of their concentration in subsidized housing projects or slums and their isolation because of inadequate public transportation and language barriers. The studies made, however, deal with prices, not with profits of the sellers. Given the problems of stores in low-income areas, it is not at all certain that profits are higher there. On the contrary, stores tend to move out of such areas. While it remains true that low-income people do suffer from disadvantages in buying durables, these disadvantages are not *necessarily* accompanied by anyone's profit advantage but are dissipated in higher costs.

The Timing of Acquisitions

Assuming that I have applied the analysis of investment theory to estimate costs and benefits and to establish priorities for my purchases of durables, how do I space the acquisitions so as to avoid spending too much too fast? And how do I compare durables with the nondurable items of current consumption in terms of benefits? Is a Christmas trip to Mexico better than buying a canoe? How do I value my estimates of future joy from a canoe, or do I discount them heavily for uncertainty?

Survey data show that families spend substantial fractions of their incomes on cars, durables, and additions and repairs to houses, and that the proportion does not vary much with income or with age. By the time the family gets one of everything, it starts replacing things or finding new items that seem attractive. A safe estimate would be that 15 to 20 percent of income should be allocated for the durable goods capital account. Young married people have difficulty in pacing their acquisitions, as evidenced by the fact that a substantial fraction of personal bankruptcies occur when family income is rising but within a few years after marriage. Apparently the desire to acquire everything at once plus difficulty in coordinating two people's plans and desires leads to overcommitment.

The use of some budget total, plus some priority list to determine the order of acquisition, should be sufficient. We have already suggested (chap. 5) that the family might want to have a separate savings or checking account into which they put some fraction of their income and from which they purchase durables. By buying the next one only when the capital account showed sufficient cash, the family would be earning a little interest between purchases instead of paying interest (at a much higher rate) all their lives.

Household Behavior

The "minimum set" of household equipment is large and growing in the United States and elsewhere. As a result, the newly married find themselves scrambling to build up their stock, purchasing even during periods when rapid price rises or other problems have driven others out of the market. Another wave of buying occurs when the family buys its first house, since they not only acquire more space but now must own, rather than rent, several major appliances. A third surge occurs when people move, since they often move to larger quarters or use the move as an occasion to replace appliances. One might think that after the stock was accumulated, the expenditures on consumer durables would taper off, but there is no evidence that this is so, except at advanced ages and then only for renters (Morgan).

The economist's approach to the market for durables, cars, and houses once focused on "saturation," particularly after World War II when the backlog of several years of low production had to be made up. But saturation, even with appliances where you need only one, is a psychological, not a physical, phenomenon. The total market is involved, and sales of new durables require only that people all along the line upgrade their investments and that some at the very end of the line scrap the ones they replace. Furthermore, a substantial number of households have found use for a second or third of a substantial number of durable items.

For these reasons, the market for the output of new cars or durables is affected by the market for used ones and for second and third ones. To sell a new car usually requires that several used ones also be sold as they "trickle down." A better export market for very old used cars would rapidly increase the sales of new cars by reducing their net price (i.e., cost less trade-in) as the prices of used cars went up.

Households are not simply dividing their income between spending and saving. They divide it among spending for current consumption, investing in houses, cars, and appliances, and saving. One can think of many household decisions as decisions about whether to invest savings in financial assets (stocks, savings accounts) or in physical assets (cars, durables), the former offering money returns and the latter "real" returns. The amount people invest in durables is largely a result of how fast their aspiration levels rise and how confident they are about their own and the country's financial future.

If one includes in consumer investments their purchases of houses, now put in the business sector of the national accounts, the year-to-year variation in consumer investment is at least as large as the variation in business investment expenditures. The original macroeconomic formulation that households saved and businesses invested no longer fits the facts. Not only do households buy most of the national output, but the fluctuations in their purchases are also the largest and the hardest to predict. Business investments, on the other hand, have longer time lags, are decided upon more formally, and are more closely related to profits and competitive situations.

In countries with lower standards of living, consumer investments are less important and more a luxury. "Luxury" refers to something on which the proportion of income spent is much higher among high-income families. In the United States, however, consumer investments are neither necessity nor luxury—the proportion of income spent on them does not vary according to family income. If anything, it seems to fall at the very highest incomes, but only because the data exclude certain things like investments in summer cottages.

Summary

What this chapter has presented is a way of looking at the decision to acquire any item that will provide a stream of services in the future. If it were easy to reverse decisions and resell things, mistakes would be cheap, but very weak resale markets for most durables and high trading costs in money, time, and discomfort (delay, uncertainty), make some investment in improving decision making worthwhile.

Operating costs may matter, but the often neglected costs of depreciation and foregone interest often outweigh any differences in operating costs, particularly with larger items like cars and major appliances.

The benefits depend heavily on how much something is used. Some sharing can be extremely efficient for items that are durable, are rarely used, and where there is some flexibility as to just when they are needed. When needs are not flexible, renting has a lot to recommend it.

More Information?
There is frequent change in the design and quality of cars and durables, in addition to the stylistic model changes; prices and availability are even more variable. Some information, though not usually naming brand names, can be expected from the Consumer Product Safety Commission and the National Bureau of Standards, and even from the Army specifications for their purchasing. But the most useful quality information comes from consumer-run product testing organizations like Consumers Union, which publishes the monthly *Consumer Reports*.

A great deal of information, for the most part stressing only the positive, is in the articles and ads in various enthusiasts' magazines devoted to cars, hi-fi, trailers, motorcycles, or general mechanical interests, such as *Popular Mechanics*. The ads in these magazines and those in the *New York Times* by New York "wholesale" or "discount" stores provide some indication of the extent to which products are being discounted. Trade association publications are also useful.

The reading list which follows contains some behavioral studies, some "how-to" publications, and a few exposés of the abuses in the market.

Alchian, Armen A. *Economic Replacement Policy*. Santa Monica, Calif.: The Rand Corporation, 1952.
American Automobile Association. *Your Driving Costs, How to Figure*. Washington, D.C.: American Automobile Association (latest edition).
Auto Dealer Costs. Available by writing to Box 708, Dept. 94, Liberty, New York 12754. Latest edition.
Caplovitz, David. *The Poor Pay More*. New York: Macmillan, 1963.
Car Fax. New York: Fax Publications, latest edition.

Center for Auto Safety. *Small on Safety: The Designed-in Dangers of the Volkswagen*. New York: Grossman, 1972.

Consumer Reports Editors. *How to Buy a Used Car*. Mt. Vernon, N.Y.: Consumers Union, 1970.

Dialogue of Discovery: A Short Course in Homemaking Equipment and Techniques. Chicago: Association of Home Appliance Manufacturers, 1972.

Ferber, Robert. "Factors Influencing Durable Goods Purchases." In *Consumer Behavior*, vol. 2, edited by Lincoln Clark. New York: New York University Press, 1955.

Harberger, Arnold, ed. *The Demand for Durable Goods*. Chicago: University of Chicago Press, 1960.

Jackson, Charles R. *How to Buy a Used Car*. New York: Chilton, 1967.

Katona, George, and Mueller, Eva. "A Study of Purchase Decisions." In *Consumer Behavior*, vol. 1, edited by Lincoln Clark. New York: New York University Press, 1954.

Lansing, John, and Hendricks, Gary. *Automobile Ownership and Residential Density*. Ann Arbor: Institute for Social Research, 1967.

Lippitt, Vernon G. *Determinants of Consumer Demand for House Furnishings*. Cambridge, Mass.: Harvard University Press, 1959.

Magnuson, Sen. Warren, and Carter, Jean. *The Dark Side of the Marketplace*. Englewood Cliffs, N.J.: Prentice-Hall, 1968.

Maynes, E. Scott. *Decision-Making for Consumers*. New York: Macmillan, 1976.

Miller, Laurence H., Jr. "The Demand for Refrigerators: A Statistical Study." *Review of Economics and Statistics* 42 (1960): 196–202.

Morgan, James N. "Consumer Investment Expenditures." *American Economic Review* 48 (1958): 874–902.

Nader, Ralph. *Unsafe at Any Speed*. New York: Bantam Books, 1965.

Nader, Ralph; Dodge, Lowell; and Hotchkiss, Ralf. *What To Do with Your Bad Car*. New York: Grossman, Penguin, 1971.

National Automobile Dealers Association. *Official Used Car Guide*. McLean, Va.: National Automobile Dealers Used Car Guide Co. (Monthly regional reports on used car prices from wholesale auctions.)

Newman, Joseph W., and Staelin, Richard. "Prepurchase Information Seeking for New Cars and Major Household Appliances." *Journal of Marketing Research* 9 (1972): 249–57. (See Katona and Mueller)

Randall, Donald A., and Glickman, Arthur P. *The Great American Auto Repair Robbery*. New York: Charterhouse Books, 1972.

Suits, Daniel B. "The Demand for New Automobiles in the U.S., 1929–1956." *Review of Economics and Statistics* 40 (1958): 273–80.

Till, Anthony. *What You Should Know Before You Have Your Car Repaired*. New York: Signet Books, 1970.

U.S. Department of Transportation, Bureau of Public Roads. *Cost of Operating an Automobile*. Washington, D.C.: Government Printing Office, February 1970.

U.S. Department of Transportation, Federal Highway Administration, Office of Highway Planning, Highway Statistics Division. *Cost of Operating an Automobile* (Suburban-based Operation). Washington, D.C.: Government Printing Office, April 1972 (later editions possible). (Inadequate analysis)

U.S. General Services Administration. *Automobile Batteries, Their Selection and Care*. Consumer's Information Series no. 1. Washington, D.C.: Government Printing Office, November 1971.

U.S. National Highway Traffic Safety Administration, Department of Transportation. *What to Buy in Child Restraint Systems*. Washington, D.C.: Government Printing Office, December 1971.

Some Projects to Learn More

1. Select some appliance and find out all you can about brands, quality, prices, etc. Tour a major city, or write to a number of catalog houses, asking for prices. What can you find out about any difference in servicing, delivery, etc.? Is there any reason to believe that the manufacturer is dumping seconds or even rejects onto a discount market?

2. Take some major appliance and make a list of the special features and options which vary between or within brands. Can you estimate the price of each from the prices of the various combinations? Can you evaluate their value to the customer?

3. Go through two years' newspapers for some town checking for appliance sales. Are there regular sales? Are they getting rid of last year's models, or actually offering current models cheaper?

4. Visit a number of stores with a particular common appliance in mind, take your time, and hint a little to see whether there is any discounting going on. Are there price differences even for posted prices?

5. Estimate the prices and the operating cost per load of gas and electric clothes dryers in your area. Plot the cost per load at various levels of use (loads per year). At what use rate is the gas dryer cheaper?

6. Do car prices really depreciate 25 percent each year? Check some prices.

7. How much variation is there for the same make, model, and year car in prices asked; and do prices vary with condition, mileage, or tread left in the tires rather than randomly?

8. Compare new and used prices of vacation trailers, campers, tent trailers, tents, and camping buses. If you kept each for five years and sold it, how would the average yearly costs compare? Does it matter if you discount the resale value to the present (at 6 percent, multiplying by 0.747)? What other cost differences are involved (extra wear on the car pulling a trailer, extra equipment required with a tent)?

CHAPTER NINE
RISKS, INSURANCE, AND ESTATE PLANNING

Everyone at some time must make important choices about whether or not to buy the service called insurance, and about what types and combinations are the best. These choices involve substantial amounts of money and require sophisticated decision making. Fortunately, understanding a few simple principles vastly improves the chances of making the proper choices.

Some Principles

Life is full of uncertain events, some of them pleasurable, but many of them potentially destructive or unsettling in their effects. When the uncertainty is regular enough so that we can assign a probability of its happening during some period of time, it is called a risk. When such a probability is reasonably independent between individuals (i.e., when the event is not contagious or does not affect many people at the same time, unlike an atomic bomb or hurricane), then it becomes an insurable risk.

Insurance eliminates the risk for any one person by pooling it with the risks of large numbers of individuals. The insurance company itself bears almost no risk of loss and has ways of coping with what little risk is left, as we shall see. The elimination of risk is possible because our ability to predict probabilities accurately (e.g., the number of accidents or deaths or the amount of average loss) increases with the number of individuals exposed to that risk. Suppose we have an age group that, according to mortality tables, loses 2 percent to death each year. If we took one hundred people of that age, we should expect that two of them would die in a year. However, there is an appreciable chance (one in fifty) that five or more would die, a very large relative error. If an insurance company could increase the pool by selling policies to 10,000 people in that age group, then the chance that 500 or more (5 percent) will die drops from one in fifty to one in five hundred. (In general, the range of likely variation in the percent who die decreases with the square root of the number of policyholders.)

For the individual, then, insurance can be thought of as exchanging the possibility of a large loss for the certainty of a small cost (the insurance premiums). It is clear that insurance is worthwhile when the possible loss from one's own assets is intolerable. We can apply the traditional economist's argument against gambling here. That argument says that even a fair gamble at even odds is not a good idea because the value of money per dollar diminishes as one has more of it. Hence, the added utility from winning $10,000 may be less than the loss in utility from losing $10,000. So a 50-50 chance of winning or losing $10,000 has a negative value. In most insurable situations, a few not-so-valuable dollars spent on premiums provide compensation against losses so large that some of those lost dollars are much more important than the premium dollars. It is not only a matter of being unable to bear the entire loss, but also whether the cost per dollar of that loss is greater than the cost per dollar of the premium. To avoid the one chance in a thousand of losing my $50,000 house is worth more to me than a $50 insurance premium.

Major Risks

What are the major risks a household faces that might require insurance?

☐ A major earner might die too early, leaving dependents.
☐ You or your spouse might live longer than you anticipated, and exhaust your savings (see chap. 5).

☐ A major earner might become permanently disabled, requiring care for him or her and provision for dependents.
☐ A mother might become permanently disabled, requiring care for her and care of children.
☐ A child might become permanently disabled, requiring extra care, and for a much longer period than a child is normally dependent.
☐ The house or its contents might suffer from fire, theft, or other damage.
☐ The car might be damaged or stolen.
☐ You might be sued for damages to others done by your car.
☐ You might be sued for damages suffered by others on your property.
☐ Anyone in the family might require extensive medical care, including psychiatric treatment.

Decisions about insurance for these risks, however, must be made against a patchwork background of overlapping and confusing possibilities and programs. Some insurance is already provided by the Social Security system, by semivoluntary group insurance connected with some jobs, etc. In addition, some losses may be compensable through a civil suit (suing someone else) or through collecting from someone else's insurance company, or through worker's compensation. The problem of insurance, then, is to cover the worst holes in the patchwork of coverage you already have.

How Much Insurance?

Insurance is necessary when the possible loss from one's assets is intolerable. It may be desirable whenever a possible loss is not easy to plan and budget for. But how much insurance? If the possible loss, say of future income in the event of an earner's death or disability, is much greater than the amount that dependents would need to be comfortable, then insurance need cover only the latter, smaller amount. On the other hand, insurance should not attempt to provide more than the potential loss. If it did, the insured would be worth more dead to survivors than alive! Insurance companies do not like to insure for more than the amount of "insurable interest" for this very reason. Life insurance should at most make one's survivors financially indifferent to whether or not one dies; no more. The amount of insurance then should be the smaller of two amounts: the amount to be lost, or the amount required so that the loss does not create suffering.

A common misconception is that insurance decisions should depend on how probable the event is. Actually, neither the need for insurance nor the amount of insurance needed depends on that probability. This misunderstanding is one of the reasons people buy airplane trip insurance, feeling that because the probability of dying is a little higher, more insurance is called for. In fact, the probability has nothing to do with the amount of insurance needed, or with the decision whether to insure at all. If an unbearable loss is possible, beyond the capacity of other resources to cover it, then insurance is called for, provided it is available at reasonable rates. In fact, the cost of special short-term insurance like flight insurance only *appears* reasonable, because the period covered is so short that the probability of death is very low. The premiums cover a great deal of administrative and selling expense spread over very little insurance and also cover the possibility of adverse selection (people taking out insurance when the weather is bad). In fact, nearly three-fourths of the premium for flight insurance is expense and profit.

Availability

Reasonable insurance rates ought to reflect the amount to be paid if the insured event occurs, times the probability that it will occur, plus some additional amount to cover insurance company expenses and a reasonable profit. The following conditions should be met if insurance is to be available at reasonable rates.

1. *There is a clear definition of the event insured*. It is usually easy to define death; it is difficult to define mental illness and disability. Hence, the premium rates for the latter must allow for expensive claims investigation, and even perhaps some fraud, which makes them very high.

2. *There is efficiency and competition in the insurance business*. There are some clues as to the efficiency of the insurance company: What fraction of revenues is paid out each year in benefits? If it is less than half, meaning the expense-profit "loading" is more than half, that insurance is probably not a good buy. Other less conclusive clues are: Does the policy pay only if other sources do not, or

reclaim its payments from other sources? If so, it is valuable only if there are not other sources. Is it a fairly standard policy, so that price competition can operate, or highly differentiated by special options? Does it list what is covered rather than what is not covered? It is easy to exclude most of the real risks this way. The best policies cover everything *except* a specific list.

Policies of a type that is renewed regularly will have lower prices than those with high lapse records.

The individual company may have better rates if it sells mostly large economy-sized policies, has good experience and steady growth, and maintains a good balance between low expenses and good individual service.

Group policies avoid agents' fees, reduce administrative costs, may well be negotiated at advantageous rates, and may be an even greater bargain if an employer absorbs some of the costs.

3. *There is not adverse selection.* If only those people likely to collect the benefits carry the insurance, it is not a good buy for the average person.

4. *The probability of the event is not affected by the fact of insurance.* Are you more careless or more likely to be sued because you are insured?

5. *The cost of the event is not raised because you are insured.* Does the doctor or hospital charge more because you are insured? Do auto repairs cost more when insurance pays? Or will the doctor keep you in the hospital longer when he or she knows it does not cost you anything?

6. *The risk is the same for you as for others in your insurance rate group.* Are you a better driver than most, or younger than most of those in a group life insurance group with fixed premium independent of age? If so, you are paying for others' higher risks.

7. *The cost is as high for you as for others.* If you can repair your own car or get a discount on doctor bills, the loss to you would be less than what it would cost the insurance company.

8. *The cost of repairing the damage is not more than the loss.* If your car is so old it would not pay to fix it if it were damaged, why pay for insurance that provides for such payments? You might enjoy getting the insurance money and using it for something else, but you would be insuring the car for more than it is really worth. Dents reduce use value and even trade-in value by less than the cost of repairing them perfectly.

Even "unreasonable" rates can be worth paying, however. In spite of the many ways in which insurance is priced above the actuarial value of the possible loss, it may still be desirable, particularly for the largest, unbearable losses.

The largest total losses possible are certainly those resulting from the permanent disability, mental or physical, of a main wage earner, since they involve extensive extra outlays for medical care as well as the loss of earnings. Yet difficulties in defining the condition of permanent disability, and the fact that insurance itself may affect probabilities and costs, make it impossible to insure adequately for these risks. A floor is provided by Social Security benefits for the permanently and totally disabled, covering a fraction of the income loss but none of the medical bills. If the disability is the result of a work injury, the employer's worker's compensation insurance may cover extensive medical costs and some fraction of income loss. But attempts to cover the remaining risk by private insurance are unlikely to be successful. Insurance companies are still wincing from their experience in the depression of the 1930s when a man could get more in disability payments than he could earn.

Life Insurance Needs

When is life insurance called for? When there is some stream of expected earnings that could stop and there are dependents who are counting on part of the future stream for their support. Nonmoney "earnings" from housework and child care are to be included too; we are discussing both parents' insurance needs here.

How much life insurance is called for? Recall that the amount needed is the smaller of two amounts: the amount to be lost, or the amount needed to prevent financial hardship to survivors. In most cases, the smaller of these two will be the needs of dependents, so it is not usually necessary to insure against the loss of the total future stream of earnings. Some part of those earnings would have been consumed by the deceased, and the remainder may well be larger than the dependents need—after other sources of support are considered, especially Social Security survivors' benefits. The needs of dependents, then, should be the basis for calculating life insurance needs. Since these

Table 16. Some Interest and Annuity Figures
(interest rate = 3 percent)

n	Present Value of $1/Yr. for n Years	Present Value of $1 Available in n Years	Accrued Value of Payment of $1/Yr.	Annual Payment, Accrued Value = $1 in n Years	n	Present Value of $1/Yr. for n Years	Present Value of $1 Available in n Years	Accrued Value of Payment of $1/Yr.	Annual Payment, Accrued Value = $1 in n Years
1	.97	.971	1.0	1.000	35	21.49	.355	60.46	.0165
2	1.91	.943	2.03	.4926	36	21.83	.345	63.28	.0158
3	2.83	.915	3.09	.3235	37	22.17	.335	66.17	.0151
4	3.72	.884	4.18	.2920	38	22.49	.325	69.16	.0144
5	4.58	.863	5.31	.1883	39	22.81	.316	72.23	.0138
6	5.42	.837	6.47	.1545	40	23.11	.307	75.40	.0133
7	6.23	.813	7.66	.1345	41	23.41	.298	78.66	.0127
8	7.02	.789	8.89	.1124	42	23.70	.289	82.02	.0121
9	7.79	.766	10.16	.0984	43	23.98	.281	85.48	.0117
10	8.53	.744	11.46	.0872	44	24.25	.272	89.05	.0112
11	9.25	.722	12.81	.0780	45	24.52	.264	92.72	.0108
12	9.95	.701	14.19	.0704	46	24.78	.257	95.50	.0104
13	10.63	.681	15.62	.0640	47	25.02	.249	100.40	.0100
14	11.30	.661	17.09	.0585	48	25.27	.242	104.41	.0096
15	11.94	.642	18.60	.0538	49	25.50	.235	108.54	.0092
16	12.56	.623	20.16	.0496	50	25.73	.228	112.80	.0088
17	13.17	.605	21.76	.0460	51	25.95	.221	117.18	.0085
18	13.75	.587	23.41	.0427	52	26.17	.215	121.70	.0082
19	14.32	.570	25.12	.0398	53	26.37	.209	126.35	.0079
20	14.88	.554	26.87	.0372	54	26.58	.203	131.14	.0076
21	15.42	.538	28.68	.0349	55	26.77	.197	136.07	.0073
22	15.94	.522	30.54	.0327	56	26.97	.191	141.15	.0071
23	16.44	.507	32.45	.0308	57	27.15	.185	146.39	.0068
24	16.94	.492	34.43	.0290	58	27.33	.180	151.78	.0066
25	17.41	.478	36.46	.0274	59	27.51	.175	157.33	.0064
26	17.88	.464	38.55	.0259	60	27.68	.170	163.05	.0061
27	18.33	.450	40.71	.0245	65	28.45	.146	194.33	.0051
28	18.76	.437	42.93	.0232	70	29.12	.126	230.59	.0043
29	19.19	.424	45.22	.0221	75	29.70	.109	272.63	.0037
30	19.60	.412	47.58	.0210	80	30.20	.094	321.36	.0031
31	20.00	.400	50.00	.0200	85	30.63	.081	377.86	.0026
32	20.39	.388	52.50	.0190	90	31.00	.070	443.35	.0023
33	20.77	.377	55.08	.0181	95	31.32	.060	519.27	.0019
34	21.13	.360	57.73	.0173	100	31.60	.052	607.79	.0016

needs are spread over many years into the future, it is necessary to estimate their present value—the amount required at death to assure such a future stream of support for dependents. Future needs must be discounted to present values, but at what interest rate? As elsewhere, we can use a relatively low rate of discount, 3 percent, on the argument that a rate of return any higher would imply an inflation that would erode everything but 3 percent; the real value of assets rises only by about 3 percent per year, on average.

Generally, the amount of life insurance needed is the present value of the dependents' needs less the other financial resources available to cover those needs. Besides the Social Security benefits, accumulated savings and other assets are also available, and these increase with the age of the insured. Needs vary too, depending upon normal living expenses, educational goals for the children, and the one-time costs associated with the death of the insured—funeral and burial expenses, taxes, and legal expenses.[1] How, then, can we calculate the amount of life insurance required?

In a childless household where husband and wife both work and neither depends on the other's income, there seems no purpose in life insurance on either spouse, unless one or both gave up some career plans on a promise of shared accumulation of assets. But if there is a child or children, one or both parents must devote time to them, a great deal for the first five or six years, somewhat less for the next twelve to fifteen years. If one partner stays home to take major responsibility for the children, it may be difficult for her or him to find a good job even after the children are gone. (Furthermore, if a surviving spouse does go to work, he or she loses Social Security survivors' benefits, though not the benefits for the children.) Thus, there is a need to insure against the difference between what the survivor could earn and the total needs of the survivor and dependents.

There are, crudely, three periods of need for a family with children: one when there are children to care for, offset by some Social Security survivor's benefits; a second after the children have gone but before the survivor is sixty-two, during which period the survivor can work but gets no Social Security survivors' benefits; and a third when the survivor is too old to work but can get Social Security survivors' benefits. Of course, there are possibilities that the needs will be met by the remarriage of the surviving spouse, or with help from the earnings of children; but most partners are likely to want to provide enough to allow the survivor independence.

Surprisingly, the net yearly amounts for these three periods of need are likely to be very similar. Suppose that the total needs amount to $10,000 per year. If Social Security in the first period, earnings in the second, and Social Security again in the third are about $4,000, then unmet needs are $6,000 per year. How much would it take to provide $6,000 a year for a survivor now aged twenty until death? The answer depends upon the interest rate used and also upon assumptions about expected length of life. As before, we use our 3 percent interest rate rule. Life expectancy is not a serious problem; the risk of living too long can be reduced by purchasing a lifetime annuity that provides a constant stream of income until death.

We can illustrate the calculations by assuming an expected lifetime of, say, seventy-six years for a woman at age twenty.[2] The present value of $6,000 needed n years from now at an interest rate of r is $\$6,000/(1 + r)^n$, but it is not necessary to do fifty-six (76 − 20) such calculations because tables of the present value of a stream are available. Table 16, second column, gives the present value of $1 per year for n years at 3 percent. (This reproduces some of the information in appendix 2.1 but adds to it and consolidates it in one place.) Table 17 gives selective present value information at various interest rates. We can tell that $6,000 per year for fifty-six years has a present value (cost) of 26.97 × $6,000, or $161,820.

Table 17. Present Value of $1/Year at Various Interest Rates, for Various Numbers of Years

Years of Payment	$r = 2\%$	$r = 3\%$	$r = 4\%$	$r = 5\%$	$r = 6\%$	$r = 7\%$
10	$ 8.98	$ 8.53	$ 8.11	$ 7.72	$ 7.36	$ 7.02
20	16.35	14.88	13.59	12.46	11.47	10.59
30	22.40	19.60	17.29	15.37	13.76	12.41
40	27.36	23.11	19.79	17.16	15.05	13.33
50	31.42	25.73	21.48	18.26	15.76	13.80
60	34.76	27.68	22.63	18.93	16.16	14.04

---

1. For a useful "worksheet" approach to calculating insurance needs, see Consumers Union, *The Consumers Union Report on Life Insurance*.

2. At age sixty-five, a woman has an expected life of about eighty-two years. The lower number at age twenty allows for some mortality before sixty-five, and for the better health of the survivors.

Notice several things about compound interest and streams from these tables: The present value of long streams is considerably less than the total amount, even at a 3 percent interest rate. Second, a few more years added to the end of a long stream do not make much difference, so mistakes of a year or two about expected life are not crucial. For example, the present value of $6,000 for fifty-seven years is only $1,100 more than the present value of $6,000 for fifty-six years. Another way to see the same point is to look at the third column of table 16, which gives the present value of a single sum of $1 payable n years hence, discounted at 3 percent; it falls to $.492 when n equals twenty-four years, to $.185 when n is fifty-seven years, and to $.094 when one must wait eighty years.

In the case of two working parents, the survivor becomes a dependent only because there are children, but we have not provided explicitly for the children's needs. Here, the major question is whether it is planned to send them to college. In any case, but particularly if the answer is yes, the yearly needs of the children get larger each year until they leave home: they eat more, wear out more clothing, require more housing space, etc. In cases where amounts needed vary, it is necessary to discount each year separately and add, but some simplification can be achieved by taking subsets of years. Suppose, for instance, that for each child we allow $1,000 per year for the first four years; $1,500 per year for the next four (ages 5–8); $2,000 per year for the next four (9–12); $3,000 per year for the next four (13–16); and $5,000 per year for the next four (17–20). The present value of each of these four-year streams can be estimated by first calculating its value at the beginning of the four years by multiplying by 3.72 (using the second column of table 16) and then discounting that value back to the present using the third column of table 16. For example, $3,000 a year for four years at 3 percent has a value at the start of the four-year period of $11,160 ($3,000 × 3.72), but that sum is not needed for thirteen years. The present value of $11,160 thirteen years from now is $7,900 (0.681 × $11,160). The same method can be used to calculate the present value of the need for each of the other four-year periods, and for calculating the surviving parent's needs if they differ between periods.

The Family Life-Cycle Pattern of Needs

At any point in time, the sum of the needs of the surviving parent and each child gives the amount needed to assure support of dependents if one spouse were to die at that point in time. But what happens to insurance needs as both parents survive each additional year? Obviously, the needs go down, because each year completed is one less year of obligation to worry about. But it is not correct to assume that the insurance needed drops each year by the amount that dependents would have required for that year. This is because all the other sums needed in the future are a year closer and consequently have a higher present value. To see this, let us return to our example of a $6,000 annual need for fifty-six years, which had a present value of $161,820. Successfully negotiating one additional year reduces the period of need by one year to fifty-five years, but the present value of $6,000 for fifty-five years is only $1,200 less than the present value of that amount for fifty-six years. So for a constant amount each year, one can think of dropping the most distant year, and the present value drops, not by the yearly amount, but by that amount divided by $(1 + r)^n$.

This does not mean that the drop in needs each year is unimportant enough to be ignored, however. The annual amounts are large, particularly during the early years when support is also needed for children, so the total amount of insurance needed drops by a substantial amount with each year successfully negotiated without death. As we shall see, it its possible to purchase insurance protection which decreases over time to match the decreasing pattern of needs.

It is sometimes suggested that the amount needed does not really drop each year, because of inflation or because family standards of living go up. We have already taken account of the first of these by using a low discount rate. Inflation will raise future living costs but will also increase the rate of return to the investment of death benefits by one's survivors. The second can be allowed for in calculating the amounts needed at later points in time, but it is unlikely that any adjustment in standards would reverse the overall tendency for the total amount of insurance needed to drop with each succeeding year.

Insurance needs depend upon total income needs of survivors, but they fall as other sources of income increase. The only other source we have taken account of is Social Security, but most families accumulate company pension rights and other assets. While these assets may be intended to supplement Social Security retirement benefits, they are available to support the survivor if one partner dies before retirement. *Any savings program that will accumulate enough to support a husband and wife in retirement will have sufficient funds long before the date of retirement to provide for a widow or widower.* (This assumes as is almost universally true, that any company retirement plan turns over the accumulated contributions and interest to the survivor if the person dies before retirement. It also assumes that the worker has the wisdom to arrange the retirement annuity so that about two-thirds of it continues to the survivor so long as she or he lives.) The implication is that the provision for the risk of living too long also helps provide for the risk of dying too early, and *the net need for insurance drops to zero several years before expected retirement age*. How can this be true when the surviving spouse has years more to live (particularly a wife, who is likely to be younger and has a longer life expectancy)? Because by then the other accumulated savings and rights will be sufficient to take care of the survivor.

The implication of accumulating assets for insurance planning is that the decrease with each passing year in the amount of insurance needed is accentuated by any amounts saved during that year plus the accumulated interest (and employer contributions) to those amounts. If the need for insurance begins when the first child is conceived, reaches its maximum amount when the last child is conceived, and drops to zero by, say, age sixty, then what is needed is an insurance policy or policies which provide this kind of lifetime pattern of insurance coverage. Notice that the Social Security survivors' benefits are in this form—so much per year for the period of need.

Life Insurance Needs for Equal Spouses

The whole set of assumptions about financial responsibility for children and surviving spouse needs careful reexamination, partly because the world is changing—more women working, more men taking day-to-day caring as well as financial responsibility for children—and partly because we have all been guilty of undervaluing housework and child care. Families today vary from the old stereotype of a male earner and female housekeeper to the new, rarer, partnership of two who share everything equally, including child care, housework, and regular jobs.

We have already looked at the insurance needs of the first kind of family. Now we will plan an insurance strategy for the equal partnership.

If two parents contribute equal dollar value of work to a family, whatever the mixtures of money and nonmoney, what would a surviving spouse need to maintain the family standard of living? The total real income is cut in half, by one partner's death, the needs cut by the value of the needs of one adult. In general, eliminating one adult cuts the cost of living by more than one-fourth and less than one-third, and cuts income by less than half after income taxes. But because income taxes ignore nonmoney earnings, they fall more when the loss is in money earnings; the survivor may want to switch from work at home to work in the marketplace, too.

The question is how much the parent was contributing to the family in money and work, how much of that would need to be replaced somehow, and what sources of help other than life insurance could be counted on. Social Security is one, lower income taxes another. It might seem that a woman's longer life expectancy would call for more insurance on the husband; but her better treatment as surviving parent under current Social Security law works the other way, so the really modern equal partnership probably needs roughly equal amounts of life insurance on each parent. The insurance should provide, with Social Security and other income from assets, a total family income of about two-thirds of what the income would have been with both partners alive. This means replacing one-third to one-half of the deceased's expected income.

What kind of contractual commitment might embody the implied financial responsibility of each parent to the children? Two eventualities need to be covered: death or departure. The analysis above indicates the amount of insurance required in case of death; this kind of a plan can take advantage of Social Security survivors' benefits and other resources. Divorce or departure requires more extensive compensation, because there is no Social Security or life insurance available. In this case, the amount required for equal protection would be the required life insurance plus the present value of the Social Security survivors' benefits. Since both are based on amounts per month for the remainder of a period, the commitment could be expressed as some amount per month for the remainder of the period until the children are all grown, or so much per month for each child until the child is twenty-one. This would leave the spouse who takes responsibility for the children with flexibility and freedom to work for money or not, and would provide for the children should both parents die or depart.

Such an arrangement is not as comprehensive as a national tax-all-parents-and-supoort-all-children policy (see chap. 3), but we need not wait for that possibility. Given the residual inequities in our laws and customs, a woman in particular would be well advised to insist on such a protective commitment from a man for each child they have. And if it is true that the number of women deserting families is increasing, a man might want a similar commitment from his equal partner.

Types of Life Insurance

Figure 13 depicts life insurance needs that begin with the conception of the first child, are maximized with the conception of the last child, and decline to zero before retirement age. What types of policies are best to meet these needs? There are two general types available from insurance companies—term insurance and cash value insurance. Term insurance provides pure life insurance: If you die, your survivors receive the "face value" of the insurance policy; if you do not die, then you and your dependents receive nothing. Cash value insurance combines pure insurance with savings. The "face value" of the policy is paid to your survivors if you die. But also a savings fund accumulates during the life of the policy so you and your dependents can receive an increasing fraction of the face amount ("cash surrender value") if you choose to cancel the coverage. "Whole life" is the most widely sold form of cash value insurance.

Term Insurance

Term insurance is pure insurance with no savings mixed in. It can be purchased for one-year, five-year, ten-year, or longer intervals. Rates rise with renewal because you are older and can expect higher mortality. By paying a higher premium, one can guarantee that the term insurance can be renewed for another term, regardless of one's health. The amount of insurance provided by term insur-

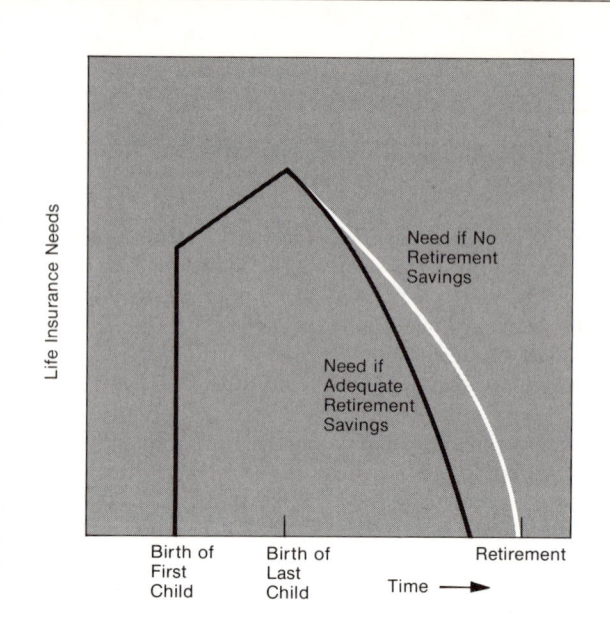

Fig. 13 Life-cycle insurance needs in a family with children. Life insurance needs are here defined as present value of needs of dependents less assets and Social Security benefits.

ance need not be constant each year. *Decreasing term* insurance, as the name implies, provides a decreasing pattern of coverage. It is the exact analogue to the Social Security survivors' provisions for wife and dependent children; both provide a stream of benefits from time of death until the end of a period. The amount of insurance in a term policy is simply the present value of the stream, so it drops with each passing year as the period to be covered gets shorter and shorter. The premiums can be kept constant during the term because the decreasing amount of insurance for the most part offsets the rising probability of dying, small accumulated reserves offsetting discrepancies.

Some combination of such decreasing term policies can provide exactly the pattern of insurance each year that is needed for a family, leaving them to accumulate their savings some other way, more flexibly and with a better hedge against inflation. To cover the changing needs spelled out in our earlier example, one policy for each spouse, providing $6,000 per year for the remainder of the forty-year period, plus one for each child providing for a twenty-year period, would be sufficient. The amounts (present values) in such policies are pictured in figure 14. Why only forty years for the spouse? Because forty years from now you will have reached age sixty, and other accumulated assets plus Social Security should have become sufficient to take care of one spouse. After all, they were

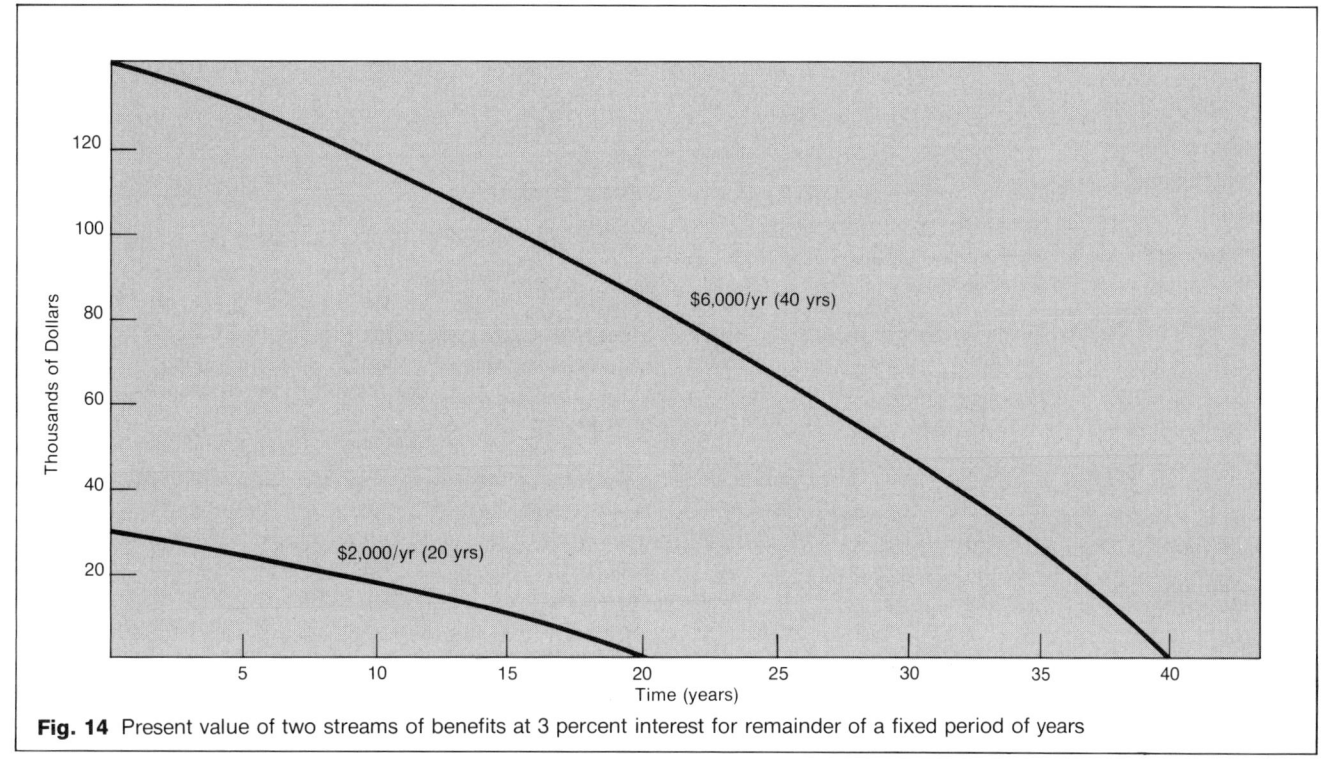

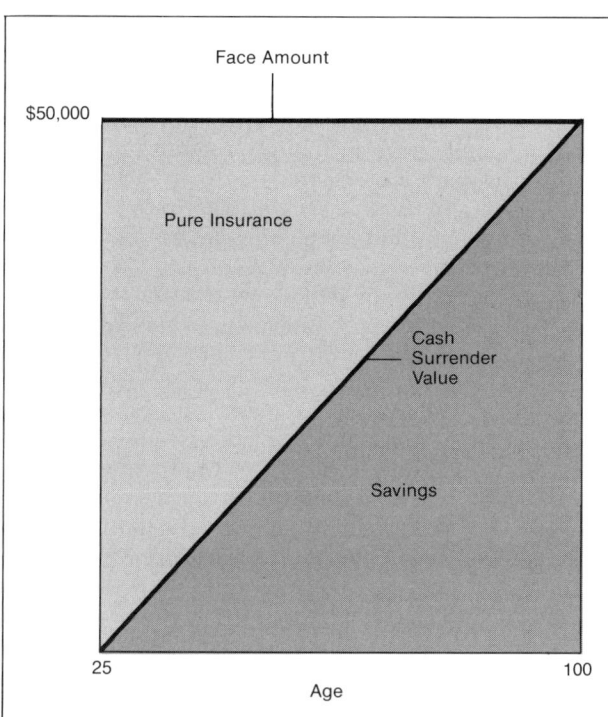

Fig. 14 Present value of two streams of benefits at 3 percent interest for remainder of a fixed period of years

Fig. 15 Insurance and savings in a whole life insurance policy

accumulated to take care of two people, and only one is left! Remember, the stream of net needs may be sixty years long at the beginning, but drops to zero in forty years.

There may be some situations where heavier needs are expected some years hence, leading to a total need that does not decline much for several years. Renewable level term policies are available to meet this pattern.

Whole Life Insurance

A typical pattern of whole life coverage is shown in figure 15. In this case, the face amount is $50,000, the coverage extends from age twenty-five to age one hundred (when the entire face amount is paid to the policyholder), and the cash surrender value increases throughout the life of the policy. A crucial fact is that the amount of insurance provided by the policy is not the face amount of the policy. Rather, it is the difference between the face amount and the cash surrender value, since the latter is available to you even if you don't die. A great many conceptual errors about life insurance can be avoided by keeping that fact constantly in mind.

The fact becomes clearer if seen from the company's point of view. The aggregate amount they must charge the policyholders as a whole to pay for each one who dies is the face value of the policy minus the reserve, which is the policyholder's own money. The policy has a declining amount of insurance each year, made up for by the policyholder's own accumulated savings plus interest, as seen in figure 15. Does the declining pattern of insurance match the declining pattern of insurance needs faced by most people? Unfortunately not, because the amount of insurance needed drops by far more than these accumulated savings go up. So even if one were willing to have all his savings tied up in a life insurance policy, most policies do not provide the needed pattern of protection. Besides, most people want some of their savings in the form of equity in their house, others want some in more accessible form, like saving accounts, while others want theirs in investments that are more likely to increase in value with inflation. A whole life policy is used as a forced saving program by many, but the money saved through a whole life policy is not likely to earn as high a return as it would if it were invested elsewhere. And, anyway, the *pattern* of insurance provided is not optimal.

Another way to look at policies that combine insurance with savings is to see what happens each year in the life of such an insurance policy. Policyholders make two kinds of payments—an explicit premium payment and, implicitly, the interest earned by the insurance company by investing policyholders' reserves. These amounts are used to cover four kinds of costs to the insurance company:

1. The pure cost of the pure insurance, paid out to the survivors of those policyholders who died. This amount is roughly the probability of dying times the face value minus the cash value.
2. Expenses (including agents' fees) and profits of the insurance company (roughly 20 to 30 percent).
3. Increase in the policy reserve and in the cash surrender value.
4. If the policy is a "participating policy," there is a dividend payment to the policyholder from the company. This, of course, is paid for by the policyholders in the first place. A dividend, then, refunds some of the excess premiums.

A variety of whole life insurance policies is offered, differing chiefly in the rate at which a reserve is accumulated and in the amount the insurance is reduced each year. Ordinary life insurance policies may become "paid up" at age eighty-five, or sixty-five, or in twenty years. "Paid up" means that the reserve is large enough that the interest earned on it is sufficient, without additional premiums, to cover three of the four items just mentioned: the pure cost of the pure insurance, the expenses and profits, and the continued increase in the reserve. The term "paid up" means no more premiums are required, but it is misleading, because the policyholder is still paying, in the form of the interest that the company is earning on his or her own money.

The sooner a policy is to be "paid up," the larger the premiums must be so that the excess can increase the reserve and thereby decrease the amount of actual insurance (and thus, the pure cost of the pure insurance). And the earlier the *age* at which the policy must be paid up, the smaller the total accumulated reserve must be, because the probability of dying is lower. The real cost of insurance is not affected by any of this. It depends on the amount of pure insurance, the probability of dying, and the company's expense-and-profit loading—not on the amount of saving built into the policy. *It is crucial to keep in mind that the premiums are not the only cost of the policy and that the face value is not the amount of insurance.*

Some policies do not just become "paid up" but can be cashed for the face amount after a specified period, sometimes as short as twenty years. These are called endowment policies and simply have such huge premiums that by the end of twenty years the accumulated reserve is equal to the face value, and there is no real insurance at all. Policies taken out on children to provide for their college education are of this sort. They combine a saving program with insurance that drops to none by the time the money is needed for college.

The crucial point about all cash value policies is not that they combine insurance with savings but that they do it so rigidly. The only way the amount of insurance is reduced over time is by building up an equal offsetting savings reserve. To meet this objection, some insurance companies offer "family income" or "mortgage protection" policies which combine the usual ordinary life insurance with decreasing amount of pure insurance. A few have gone the whole way, providing straight decreasing term insurance ("income protection").

There are a variety of other special provisions in whole life insurance policies, but they are largely selling devices and methods of making it difficult to compare prices. Each provision has an actuarial value that is often difficult to estimate. Some are totally unjustified.

"Mortgage protection" policies, for example, add to the face value of the life insurance an amount equal to the remaining mortgage on the house. But what is there about a mortgage that changes the amount dependents would need for their support? Nothing. This is just one example of the folly of insuring bits and pieces, or treating some needs as different from others, rather than insuring to cover the total need. For a small added sum one can have a "disability waiver of premium" clause, which continues the policy without further premiums if the insured should become permanently and totally disabled. This is not a proper disability insurance policy, but only the small amount of disability insurance needed to pay the life insurance premiums. But what is the point in carrying life insurance on someone permanently and totally disabled? Unless a disability insurance policy replaces some of the lost earnings, there is no longer a stream of future income that will stop if the person dies. Indeed, a stream of *costs* will end if the person dies; the survivors, sad to say, would be better off economically if the person did die. It would make more sense to cash in the policy in the event of disability, unless one felt certain the person would die shortly. But that would be gambling, not insurance, and only emphasizes that keeping such insurance makes the person "worth more dead than alive."

For other (nonproducing) family members, there is no point in life insurance. If children were really expected to repay their parents' "investment" by supporting them later, life insurance on the children might make sense. But the loss occasioned by the death of a child is usually emotional, not economic. Yet many poor families carry insurance on everyone in the family or, worse still, everyone except the main earners. A small amount might be justified as burial insurance, but even this violates the principle that the cost of the event should not be increased by the fact of insurance. Funerals tend to cost what the insurance will pay.

Evidence on Life Insurance Costs

Despite vast assemblages of published details about premiums, dividends, and cash values, the complexities of policies make it difficult to compare prices (Belth, 1966). The prices of cash value insurance policies are especially difficult because those policies combine insurance protection and a return on savings. It is impossible to price both simultaneously. One can make assumptions about the return on savings and then calculate the implied price of protection. "Twenty-year net cost" figures exemplify this method, assuming a zero interest rate. "Interest-adjusted costs" assume some rate like 5 percent. The alternative is to calculate the return on savings after making assumptions about the price of the pure insurance. Prices of term insurance are used for this purpose. Although the interest-adjusted cost and return-on-savings methods produce a similar ranking of actual insurance policies (Belth, 1968), the rate of return calculation would seem to be more useful to consumers, who can then compare that return with the return on alternative financial investments.

Twenty-year net cost is arrived at by taking the premiums for twenty years, subtracting estimated dividends (based on past experience or on the present rates), and then subtracting the cash surrender value at the end of the period. It should be clear that this is not a true cost estimate, because the interest earned on the reserve has been omitted. This becomes obvious sometimes when the twenty-year net cost comes out negative! Furthermore, even for the same kind of policy, it is easy to make the net cost figure low by charging slightly higher premiums and thereby accumulating a larger reserve, which earns more interest *and* reduces the pure insurance costs by reducing the amount of real insurance. One can also make net costs look low by paying no dividends for the first two years, which has the same effect without even making the premiums higher. Note that such rapid accumulations of reserves do double duty: they not only earn interest but also reduce the amount of benefits that must be paid out of premiums, because each death benefit has a larger component of the policyholder's own money.

In response to objections to the ignoring of interest in twenty-year net cost comparisons, interest-adjusted cost indexes were developed, tested for consumer acceptance by the Federal Trade Commission, and are published annually by the National Underwriter Company (Gaines and Casson). The particular interest rate used will, of course, affect the absolute and even relative insurance cost estimates of the individual companies. The use of 5 percent for 1979 when market interest rates were 6 to 12 percent clearly makes the insurance look cheaper than it is, and makes insurance policies with larger saving features look better than others. Indeed, the complexity of policies with saving features and dividends allows a variety of manipulations to make them look cheaper, and a continuing battle goes on within the industry about this, particularly through the efforts of Joseph M. Belth and his publication, *The Insurance Forum*.[3]

The insurance cost-adjusted interest rate on the savings in the policy is the alternative way of pricing cash-value insurance policies, less subject to manipulation and more understandable to the consumer. Such estimates of return on the savings element in cash-value life insurance were proposed many years ago by M. Albert Linton. Recent discussion suggests that even they can be misleading unless carefully interpreted (Belth, 1968). But most such studies reveal rates of return that are generally, but not always, smaller than passbook savings account rates, particularly over short periods and for older nonparticipating policies taken out when interest rates were lower. (Interest earned on insurance policies escapes income tax, so these calculated rates of return on savings are comparable to the after-tax rates of return of alternative investments.)

A recent staff report of the Federal Trade Commission (FTC, 1979) reaches very negative conclusions about the pricing practices of insurance companies. They include:

The life insurance industry is a major repository of consumer savings, holding over $140 billion in 1977. Yet in 1977, the industry paid its policyholders less than 2 percent on their savings in a year when the rate of inflation was around 10 percent and in which all other savings institutions were paying higher rates. Life insurance companies paying 2 percent *after twenty years* compete successfully against companies paying 5 percent. Penalties for early withdrawals are remarkably severe but unannounced. We recommend that the life insurance industry be required to disclose the rate of return and several other items of information to their policyholders in a simple and effective manner. Price competition can only be effective when some significant fraction of the market is *able* to compare prices, and this is what the disclosure system is designed to do. (U.S. Federal Trade Commission, p. 182.)

The report points out that the rate depends on how long one holds a policy since various administrative costs are being spread over various numbers of years, but chides the companies for ignoring the service charges entirely when announcing rates of return on annuities. It also points out that the profits of the insurance industry have not been excessive. This raises the question of how more price competition would produce a net benefit for all consumers. Presumably, the improvement would result partly from consumers making better choices to meet their own needs, but largely from driving out inefficient companies and forcing increases in efficiency on the rest. The report also points out that federal regulations have kept interest rates paid by banks and savings and loan associations down to 5 and 5.25 percent when open market interest rates were 9.5 to 10 percent, and even the latter were barely covering the current rate of inflation. Inflation has served to dramatize and amplify the extent to which regulation and lack of competition have injured consumers who saved their money in traditional ways, like insurance and savings accounts.

Rules of Thumb

Some rules of thumb about life insurance needs might be useful, even though they do not apply to all situations. Let us assume that the decision to purchase life insurance is made at the point when a couple is in their twenties. Both partners assume that they are making some commitments and career sacrifices and should have some claim on their partner's future income (or an equivalent amount if the partner dies or departs). Assume also that for each child conceived, the commitment increases by the amount each partner is expected to contribute (in time and money) to the raising of the child.

Each spouse or partner should start with a forty-year decreasing term policy on his or her own life that replaces about a fourth of his or her market and nonmarket income. That fraction is somewhat arbitrary but represents an estimate of the amount that is sacrificed in a marriage or other partnership. Since the present value of a forty-year stream is twenty-three times the annual amount (see app. 2.1), this means the initial insurance amount in the

---

3. *The Insurance Forum* is published monthly by Insurance Forum, Inc., P.O. Box 245, Ellettsville, Indiana 47429.

policy should be about 23 × 0.25 = 6 times the person's income. Thus, a spouse earning $20,000 per year should have about $120,000 worth of forty-year decreasing term insurance. For each child, a twenty-year decreasing term policy should be taken out by each parent, replacing some eighth of his or her income. Since the present value of a twenty-year stream at 3 percent is about fifteen times the annual amount, this means the initial insurance amount in the policy should be about 15 × 0.125 = 2 times each parent's income. Hence, for a family with two very young children, each partner should be carrying a set of decreasing term policies with starting insurance amounts equal to about ten years' income.

As time passes, the needs decrease, but so does the amount of the insurance provided in a decreasing term policy. Only changed family obligations or inflation will alter the picture. In the case of inflation, additional policies, also decreasing term but only for the remainder of the period, can be taken out periodically. The amounts in the supplemental policies should be enough to provide annual incomes equal to the inflation rate times the annual incomes provided in the original policies. For example, suppose five years after the initial purchase the price level is 20 percent higher. Then each partner needs an additional thirty-five-year decreasing term policy equal to 0.20 times 6 times initial income and an additional fifteen-year decreasing term policy for each child equal to 0.20 times 2 times his or her initial income.

What about real increases in income and in living standards? These can be handled as similar to inflationary increases. But rather than treating inflationary and real income increases separately, we can assume that increases in nominal income reflect both inflation and rising standards of living. Then additional policies (for shorter remaining periods) could be taken in amounts equal to the percentage increase in income times the original income amounts.

Social Security will cover some of these insurance needs. Social Security survivors' benefits are like decreasing term insurance since they pay so much per month until the children leave home or school or reach eighteen. But they assume that after that the surviving spouse needs nothing until retirement, and they provide a benefit based on previous income only up to a modest level. The present value of the expected survivor benefits can be estimated with information from a local Social Security office and subtracted from the total insurance need.

More Details about Life Insurance

The combination of saving and insurance in cash-value policies allows the agent to lead the semi-sophisticated customer through the following misleading exercise: Let us compare term insurance with ordinary life insurance, says the agent. If we take the premiums for a $10,000 ordinary life policy, minus dividends, minus the cash value at the end of twenty years, and compare that with the premiums minus dividends on $10,000 of term insurance each year for twenty years, look how much cheaper the former is. The customer then reminds the agent that the company has had some of his or her money during the twenty years—money on which he could have earned interest. Yes, says the agent. But suppose we deduct from the premiums minus dividends of the ordinary life policy each year the premiums minus dividends of the term policy. This stream of extra premiums accounts for the cash value of the ordinary life policy at the end of the twenty years. The cash value is larger than the sum of the extra premiums. What interest rate is implied by that fact? It will turn out to be 4 to 6 percent.

The trick, of course, is that the agent is not comparing like with like. The ordinary life policy involves $10,000 in pure life insurance only during the first year; after that, the amount of insurance is progressively less. A level premium is paying for a decreasing amount of term insurance each year. It is essential to remember that the amount of insurance is not equal to the face value of the policy. If one did the above calculation correctly, the interest earned on the whole life savings component would prove to be small. Moreover, the customer who separated his insurance program from his savings program could invest the savings in something with a much higher yield, and perhaps with a hedge against inflation.

Having gotten this far, many tracts on life insurance then plump for regular term insurance. But this ignores all we have learned about the pattern over time of the amount of insurance needed—that amount declines rapidly. It is possible to take out renewable term insurance and renew only the fraction of it that then seems appropriate, but the fee structure needs to be considered if you do this. The agent typically gets 55 percent of the first year's premium and 5 percent of the next nine renewal premiums. What seems appropriate for most people is some combination of decreasing term policies, perhaps supplemented by a fixed-amount term policy of limited duration.

It is often suggested that people take out insurance before they need it, for fear they might become ill and thus uninsurable later. Life insurance usually requires a medical examination, and each policy application asks whether the applicant has even been refused insurance, so it is prudent to see one's own private doctor first, in order to avoid that first turn-down that could lead to a general inability to get insurance. Some companies issue special-risk policies to people with health problems, but they are very expensive.

It is sometimes argued that one should take out insurance when young because the premiums are lower then, and remain lower all one's life. This is deceitful, since the cost of any amount of insurance depends on the probability of death. Carrying insurance for several years before one really needs it adds an unnecessary cost and makes later insurance look cheaper, for the same two reasons: interest on a larger reserve, and less real insurance because of the reserve.

Finally, there is the recommendation that the amount of insurance should increase with increases in a family's living standards. But when a family gets affluent enough to worry about this, they would do better to increase their saving program, rather than their insurance, since their standard of an adequate retirement must also have risen at the same time. Chapter 5 suggested some rules about spreading income increases into retirement years.

Why do insurance companies and agents keep on selling people the wrong kind of insurance, knowing that they will usually have insufficient insurance in their early years because of the extra "cost" of the saving part, and perhaps too much later? Partly because they believe people should be forced to save. Partly because the hidden interest can make policies look cheaper and easier to sell. Agents generally receive larger fees for the high-saving policies, but they also frequently appear to believe the spurious arguments they produce in their favor.

Books critical of insurance companies are unfair in some instances. They accuse the companies of using out-of-date mortality tables with higher death rates than actually exist, and certainly higher than exist for their carefully screened policyholders. But this is irrelevant if the company's expense loading is not exorbitant and if the extra charges are repaid as dividends. They also accuse the companies of refusing to repay the full reserve when a man cancels his policy, but there are real costs connected with lapsed policies and these should not be borne by the faithful remaining policyholders.

One of the reasons so little has been said here about shopping for life insurance is that it is far more costly to buy the wrong type or the wrong amounts of insurance, or to insure the wrong people, than it is to select the wrong company. Insurance companies are heavily regulated, particularly in some states, so that almost any national company licensed to do business in a large state like New York is safe. If you are looking for decreasing term insurance, the problem is more one of finding a company that handles it in proper varieties than of finding the cheapest one. The use of twenty-year net cost figures, even interest-adjusted, tends to make the price differences look dramatic (National Underwriter Company Bulletin). Yet a careful examination of comparative pricing done in different years shows substantial instability in the ranking of insurance companies over the years. And as we said earlier, even the interest-adjusted rates are imperfect measures (Josephson).

There are some "bargains" in insurance: GI insurance, savings bank life insurance in a few states, and group life insurance negotiated efficiently and competitively and with minimum fees by the employer or some organization. In a period of rising interest rates, the right to borrow on one's reserves at a fixed low interest rate may be an advantage. Conversely, a policy taken out when interest rates are high may have options to convert it to an annuity at a favorable rate that make the policy worth keeping. Both of these possibilities are more likely with nonparticipating policies, where the company's errors in predicting future interest rates cannot be offset by a reduction in the dividends.

It is important to know that some life insurance agents sell insurance for more than one company and hence may be better able to advise you about their differences. But there is probably no better way than to decide how much insurance you want and of what kind, then to price it with different companies. It also pays to keep in mind that the agent's fee is a substantial part of the first year's premium and a small percentage of renewal premiums, so creating a flexible decreasing term coverage by buying multiple policies and dropping some may well prove to be inefficient.

To summarize the main points again:

1. The amount of life insurance needed is the smaller of two amounts—the amount needed by survivors, or the present value of the amount of income lost less what the deceased would have consumed.

2. Accumulations to handle the risk of living too long also serve in case one partner dies early, and should be deducted from insurance need.

3. Every year passed is one less year of risk, so the amount of insurance needed tends to start high and decrease, usually to zero long before retirement, because savings to take care of two people in retirement are enough for one long before retirement.

4. Life insurance policies with savings features are unlikely to provide the proper pattern either of saving or of insurance with the passing years. Insurance need drops faster than savings can accumulate.

5. Pricing a joint product is always difficult. Combining savings with insurance confuses people, since the amount of insurance is not the face value of the policy but—at most—the face value minus the cash value. Ignoring the interest earned by the company on the accumulating savings underestimates the cost of the policy.

Automobile Liability Insurance

Next to death or disability, the next largest risk an individual faces is probably the risk of being sued for damages to other people's property or persons resulting from negligent operation of your car. People feel so strongly that auto accident victims should be compensated that there is pressure to use the damage suit combined with liability insurance as a way of doing this. In fact, laws dealing with damages (tort laws) stipulate that compensation is supposed to be paid to the victim only if the other driver was negligent and the victim was not also negligent (contributory negligence), or if the victim was also negligent, the other driver still had a last clear chance to avoid the accident.

Given negligence, the guilty driver is responsible for property damages, medical costs, lost income resulting from death or disability, and even a dollar amount for "pain and suffering." The present value of a stream of income lost through death or disability is potentially the largest of the amounts. Some delicate writings on the value of a human life arise from such cases, including estimates of the future earnings of young people whose educations have barely begun.

Since few individuals have assets sufficient to cover large damage awards, most carry liability insurance, although very few carry an amount adequate to cover major losses. For this reason, people have exaggerated notions of what they can collect in an auto accident case. Newspapers publish huge jury verdicts, many of which are never paid in full because they are later reversed or modified, or because the guilty driver has inadequate insurance, or none. And most payments made pursuant to court awards are larger than the much more numerous out-of-court settlements. In even more cases, there is no tort claim at all (Conard).

Many people have very few assets that can be attached if they lose such a case. Most have their savings tied up in retirement plans, a house, or life insurance. If one attaches (garnishees) their wages, they may well be fired, drying up that source. If a person has only $20,000 in liability insurance, all you can get from a suit may turn out to be $20,000 minus your own lawyer's fee of $5,000 or more. A suit is usually handled by a lawyer who takes a "contingent fee"—if the lawyer loses, he or she gets nothing—so it is difficult to get a lawyer to take a small case. On the other hand, the system does discourage a lawyer from taking on cases where liability is difficult to establish.

Despite this, however, the amount you can be sued for is not exaggerated. Many people innocently say, "Since I have only $10,000 in assets, I need only $10,000 in liability insurance." The absurdity is obvious: *you can lose your own funds if the award is larger than your insurance coverage*, e.g., if you have $10,000 in insurance and are successfully sued for $20,000.

The logic behind applying tort liability to auto accidents seems to be that accidents are the avoidable consequence of negligence, and the negligent should be punished. It does not work that way, of course, since insurance relieves the guilty driver of punishment and spreads the cost among all drivers, including the innocent. The guilty may be punished by higher insurance rates or for negligent homicide, but they are not really made to pay the full costs of their misdeeds. Spreading the costs through insurance was felt to be justified in order to assure that victims would be compensated, and by a system that put the costs of such compensation upon the activity of driving where it belonged. But the logic of this also was faulty. The easiest way to see why is to categorize accidents arbitrarily into two types: avoidable accidents arising from negligence, and unavoidable accidents that are simply the inevitable result of a lot of cars and the combinations of chance events.

Avoidable accidents are often uncompensated, and the largest and most serious ones are the most seriously undercompensated. The compensation comes mostly from insurance charges paid by the good, safe drivers, when it should come in part from a government that does not have the wisdom or courage to keep drunk drivers off the roads.

The unavoidable accidents, on the other hand, are not compensated at all; yet they are obviously part of the overall cost of driving and should be compensated out of charges on all drivers, in proportion to the extent to which they expose themselves and others to risk (mileage, safety of their car). Yet these costs are not put upon the activity of driving at all. Since the tort law applies only to cases involving negligence, the costs of unavoidable accidents are borne largely by the particular victims and whatever other compensation systems come into play (medical insurance, life insurance, disability insurance, welfare). A little is covered by collision insurance and auto passenger medical payments insurance, but not much.

From an economist's point of view, the auto liability insurance system leads to poor pricing and cost allocation and to erratic losses by the victims of most accidents, since guilt is often difficult to prove. In addition, the system itself introduces very high costs—costs of determining guilt, selling insurance, determining amounts of compensation, etc. Only a few cases go to court, and only a few of these go to trial and judgment, but expenses are very high, as in any adversary system. Auto insurance premiums themselves are more than twice the benefits paid out, and there are further court costs borne by the state (Conard; Volpe).

There are other problems: delay in the courts (up to three years for filing and additional time if postponements); delay in rehabilitation; overcompensation of small nuisance claims; compensation for "pain and suffering" erratically given; waste, when repairs cost more than the value of the car is increased; inequity, when insured repairs are billed at higher rates than uninsured repairs; and all the tribulations of a system that requires the victim to magnify his troubles and wait endlessly for his compensation. The guilty driver, on the other hand, is often unaffected, and in many cases does not even know whether his victim was ever compensated, or how well. It is all handled by his insurance company.

Any such system has its vested interests which assert sophisticated reasons for the system, and resist changing it. The automobile companies benefit when the costs of car insurance do not include all the costs of driving, including the costs of the unavoidable accidents. The insurance companies want to stay in business insuring tort liability, even though they recognize soaring costs and rates and are helpless to do much about them. They cannot encourage the design of safe cars because it is the safety of the car of the victim, not the person they insure, that affects their claims costs.

Trial lawyers, however, represent the main resistance to change. One paper, by a professor of law, proposing a reform of liability insurance laws, was even removed from the program of the meeting of the Trial Lawyers Association in Florida a few years ago. Since lawyers are heavily represented in state legislatures, where both auto insurance laws and tort liability laws are made, any change opposed by lawyers is difficult.

What proposals for reform have been made? Perhaps the simplest is to eliminate from tort liability any damages compensated through some other system, making only the residual loss collectible in tort. With the growth of other compensation systems—such as medical insurance and disability incomes—this could lead to the gradual decline of the auto damage suit system. Some advocate turning the whole compensation system over to Social Security. But this is regressive, since the financing of Social Security is somewhat regressive, and poor pricing, since it does not charge the activity of driving with some of the costs it creates, and perhaps too radical, since it would be opposed by both the lawyers and the private insurance companies.

The most elaborate, ingenious, and economically sensible reform was proposed by two law professors, Robert Keeton of Harvard and Jeffrey O'Connell of Illinois. The essence of their proposal, often called "no-fault" insurance, was to exempt the first $10,000 of property damage and personal injury liability from tort law and have everyone carry his or her own insurance for that. This removes the bulk of accidents from the expensive tort liability system and covers them with "first person" insurance. The legal implications need not concern us; they are carefully worked out, including interstate complications. The economic implications are more interesting: there is no longer, for most accidents, any necessity of determining guilt. The accidents in which guilt would be hardest to establish, the unavoidable ones, would now be covered by insurance, with the cost spread among all drivers, as it should be, probably in proportion to their exposure to risk.

The individual would collect from his or her own insurance company; since they would have a continuing business relationship, both parties would tend to be more considerate of each other. Guilty drivers could still be punished, under both criminal law and tort law, but the high cost of trials whose purpose is mostly to get compensation would be eliminated. Since rights to compensation would be clear, there would be no delay in getting medical care and rehabilitation.

Under present law, compensation under personal tort liability must be total and cannot involve coinsurance (where the insured individual and the company share the cost) or extra awards as incentives to safe driving. But if you carried your own insurance, you could coinsure, and you would have an incentive to be economical; the overall effect would be to keep premiums down. And the insurance company could even agree to pay 90 percent, instead of 80 percent, of personal injury losses if you had your seat belt fastened.

Even more interesting is the possibility that in their own interest insurance companies would introduce incentives toward safer cars, safer driving, and economy in the use of compensation funds. Insurance companies have in the past varied premiums according to the nature of the car only in a limited way. The personal injury they compensate is to people in some other, unspecified car, but the companies have been able to allow only for the safety of the car of their own client in setting insurance rates. But if they insured a particular car and its occupants for personal injury, medical costs, and lost earnings (up to $10,000 in any accident), they could pay more attention to the design of the car. If an insurance company is willing to offer a lower insurance rate on a car they think is safer for its occupants, in effect betting its profits on that decision, then the auto companies face not an arbitrary government regulation but a careful and impartial assessment of their product. A customer, told that a car costs a little more but is safer and will return the difference in lower insurance premiums, might well be motivated to choose the safer, better-built car. This would put market forces and prices behind the drive for safety, replacing the government regulatory agencies, whose record in this and other areas has been less than brilliant.

One immediate result would be higher insurance costs for smaller cars because their occupants are exposed to more risk. Some may decry this, arguing that they are risky only because other people insist on driving around in big heavy cars. But one cannot eliminate heavy cars or trucks, and at present people are deceived about the costs of the risks to which they expose themselves in driving lightweight cars. There might also be more variation of premiums according to the amount and kind of driving done.

A few states have passed some form of no-fault auto insurance law, but most are compromises and are still being fought by the trial lawyers.[4] A federal law has been proposed, but the outlook for major reform is not good, and the individual household has to face more immediate

---

4. It has also been proposed that the no-fault insurance principle be extended to all kinds of accidents on an elective basis, cutting down on malpractice and product-liability suits. See O'Connell's articles.

problems. Auto insurance rates keep rising with increasing costs of repair, of medical care, and of handling claims. Companies are trying to keep premiums down by getting rid of their bad risks—cancelling policies or raising rates of those with any accidents. Since the biggest risk is personal liability for damages and injuries to others, the important thing for the individual is to carry a very large amount of such insurance. The rates do not go up appreciably for the larger amounts. Since it is crucial to keep that coverage, it is obviously unwise to use one's insurance to pay for minor damages done in accidents that do not involve personal injury. In fact, coverage for such minor claims is illusory, since most companies raise rates after a minor claim or two, and can even cancel insurance, leaving one with no liability coverage. The sensible thing to do in minor accidents where one is at fault is to pay the damages directly (asking for three bids as the insurance company would) turning the matter over to the insurance company only when the other driver is unreasonable or the amount is very large (several years' premiums).

Insurance for Damages to Your Own Car or Its Occupants

Besides liability, auto insurance policies also include coverage for theft of the car, for medical payments to occupants, and "collision insurance" for accident damage not collectible from someone else. The value of any of these depends on the amount at risk and on one's ability to shoulder the possible loss. It also depends on other sources of compensation. The main reason for medical payments is probably to cover one's sense of responsibility for occupants in those cases when the other driver involved in an accident cannot be made to pay, but the occupants may well have their own medical insurance. Theft coverage is reasonable until a car is four or five years old, at which time its value is not all that great.

The federal income tax law allows deductions from taxable income for casualty losses, so the value of casualty insurance is reduced because an uninsured loss net of tax reductions is less than the full loss the insurance would have to cover. For instance, suppose the probability of theft were 0.01 in a year, the car was worth $1,000, and your marginal tax rate was 30 percent. Insurance, with 50 percent expense loading, would cost about $20, but the actuarial value of the expectation of loss to you is 0.01 times $700 ($1,000 minus an estimated tax offset of $300), or $7, so the insurance would cost not twice its actuarial value but nearly three times.

Collision insurance also fails to meet many of the conditions that determine whether insurance is likely to be available at reasonable rates. Some of the drawbacks are:

1. *Adverse selection.* People who carry it are more likely to have claims than others. Careful drivers who do not expect accidents except when someone else is to blame are less likely to carry it. It is also probably carried more by people with very expensive cars, and the rates are not fully adjusted to the differences.

2. *The cost to the insurance company is affected by the fact of insurance.* Substantially higher costs are likely when the repair job is insured, and three "competing" bids will not solve this problem.

3. *The amount of insurance benefit payable may not represent the real loss.* The insurance must make good the damage (unless the market value of the car before the accident was less than this), but many a driver would prefer to use the money on a new car, or on something else. If one has an old car, worth say $500, it makes economic sense to leave the dents in it, since they will reduce its trade-in value by far less than the cost of repairing them.

4. *There tends to be cheating on the deductibles, the garage writing a bill larger than its real bill by the amount of the deductible, and then excusing the customer from paying the deductible amount.* The expenses of claims adjustment and of keeping down cheating by repair garages or customers are substantial.

Buying Auto Insurance

There are differences in auto insurance rates among companies, but they are difficult to assess because some companies have a high first-year charge (covering most of the agent's fee), and others seem to have a practice of charging very low fees but raising them rapidly, particularly if there are any claims. Furthermore, you are paying for service as well as insurance. You want the company to be careful and not "taken" by absurd claims, and you need to know whether they pay valid claims promptly and fairly, either to you or to someone else. One source of information about this comes from questionnaires returned by members of Consumers Union and reported at intervals in *Consumer Reports*. They represent a very special group of alert, educated, concerned consumers, but their relative ratings of insurance companies should not be biased by that.

Insurance is also combined with other services in auto clubs. The quality of these clubs varies from state to state, as does the quality of their insurance, since the American Automobile Association (AAA) is really a federation of state auto clubs, each with its own insurance aggrangement.

When the children start to drive, it may be necessary to reexamine insurance and shop again, since companies vary in their treatment of teenage drivers. When the family acquires a second car, there should be some discount because the total mileage (exposure) is not doubled by having a second car. (On the other hand, one must remember that with two risks a large loss can happen three ways: a large loss on either car, or a moderate loss on each of them.)

In response to growing public clamor against rising auto insurance rates, group coverage has been proposed, but this can save only a little of the agents' fees. Short of turning all compensation (whatever the cause) over to a single national system and taxing drivers for the costs which auto accidents add to that system, the most appropriate compromise solution seems to be the Keeton-O'Connell proposal of no-fault, first-person insurance. In the meantime, the driver needs a lot of liability insurance and a skeptical attitude toward the other coverages. No amount of liability insurance is enough, given the open-ended nature of the possible damage claims. A person should carry an amount so large that no one is likely to win a damage award against him larger than that, provided he has anything at all to lose. This means half a million dollars, if one can get it.

Medical Insurance

Hospital and medical costs form a queer statistical distribution, with small costs for large numbers of people (or for most years for one person), but always the small chance of bills large enough to wipe out a family's assets. It is very important to make the distinction between the small, relatively predictable items that should be budgeted for rather than insured, and the large, rarer disasters that are a proper field for insurance. Historically, however, medical insurance has spread rapidly in a form that covered all illnesses but was limited to hospital costs, since these were more easily defined (eligibility being determined by doctors, and legitimate costs more easily determined, etc.) A fear of discouraging people from seeking early care restricted the use of deductibles or even coinsurance. In negotiating plans for their members, trade unions stressed the coverage of small items lest their members be impoverished by a series of small bills; they were less concerned about the large catastrophes, since most of their members had no estates to lose anyway.

For anyone with any assets at all, however, and any flexibility to budget for mildly erratic costs, there is a strong case to be made for medical insurance that will cover the very large catastrophic bills, but with deductibles or coinsurance for the more budgetable risks to keep the premiums down. (Premiums are also kept down by reducing the costs of policing and of handling a lot of small claims.) There are problems of defining the unit for a deductible. The most sensible arrangement is probably to have the insurance cover the costs above some stated total in any three-month period, rather than trying to define one illness or incident. The policy should also cover the family as a unit, and not apply a separate deductible to each member. Coinsurance, where you pay some fraction (perhaps 20 percent) of bills beyond the deductible, is also suggested to motivate economy.

The familiar problems arise also with medical insurance: the amount used and the price may both be enlarged by the fact of insurance. Even where the doctor determines the length of hospitalization, he can easily be influenced by the presence or absence of insurance in making his recommendations. There is evidence both that the uninsured get less care than they should have and that the insured sometimes get more than they need (McNerney). Both the likelihood of needing medical care and the likely length of hospital stays increase dramatically with age, so insurance that does not adjust premiums with age may well be a bargain for older people and overpriced for younger ones.

The complexity of medical care, and the open-ended nature of some risks, have led to attempts to cut insurance premiums by excluding specific illnesses from policies. One might think that a policy which lists exclusions is bad. In fact, a policy which lists what it covers may well be worse. There are so many things to be covered that a policy covering "all medical costs except" will resolve all uncertainties in your favor and include all those things you would never have thought to look for in a list of covered illnesses or conditions. Of course, explicitly excluding the large risks is also likely to be disadvantageous, whether by name or by limits on the number of days in the hospital, or by the total amount payable. As in any insurance, a critical question is what fraction of the premiums (plus interest the company earns on them) is paid out in benefits. In the case of medical malpractice insurance, this fraction has been estimated to be 16 to 17 percent; Blue Cross group plans pay out around 97 percent![5]

Worker's Compensation Insurance

You have no choice to make about it, but since worker's compensation insurance covers some of the same risks as other insurance, it deserves a brief discussion. Worker's compensation insurance is the earliest social insurance in this country, being introduced state by state starting early in this century. The state laws generally required employers of more than some minimum number of workers to carry insurance, or prove capacity for covering their own risk, to cover medical care and partial replacement of lost wages for workers injured in the course of employment.

What these laws really did was remove the right of a worker to sue his employer for negligence (e.g., unsafe equipment) in return for guaranteeing him a more limited compensation without question of fault. It was felt that employees would not dare sue their employers anyway, or could not afford the loss of income during the trial. It was also argued that it would be efficient since there would be no expensive court determination of either guilt or the amount of compensation. (It has not quite worked out that way, since workers often engage lawyers to fight about whether the injury was compensible—arose in the course of employment—or about the amount.)

On a broader scale, it was argued that such insurance properly placed on each industry the costs of its work accidents and saw to it that they became part of the price of that product. Experience rating by the insurance companies—raising rates on companies with bad records—was expected to induce companies to install safety devices.

The details vary from state to state, with the poorer states tending to have less adequate levels of compensation. Medical care is covered, but only some fraction of the lost wages is paid, in the belief that this will encourage return to work. There may even be a dollar limit on the compensation payments, which tends to become more and more inadequate as prices and real wages continue to rise. With increased coverage from other forms of compensation such as medical insurance, unemployment compensation, and liability insurance, state legislatures have been reluctant to improve worker's compensation benefits, particularly in the face of anguished cries that the rising insurance costs would put that state's insurance industry at a competitive disadvantage. Such worries demonstrate the difficulties of state responsibility, and attempts to promote uniform national standards have not succeeded (Cheit and Gordon).

An additional problem with worker's compensation arises because most state laws allow the injured worker to settle all his claims for future medical care and wage replacement in a single lump-sum settlement. In the case of permanent disabilities, this was intended to allow investment in retraining for a new career or for starting an independent business. There was also an assumption that with no more regular payments depending on a continuing disability, the disability might disappear. Bad backs in particular often are difficult to diagnose and are suspected of being partly psychological. The various participants are all motivated to settle—the worker's lawyer because the whole fee comes immediately out of a settlement, the company because their risk of further injuries and claims is ended, and the insurance company because it can get the case off its books. Most of all, the worker is

---

5. A pamphlet on the loss ratios of 327 of the largest health insurers is available from the Research Institute for Quality Health Plans, 1611 Foster Street, Lake Charles, Louisiana 70601 ($1.50).

enticed because it is difficult to get along on the weekly disability payments.

However, when those who accept such settlements are followed, located, and interviewed a year and a half later, it turns out that even those with bad backs mostly did *not* go back to work when the weekly payments stopped (Morgan, Snider, and Sobol). Nor were the settlements used to start businesses—they mostly went to pay accumulated debts, including those to the welfare department, which can insist on recouping its contributions. Whether or not the disabilities were psychological, the removal of any economic incentive to stay disabled did not get people back to work. In many cases, of course, a substantial fraction of the settlement also went to pay a lawyer's fee.

The most likely solution to this situation is probably the gradual replacement of worker's compensation with other forms of compensation not dependent upon the employment connection. In the meantime, the ordinary household can do little.

Household Insurance

Like auto insurance, household insurance covers personal liability for damages sustained by others on your property—from slipping on your sidewalk, for instance—and compensation to you for casualty damage sustained from such causes as theft, vandalism, fire, wind, and hail. In addition to the usual rules of liability, householders with swimming pools or nice trees to climb face a doctrine of "attractive nuisance," under which one is responsible for what happens to young children even if they have been warned to stay away. Even so, the probability of being sued is low, except in our three most litigious states of New York, Florida, and California, so the cost of liability insurance is quite low. The amounts to be lost in house and furnishings are large enough to justify casualty insurance.

The other coverages are straightforward enough, usually including theft of such property as bicycles and lawn mowers and theft of personal belongings while traveling (within the United States). There are two complications. Many policies have a "coinsurance" clause, which says that if you insure for less than 80 percent of the current replacement cost of the property, then the insurance company will pay only the fraction of 80 percent that you insured. For example, if you insured your house and its contents for 50 percent of its market value, the company would pay only 50/80 of your losses. (This should not be confused with two other uses of the term coinsurance: where you pay, say, 20 percent of the costs, as with 80 percent coinsurance in major medical insurance; or the practice of insurance companies of dividing large risks among themselves, several companies jointly insuring each.)

A special risk is connected with buying or building a new house. The title to the land may be faulty, in which case the real landowner ends up owning your house as well, without having to pay for it. You can take out title insurance to cover this (see chap. 4).

In an attempt to cut selling costs and perhaps paper work, insurance companies have been selling "package policies," which cover several things at once. Whether they are bargains depends on the individual situation, but as in most package sales, it is difficult for the customer to make price comparisons and to know how much he is paying for what.

Household Behavior

There is evidence that many of us behave irrationally when risks are involved, overestimating likelihood of some events, underestimating the chances of other events. There is a lack of symmetry in our behavior toward the events with bad outcomes or good outcomes, and it would help us all to plan insurance if we understood our own foibles (Kahneman and Tversky). Most people underinsure the largest risks, such as death of a main earner with many children, which explains why the survivors' benefits were added to the Social Security system rather early. Among those under forty-five and with children under six, who have the maximum risk, not one in ten carries as much as a few years' income worth of life insurance. At the other extreme, a substantial number of people with no children or who are retired still carry life insurance. Even with the example of Social Security survivors' benefits tailored to needs, many people still tend to accumulate more insurance as they grow older and more affluent even though their insurance needs are dropping. And many still purchase high-priced airplane trip insurance.

Regulating the Insurance Industry

We have already mentioned that the regulation of insurance company investments to assure the companies' stability keeps the interest yield low. Regulation of some insurance rates probably does not keep the rates low overall, although it may prevent some excessive rates by some companies. It is important to realize that almost all this regulation is by the states, not the federal government, and thus can vary in quality and detail, leaving consumers in a difficult position if they have insurance with a company not registered and regulated in their own state, but sold by mail from another. It is easy to find out from the state insurance commission whether a particular company is licensed to do business in your state and perhaps whether it has ever been in any difficulty with the commission.

Just as with the regulation of consumer credit and lenders, there is an open question whether increasing competition and information—by demanding clear policy terms, standard policies, and reasonably free entry into the business—might not do consumers more good than attempting to fix rates. Regulation for safety and solvency is crucial, of course, particularly where large amounts to needy survivors are at stake. But the history of regulating prices and rates to drive profits down to normal is not encouraging. We must remember, thinking more broadly, that we all pay the costs of regulation, in taxes if not in rates, so it is necessary to look at the total costs and benefits of regulation in the long run to decide how enthusiastic we should be for what kinds of regulation.

The move toward no-fault auto insurance is an example of an attempt to improve the overall benefit-cost picture while preserving or improving equity. Skyrocketing insurance costs to doctors and hospitals for malpractice liability suits, and to producers for liability for products that injure consumers, have led to proposals for insurance that would cover losses without the expensive determination of fault, and without the erratic lack of compensation where fault is difficult to prove. Punitive damages to cover "pain and suffering" are charged with being a tax on all consumers for the benefit of a very few successful plaintiffs and their lawyers.

It is likely that important changes may be made in the combinations of insurance and damage suits available to compensate different kinds of accidents and losses, and consumers need to keep up with these changes. Interpreting them in terms of how they benefit consumers in general, or any individual consumer, may be difficult but necessary both for the occasional chance to vote for or against, and for realigning one's own insurance portfolio.

Gambling

Sometimes people purposely increase the risks in a situation rather than avoid, or insure, or bear them. There seem to be two reasons—the lure of a very large possible gain which might totally alter one's life, and the sheer excitement, often combined with a belief that one can beat the system. Even if one gambles for fun, the notion of "loading" (expenses and profit of the "house") is still appropriate. What fraction of the money bet ever gets won by someone, rather than appropriated by whoever is running the game? Except in a few areas where gambling is legalized (on-track betting on horse races, state lotteries), that fraction is difficult to find out.

Why should anyone gamble and carry insurance at the same time? Perhaps some believe the odds are better than they are, or that they have a system, or that they know a lot about horses (Kahneman and Tversky). Perhaps the lure of a very large gain prevents people from seeing that, multiplied by a very low probability, it has a very modest "expected value." Some of the lure, as with bingo games, is social, plus a feeling that the profits are going to a church or other worthy cause. In American colonial days, churches were often built with the proceeds of lotteries.

A declining number of gambling methods are still illegal, partly because of moral objections and partly because it is one of a class of behaviors which some people overdo to their own and their families' misery. The result is to raise the "price" (i.e., the "loading"), because it has to cover the costs of running an illegal operation (bribes, fines, secrecy, etc.) and because the restriction of the supply of gambling opportunities allows the profits to be higher.

Worse still, gambling is in a class of behaviors which is made illegal but in which a large number of people want to engage. This puts the police in the middle, asked by some to enforce a law which others do not want enforced. Partly in response to this, partly because of changed public attitudes, a number of states have eased their restrictions and allowed various forms of gambling. The most common way has been to put the state into the gambling business by running a state lottery, the profits from which go into the state treasury, sometimes assigned to specific purposes. The ratio of total prizes paid to total amount bet is much lower in state lotteries than in most other gambling—less than half in some states. The hope was that lotteries would discourage illegal gambling, though so far its effect seems to have been small, and it is possible that it may legitimize gambling for people who would not otherwise have done it (Kallick and Suits). Indeed, the kinds of lotteries run by most states, with small bets, seem to be patronized largely by lower-income, less educated people—a kind of regressive tax, if politically more acceptable than the sales tax.

At any rate, the crucial question for the bettor is: what fraction of the total amount bet is ever paid out to winners?

Funerals

Part of the cost of death and of the need for insurance is the cost of the funeral. Recurrent muckraking aside, it remains true that grief-stricken survivors often make decisions they would not have made in a calmer moment, and spend more than the deceased ever wanted them to (Mitford; Bowman). Religious institutions exist in an uneasy truce with the funeral directors, wishing their members would use the church or equivalent, but unable to intercede. There are even laws in some states making it illegal for a minister to negotiate a funeral with a funeral director.

In this situation, many concerned people advocate preplanning and the depositing of instructions with some minister or burial society. Legally, these desires are not binding on the survivors, who may do anything they want, but they are likely to be useful (Ernest Morgan). The instructions may include donating one's body to a medical school for research and teaching, or parts of it to eye or ear banks.

Over the years, laws have been passed in many states making it difficult for people to economize on funerals, and impossible for them to engage in do-it-yourself burials. (One state passed a law making it illegal to bury someone within two days of death, in case an autopsy might be required to check for foul play, and then a week later passed another law which said that if the body was not buried within twenty-four hours, it had to be embalmed!) Bodies cannot be transported except in licensed vehicles; cremation may be illegal except in a casket; the list goes on and on.

Within all these limits and restrictions, it is still possible, particularly with a small cooperative society, to work out arrangements with cooperative undertakers. The important thing is that the plans be made by each individual in advance. Some burial societies arrange to take most of the burden of arrangements off the hands of the survivors. Others, formed in religious groups, actually arrange memorial services far more personal and appropriate than the commercial ones, often with testimony by the deceased's friends. The Seattle office of the Federal Trade Commission issued a handbook on how to do a local survey on the costs of burials, cemeteries, and grave markers (U.S. Federal Trade Commission).

Prepare Now, Go Later

Assuming that you have an adequate combination of assets and insurance to provide for survivors, and have made some plans or commitments about how your funeral is to be arranged, there are still some things that can be done to save taxes and to make things easier for those you leave behind. However small your "estate," the state laws will require some accounting and probably a formal probate to see to it that everything is accounted for and properly distributed. Everyone should do at least the first few things on this graduated list; the later ones should also be done by the wealthy:

1. Leave a set of financial records, including the location of will and other records, names of insurance agents and companies, stockbroker, lawyer, etc.
2. Leave a proper will for each adult on file with your lawyer, burial society, or bank—but *not* in a safety deposit box, which will be sealed when you die.
3. Have an agreement with one or two people to serve as executors of your estate, including their fees.
4. Make sure that the ownership and the source of funds for acquisition of every asset is clear.
5. Set up one or more trusts.

Before taking these up in order, some general remarks are needed. There is a federal transfer tax on the deceased's estate and on gifts during his or her lifetime, plus state taxes on the heirs' individual inheritances received and sometimes also on the estate itself. Since the state inheritance taxes are smaller and partly deductible as a credit against federal taxes up to a maximum of about 10 percent of the taxable estate, it is wise to ignore them at first and to try to minimize the federal transfer tax. The laws about ownership of assets, however, are state laws, so that we cannot be too specific about dealing with the federal tax.

Estate and gift taxes are not a worry for most people. As of 1979, there were no estate taxes for single persons with estates valued at less than $175,000 or for married persons with estates valued at less than $350,000, if the married person bequeaths at least half of it to the spouse.

For those with estates larger than these limits, estate taxes can be minimized with gifts to children ($3,000 or less per child per parent per year) or with trusts. We will not detail the bewildering array of trusts that can be set up, although it is useful to distinguish "living" trusts, which entail management fees and tax reports before death, from a residuary trust that is set up before death but does nothing until the will places the estate into it. Trusts usually do avoid substantial estate taxes and some probate costs, but do cost something to set up and require expert legal help. Any active trust requires management charges and compensation for the trustee. Most advice about trusts and estate planning comes from trust lawyers, insurance salesmen, or "estate planners" (who are usually insurance agents). All of these types have something to sell, so the consumer needs to be certain that it is really needed.

In general, the whole process of estate settlement can be regarded as a ghoulish scramble for your assets after you die. Burial and legal expenses and executor's and probate and appraisal fees all come out first, and so reduce the estate tax; in a sense they come out of what the federal government would otherwise get. Since the marginal estate tax rates go up to 70 percent and are above 50 percent on estates over $2.5 million, it is easy to see why people billing an estate might feel that the federal government would pay much of the bill. State laws are often designed to maximize the amount of state revenue that is taken by reductions in the federal estate tax revenue rather than out of the net estate. Since state taxes are deductible before calculating the federal tax, this is easy.

Elaborating on our list of possible preparations:

1. Financial records are crucial for those who administer the estate. And the mere act of systematically recording transaction dates and sources of assets may uncover gifts subject to tax, or allow proof that they were within the $3,000 limit. Prior tax returns are most useful, since they contain lists of assets producing income.

It is also important for survivors to know where your birth and marriage certificates are, the names and addresses of living relatives, and where your most recent will is. Your burial instructions and commitments or even prepayments should be where they will be found in time, even though they do not legally bind the survivors. (Survivors can take your money and give you any kind of funeral they like.)

2. A will is universally advised, even if it simply appoints an executor or executrix and makes sure that the surviving partner gets half the taxable estate or $250,000, whichever is larger. A simple will is not expensive, and the recent changes in regulations regarding lawyer advertising has introduced some price competition into the legal market for routine services such as wills. Without a living executor/executrix appointed (often a resident of the same state is required), the state will appoint an administrator to do the same job and fix a fee for it. There will be an added cost of bonding the appointed administrator.

The main argument for a will is that without it state law specifies the distribution of the estate. Parents take precedence even over spouses, and a surviving spouse with children sees half or two-thirds go directly to the children. The court will appoint a guardian if funds go to minor children, and when one of the children dies, its *natural* parent inherits its money—even an estranged or divorced spouse!

3. There are fees set by the state for the executor/executrix or administrator, as well as for other things, but the former can be replaced by a more modest prearranged fee. This is particularly useful if a family member is made co-executor with a lawyer and there is an agreement with the lawyer about fees for legal services.

4. Given the possible liability for transfer taxes from an innocent act of buying some asset and putting it in joint tenancy, and the fact that assets in the name of the surviving spouse are entirely outside the estate, it is important to have a clear set of records. The fact that the source of a family's savings is ambiguous, and that the total could be attributed (at the margin) to either spouse, will probably be increasingly recognized by law; but in the meantime, the law can treat women badly by assuming that all the money to purchase the house was provided by the husband.

The mere act of sorting out assets and ownership now may make it clear that something needs to be changed in order to reduce potential transfer taxes. It used to be that so few people had to pay estate taxes that they were hardly worth mentioning; since the deduction and exemption levels have been raised to allow for inflation, that time has returned. Merely distributing assets in the names of husband, wife, husband and wife jointly, and children, may be enough for most people, without the need to become involved with trusts at all.

There are many people in the United States who have accumulated substantial wealth in the last decades, without much, if any, help from inheritances. Many of them have doubts about the wisdom of bequeathing large sums to children, as distinct from investing in their education and training and initial ventures now. For these people, charitable bequests are an attractive option, again because such bequests are tax free. This means that a favorite charity can get a great deal more than the family would be able to keep after estate taxes. A wealthy man with a wife and no other close relatives can give half to the wife and half to charity and pay no estate taxes; or he could set up a charitable trust to support the wife until she dies, with everything going to charity afterward. Charity "bargains" may be even greater than those from giving now and saving on income taxes.

Summary

It should be clear now how important it is to understand the principles of insurance if one is to deal intelligently with risks. Of course, the best thing to do about risks is to avoid them. But if they cannot be avoided, and you have anything to lose, and someone will really suffer if it is lost, and if insurance is available at reasonable rates, then you are in the market.

At one time there were religious objections to carrying insurance ("Take no thought for the morrow," "Consider the lilies . . ."). Today the objections are likely to be more pragmatic—high expense loadings, adverse selection, effects of insurance status on probabilities or costs, or tax considerations in casualty losses.

The crucial things one must understand about insurance are few and relatively simple:

The amount of life insurance one needs is the smaller of two amounts—the amount that could be lost, or the amount needed so that the loss causes no suffering. If either is zero, no life insurance is needed. Whenever insurance is combined with saving, as with a whole life insurance policy, the amount of real insurance is the amount paid if the loss occurs *minus* the amount of one's funds held by the insurance company. The annual cost of the insurance is the premium *plus* the foregone interest on the funds held by the company.

Dying too early and living too long are both risks, but the funds accumulated to take care of the latter can also take care of survivors if one dies too early. Any saving program that will take care of two people from age sixty-five on will provide for one survivor long before that. For this reason, the need for life insurance drops to zero long before the insured person retires.

Under almost any reasonable assumptions, the amount

of life insurance needed reaches a peak when the last child is conceived and declines rapidly from then on, as each year is successfully passed and as other funds accumulate. The amount of insurance needed does not depend on the risk (probability of some disaster). If the risk gets sufficiently great, however, it may be cheaper to budget for it than to insure. There is no purpose in insurance to cover parts of a risk, nor to cover a risk already covered by some other insurance. Neither the existence of a mortgage nor plans to take a plane trip, for example, justify altering the amount of one's life insurance.

Insurance is really part of estate planning and needs to be accompanied by planning that will avoid needless waste or taxes.

More Information?

Libraries have compendiums of insurance companies listing their premium schedules and other information—Best's *Insurance Reports*, for example.

The general treatments by Belth and by Consumers Union (see the reading list) combine technical precision with good sense and readability. Insurance texts sin by omission, being directed toward selling insurance; the passionate critics are frequently careless and even incorrect.

A general agent who handles more than one insurance company, particularly if the firm also handles mutual funds, Independent Retirement Accounts, and other investments, is likely to be a less biased source of information about differences in companies and about policies with and without saving-investment features. If you know exactly what you want, it might be interesting to ask how much the agent gets out of the first year's premium, in case it might be shared with you, directly or in some other way.

Your state insurance commissioner has a list of approved insurance companies, and keeps a file of their reports giving total benefits paid versus total premium and other income; the ratio of the two should be of interest to you.

The Institute of Life Insurance serves the insurance companies but is a useful source of general information.

American Institute for Economic Research. *Life Insurance from the Buyer's Point of View.* Great Barrington, Mass.: American Institute for Economic Research, latest edition.

Arvia, Raymond P. *The Cost of Dying and What You Can Do About It.* New York: Harper and Row, 1974.

Belth, Joseph M. *Life Insurance: A Consumer's Handbook.* Bloomington: Indiana University Press, 1973.

Belth, Joseph M. *The Retail Price Structure in American Insurance.* Bloomington: Bureau of Business, Graduate School of Business, Indiana University, 1966. (Six methods of comparing prices make a difference, and traditional method distorts. Difficult in any case, and interest rate used matters.)

Belth, Joseph M. "The Rate of Return on the Savings Element in Cash Value Life Insurance." *Journal of Risk and Insurance* 35 (1968): 569–81.

Best, Alfred M. *Insurance Reports, Life/Health.* Morristown, N.J.: Best Company, annually.

Bowman, Leroy. *The American Funeral: A Study in Guilt, Extravagance, and Sublimity.* Washington, D.C.: Public Affairs Press, 1959.

Cheit, Earl F., and Gordon, Margaret. *Occupational Disability and Public Policy.* New York: John Wiley and Sons, 1963.

Chernik, Vladimir P. *The Consumer's Guide to Insurance Buying.* Los Angeles: Sherbourne Press, 1970.

Conard, Alfred, et al. *Automobile Accident Costs and Payments.* Ann Arbor: University of Michigan Press, 1964. (The main factual base on which no-fault insurance was proposed)

Consumers Union. *The Consumers Union Report on Life Insurance.* Rev. ed. Mt. Vernon, N.Y.: Consumers Union, 1977.

Cooper, George. *A Voluntary Tax? New Perspectives on Sophisticated Estate Tax Avoidance.* Washington, D.C.: Brookings Institution, 1979.

Dacey, Norman F. *What's Wrong with Your Life Insurance.* New York: Collier Books, 1963 (paper edition 1966).

Denenberg, Herbert S. *The Insurance Trap: Unfair at Any Rate.* Racine, Wis.: Western Publishing Company, 1972.

Denenberg, Herbert S. *A Shopper's Guidebook to Life Insurance, Health Insurance, Auto Insurance, Homeowner's Insurance, Doctors, Dentists, Lawyers, Pensions, etc.* Washington, D.C.: Consumer News, Inc., 1974.

Denenberg, Herbert S.; Eilers, Robert D.; Melone, J. J.; and Zelten, R. A. *Risk and Insurance.* 2d ed. Englewood Cliffs, N.J.: Prentice-Hall, 1974.

Ehrlich, Isaac, and Becker, Gary S. "Market Insurance, Self-Insurance, and Self-Protection." *Journal of Political Economy* 80 (1972): 623–48. (A theoretical treatment.)

Flaherty, Patrick F., and Zieller, Richard S. *Estate Planning for Everyone.* Rev. ed. Scranton, Pa.: T. Y. Crowell, 1979.

Gaines, Price, and Casson, Louise. *1979 Interest-Adjusted Index.* Cincinnati, Oh.: The National Underwriter Company, 1979.

Gilbert, Albert E. *Insurance and Your Security.* New York: Rinehart, 1948. (One of the earliest critical books, overdoes it.)

Gillespie, Paul, and Klipper, Miriam. *No-Fault: What You Save, Gain, and Lose with the New Auto Insurance.* New York: Praeger, 1972.

Gollin, James. *Pay Now, Die Later.* New York: Random House, 1966. (Subtitle: What's Wrong with Life Insurance: A Report on Our Biggest and Most Wasteful Industry)

Gordon, George Byron. *You, Your Heirs, and Your Estate.* Rockville Centre, N.Y.: Farnsworth Publishing, 1973.

Gorer, Geoffrey. *Death, Grief, and Mourning in Contemporary Britain.* New York: Doubleday, Cresset Press, 1965.

Guarino, Richard, and Trubo, Richard. *The Great American Insurance Hoax: How to Protect Yourself Against Insurance Fraud.* Los Angeles: Nash Publishing Corporation, 1974.

Hamilton, Richard T. *The Confidence Games—Game 1: The Insurance Game.* Jericho, N.Y.: Exposition Press, 1971.

Hendershot, Ralph. *The Grim Truth About Life Insurance.* New York: G. P. Putnam's Sons, 1957.

Holmes, R. A. "On the Economic Welfare of Victims of Auto Accidents." *American Economic Review* 60 (1970): 143–52. (A study in British Columbia)

Huebner, S. S., and Black, Kenneth Jr. *Life Insurance.* 7th ed. New York: Appleton-Century-Crofts, 1969. (A standard text for teaching sellers)

Institute of Life Insurance. *A List of Worthwhile Life and Health Insurance Books.* New York: Institute of Life Insurance, 1972.

Insurance Forum (monthly newsletter). P.O. Box 245, Elletsville, Indiana, 47429.

Josephson, Halsey D. *Life Insurance and Price Disclosure.* Lynbrook, N.Y.: Farnsworth Publishing, 1972. (Challenges the interest-adjusted method of pricing as deceptive)

Kahneman, Daniel, and Tversky, Amos. "Prospect Theory: An Analysis of Decision Under Risk." *Econometrica* 47 (1979): 263–91.

Kallick, Maureen, and Suits, Daniel. *A Survey of American Gambling Attitudes and Behavior.* Washington, D.C.: Government Printing Office, 1976; reprinted by Institute for Social Research, Ann Arbor, 1979.

Keeton, R. E., and O'Connell, J. *Basic Protection for the Traffic Victim.* Boston: Little, Brown, 1965. (The classic document on no-fault auto insurance)

Keeton, R. E., and O'Connell, J. *After the Crash.* Homewood, Ill.: Dow Jones-Irwin, 1967.

Keeton, R. E.; O'Connell, J.; and McCord, John H. *Crisis in Car Insurance.* Urbana, Ill.: University of Illinois Press, 1970.

J. K. Lasser Tax Institute. *How to Get the Most Life Insurance Protection at the Lowest Cost.* Larchmont, N.Y.: Cunnion Business Reports, Inc., 1968.

Maynes, E. Scott, and Geistfeld, Loren. "The Life Insurance Deficit of American Families: A Pilot Study." *Journal of Consumer Affairs* 8 (1974): 37–60.

McDonald, D., ed. *Medical Malpractice: A Discussion of Alternative Compensation and Quality Control Systems.* Center Occasional Paper. Santa Barbara, Calif.: Center for the Study of Democratic Institutions, 1971.

McNerney, Walter, ed. *Michigan Hospital Studies.* 2 vols. Chicago: Educational Trust, 1962.

Mitford, Jessica. *The American Way of Death.* New York: Simon and Schuster, 1963.

Morgan, Ernest. *A Manual of Simple Burial.* 5th ed. Burnsville, N.C.: Celo Press, 1971.

Morgan, James N. "Who Uses Seat Belts?" *Behavioral Science* 12 (1967): 463–65.

Morgan, James N.; Sirageldin, Ismail; and Baerwaldt, Nancy. *Productive Americans.* Ann Arbor: Institute for Social Research, 1966.

Morgan, James N.; Snider, Marvin; and Sobol, Marion. *Lump Sum Redemption Settlements and Rehabilitation: A Study of Workmen's Compensation in Michigan.* Ann Arbor: Institute for Social Research, 1959.

Nader, Ralph. *Unsafe at Any Speed.* New York: Crossman, 1965.

National Funeral Directors Association. *Funeral Facts and Figures.* Milwaukee, Wis.: National Funeral Directors Association, 1967.

National Underwriter Company. *Cost Facts on Life Insurance: Interest-Adjusted Method.* New York: National Underwriter Company, 1970. (Look for later edition.)

Nonte, George C., Jr. *To Stop a Thief: The Complete Guide to House, Apartment, and Property Protection.* New York: Follett, 1975.

O'Connell, Jeffrey. "Expanding No-Fault Beyond Auto Insurance: Some Proposals." *Virginia Law Review* 59 (1973): 749–829.

O'Connell, Jeffrey. "Elective No-Fault Insurance for All Kinds of Accidents: A Proposal." *Insurance Law Journal,* September 1973, pp. 495–515.

O'Connell, Jeffrey. *Ending Insult to Injury: No-Fault Insurance for Products and Services.* Urbana, Ill.: University of Illinois Press, 1975.

O'Connell, Jeffrey, and Simon, Rita James. *Payment for Pain and Suffering: Who Wants What, When, and Why?* Santa Monica, Calif.: Insurors Press, Inc., 1972.

Oehlbeck, J. Tracy. *The Consumer's Guide to Life Insurance.* New York: Pyramid Books, 1975.

Research Institute for Quality Health Plans. *Loss Ratios of 327 of the Largest Health Insurors*. Lake Charles, La.: Research Institute for Quality Health Plans, periodically.

Rokes, William Park. *No-Fault Insurance*. Santa Monica, Calif.: Insurors Press, 1971.

U.S. Department of Health, Education, and Welfare, Division of the Actuary. *Estimated Amount of Life Insurance in Force as Survivors' Benefits Under OASI in 1957*. Actuarial Study 47. Washington, D.C.: Government Printing Office, 1959.

U.S. Department of Labor, Employment Standards Administration. *State Workmen's Compensation Laws, A Comparison of Major Provisions with Recommended Standards*. Bulletin 212, rev. Washington, D.C.: Government Printing Office, 1971.

U.S. Department of Transportation. *Economic Consequences of Automobile Accident Injuries*, 2 vols. Auto Insurance and Compensation Study. Washington, D.C.: Government Printing Office, 1970.

U.S. Federal Trade Commission, Bureau of Consumer Protection and Bureau of Economics. *Life Insurance Cost Disclosure*. A Staff Report to the Federal Trade Commission. Washington, D.C.: Government Printing Office, 1979.

U.S. Federal Trade Commission, Seattle Regional Office. *The Price of Death: A Survey Method and Consumer Guide to Funerals, Cemeteries, and Grave Markers*. Consumer Survey Handbook, no. 3. Seattle, Wash.: U.S. Federal Trade Commission, n.d.

U.S. National Commission on Product Safety. *Final Report*. Washington, D.C.: Government Printing Office, 1970.

Volpe, John A. *Motor Vehicle Crash Losses and Their Compensation in the United States*. A Report to Congress and the President. Washington, D.C.: Government Printing Office, 1971.

Some Projects to Learn More

1. Use the library to see what data are available on prices for some kinds of insurance. Can you find any data on the ratio of benefits to premiums-plus-interest?

2. Get from several insurance agents recommendations for your own insurance program. Compare and evaluate them. Ask each agent at the end of the discussion about decreasing term life insurance and see what he or she says.

3. Take a damaged car to repair shops for estimates of repair costs, varying the story about who is paying for the repairs. For some large, busy shops you may be able to return to the same shop with a different driver and a different story. Compare prices. Then calculate the advantages of collision insurance, taking account also of 50 percent loading, and tax deductibility of casualty losses.

4. Which auto insurance rates vary with the age or value of the car? Does this lead to any strategies concerning when to carry each type?

5. Follow the current controversy over reform of auto insurance from tort liability laws to "no-fault." Form and write an appraisal of the situation.

6. Take two or three standard texts in life insurance and evaluate them in the light of what you have learned in this chapter.

7. Visit the office of the State Insurance Commission and ask to see the filed reports of a few companies with whom you have or would like to have insurance. Can you tell what fraction of total premiums-plus-interest earnings are paid out in benefits?

8. Read the latest articles on tax reform. What do recent and proposed charges mean for consumer decisions about insurance and estate planning?

CHAPTER TEN
MEDICAL CARE

Medical care is not the next-largest item of consumer expenditure after housing and durables, but it is one of the most troublesome for a number of reasons. Medical care has aspects of both current consumption and capital investment, since some of it is investment in one's future health. It has both public and private aspects, since the government and voluntary organizations have always been involved in providing medical care or paying for it. It involves both insurance problems and budgeting problems, the former already discussed in chapter 9. The consumer faces difficult problems of inadequate information in attempting to buy medical care. It will not be possible to separate entirely the consumer problems from the public policy issues, but the discussion will begin with the former, bringing in the latter where they fit.

The household has problems of information and of strategy, not only in paying for medical care, but also—perhaps more important—in reducing the need for medical care, in getting proper care when it is needed, and in handling the income loss that may also be involved.

Reducing the Need For Care

A great deal of illness and disease is preventable, often at lower cost than the cost of cure. The most obvious examples of preventive care are vaccinations, inoculations, periodic checkups, and early diagnoses. People with very tight budgets or particularly bad eating habits also could benefit from improved nutrition; moreover, attention to proper nutrition is important even among the affluent.

Nutrition

Nutrition is too complex a subject to cover thoroughly here, but it is important to remember that a wide range of diets is still nutritionally adequate; the human body has a remarkable ability to adapt to variety. Also, there are complex interactions among nutritional elements which make it difficult to specify absolute ideal levels for each one. Often several elements must be present simultaneously for the body to receive the full nutritional benefits of each. In addition, it is difficult to know the nutritional composition of some foods, since it depends heavily on just where they were grown, how they have been treated since then, and how fresh they are. (Indeed, there is evidence that food grown in tropical climates is deficient in B vitamins [de Castro].) A wide distribution of both food types and colors may be more important to adequate nutrition than a detailed, prescribed diet, because vitamin content is often revealed more by color than by food name, and variety minimizes the chances of imbalance. Most experts claim that for those who eat well and with some variety, supplementary vitamins are unnecessary and even wasteful.

Despite some fantastic claims to the contrary, there is no convincing evidence of any unique health benefits resulting from the ingestion of a large excess of any one nutrient. In fact, nutritional deficiencies are encountered primarily in populations with a limited choice of foods, indicating that variety is important. (See appendix 10.1 for information on vitamins and recommended dietary allowances.)

An individual who wants to get a proper protein intake with foods less expensive than red meat must do some complex planning and problem solving. The body can use protein only if the protein is properly balanced as to essential amino acid components, and some of the most popular substitutes for meat, such as soybeans, are quite inadequate by themselves. There are twenty-two different amino acids, eight of them essential in that they must be present in the right proportions if the protein is to be fully usable. Some can be manufactured in the body. What this means is that achieving a proper diet efficiently is a complex task requiring knowledge of what combinations of vegetable protein sources will provide a "complete protein" balance. Adequate supplies of vitamins, minerals, fats, and carbohydrates can be provided cumulatively, but protein balance must be at the same meal. The simple rule about combining a grain with a legume or milk product in the same meal is a handy shorthand way of remembering how to do it. Grains, nuts, and seeds are all low in some of the amino acids that are plentiful in milk and in legumes (soybeans, lentils, other beans). The grains—wheat, rice, barley, oats—are like the nuts and seeds, so the "beans and rice" combinations offer a wide range of possibilities for protein balance, as well as some fun in the experimenting.

The leading proponent of such diets has been Frances Moore Lappé, in her book, *Diet for a Small Planet*. Lappé gives recipes as well as the theoretical explanation. Using the less expensive sources of protein, rather than eggs and meat, has other advantages. It reduces fat intake and also helps reduce world pressure on land and resources; it takes several pounds of grain to produce a single pound of meat. However, lest you think that it is enough to know the chemical analysis of amino acids and the food combinations that provide a balance chemically, there is a substantial discrepancy between the chemical analysis, results of nutrition experiments on rats, and experiments with human beings (United Nations Food and Agriculture Organization). Foods that appear excellent chemically may perform poorly in practice, and vice versa. (For those who like peanut butter, it can be said that it is one food that seems to produce better nutrition than its chemical analysis would indicate!) The more general point is that nutrition research is not all that definitive yet. There is even reason to believe that individuals differ as to what they can metabolize effectively. We know, for example, that some of us lack the enzymes to digest cow's milk properly, and that some entire tribes manage to survive on apparently inadequate diets. Better diets may be made easier to attain by a number of new scientific developments. One is a cross between rye and wheat called Triticale, which contains more total protein and more of two essential proteins, lysine and methionine. Another is a cross between a cow and a buffalo that produces meat with less cholesterol. Some new animal feeds do the same thing.

Great attention has been given to reducing cholesterol in the diet because of its apparent association with heart disease. Unfortunately, many of the nonmeat protein diets proposed by conservation enthusiasts are high in cholesterol because of their reliance on cheese and eggs. Luxury foods like beef, butter, blue cheese, crab, and shrimp also tend to be high in cholesterol. On the other hand, it is the more expensive oils like safflower, sunflower, and corn oil that contain less saturated fat than the other vegetable oils. The hydrogenation necessary to solidify oils into hard margarine or shortening increases the proportion of saturated fat in all vegetable oils (see app. 10.3).

If you have solved the complexity of balanced proteins, there are still the minerals and vitamins, and the need for enough calories for energy. Calories come from carbohydrates, fats, or proteins and are of real concern only to those who need to gain or lose weight. But there are some twenty-three minerals, sixteen of them needed only in trace amounts (that includes iron), the other seven in less microscopic quantities, the most familiar being calcium. Obviously, a variety of foods is the only way most of us can be sure of receiving all those elements.

There are twelve important vitamins, some with two names, like ascorbic acid (C), thiamine (B_1), riboflavin (B_2), and pyridoxine (B_6). The four fat-soluble vitamins (A, D, E, and K) can accumulate in the system, and overdoses can be dangerous, whereas huge doses of vitamin C (as recommended, with inadequate evidence, by some) tend to flush right through. Again, eating a variety of foods seems the only way—without a large household computer—of assuring adequate nutrition. Experts like Jean Mayer recommend variety, moderation, exercise, and lower salt intake. The reason for cutting sodium is that it is associated with hypertension and heart disease and is certainly no longer necessary for food preservation, as it once was. Most of the other spices are safer and can substitute for salt.

The amount of each nutrient needed varies according to age and sex, and standards are recommended by two groups of experts, who give slightly differing advice. The United States Department of Agriculture's "Recommended Daily Allowances" are used in the Food and Drug Administration's dietary labeling regulations (see app. 10.2). The other "Recommended Dietary Allowances" provides more detail. It is issued by the Food and Nutrition Board, National Research Council, National Academy of Sciences. (See app. 10.4.)

Exercise

There is a growing belief that exercise may be even more important than diet in maintaining good health. High cholesterol may result from excessive intake of saturated fat combined with nervous strain, but only when exercise is inadequate to burn it up. Of course, one should consult with a doctor before beginning any program of vigorous exercise.

The accumulating body of evidence about the beneficial aspects of exercise is impressive. There are even extreme examples of people overcoming handicaps of one sort or another by persistent effort. But single case studies are less persuasive than large-scale scientific studies. Perhaps the most interesting of these was a longitudinal study of London bus drivers and ticket takers, who worked for the company for many years and who were issued uniforms, requiring records of their weight and girth. Over the years, the ticket-taking "squirrels," who went up and down stairs on the double-decker buses collecting fares, remained slim and healthy. The drivers, who sat, got heavier and suffered far more heart attacks and other illnesses. One could argue that the London traffic caused the drivers a lot of nervous strain, but the "squirrels" also suffered strain, keeping track of a changing mix of passengers, dealing with unruly ones, and answering questions.

Another result of lack of exercise is "back trouble," variously referred to as lumbago, slipped disc, pinched nerve, neuralgia. Poor muscle tone or deterioration of the discs allows the fibrous discs between the vertebrae to slip and pinch the nerve fibers that run down through the vertebrae. The nerve then causes various muscles to go into spasm, which usually increase the pinching in a reinforcing cycle. The standard prescription—aspirin, heat, rest, and mild exercise when it is possible—is not only for comfort but to break the cycle. Most doctors say that a regimen of relatively simple exercises, regularly adhered to, will usually prevent the problem or a recurrence. It turns out that the prescribed exercises for lower back problems mimic those of pushing a lawn mower or hoeing a garden!

Older people tend to be plagued with circulatory problems, also made less serious with regular exercise. Analogies with animals are always imperfect, but there are very impressive studies of rats showing that they live a great deal longer when they are hungry and active much of the time.

One of the perils of affluence is that we tend to pay machines or other people to do all the things that exercise our muscles, leaving us with the tension-producing tasks like fixing things or earning the money to pay for them. Even power steering and automatic transmission, for all their convenience, remove most of the mild exercise that driving used to call for. Substituting tennis or jogging or other sports tends to produce too much strain at irregular intervals, or for only selected muscles. Some real planning and discipline may be called for, particularly for those in "sedentary occupations."

Safety, Prevention, and Strategy

Avoidable accidents account for some medical costs, because people seem to undervalue the probabilities that they will occur, or the possible costs if they do. The evidence on the value of seat belts is clear, but apparently not convincing. People still leave overturned boats to swim for shore, go boating without life preservers, and live with frayed electric cords and other hazards. Would they buy a lawn mower that was safe but, according to Consumers Union, costs twice as much? This raises the tricky question of whether laws should mandate expensive safety.

Preventive medicine is proving especially necessary for world travelers, particularly when they leave a highly sanitary society, and the germs from which they have developed immunity, and expose themselves to new dangers. Virulent strains of malaria, typhoid, amoebic dysentery, and hepatitis are the main examples of diseases arising from travel in countries with less concern for sanitation (Consumers Union, 1964).

Much is written about checkups and preventive medical care, and they are important. Yet going through a full inventory of available tests is difficult, expensive, and perhaps not even necessary. Some tests are costly or even dangerous and might be used more selectively. As to symptoms, after sixty years of age, the usual medical signs do not predict accurately, so specialists in geriatric medicine are needed to decide what to test for. The proper strategy has to be based on some assessment of the probabilities of various illnesses or diseases and the costs of not finding them early. In many cases there are early warning indicators which can increase the precision of our probabilities and lead to more effective choices. What the public needs is a strategy: which symptoms should indicate which further investigation? At what ages should there be assessments looking for certain common troubles?

In the case of a bad back, there are remarkably clear and unambiguous indications as to whether the problem is a simple muscular strain or involves a pinched nerve (slipped disc), because in the latter case the pain travels along the nerve down a leg or arm. The potential problems are serious, and medical care is essential; yet there has been no attempt to educate the public on how to recognize the symptoms.

In small children, symptoms of illness are often dramatic, but the doctor usually cannot produce a useful diagnosis until a fever has persisted for at least a day or two. The error of waiting too long needs to be avoided, but so should the error of running for help too early. Self-education in medical matters needs to focus on knowing enough to know when one needs a doctor, and when one does not.

Mental Health

Avoiding the need for medical care has the highest payoff in the area of mental health, where the potential costs are immense and mostly uninsurable. There are books, a proliferation of them, on methods for staying sane, achieving inner peace, or just being happy. There are also organizations, movements, and cults. That few of them have any scientific credentials or evidence, and that most of them are highly profitable to their founders or managers, has apparently not stifled their growth. The quantitative evidence on the beneficial effects of legitimate psychotherapy is not much better, although some of the biofeedback people and meditation experts can show some physiological changes produced by their methods, with at least some selected individuals.

Some of the traditional psychology books may be useful in suggesting ways of staying out of emotional trouble and listing "early warning" signs that indicate a need for help. There are two main indicators to watch for in yourself and your friends: *overreacting*—responding in intensity or manner out of all proportion to the stimulus, and *stubbornness*—continuing some pattern of behavior in the face of repeated experience that it does not produce desired results (J. J. B. Morgan). The very emotional difficulties that call for help may make it difficult for us to realize we need it, however. Indeed, there is evidence that even spouses, close relatives, and friends tend to overlook or excuse obvious indications of trouble until it is too late for therapy to be effective, or some damage has been done. People who end up on shooting sprees or who require institutionalization frequently have a long known history of bizarre behavior, covered up by loved ones.

One other common strain running through much of the literature on mental health is a generalization that too much concern with oneself and one's own feelings, and too much isolation from others, can itself cause or accentuate emotional difficulties. The Russians claim that during the 800-day siege of Leningrad during World War II, when millions died of bombs or starvation, there was not a single recorded case of suicide. People were too busy trying to keep the invaders out and trying to survive! But others insist that organizations require, perhaps for efficiency, that people conform and give up some individuality and freedom, and some people find this difficult. The great efficiencies from division of labor and specialization also require that we cooperate and conform even in such mundane things as working regular hours.

A third line of explanation of emotional difficulties focuses on guilt and conflict between values we were supposed to have and things we ended up doing. Whether openly rejecting the values of the past eliminates this problem without substituting others is unclear.

For a person who realizes that help is needed with mental or emotional problems, however, there is no buyers' guide to good psychiatric care. A psychiatrist, who has an M.D. degree as well as some psychiatric training, may be more likely to distinguish organic medical problems from emotional ones. Psychologists are licensed to do clinical work in some states, and degrees in clinical psychology, guidance and counseling, or social work indicate the amount of formal training. More and more ministers and staff people in social agencies are being trained in guidance and counseling, and they are presumably responsible and competent. Beyond that, there is the proliferation of self-accredited experts, gurus, etc., who may well be excellent—one just does not know. Occasional scandals indicate that there are problems. These can occur even with well-trained counselors, but (it is hoped) not as often.

Public Policy Aspects

Whenever individuals behave in ways that cause problems for themselves or others, society tends to step in. Preventive medicine is one area in which government has been active. Public efforts to clean up water supplies or assure adequate treatment of sewage, or to encourage or supply inoculations and vaccinations, have gone on for a long time. Sometimes they run up against "private enterprise" and retreat, encouraging people to purchase their "prevention" privately, as in the case of polio shots. The result is often that the poor and uneducated do not get the preventive care, which creates problems for themselves and for others. Like any other attempt at change, public health measures can rely either on subsidy (providing free or subsidized services) or on coercion (mandating the adequate treatment of sewage, or certain vaccinations).

Even a household which is successfully handling its own regimen of preventive medicine has an interest in what others do, since no one lives in a vacuum. It is difficult in the present state of knowledge to put price tags on the benefits of preventive medicine, and in any case, they are often mixed up with other benefits such as a more pleasant environment, freedom from pollution, etc. The strategy of publicly-financed screening, such as mass chest X-rays, has been questioned because it is not at all clear that the same funds used to take care of the known sick, or making sure those with clear symptoms get help, might not produce more benefit.

One discouraging phenomenon in the field of preventive medicine has been the public resistance to adding fluoride to water supplies, in the face of convincing evidence of its effectiveness. Even the support of the American Dental Association, which put its professional ethics ahead of self-interest, has not helped. When forced to local option, fluoride has lost more times than it has won.

Getting Medical Care

When the symptoms call for medical care, or there is good reason for a checkup, how does the individual know where to go and what to do? There is no consumers' protective league that rates doctors and hospitals. In fact, the only policing of the medical profession is by the profession itself, and even when problems are recognized, they are handled quietly and privately. There are "academies" and societies which accredit hospitals and specialists, and most libraries have copies of *Directory of Medical Specialists* (see also Placere and Marwick). But the consumer's main aid must necessarily be an expert inside the system, which means a good general practitioner. The value is not only the care the general doctor provides in ordinary illnesses, but the skill in diagnosis and referral to competent specialists when one needs them. Unfortunately, most consumers do not appreciate the value of diagnosis and referral; the big rewards in fame and money go to the specialists. It is proving difficult to get doctors to go into general or family practice and stay there for this reason.

It is against the ethics of the profession to solve this problem by allowing the specialist to remit part of his fee to the doctor who referred the patient to him (fee-splitting). The reason is obvious—how can one trust a doctor to refer a patient to the best specialist, and only when necessary, if the referring doctor receives a payment only upon referral, and perhaps a larger split if the specialist needs the business? Perhaps people will begin to realize the value of good diagnosis and expert referral (and follow-up), demand more of it, bid up its price, and, as a result, induce more doctors to go into general practice.

How is one to select a general practitioner? Word of mouth tends to get many patients for the popular doctors. But do people really assess their doctors on the basis of their care in diagnosis, careful records, and frequent updating of their knowledge? One can assess for oneself on the first visit whether a doctor takes a good medical history, collects symptoms methodically, and explains things adequately. Since it is difficult to change doctors, and since good care requires that the doctor be familiar with your medical history, the initial selection process is crucial. To avoid having to repeat the process, or being turned over to another doctor one did not select, it may be wise to select a doctor not much older than oneself.

More and more doctors are practicing in groups, so the consumer needs to consider the quality of the whole group. The best group situation is the one in which each member of the group has primary patients and takes others only when their main doctor cannot. The older, more autocratic group of one senior doctor and his (sometimes exploited) assistants is not as good.

Malpractice

The local medical societies in many counties have committees watching over the medical ethics of their members, and grievances can often be taken to them. Unfortunately, the trend has been to malpractice suits, forcing the issue into adversary proceedings and expensive legal confrontations. The patient sees the situation as unfair, since it is difficult to get one doctor to testify against another. The doctor sees the growing likelihood of unjustified and nuisance suits as a threat, covered only by expensive insurance. A California study, however, indicated that malpractice suits were largely against rather authoritarian doctors who were not candid with their patients and even tried to cover up errors, and largely by relatively hostile and unusual patients (Blum).

As with auto accidents, the combination of laws governing malpractice suits and insurance makes little economic sense. If it were only a few bad doctors who were the problem, presumably they could and would be refused insurance; but in fact certain combinations of medical specialty, patient, and lawyers lead to very large settlements. These are ultimately paid for by all patients in the form of the higher doctors' bills necessary to cover the costs of malpractice insurance. Justice is not cleanly served, and the inefficiency is substantial. One expert estimated that only 16 to 17 percent of the premiums paid for malpractice insurance ever went to injured patients (see chap. 9). The explosion of such suits has dramatized a problem that could be ignored when they were rare. It is clear that some kind of no-fault insurance is in order. In the meantime, attempts have been made to use voluntary arbitration. The patient is asked to sign an agreement in advance to submit claims or disputes to arbitration under the rules of the American Arbitration Association. The panel is usually three persons—a lawyer, a doctor or hospital administrator, and a layperson. There are some costs to arbitration, of course, but usually much less than filing a suit under tort law.

One of the worst effects of malpractice suits is their distortion of medical practice in a defensive attempt to avoid them. Unnecessary precautions, from X-rays to elaborate records to very conservative treatment, have been stimulated. Perhaps most wasteful has been the reluctance of doctors to use paramedical personnel for initial screening, administration of injections, explanations, and so forth.

Costs of Medical Care

One also wants a reasonably priced medical care. It avoids worry and some unpleasant surprises to ask about the likely cost of any treatment or special examination before it is undertaken. A good doctor considers it proper medical practice to discuss fees beforehand. Both fees and quality vary widely from area to area, as well as within areas. The level of surgeons' fees in southern California is notoriously high. The quality of medical care in most of the poorer states is also said to be bad. Since doctors usually go to medical school and practice in the state where they grew up, a state with a poor medical school gets the kind of medical service it pays for. Going to medical school in a different state is difficult, because medical education is heavily subsidized, largely by state funds, and out-of-state students are not encouraged. The net result is a perpetuation of a poor geographic distribution of doctors.

The supply of doctors also is affected by a number of things. The cost of a medical education in time and money is very heavy; although it has traditionally been subsidized, the subsidy has not covered all the costs, particularly if one considers foregone earnings. Students have paid some costs in tuition and in long periods of no earnings or substandard earnings as interns and residents.

The medical profession itself has encouraged restricting the supply of doctors, usually by focusing on the need for high quality and long training periods. The lure of the high-paid specialties, or of careers in research or public health, where one's total contribution looked greater, has attracted many of the limited number of medical school graduates away from general practice. One result of the perceived shortage of doctors has been an influx of doctors trained abroad, who do their internship and residency training here and then stay here to practice. While this provides an additional supply of interns, it of course exploits the country that provided the subsidized medical school education without getting a doctor later. Because it also reduces control over the quality of medical education received by doctors practicing in the United States, the flow is gradually being cut off; even that alternative supply will will not be available.

The supply of medical care, as distinct from the supply of doctors, can be expanded by increasing the efficiency with which we use doctors. Two main ways are group practice and the increased use of paramedical personnel. Both mean more division of labor and specialization. Group practice in this case means not a few doctors of the same specialty sharing an office but a mix of medical specialists combining to keep joint records, make the referral process and the feedback to the diagnostician more effective, and share certain expensive facilities and services. There is a lot to be said in favor of this kind of group practice. The mere fact that each specialist's work is being subjected to closer scrutiny by fellow professionals increases the likelihood that it will be carefully done. It is possible to redress legally the salary imbalance between diagnosticians and surgeons. Any loss of "free choice of physician" is negligible, since one can still specify which doctor one wants to see; there is rarely much choice of specialists, anyway.

Group practices are not necessarily affiliated with prepayment plans or group insurance schemes. Indeed, their connection with prepayment schemes may well have slowed down the development of group practices. The American Medical Association for years strongly opposed any group practice schemes and even lost an antitrust suit over the matter. The new health maintenance organizations do combine group practice with prepaid fees for total care rather than for each service (see p. 175).

If doctors were willing to delegate more functions to nurses, secretaries, and other specialists, they could presumably concentrate on the things for which they got all that expensive training.

Drugs

A major part of the cost of medical care is drugs, particularly prescription drugs. There is a long history of controversy over retail price maintenance and the use of the law to increase the power of producers over the retail prices of their products. Substantial retail markups were buttressed by the various licensing regulations on pharmacists. Legal breakthroughs that make the posting of prices permissible or even mandatory are helping, as is the growth of mail-order companies selling even prescription drugs (except narcotics) at much lower prices.

It is difficult for an individual to shop around for drugs, particularly when he is in pain and anxious for relief. Some groups have conducted local drug price surveys in an attempt to increase competition and decrease prices. *Consumer Reports* published a list of the most frequently used drugs, four of them nonprescription insulin preparations used continually for diabetes, with illustrative amounts and prices from the Chicago area, illustrating the wide spread in prices. The Seattle Regional Office of the Federal Trade Commission issues a handbook for use in community drug price surveys with instructions and a list of twenty-five drugs with quantities, three of them generic—that is, not brand names restricted by patents (U.S. Federal Trade Commission, 1975). They also suggest checking on nine services that might affect costs and what you get for your money, such as delivery, acceptance of checks or credit cards, and discounts for senior citizens. Consumers are often urged to get their doctor to prescribe by generic drug name rather than brand name, and some states have passed laws allowing pharmacists to substitute generic drugs if asked. There are, however, a substantial number of new drugs still available only as brand-name drugs.

Paying for Medical Care

In chapter 9, in the discussion of paying for medical care by medical insurance, it was pointed out that for the more frequent, less costly items there was a clear advantage in some budgeting or reserve funds rather than insurance. Actually, however, most people prefer insurance that covers everything; this does eliminate the problem of negotiating the medical charges, which is done by the insurance managers. This is not really insurance but budgeting, and is justifiable only if there is also some genuine insurance against the very large risks. Often it seems free, because an employer pays for it, without offering alternatives.

One long-standing controversy is whether the government should assure that people get adequate medical care by forcing everyone to have medical insurance. Opponents have called this socialized medicine, but actually most plans would leave the private market relatively intact, provide the sellers of medical services with an assured market, and to some extent force some people (low income) to pay for medical care they had been getting free.

There have long been many sources of payment for medical bills besides the patient's pocket at the time. There has always been some charity medical care, originally provided by doctors and hospitals themselves or by charitable organizations. More recently it has been paid for by welfare agencies as well as the Veterans Administration and the Department of Health and Human Services. There is very little really free, meaning unpaid for, medical care any more. The sources of payment are just more varied (table 18).

Medical costs are also covered under tort law if some negligent driver or homeowner is responsible (and insured), or under the worker's compensation law of the state if the injury occurred in the course of employment or the illness resulted in part from the employment. Employers often provide medical insurance, or partly subsidize it, or negotiate it for groups at more favorable rates. The vast majority of people have at least some kind of hospitalization insurance. The fraction of doctor and hospital bills actually covered by insurance is difficult to determine; when it has been estimated by surveys, it is usually considerably smaller than the fraction of people covered, because insurance does not cover everything and usually has upper limits.

Private medical insurance plans cannot handle the inability or unwillingness of the poor and the aged to pay for their own insurance. In some states Blue Cross originally subsidized the aged, by collecting excess premiums from those under sixty-five to pay for the excess medical costs of those over sixty-five. This practice gradually broke down as the young, particularly those represented by labor unions, objected to helping the aged in this way. Of course, those with no coverage did not get the care they needed.

The inadequacy of private insurance, particularly for the poor, who are pressured by more immediate needs, and for the aged, whose medical needs are so extensive that insurance seems unbearably expensive for them, led to two federal programs, Medicaid and Medicare. The first is a federally aided state transfer system for providing

Table 18. Per Capita Personal Health Expenditures by Use and Source, 1975

Uses	Under 19	19–64	65+	All Ages
Hospital	$ 71	$230	$ 603	$215
Physicians	70	100	218	102
Dentists	21	45	24	35
Other Professionals	6	10	20	10
Drugs	28	49	118	49
Eye Glasses	5	12	23	11
Nursing Home Care	3	9	342	42
Other	7	18	13	14
Total	$212	$472	$1360	$476

Sources	Under 65	65+	All Ages
Direct Payment	$128	$ 390	$155
Private Health Insurance	132	73	126
Philanthropy and Industry	6	5	6
Government	108	892	189
Total	$375	$1360	$476

Source: U. S. Department of Health, Education and Welfare, Social Security Administration, Office of Research and Statistics, "Age Differences in Health Care Spending, Fiscal Year 1975," by Marjorie Smith Mueller and Robert M. Gibson; see also Robert M. Bigson and Marjorie Smith Mueller, "National Health Expenditures, Fiscal Year 1976," in *Social Security Bulletin* 40 (April 1977), pp. 3–22; Marjorie Smith Mueller, "Private Health Insurance in 1975: Coverage, Enrollment and Financial Experience," *Social Security Bulletin* 40 (June, 1977) pp. 3–21. (Insurance covers 75 percent of hospital care costs, less than half of physician service costs, less than a tenth of the rest.)

medical care for the indigent, leaving each state to design its own program and to define "unable to pay." The result initially was that the more prosperous and progressive states, able to provide the matching funds, set up very liberal programs and absorbed a large part of the federal funds, even though the system was intended to send the bulk of the funds to the poorer states. The system has, however, vastly increased the provision of medical care to the poor in some states.

Medicare was added to the Social Security system as an efficient form of medical insurance for the retired. It is administered through some private organization in each state, an insurance carrier or Blue Cross. The result of these plans has been an explosion in the demand for care, as well as the ability to pay for it, that ran up against an inadequate supply. The supply of medical care cannot be increased soon or without a major capital investment. The inevitable consequence has been a dramatic increase in the price of medical care.

In response to the exploding demand for care, much attention has been given to increasing the efficiency of health care delivery. All kinds of proposals, from economic incentives to new technology (e.g., cable television), have been suggested. Given the high labor costs in a hospital, a new hospital designed to minimize human labor can "pay for itself" relatively fast. Also being tried in some areas are groups called health maintenance organizations (HMO), which are essentially a combination of group practice and prepayment schemes. Rather than purchase health insurance, the subscriber pays a monthly fee to the HMO group, whose doctors he must use. Some HMOs also maintain hospitals. The idea is that if your payment covers the cost of keeping you healthy, the providers (doctors and hospital) will practice more preventive medicine, since their fees do not depend upon providing more service. They lose money if they provide services that are no longer needed. The regulations for becoming an official HMO are sufficiently restrictive that similar unofficial arrangements are also being tried.

One must be careful in using the term "cost" when one means price. Discussions of the cost of socialized medicine in Britain, or of any similar provision in this country, seem to assume that these costs are equivalent in meaning to the cost, say, of a new military missile. In fact, the amounts mentioned are not really costs but transfers—money taken from a large group of tax or fee payers to pay for the medical care of a smaller group, those who need care. Insofar as any such redistribution of income has costs, they are the costs of administering the system and the impact of any market distortions or disincentive effects caused by the taxes or fees collected. The costs per person of administering a universal government health system are much lower than the costs of group insurance, and group insurance is much less costly per person than individual private insurance, since there are economies of scale as well as fewer agents and salesmen to be paid.

The provision of medical care is, of course, a real cost to a society, to be balanced against the benefits. But that cost remains, regardless of who pays for it. If medical care is provided where it was not previously, that increased cost must be weighed against the increased benefits, not treated as a total loss. In the case of medical care, some of the benefits are return to investment in human capital, measurable by increased production and earnings, less time lost in the workplace, less need for nursing care. Others are in increased happiness of individuals, which should be considered part of the national "income" even if we cannot measure it. This is one reason we provide medical care even for old people who do not produce anything, and not just for the younger, more "valuable" members of society (Titmus; Somers and Somers).

Handling the Income Loss

Medical care may reduce or eliminate future income loss, but illness is often accompanied by loss of current earnings. Some of the same systems that pay for medical care also compensate for some of the income loss—tort liability of negligent drivers or homeowners, workers' compensation. Some states have, in addition to unemployment compensation, a system of cash sickness benefits for workers. Many employers provide paid sick leave. In extreme cases, there is also disability coverage under Social Security, some private disability insurance, and general welfare.

In Britain the provision of medical care requires centralized records, which allowed a study to be conducted comparing the work loss and illness experience of workers who did or did not have any income maintenance payments when they were out sick. As expected, those whose income did not stop entirely were somewhat likely to be sick more often; but their total days lost from work were slightly *fewer* than those not so covered. The implication is that those whose income stopped whenever they stayed home sick waited until they could not possibly get to work—but it then took them longer to recover. This is one of the few bits of evidence for the economic value of early care, and the disadvantages of monetary barriers to it.

Public Policy

We have already discussed a number of public policy issues, but a more systematic treatment of them as alternative strategies is in order. Most public actions have been attempts to increase the amount and quality of medical care and thus the health of the nation. This has been done, not by directly interfering with the marketplace, but by subsidizing the supply and subsidizing the demand. Obviously, if one subsidizes only the demand in a situation where the supply responds slowly, if at all, the main result is rising prices rather than more or better medical care. On the other hand, merely providing hospitals and training many doctors might lead to wasteful underemployment of resources if people were not encouraged to seek the care. Price competition does not seem to work well in the medical care industry.

When it is a matter of public concern that people get certain care because the health of others is affected, it can be brought about by coercion, as with inoculations. In general, however, we have tried to induce and bribe rather than coerce. Hospitals were originally subsidized by private charity, including the unpaid work of the religious orders. They were also subsidized in a sense by the very low wages they paid, until the combination of unionization and better financing revealed what a market wage really was. Federal subsidy today largely takes the form of construction costs. A full and complicated analysis of the system of subsidies and an assessment of the taxes that pay for it is beyond the scope of this book, and is in a process of transition, anyway.

The subsidy to medical education has been shifting from the states to the federal government. The unpaid or underpaid work of the doctors in training may seem like a subsidy paid by the doctors themselves, but it is less a subsidy than a postponement, recouped out of the later earnings of doctors. Would both society and the doctors be more comfortable with a system that paid them more, early in their training? It seems likely that the medical schools would have a broader choice of students if they were not restricted to those willing either to postpone earning much for a long period or able and willing to receive subsidies from their parents. There is already a trend toward more adequate salaries for interns and residents in training. This would not necessarily reduce doctors' later earnings, so long as doctors are so scarce. One way to do that and help fund medical education would be a surtax on the individuals who receive the education, as a way to recoup the costs from their later earnings. This would require taxing different individuals at different rates and would require some legal ingenuity, but would allow society to assure proper medical care without subsidizing some small subgroup.

Coming back to the supply of medical care, we find great concern for the efficiency of the delivery of care, now that funding has driven up the demand and the prices. One complication is that if one looks at the cost of *providing* the service rather than the cost of *receiving* it, one ignores the costs that do not appear on the books of the hospital or doctor. For example, the costs of hospital care can be cut by building a new efficient hospital on cheaper land outside of town. The increased costs to patients in getting there are ignored. Similarly, if the costs to patients of time spent waiting in doctors' waiting rooms are not accounted for, the apparent costs of care can be cut by arrangements that increase that waiting time and thereby increase patients' costs—perhaps even more than they reduce the costs of doctors and hospitals.

The supply of medical care is increased also by public health activities and by research that presumably makes the doctors and medicines much more effective. Here again, government activities have paralleled a private market-private enterprise system. Frictions arise, of course, when this happens. The pharmaceutical producers and the retail druggists in particular have fought to maintain their own interests; the extensive advertising by the former in the *Journal of the American Medical Association* has raised ethical questions. Any large-scale provision of medical care raises the possibility of bulk buying of medicines to save money, a threat to manufacturers and, even more, to retail druggists.

The pharmaceutical manufacturers have justified their large markups on the basis of the costs of their research, but critics have pointed to their extensive expenditures on promotion: advertising, and the "detail men" who visit doctors regularly to keep them up on the latest products and give them free samples. Critics have also raised questions about the tendency of doctors to rely on clearly biased information, corrected by research articles in the medical journals, sometimes only after long delays. To fill the gap, one independent organization, founded by a former director of Consumers Union, now issues a *Medical Letter on Drugs and Therapeutics* for doctors, providing unbiased assessment of pharmaceuticals and rapid summaries of the latest independent findings on their effectiveness and side effects. Cases of continued use of drugs after unfavorable assessments, in one case a drug known to produce irreversible deafness in some fraction of patients, certainly justify concern about the relation of private producers and salesmen to medical care.

The lack of concern on the part of many doctors about the prices of drugs is based partly on ignorance of what those prices are, partly on the fact that the doctor has free samples he can dispense wherever he feels the patient may have trouble paying, and partly on the fact that there are now many insurance sources to pay for them anyway. Doctors who know that prescriptions can be given to their patients and then filled by mail at vastly reduced prices, seldom mention the fact to their patients, even when the prescription must be refilled many times. Some are turning to prescribing by generic drug name rather than brand, however, to save patients money. Attempts to prove the branded drugs are of higher quality have not been convincing. Doctors do receive certain services from local druggists (nothing illegal like kickbacks), but mostly they seem unconcerned about drug prices, or convinced that even at the high price the medicine is worth it.

Public policy discussions about medical care are sometimes tinged with emotionalism that leads to poor economic analysis. The cry is for "the best quality medical care for everyone." But there are more and more new techniques, procedures, treatments, and medicines which are not only very expensive but have a low probability of doing much good. In such a situation there should perhaps be some limit to the amount invested in any one patient, particularly when there is some aggregate limit on the resources available for medical care. The question is easily raised, for instance, whether the amount of resources put into some transplant operations might not have saved more lives or produced more benefits if put into other kinds of care.

Even more difficult questions arise in deciding about some of these expensive and "marginally useful" procedures, about whether preference should be given to patients whose future productivity may be affected (where there is an economic payoff), as against the aged or those who will remain disabled in any case. Should some of the expensive, doubtful new procedures be restricted in that way? Or should they perhaps be restricted as in the past to the wealthy who are willing to spend their own money on them? The latter alternative may seem unfair until one reflects how unlikely the benefits are; it would certainly put a more critical eye on these new procedures if someone other than the government or insurance companies had to pay for them!

All in all, there are problems in applying good economic analysis to a part of the economic system where the government and private philanthropy are both active, emotions run high, and a whole series of vested interests exist. Compounding the difficulty is the delegation of function to states; this results in a great disparity between states, and often inadequate standards in some of them.

The ordinary household may appear a defenseless pawn in this struggle among the various vested interests and professional prides. The only defense in the short run is keeping informed about the various systems and interests one must deal with. In the long run, the consumer may want to have more to say about a system controlled by those who supply the main services, for private remuneration, however professional and socially concerned those groups try to be.

The combination of increased government participation, more insurance, and rising prices for medical care has meant an explosion in the aggregate expenditures for medical care, even as a percent of gross national product (GNP), from 4.5 percent of GNP in 1955 to 8.4 percent in 1975 (Gibson and Mueller). The fraction of total medical expenditure (including construction and research) paid for by public funds increased in the same period from 25.5 percent to 41.6 percent. This represented a kind of socialization of medicine but with minimal interference with its administration or operation.

Eighty-seven percent of the aggregate medical expenditure is for personal health care, and we have already seen in table 18 that most of it goes to hospitals and doctors. It is paid for by government (particularly for the aged), insurance, and direct payments, with a little philanthropy thrown in. Over time the government share has grown dramatically, insurance remained about a fourth, and private direct payments have dropped to a third of the total (Gibson and Mueller).

Governments have also tried in various ways to reduce the need for medical care: public policy is increasingly seen as important in monitoring the use of chemicals that pollute the air and water. A few dramatic cases of methyl mercury or polyvinyl chloride poisoning, and the discovery of chlorinated hydrocarbons like DDT and other long-lived chemicals in foods, precipitate action; but it is a long, slow process to identify pollutants and design methods to discourage their introduction. Most economists favor the use of taxes or effluent charges for polluting firms, to maximize freedom in the choice of methods to reduce the problem. In some cases, it is a matter of reducing the total rather than abolishing all effluents, since air and water can absorb and recycle some amounts of some pollutants. It seems most effective to concentrate on those for whom it is easiest to reduce effluents. Charges based on the amount of oxygen required to render the pollutant inert have been suggested.

Governments have long been involved in assuring the proper treatment of garbage and waste, assuring good water supplies, and monitoring the foods and drugs we use. They have also been concerned with safety from accidents on the job, at home, and on the highways. Occupational safety has been improved by the Occupational Safety and Health Act, and the safety of products by the Consumer Product Safety Commission. Indeed, the consumer has benefited greatly from such government activities, as will become apparent to anyone observing the quality of milk, market sanitation, or worker safeguards in less developed countries. Of course, individuals or groups must continue to point out slippages or remaining problems.

Fads, Quacks, Nostrums, Food Additives, New Nonprescription Drugs

For years the medical profession and the federal government have been trying to keep people from wasting their time and money and risking their health on fads, nutritional and other, or on medical quacks and their "patent medicines." So long as no false claims are made and the stuff is not harmful, it is difficult to stop. The Federal Trade Commission, the Food and Drug Administration, and the Public Health Service have campaigns of both education and law enforcement to keep the problem in check. Particularly in the more painful or hopeless situations like arthritis or cancer, it is understandable that people would turn to anything that promised relief. When a return of youth is promised, even the well educated may be willing to part with large sums for treatments of the most untested sort. When such nostrums are merely wasteful and the victims can afford it, no one need interfere, but when there is danger, including the danger of failing to get proper treatment, or when they mulct the poor, it is clear that a societal problem exists.

The situation is different with food additives and new "nonfood food" products. In these cases, private industry wants to sell something, or reduce spoilage, and the policy issue is how conclusive the proof must be that the additive is safe before it is allowed. Purists will insist on perfection. The economist might balance some risks against some advantages when there are apparent benefits, but argue for tighter security precautions when the additive produces no real benefits aside from appearance or a competitive advantage.

The problem of the efficacy and safety of new drugs hit the nation with new force when the thalidomide scandal erupted in the 1960s, and as a result, new attention has been paid to DDT and some sweetening and coloring agents; there appears to be a new courage by government agencies to ban things. The story of the pending reforms in the Food and Drug Act being saved from extinction by the thalidomide story makes interesting reading, as do the books which periodically stir the public conscience (Carson; Nader).

There is another side to the problem of regulating drug use. The necessity of Food and Drug Administration approval, and the reliance on private enterprise to develop and market new drugs, inhibits the development of some products. Only those drugs that can be sold to a mass market, or to patients so desperate that cost is no object, are economically worth the very large investment necessary to develop, test, and secure approval. Some apparently effective pharmaceuticals widely used elsewhere are not approved for use in the United States. An apparently excellent medication to control seizures (sodium valproate) was cleared in this country only when national television made an issue of it. So the Food and Drug Administration has to avoid two kinds of error: accepting bad drugs and preventing good drugs from reaching the market. To avoid the second, drugs that save lives but have no mass market could be tested at government expense, even if they are sold for profit later. On the other hand, there are countries where social insurance covers the cost of most drugs and where doctors are under pressure to dispense a large variety, most of them presumably harmless, but many also unnecessary.

Summary

The individual needs to know how to avoid the need for medical care, how to find adequate care when it is needed, and how to pay for it. The overlapping and rapidly changing mix of ways of providing and paying for care require attention to new opportunities and dangers. Without medical insurance, for example, you may be vulnerable economically.

Medical care in general is a problem of supply and demand; we want to increase both. In a classic problem of pricing and resource allocation, we think there should be more and better medical care for everyone, but every proposal to achieve that objective has implications for equity of the system—that is, who pays? While it is conceivable that we could *force* everyone to get better medical care, going far beyond the public health measures we now have, it is more likely that we shall rely on bribery, subsidizing medical education, subsidizing medical care for some, and promoting private insurance arrangements and prepayment plans.

The basic resource allocation questions remain. How much medical care is enough? What is the proper allocation among medical care, prevention and public health, and medical research? Will reducing pollution do more good than research on cures, for example?

Finally, there is the question of how much of such an important "industry" can be left to the marketplace and free enterprise. Can the government continue to pay for basic medical research and education, while the pharmaceutical houses develop and sell drugs for high profits, and doctors control the system that employs them? Can their charges continue to rise indefinitely? Can the medical professions police themselves for both quality and ethics? Can we get along with the inequities that arise out of the overlap among a bewildering variety of systems of providing and paying for care? Why are we insuring every minor medical bill but allowing family savings to be wiped out by major medical catastrophes or mental illness?

More Information?

The medical care situation is changing, both in education and in institutional arrangements and systems for paying for care. Experiments with payment or delivery systems will come and go, given the basically incompatible mixture of private enterprise and public programs. Finding good care and paying for it will require keeping up with the local scene, and asking questions about the costs and benefits of any arrangement. Unfortunately, most of the published material is about national issues that consumers can affect only by voting.

American Medical Association. *What Americans Think of the Medical Profession*. Chicago: American Medical Association, 1956.

Anderson, Ronald. *A Behavioral Model of Families' Use of Health Services*. Chicago: Center for Health Administration Studies, Graduate School of Business, University of Chicago, 1968.

Anderson, Ronald; Lion, Joanna; and Anderson, Odin W. *Two Decades of Health Services: Social Survey Trends in Use and Expenditure*. Cambridge, Mass.: Ballinger Publishing Company, 1976. (Gradual improvement in service, and insurance coverage, and in such things as seeing a physician in the first trimester of pregnancy; 65 to 83 percent 1953 to 1970, p. 57.)

Annas, George J. *The Rights of Hospital Patients*. American Civil Liberties Handbook. New York: Discus Books, 1975.

Axelrod, S. J., and Patton, R. E. "The Use and Abuse of Prepaid Comprehensive Physicians' Services." *American Journal of Public Health* 42 (1952): 566–74.

Becker, Harra, ed. *Prepayment and the Community*. New York: McGraw-Hill, 1955. (Analysis of 50,000 Blue Cross bills)

Best's *Accident and Health Buyers' Guide*, periodically.

Blum, Richard N. *The Psychology of Malpractice Suits*. Prepared for the Medical Review and Advisory Board of the California Medical Association, 1957.

Brozen, Yale. "No Scarlet Letter." *Barrons*, 28 February 1972. (States with fewer restrictions on advertising had the lowest prices on eyeglasses.)

Burack, Richard, and Fox, Fred J. *The New Handbook of Prescription Drugs*. Rev. ed. New York: Ballantine Books, 1975.

Burns, Eveline M. *Health Services for Tomorrow: Trends and Issues*. New York: Dunellen, 1973.

Cady, John F., and Andreasen, Anan R. "Price Levels, Price Practices, and Price Discrimination in a Retail Market for Prescription Drugs." *Journal of Consumer Affairs* 9 (1975): 33–48.

Carter, Richard. *The Doctor Business*. New York: Doubleday, 1958.

Consumers Union. *Health Guide for Travelers*. Mt. Vernon, N.Y.: Consumers Union, 1964.

Consumers Union. *The Medicine Show*. 5th ed. Mt. Vernon, N.Y.: Consumers Union, 1980.

Cooper, Barbara S., and McGee, Mary F. "Medical Care Outlays for Three Age Groups: Young, Intermediate, and the Aged." *Social Security Bulletin* 34 (1971): 3–14.

Darsky, B.; Sinai, N.; and Axelrod, S. J. *Comprehensive Physicians' Service Under Voluntary Health Insurance*. Cambridge, Mass.: Harvard University Press, 1958.

de Castro, Josue. *The Geography of Hunger*. London: Victor Gollancz, 1952.

Deutsch, Ronald M. *The Nuts Among the Berries*. Rev. ed. New York: Ballantine, 1967.

Ehrenreich, Barbara John. *The American Health Empire: Power, Profits, and Politics*. New York: Vintage, 1970.

Fein, Rashi. *The Economics of Mental Illness*. New York: Basic Books, 1958.

Fein, Rashi. *The Doctor Shortage*. Washington, D.C.: Brookings Institution, 1967.

Feingold, Eugene, ed. *Medicare: Policy and Politics*. San Francisco: Chandler Publishing Company, 1966.

Feldman, Jacob J. *The Dissemination of Health Information*. Chicago: Aldine, 1966. (National survey of knowledge about disease symptoms)

Fletcher, F. Marion. *Market Restraints in the Retail Drug Industry*. Philadelphia: University of Pennsylvania Press, 1975.

Gibson, Robert, and Mueller, Marjorie. "National Health Expenditures, Fiscal Year 1976." *Social Security Bulletin* 40 (1977): 3–22.

Greenberg, Selig. *The Quality of Mercy*. New York: Kingsport Press, 1971.

Gregg, John. *The Health Insurance Racket and How to Beat It*. Chicago: Regnery, 1974.

Gross, Martin L. *The Doctors*. New York: Random House, 1966.

Gumbhir, Ashok K., and Rodowskas, Christopher A. Jr. "Consumer Price Differences Between Generic and Brand Name Prescriptions." *American Journal of Public Health* 64 (1974): 977–82.

Harvard Medical School. *The Harvard Medical School Health Letter*. Cambridge, Mass.: Harvard Medical School, monthly.

Health Information Foundation. *Progress in Health Services* 15, March-April 1966. (Reports on surveys in 1953, 1958, 1963)

Jacobson, Michael F. *Eater's Digest: The Consumer's Fact Book on Food Additives*. New York: Doubleday, 1972.

Jacoby, Jacob; Chestnut, Robert W.; and Silberman, William. "Consumer Use and Comprehension of Nutrition Information." *Journal of Consumer Research* 4 (1977): 119–28.

Kennedy, Edward M. *In Critical Condition: The Crisis in America's Health Care*. New York: Simon and Schuster, 1973.

Kunnes, Richard. *Your Money or Your Life*. New York: Dodd, Mead, 1971.

Lappé, Frances Moore. *Diet for a Small Planet*. New York: Ballantine, 1971.

Lasagna, Louis. *Life, Death, and the Doctor*. New York: Collier, 1963.

Lewis, Howard and Martha. *The Medical Offenders*. New York: Simon and Schuster, 1970. (Based primarily on a 1960 AMA Disciplinary Committee Report)

McClure, Frank J. *Water Fluoridation*. Bethesda, Md.: National Institute of Health, Department of Health, Education, and Welfare, 1970. (Government Printing Office, 1970.)

Mayer, Jean. *Overweight: Causes, Cost, and Control*. Englewood Cliffs, N.J.: Prentice-Hall, 1968.

Mayer, Jean. *A Diet for Living*. New York: David McKay, 1975. (Paperback from Consumers Union)

Mitford, Jessica. *The American Way of Death*. New York: Simon and Schuster, 1963.

Morgan, John J. B. *How to Keep a Sound Mind*. New York: Macmillan, 1946.

Nader, Ralph. *Unsafe at Any Speed*. New York: Crossman, 1965.

National Academy of Sciences, Academy Forum. *Improvement of Protein Nurtiture*. Washington, D.C.: National Academy of Sciences, 1974.

National Academy of Sciences, Academy Forum. *Sweeteners: Issues and Uncertainties*. Washington, D.C.: National Academy of Sciences, 1975.

National Research Council. *Recommended Dietary Allowances*. 9th rev. ed. Washington, D.C.: National Academy of Sciences, 1979.

National Technical Information Services. *A Study of Health Practices and Opinions: Final Report*. Springfield, Va.: National Technical Information Services, June 1972. (Study made for Food and Drug Administration on worthless and potentially harmful nonprescription drugs)

Perlman, Mark, ed. *The Economics of Health and Medical Care*. Proceedings of a conference of the International Economics Association, Tokyo. New York: Halsted Press, 1974.

Pharmaceutical Manufacturers Association. *Brands, Generics, Prices, and Quality: The Prescribing Debate After a Decade*. Washington, D.C.: Pharmaceutical Manufacturers Association, 1970.

Placere, Morris N., and Marwick, Charles S. *How You Can Get Better Medical Care for Less Money*. New York: Walker and Company, 1973. (Barnes and Noble paperback in 1974)

Paul Revere, DDS [pseud.]. *Dentistry and Its Victims*. New York: St. Martin's Press, 1970.

Ribicoff, Abraham, and Danaceau, Paul. *The American Medical Machine*. New York: Saturday Review Press, 1973.

Schorr, Daniel. *Don't Get Sick in America*. New York: Aurora, 1970.

Schwartz, Harry. *The Case for American Medicine*. New York: David McKay, 1973.

Scitovsky, Anne A., and Snyder, Nelda M. "Effect of Coinsurance on Use of Physicians' Services." *Social Security Bulletin* 35 (1972): 3–19. (Reduced use, but also the number of annual physical exams. Another article in the same issue by Phelps and Newhouse uses multivariate analysis with same results.)

Smith, Victor. *Electronic Computation of Human Diets*. East Lansing, Mich.: Bureau of Business and Economic Research, Graduate School of Business Administration, Michigan State University, 1964.

Somers, Herman M., and Somers, Anne R. *Doctors, Patients, and Health Insurance*. Washington, D.C.: Brookings, 1961.

Sorenson, James R. *Social Aspects of Applied Human Genetics*. New York: Russell Sage Foundation, 1971.

Stare, Frederick J., and McWilliam, Margaret. *Living Nutrition*. 2d ed. New York: John Wiley and Sons, 1977.

Stevens, Rosemary. *American Medicine and the Public Interest*. New Haven, Conn.: Yale University Press, 1971.

Stigler, George J. "The Cost of Subsistence." *Journal of Farm Economics* 27 (1945): 303–14.

Strickland, Stephen P. *U.S. Health Care: What's Wrong and What's Right*. Washington, D.C.: Universe Books, 1973.

Tancredi, Laurence R., ed. *Ethics of Health Care*. Papers of a conference organized by Institute of Medicine. Washington, D.C.: National Academy of Sciences, 1974.

Tinkleberg, J. R., ed. *Marihuana Health Hazards*. New York: Academic Press, 1975.

Titmus, Richard M. *Essays on the Welfare State*. Boston: Beacon Press, 1969.

Tushnet, Leonard. *The Medicine Men*. New York: St. Martin's Press, 1971.

United Nations Food and Agriculture Organization. *Amino Acid Content of Foods and Biological Data on Proteins*. Rome, Italy: Food and Agriculture Organization, 1972. (Compares chemical analysis, rat and human studies)

U.S. Department of Agriculture. *Dietary Levels of Households in the United States*. Household Food Consumption Survey, 1955, Report No. 6. Washington, D.C.: Government Printing Office, 1957.

U.S. Department of Agriculture. *Nutritive Value of Foods*. New ed. Washington, D.C.: Government Printing Office, 1975.

U.S. Department of Agriculture. *Family Economics Review*. Washington, D.C.: Government Printing Office, periodically. (Regularly prices weekly food costs by age and sex)

U.S. Department of Agriculture, Consumer and Marketing Service. *Home and Garden Bulletins*. (Various publications entitled, "How to Buy . . .")

U.S. Department of Commerce, National Bureau of Standards. *Safety for the Household*. Washington, D.C.: Government Printing Office, 1947.

U.S. Department of Health, Education, and Welfare, Public Health Service. *Mental Retardation: Its Biological Factors*. Washington, D.C.: Government Printing Office, 1972. (Genetic counseling)

U.S. Department of Health, Education, and Welfare, Public Health Service. *National Drug Code Directory*. 4th ed. Washington, D.C.: Government Printing Office, 1972.

U.S. Department of Health, Education, and Welfare, Public Health Service, Food and Drug Administration. *Consumer Nutrition Knowledge Survey*, *Report 1, 1973–74*, and *Report 2, 1975*. DHEW Publication No. (FDA) 76-2058 and 76-2059. Washington, D.C.: Government Printing Office, 1976. (A nationwide interview survey)

U.S. Department of Health, Education, and Welfare, Social and Rehabilitation Service, Office of Consumer Services. *Nursing Home Care*. Consumer Information Series, no. 2. Washington, D.C.: Government Printing Office, 1972. (List to check)

U.S. Federal Trade Commission. *Prescription Drug Price Disclosures*. Washington, D.C.: Government Printing Office, 1975. (Proposes rules governing retail price disclosures and gives data on spreads)

U.S. Federal Trade Commission. *Prescription Drug Prices*. Consumer Handbook no. 2. Seattle: Seattle Regional Office, U.S. Federal Trade Commission, 1974.

U.S. Federal Trade Commission. *Consumer Bulletins*. Washington, D.C.: U.S. Federal Trade Commission, 1971. (Various topics)

Walker, Hugh D. *Market Power and Price Levels in the Ethical Drug Industry*. Bloomington: Indiana University Press, 1971.

Wilson, Eva D. *Principles of Nutrition*. 3rd ed. New York: John Wiley and Sons, 1975.

Winter, Ruth. *Poisons in Your Food*. New York: Crown, 1969.

Winter, Ruth. *How to Reduce Your Medical Bills*. Greenwich, Conn.: Fawcett Publications, 1970.

Young, James Harvey. *The Medical Messiahs*. Princeton, N.J.: Princeton University Press, 1967.

Some Projects to Learn More

1. See what you can find out about the ratios of benefits paid to premiums collected for various types of medical and hospital insurance policies. The state insurance commission may have data to supplement the library sources. How do you interpret these data?

2. Plot the trends in costs of medical care, and explain them. Where will they go in the future, and why?

3. Make a historical study of what the President has requested and what Congress has appropriated, and what has actually been spent each year by the National Institutes of Health. Compare these expenditures with estimates of national expenditures for medical care, drugs, etc.

4. Visit your county health officer, and analyze the costs and benefits of his office and its functions.

5. See what you can find out about the various sources of compensation for medical care costs (insurance, workers' compensation, tort suit). Which ones pay regardless of who else is paying? Which ones pay but then recollect if they can from some other place (called *subrogation* in the case of claimed damages)? Which ones pay only if no one else pays? What difference does this make?

6. Ask your doctor to name five common prescriptions. Ask him or her to estimate their cost, and to indicate whether there is any way to get them cheaper. Then ask five drug stores and one hospital pharmacy to price them. Then get four friends to ask their doctors to estimate the cost of the five prescriptions, and whether there is any way to get them cheaper. Finally, send off to one or two mail-order cut-rate prescription houses copies of the prescriptions and ask them for price quotations. Or use the FTC (Seattle Regional Office) list and methods.

7. Use the nutritive content labels on some food product like breakfast cereal to calculate the cost per gram of protein, or carbohydrate, or the cost per calorie of alternatives such as oatmeal, corn flakes, special high-protein cereals, or granola-type mixtures.

Appendix 10.1

A Primer On Vitamins[1]

G. Edward Damon

Vitamins are essential to human life, but their true role in the body and in nutrition is often misunderstood. This primer on vitamins explains what vitamins are and how they work. It is part of FDA Consumer's *continuing efforts to present scientific information about areas regulated by FDA.*

Vitamins are organic compounds which are necessary in small amounts in the diet for the normal growth and maintenance of life of animals, including man.

They do not provide energy, nor do they construct or build any part of the body. They are needed for transforming foods into energy and body maintenance. There are 15 or more of them, and if any is missing, a deficiency disease becomes apparent.

Vitamins are alike because they are made of the same elements—carbon, hydrogen, oxygen, and sometimes nitrogen. (Vitamin B_{12} contains cobalt, an essential mineral.) They are different because their elements are arranged in different combinations, and each vitamin performs one or more exclusive functions in the body.

In the early 1900's, it was thought that three compounds were needed in the diet to prevent beriberi, pellagra, and scurvy. They originally were believed to be a class of chemical compounds called amines and were named from the Latin *vita*, or life, plus *amine*. Vitamine. Later, the "e" was dropped when it was found that not all of the substances were amines.

At first no one knew what they were chemically, and they were identified by letters. Later, what was thought to be one vitamin turned out to be many, and numbers had to be added; the vitamin B complex is the best example.

Then, some vitamins were found unnecessary for human needs and were eliminated from the list, which accounts for the gaps in the numbers. The present trend is to use the chemical names and eliminate the confusion of the past.

Vitamins are measured in extremely small amounts, because it takes very little to be effective in generating the needed chemical reactions. Some vitamins are described in I. U.'s—International Units—which means a given amount of activity that can be measured. Others are expressed by weight only, in milligrams or micrograms.

To illustrate the small amounts needed by the human body, let's start with an ounce of vitamins, which is 28.3 grams. One gram, then, is about 35/1000 of an ounce; a milligram is 1/1000 of a gram, and a microgram is 1/1000 of a milligram.

To look at it from another direction, the recommended allowance of vitamin B_{12} for adults is 6 micrograms a day. Just 1 ounce of this vitamin would satisfy the daily needs of 4,724,921 people!

Getting enough vitamins is essential to life. But the body has no use for excess vitamins. Many people believe, however, in insurance. So it is easy to understand why they, fearful of not eating a well-balanced diet, take extra vitamins.

So-called average or normal eaters probably never need supplemental vitamins, although many think they do. People eating *known* deficient diets require them, as do those recovering from a specific illness or vitamin deficiencies that have been identified by a physician.

Every adult consumer interested in nutrition and good health should become familiar with the initials U.S. RDA. "United States Recommended Daily Allowances" were established by FDA for use in nutrition labeling. They are the amounts of vitamins, minerals, and other nutrients from food that a person should eat every day to stay healthy.

The accompanying table lists the U.S. RDA's for vitamins used in nutrition labeling of foods, including foods that are also vitamin supplements. The table is not complete because it lists only vitamins. Minerals and other nutrients are part of the complete table.

United States Recommended Daily Allowances

	Unit[a]	Infants (0–12 mo.)	Children under 4 yrs.	Adults and children 4 or more yrs.	Pregnant or lactating women
Vitamin A	IU	1500	2500	5000	8000
Vitamin D	IU	400	400	400	400
Vitamin E	IU	5	10	30	30
Vitamin C	mg	35	40	60	60
Folacin	mg	0.1	0.2	0.4	0.8
Thiamine (B_1)	mg	0.5	0.7	1.5	1.7
Riboflavin (B_2)	mg	0.6	0.8	1.7	2.0
Niacin (B_5)	mg	8	9	20	20
Vitamin B_6	mg	0.4	0.7	2	2.5
Vitamin B_{12}	mcg	2	3	6	8
Biotin	mg	0.05	0.15	0.3	0.3
Pantothenic acid	mg	3	5	10	10

Note: The U.S. RDA system was developed by FDA for its nutrition labeling and dietary supplement programs. This table for use in the labeling of dietary supplements lists only vitamin requirements, for the purpose of this article.

[a] IU = International unit; mg = milligram; mcg = microgram

1. Reprinted from *FDA Consumer,* May, 1974, pp. 5–11.

Vitamin A—Retinol
Vitamin A is one of the oil soluble vitamins (A, D, E, and K), and is stored principally in the liver.

This vitamin is necessary for new cell growth and healthy tissues and is essential for vision in dim light.

In addition to night blindness and other eye injuries, vitamin A deficiency causes a dry, rough skin which may be more susceptible to infection. Too much vitamin A causes headache, nausea, and irritability. More severe ailments include growth retardation in children, enlargement of the liver and spleen, loss of hair, rheumatic pain, and disturbance of the menstrual cycle.

Children and young people who have been given large does of vitamin A have developed an intracranial pressure that mimics a brain tumor so realistically that unnecessary surgery has been performed.

Vitamin A is found most abundantly in liver, fortified margarine, eggs, butter, and whole milk. Green and yellow vegetables and yellow fruits are the best sources of carotene, which the body converts to vitamin A.

Vitamin B_1—Thiamine
This vitamin is water soluble as are all in the B group. Thiamine is required for normal digestion. It is necessary for growth, fertility, and lactation, and the normal functioning of nerve tissue.

Vitamin B_1 deficiency causes beriberi, a dysfunctioning of the nervous system. Other deficiency problems are loss of appetite, body swelling, growth retardation, cardiac problems, nausea, vomiting, spastic colon, and pain in the calf and thigh muscles.

Thiamine is found abundantly in pork, beans, peas, nuts, and in enriched and whole-grain breads and cereals.

Vitamin B_2—Riboflavin
Riboflavin helps the body to obtain energy from carbohydrates and protein substances. A deficiency causes lip sores and cracks, as well as dimness of vision. This vitamin is found abundantly in leafy vegetables, enriched and whole-grain bread, liver, cheese, lean meat, milk, and eggs.

Niacin
This vitamin has been called B_5 as well as PP (pellagra preventive). Both terms are obsolete.

It is necessary for the healthy condition of all tissue cells. A niacin deficiency causes pellagra, which was once the most common deficiency disease next to rickets. Pellagra is characterized by rough skin, mouth sores, diarrhea, and mental disorders.

Niacin is one of the most stable of the vitamins, the most easily obtainable, and the cheapest.

The most abundant natural sources are liver, lean meat, peas, beans, whole-grain cereal products, and fish.

Pantothenic Acid
Once called B_3, pantothenic acid is needed to support a variety of body functions, including proper growth and maintenance of the body.

A deficiency causes, among other things, headache, fatigue, poor muscle coordination, nausea, and cramps.

Pantothenic acid is found abundantly in liver, eggs, white potatoes, sweet potatoes, peas, and peanuts.

Folic Acid (folacin)
Folic acid helps to manufacture red blood cells and is essential in normal metabolism which is, basically, the converting of food to energy. A deficiency causes a type of anemia.

The most abundant sources are liver, navy beans, and dark green leafy vegetables. Other good sources are nuts, fresh oranges, and whole wheat products.

Vitamin B_6—(Pyridoxine-Pyridoxal-Pyridoxamine)
This vitamin is involved mostly in the utilization of protein. As with other vitamins, B_6 is essential for the proper growth and maintenance of body functions. Deficiency symptoms include mouth soreness, dizziness, nausea, and weight loss, and sometimes severe nervous disturbances.

Pyridoxine is found abundantly in liver, whole-grain cereals, potatoes, red meat, green vegetables, and yellow corn.

Vitamin B_{12}—Cyanocobalamin
Vitamin B_{12} is necessary for the normal development of red blood cells, and the functioning of all cells, particularly in the bone marrow, nervous system, and intestines.

A deficiency causes pernicious anemia, and if the deficiency is prolonged, a degeneration of the spinal cord occurs.

Abundant sources are organ meats, lean meats, fish, milk, and shellfish. B_{12} is not present to any measurable degree in plants, which indicates that strict vegetarians should supplement their diets with this vitamin.

Biotin
Once called vitamin H, biotin is now the sole descriptive term for this vitamin which is actually a member of the B complex. It is important in the metabolism of carbohydrates, proteins, and fats.

Most deficiency symptoms involve mild skin disorders, some anemia, depression, sleeplessness, and muscle pain. As with many vitamins, deficiency is very rare.

Abundant sources include eggs, milk, and meat.

Vitamin C—Ascorbic Acid
This least stable of the vitamins promotes growth and tissue repair, including the healing of wounds. It aids tooth formation, bone formation, and repair. When used as a food additive, vitamin C acts as a preservative.

A lack of this vitamin causes scurvy, one of the oldest diseases known to man. The signs of scurvy include lassitude, weakness, bleeding, loss of weight, and irritability. An early sign is bleeding of the gums. Long before the 16th century, American Indians knew that scurvy could be cured by a tea made with spruce or pine needles.

Abundant sources are citrus and tomato juices, strawberries, currants, and green vegetables such as lettuce, cabbage, broccoli, kale, collards, mustard and turnip greens, and potatoes. You can get all the vitamin C your body can use, for example, by drinking 5 or 6 ounces of orange or tomato juice a day.

Vitamin D—Calciferol
Vitamin D aids in the absorption of calcium and phosphorus in bone formation.

Vitamin D deficiency causes rickets. The earliest obvious signs are skeleton deformation—bowed legs, deformed spine, "potbelly" appearance, and sometimes flat feet and stunting of growth.

Too much vitamin D causes nausea, weight loss, weakness, excessive urination, and the more serious conditions of hypertension and calcification of soft tissues, including the blood vessels and kidneys. Bone deformities and multiple fractures are also common.

Abundant sources are canned fish such as herring, salmon, and tuna; egg yolk, and vitamin D fortified milk. People who spend part of their time in the sun need no other sources of vitamin D, since it is formed in the skin by the sun's ultraviolet rays. Foods which are fortified with vitamin D are intended mainly for infants and the elderly who lack outdoor exposure to sunlight. The daily dietary requirement of vitamin D is very small, and any excess is stored in the body.

Vitamin K
There are several scientific names for vitamin K, which is essential for clotting of the blood. One type is found naturally in food. Another is made in the intestinal tract, and a third is made synthetically.

A deficiency causes hemorrhage and liver injury. Vitamin K is found in spinach, lettuce, kale, cabbage, cauliflower, liver, and egg yolk.

Vitamin E—The Tocopherols
Vitamin E in humans acts as an antioxidant which helps to prevent oxygen from destroying other substances. In other words, vitamin E is a preservative, protecting the efficiency of other compounds such as vitamin A. No known clinical symptoms are associated with very low intake of this vitamin in man. A rather rare form of anemia in premature infants, however, responds to vitamin E medication.

Abundant sources are vegetable oils, beans, eggs, whole grains, liver, fruits, and vegetables.

Vitamin E is not the most important vitamin, but it is one of the most talked about.

To some extent the wild and unsubstantiated claims made for vitamin E have come from a combination of misinterpretation and hope.

The Committee on Nutritional Misinformation of the National Academy of Sciences has issued a report about vitamin E. Three statements are quoted here:

"Surveys of the United States population indicate that adequate amounts of vitamin E are supplied by the usual diet."

"Careful studies over a period of years attempting to relate these (test animal) symptoms to vitamin E deficiency in human beings have been unproductive."

"Self-medication with vitamin E in the hope that a more or less serious condition will be alleviated may indeed be hazardous, especially when appropriate diagnosis and treatment may thereby be delayed or avoided."

Science, as such, is a mystery to most of us; we view scientific knowledge with awe, and we are quite justified, considering the scientific achievements of our age. Misconceptions about vitamins and their proper functions are understandable, but no primer would be complete without clearing up some of these misconceptions:

☐ "Synthetic" vitamins manufactured in the laboratory are identical to the natural vitamins found in foods. The body cannot tell the difference and gets the same benefits from either source. Statements to the effect that "Nature cannot be imitated" and "Natural vitamins have the essence of life" are without meaning.

☐ Vitamins will not provide extra pep, vitality beyond normal expectations, or an unusual level of well-being.

☐ Excess vitamins are a complete waste, both in money and effect.

☐ Anyone who eats "all over the store," meaning a reasonably varied diet, should normally never need supplemental vitamins. Vitamin sources are varied and abundant and have been for many centuries; if they weren't, our present population would not be here.

The abundant sources that have been listed give some idea of how difficult it is to be undernourished from lack of vitamins.

Each of these is a source of one or more vitamins:

Liver, eggs, cheese, fortified margarine, butter, whole milk, fortified milk, fish, egg yolk, yellow vegetables, green leafy vegetables, yellow fruit, beans, peas, nuts, whole-grain foods, red meat, lean meat, pork, shellfish, fresh vegetables, white potatoes, sweet potatoes, yellow corn, rice, strawberries, currants, citrus fruit and juices, tomatoes and juices, other fruits, juices, and berries, canned herring, salmon, and tuna, lettuce, fresh oranges, cabbage, spinach, cauliflower, and vegetable oils of several kinds. And these are just the *abundant* sources!

Even though the widely seen and identified vitamin deficiency diseases of 30 years ago have all but disappeared, the American consumer is approached from all sides with misinformation about the almost-universal "need" for supplemental vitamins.

Is there really a need? Each person can answer this *only* after learning what vitamins do and do not do, plus their presence in foods.

If some vitamins have additional value in preventing or treating conditions of ill health, these values will be discovered by professionally trained and dedicated clinicians. And they will then become known to the public.

Appendix 10.2

Nutrition Labels: A Great Leap Forward[1]

Arletta Beloian

The Food and Drug Administration has undertaken one of the most ambitious programs in its history—one called nutrition labeling—to see that consumers are told, right on the label, what nutrients are in the food they buy. The new food labels will list not only the ingredients, but—in a standard format—what nutrients the food in the package will provide, and in what quantities.

Uniform presentation of this information will enable consumers to compare the nutritional values of different foods and to compare new food products with more familiar ones. Nutrition labeling will not force anyone to eat anything he or she does not want to. But it will, for the first time, make nutrition information readily available to everyone who wants to use it.

Nutrition labeling will have a broad impact, even though, in most cases, it will be voluntary. Several major food processors and supermarket chains are using it already, and most others are expected to follow suit, by choice or because of competitive pressure.

The regulation requires a manufacturer to use nutrition labeling when he adds any nutrient to the food or when he makes some nutritional claim for it on the label or in advertising. Offers to provide nutrition information on request do not make nutrition labeling mandatory on the label, but the information supplied must follow the specifications and format for actual nutrition labeling.

In brief, the nutrition panel on a food package will list how many calories and how much protein, carbohydrates, and fat a serving of that food will provide. It will also show what percentage of the U.S. Recommended Daily Allowance (U.S. RDA) of protein and seven essential vitamins and minerals a serving will provide. The label may also list how much unsaturated and saturated fat, cholesterol, and sodium the food contains, and may give the percentage of the U.S.

1. Reprinted from *FDA Consumer,* September, 1973, pp. 10–16.

RDA for another dozen vitamins and minerals.

Nutrition labeling is only part of the package of new regulations designed to better inform the consumer about food through labels.

Other important sections of the food labeling regulations will:

☐ require specific information on the labels of foods for special dietary use;
☐ require specific information on the labels of dietary supplements of vitamins and minerals;
☐ remove the "imitation" stigma now applied to some new foods by permitting common names for those which resemble and are used in place of older foods but are not nutritionally inferior to them;
☐ outline conditions under which foods may be labeled for saturated and unsaturated fat content and cholesterol;
☐ permit a label to state that the product meets specific nutritional guidelines established by FDA for certain classes of foods;
☐ and prescribe more informative labeling of flavors and spices in other foods or as separate products.

Some parts of the regulations on the food labeling package evolved from more than 10 years of study, public hearings, and discussion with consumers, health professionals, and the food industry. Others reflect FDA's response to the increasing demands of consumers for more and better information about foods and dietary supplements.

Understandable Units

FDA has designed the nutrition labels to be as easily understood as possible. Quantities of nutrients must be expressed in terms of a serving of food, which FDA has defined to be a reasonable amount usually eaten by an adult male engaged in light physical activity. This is easy to understand for most foods, but if the food is to be used as an ingredient in the preparation of some other food, for example, tomato paste, the quantity may be expressed in terms of a portion. The first line of the label will define the size of a serving or portion.

The next line of the nutrition information panel tells how many servings or portions are in the container.

Both of these label statements must be in units that can be easily understood by the consumer. For example, servings might be expressed as ounces, slices, muffins, or cupfuls. These foods, if usually used only once a day, will have the standard nutrient list on the left and one column of figures for the quantity per serving or per portion on the right.

Some foods, such as bread and milk, are commonly consumed more than once a day. For these kinds of food the label may include a second column of nutrient figures showing the quantities contained in the amount to be consumed in a day as well as in a single serving.

Other types of foods are also permitted to show two columns of figures for the nutrient quantities. Nutrient quantities for these foods must be given for one serving of the food, as purchased, but may also be given for the food after cooking or other preparation in the home. However, the method of preparation must be specified. For another situation, a food to which other ingredients will normally be added (such as a cake mix, to which will be added milk and eggs), the second column may show the nutrient quantities per serving for the finished product.

Macronutrients

Immediately after the serving and package contents information will come a breakdown of calories, protein, carbohydrates, and fat.

Calories will be expressed in two-calorie increments up to 20 calories, in five-calorie increments from 20 to 50 calories, and in 10-calorie increments above 50 calories.

Quantities of protein, carbohydrates, and fat will be expressed to the nearest gram. (The gram, a unit in the metric

The Why and How of Nutrition Labeling

How did FDA's Nutrition Labeling Regulation come about?

What immediately precipitated it was the White House Conference on Food, Nutrition, and Health, held in Washington, D.C., in December 1969. The Conference recommended that FDA consider the development of a system for identifying the nutritional qualities of food: "Every manufacturer should be encouraged to provide truthful nutritional information to consumers about his products to enable them to follow recommended dietary regimens."

The Conference itself was a result of the increasing demands by consumers to be provided with more information on food labels about nutrition and by health professionals concerned about the kind and quality of nutrients in the food supply.

Public concern had been aroused by results from nationwide studies in the 1960's which showed the U.S. diet to be poorer than it should be. Study by the U.S. Department of Agriculture on food consumption by households found an apparent increase from 1955 to 1965 in the number of families that had "poor" diets. The problem was found to be more pronounced among families in lower income groups but existed to some extent in the higher income groups. The nutrients most often short were calcium and vitamins C and A. From data by season, more families had low calcium in their diets during the summer. Vitamin A was more frequently below the allowances used for comparison in two seasons, spring and winter; low vitamin C was more frequent in spring and fall.

Another study stimulating concern was the 10-State Nutrition Survey conducted by DHEW between 1968 and 1970. Nearly 30,000 families living in low-income areas were studied to determine the magnitude and location of malnutrition and related health problems in this country. The occurrence of iron deficiency anemia and low iron intake data showed a widespread problem within the population surveyed. In the past it was thought that only females had a low iron intake in their diet. A particularly surprising result of this survey was the high prevalence of low iron intake among males.

This same study in low-income areas demonstrated other problem nutrients for population groups. Marginal protein intake was suggested among pregnant and lactating women. Based on biochemical measurements and analysis of dietary intake data, Spanish Americans had a major problem in regard to vitamin A. Less serious, but still a problem, low levels of vitamin A were found to exist among young people in all subgroups. Although vitamin C was not a major problem, the prevalence of poor status for this nutrient increased with age.

These findings and other publicized reports, along with public statements by nutritionists and welfare workers, heightened the public concern about the family diet and led to the 1969 White House Conference on Food, Nutrition and Health.

FDA responded to the Conference's recommendation by beginning work on a regulation. They employed information, although limited in scope, from two studies completed in 1970. One of the studies indicated a general opinion among professional nutritionists that a standardized system should be used to provide nutrition information on food labels. The other study indicated that consumers were receptive to and used nutrition information on food labels in selecting purchases.

From this preliminary information, FDA outlined several methods of nutrition labeling. These were evaluated for scientific correctness by representatives of the Food and Nutrition Board of the National Academy of Sciences—National Research Council, the American Dietetic Association, and the American Institute of Nutrition. After comments, six alternate approaches, were sent to groups representing professional nutritionists, consumers, the food industry, home economists, and dietitians. These approaches were tested among consumers by a nonprofit research group to determine which forms of nutrition labeling were suitable for further study. Six methods were reduced to three appearing the most feasible.

In this final testing period, a procedure was developed to study consumer response to nutrition labeling, both formally and informally, by those who had an interest in consumer reaction. After this involved procedure, the format for nutrition labeling was finally published in the *Federal Register*, March 30, 1972, for the first time.

---

system, is used because the quantities are so small. A gram is about 1/28 of an ounce, or about the weight of a paper clip.)

The statements about fat content must also give the percentage of calories from fat. An optional statement to follow total fat, on the amounts of polyunsaturated and saturated fats, may be reported (to the nearest gram) but can only be made if the food contains 10 percent or more total fat on a dry-weight basis and not less than two grams of fat in a serving.

Next, after the component parts of fat, the manufacturer may state cholesterol content. Any mention of either fat components or cholesterol makes use of the entire nutrition label mandatory.

When cholesterol content is stated, it must be given to the nearest five-milligram increment per serving and to the nearest five-milligram increment per 100 grams of the food. (A milligram is 1/1,000 of a gram.)

When the cholesterol content or fat composition is stated, this statement must appear on the label: "Information on cholesterol [and/or fat] content is provided for individuals who, on the advice of a physician are modifying their total dietary intake of cholesterol [and/or fat]." FDA is not taking a position in the debate over the role of fats and cholesterol in cardiovascular disease; it is merely allowing such information about food to appear on the label.

Micronutrients

Next on the nutrition information panel will come the statement of protein, vitamin, and mineral content in percentages of the U.S. Recommended Daily Allowance (U.S. RDA) for each. This list includes two groups of nutrients. The first is a group of eight, consisting of protein, vitamin A, vitamin C, thiamine, riboflavin, niacin, calcium, and iron.

In most cases, all eight of these nutrients will be listed. If less than 2 percent is present for four or less of the nutrients, it will be allowable to show quantities present in minute amounts in either of two ways: by a zero, or by an asterisk referring to a statement at the bottom of the table saying they are present at less than 2 percent. If five or more nutrients are below the 2 percent level, the low nutrients may be deleted from the list and specified at the bottom of the table in a statement, "Contains less than 2 percent of the U.S. RDA of _____."

FDA feels that a person who eats foods containing all of the nutrients in this first group is likely to obtain the necessary amounts of the 12 other essential vitamins and minerals in the second group, shown below:

vitamin D	iodine
vitamin E	magnesium
vitamin B_6	zinc
folic acid	copper
vitamin B_12	biotin
phosphorus	pantothenic acid

Listing any of these, in part or in total, is optional. However, if any of them are added to the food, they must be listed.

Understanding the U.S. RDA
In all cases, the quantities of the protein, vitamins, and minerals will be given as percentages of the U.S. RDA rather than as absolute amounts. Thus consumers will not have to memorize or constantly refer to a table of the U.S. RDA to know if they are getting enough of any given nutrient; instead, they can simply add the percentages for all the foods they have eaten that day.

And even this process need not be rigid. FDA derived the U.S. RDA from the Recommended Dietary Allowances of the National Academy of Sciences-National Research Council. In most cases, FDA took the highest of nearly 20 values the Academy has recommended for sex and age differences for each nutrient. Thus many normal, healthy people may not need the full 100 percent of the U.S. RDA of a given nutrient on a given day, and falling short of this level may not be a cause for alarm.

On the labels, the percentages of the U.S. RDA for protein and the various micronutrients will be expressed in 2 percent increments up to 10 percent, in 5 percent increments from 10 to 50 percent, and 10 percent increments above 50 percent.

No claim can be made that a food is a significant source of a nutrient unless the nutrient in the food equals or exceeds at least 10 percent of the U.S. RDA for that nutrient. No claim can be made that one food is superior to another as a source of any given nutrient, unless it contains at least 10 percent more of the U.S. RDA for that nutrient than does the other food.

> **There's Protein— and Then There's Protein**
> The avid reader of nutrition labels will quickly discover that meat and milk products supply larger proportions of the U.S. RDA for protein than other foods. This difference is related not only to the quantity of protein, but the quality as well. The quality of protein in the foods you eat determines to some degree the quantity you need. If the quality is excellent, less protein is required than if the quality of protein is poor.
>
> Quality of protein in foods is determined largely by the kinds and proportions of the amino acids they contain. The amino acids are the building blocks of the larger protein molecules. The human body needs 22 amino acids to function properly; of these, it can manufacture 14. Foods are the main source of the remaining eight amino acids. These eight are called the essential amino acids, and their presence in varying combinations determines protein quality in food.
>
> Protein is the only nutrient on the information panel which is shown in terms of both total content of a serving and the percentage of the U.S. Recommended Daily Allowance (U.S. RDA). The percentage figure takes into account the quality of protein in foods, and its purpose is to make balancing a diet easier for the consumer.
>
> The principal protein in milk, known as casein, has been adopted by FDA as the standard of comparison for quality. Thus, when protein is equal to or better than the quality of casein, the U.S. Recommended Daily Allowance is 45 grams; for protein with lower quality than casein, the U.S. RDA is 65 grams. Having a specific U.S. RDA for every kind of protein would be too cumbersome and time-consuming for the consumer. So just the two U.S. RDA's for the adult population have been established. For those who are curious how the percentage of the U.S. RDA for protein is obtained, it is a simple calculation. For foods supplying a high quality protein, the total protein in grams (per serving) is divided by 45 grams. When the quality in food is lower, the total protein is divided by 65 grams.
>
> The above method for determining the percentage of U.S. RDA for protein has been simplified from a very complex one.
>
> Even though this is simplified, the concept is admittedly still complicated. But you really don't need to understand all the specifics about protein to use nutrition labeling. Just plan to follow an eating pattern that will bring you close to 100 percent of the U.S. RDA. If you fall short some of the time, there is no cause for alarm, because the U.S. RDA's include a fairly generous margin.

In the case of calories, carbohydrate, and fat, no U.S. RDA has been specified, that is why no percentage of U.S. RDA is on the label. Required amounts of these macronutrients, which serve principally as sources of body energy, are difficult to assess. Further, as energy sources, the amounts needed by individuals depends upon many factors, such as age, sex, height, weight, body metabolism, and degree of activity. This does not lessen the importance of calories, carbohydrate, and fat in the diet but does affect the way the content in food is reported. Since it is very easy to get excesses of these macronutrients in the diet, they must not be more than 20 percent above the amount declared on the label.

When FDA evaluates the nutrient content of food for compliance with labeled amounts, the nutrient quantities declared will be allowed some variation. Reasonable shortages of calories or fat will be acceptable within good manufacturing processes. In contrast, reasonable excesses of the vitamins, minerals, and protein will be acceptable.

Exceptions to the Rule
Some specific kinds of foods either are subject to special labeling requirements or are exempt from nutrition labeling requirements.

Infant, baby, and junior-type foods, although not expressly covered by the previously discussed regulations, must carry nutrition labeling with a slight change. For such foods, the term "serving" shall mean a reasonable quantity for an infant or baby. A special set of U.S. RDA's for infants and children will be used instead of the adult table that will be used for most foods.

Any food represented for use as the sole item of the diet or any food represented for use solely under medical supervision in the dietary management of specific diseases will be labeled according to the specific regulation on foods for special dietary use.

Nutrition labeling is not required in the following categories. These items may be listed by their proper names in the ingredients statement if they are not otherwise mentioned on the label or in advertising:

☐ iodized salt when used as an ingredient and neither iodine or iodized salt is given special mention on the label;

☐ nutrients, such as vitamin C, when used to prevent discoloration of fruit and included in food solely for technological purposes;

☐ or a standardized food, containing an added nutrient such as enriched flour, which is included in another food as a component and listed as an ingredient.

Two other exemptions from nutrition labeling are provided for:

☐ food products shipped in bulk for use solely in the manufacture of other foods;

U.S. RDA vs. MDR
One of the significant contributions of nutrition labeling is the establishment of the U.S. RDA. With this tool a concerned consumer will find it possible to determine which nutrients he is getting in a food and how much a serving or portion will contribute to his daily needs.

The U.S. RDA have replaced the Minimum Daily Requirements (MDR), which had been specified in earlier FDA regulations for declaring the nutrient values in foods for special dietary use and for dietary supplements of vitamins and minerals.

The decision to switch to the U.S. RDA arose from dissatisfaction with the MDR system because: (1) FDA and others felt the term MDR was misleading to many consumers, who did not realize that minimum requirements were chosen for legal reasons and formed only a basis for past labeling regulations; (2) the U.S. RDA is not only a more modern development, but standards for more of the essential nutrients have been worked out than in the MDR system; (3) in contrast to the MDR, the U.S. RDA generally call for somewhat higher nutrient values which are likely to be abundant for many and sufficient for everybody.

The U.S. RDA's represent the amount of nutrients needed every day by healthy people, plus an excess of 30 to 50 percent to allow for individual variations. Many adults need only two-thirds to three quarters of the U.S. RDA for several nutrients, and children only about half.

The following chart lists the U.S. Recommended Daily Allowances for use in nutrition labeling (g-gram, IU-International Unit, mg-milligram, and mcg-microgram).

	Adults and Children		Adults and Children
Protein	65 g[a]	Vitamin B_6	2.0 mg
Vitamin A	5,000 IU	Folacin	0.4 mg
Vitamin C	60 mg	Vitamin B_{12}	6 mcg
Thiamine	1.5 mg	Phosphorus	1.0 g
Riboflavin	1.7 mg	Iodine	150 mcg
Niacin	20 mg	Magnesium	400 mg
Calcium	1.0 g	Zinc	15 mg
Iron	18 mg	Copper	2 mg
Vitamin D	400 IU	Biotin	0.3 mg
Vitamin E	30 IU	Pantothenic Acid	10 mg

[a]If protein efficiency ratio of protein is equal to or better than that of casein, U.S. RDA is 45 g.

☐ and food products containing an added vitamin, mineral, or protein, or foods otherwise subject to nutritional labeling but which are supplied for institutional food service only. Current nutrition information, however, must be supplied directly to the institutions on a current basis.

Prohibited Claims
The regulation not only spells out what is to appear on nutrition labels, it expressly forbids certain claims about nutrition and diet. FDA has long been concerned with misleading claims made to promote the sale of some foods and dietary supplements, and will consider foods misbranded if their labels violate the regulation.

Thus FDA is trying to do two things with the nutrition labeling regulation: provide the public with more information about the nutrients in food, and protect the public from misinformation.

Under the regulation, a label will not be allowed to say or even imply:

1. that a food can prevent, cure, mitigate, or treat any disease or symptom;

2. that a balanced diet of ordinary foods cannot supply adequate amounts of nutrients;

3. that a lack of optimal nutritive quality of a food, because of the soil on which that food was grown, is or may be responsible for an inadequacy or deficiency in the daily diet;

4. that storage, transportation, processing, or cooking of a food is or may be responsible for an inadequacy or deficiency in the daily diet;

5. that a natural vitamin is superior to an added or synthetic vitamin;

6. or that a food contains certain nutrients when such substances are of no known need or significant value in human nutrition. This prohibition is aimed at rutin, other bioflavonoids, para-aminobenzoic acid, inositol, and similar substances. These items have been promoted in the past as having nutritional properties; they have not been proven to be essential in human nutrition, and therefore FDA will not permit them to be mixed with other vitamins or minerals or mentioned on a label. They may be sold separately if no nutritional, dietary, or therapeutic claim is stated or implied.

FDA states that these prohibitions are intended to stop unsupported generalizations about nutrient losses because of soil quality, transportation, processing, and so on. A manufacturer who has adequate scientific data, which proves his product has a higher nutrient retention than a competitor's, may make that claim. If adequate scientific data proves that a particular food has a higher nutrient content than usual because of unusual soil conditions, then that claim may be made. The burden of proof will rest with the manufacturer.

Timetable
Nutrition labels have begun to appear on some food packages, but the program will not swing into high gear for at least another year. Before labels can be printed with the nutrient content of food, processors must analyze their products. For some foods, obviously this cannot be done until harvest.

Many manufacturers order their labels printed in large quantities to last a long time, and may still have stocks of labels made prior to the date of these new food labeling regulations. The regulation, therefore, provides for a period of adjustment by stating that any labeling ordered after December 31, 1973, must comply, and any food shipped interstate after December 31, 1974, must comply.

In the meantime, FDA is doing all it can to acquaint consumers with the new program. A media campaign will be conducted to explain the program. Consumer specialists across the country will be alerting consumers. And a number of food processing and marketing companies will be conducting their own educational campaigns.

Appendix 10.3 Fats in Food and Diet[1]

Diet is only one of many factors associated with the development of atherosclerosis and increased risk of coronary heart disease. Other factors include heredity, obesity, high blood pressure, high blood cholesterol and high blood lipids, cigarette smoking, lack of exercise, stress, and certain metabolic diseases such as diabetes.

Scientific opinion varies as to the specific role played by different foods and nutrients, especially fats, in increasing or decreasing the risk of atherosclerosis.

There is consensus, however, about the importance to health at every age of—

☐ A balanced diet suitable for one's age and activity.
☐ Maintaining desirable weight.
☐ Moderation in the total amount of fat in the diet.
☐ Variety in the kinds of fat or fatty acids in the diet.

These factors and the cholesterol content of foods are discussed on the following pages.

A Balanced Diet

A balanced diet is one that includes the kinds and amounts of food which will provide the needed quantities of essential nutrients and energy. Amounts of protein, calories, vitamins, and minerals needed by different sex-age groups for nutritional well-being are recommended by the Food and Nutrition Board of the National Academy of Sciences-National Research Council and referred to as Recommended Dietary Allowances (RDA's).

USDA nutritionists have translated these nutrient recommendations into food recommendations in "Food for Fitness—A Daily Food Guide" (Leaflet 424).[2] In the Guide, foods are grouped according to their nutrient content into the Vegetable-Fruit Group, Milk Group, Meat Group, and Bread-Cereal Group. The Guide recommends the minimum daily number of servings from each group needed to provide a substantial proportion of the RDA's.

Other foods or additional servings selected from the four food groups, or both, are expected to supply additional amounts of the nutrients and meet energy needs. The Guide permits as wide a choice as possible within each food group and allows free choice in selecting additional foods.

Limitation in Total Calories

This means seeing that the total caloric intake from food (and alcohol) does not exceed a person's energy need. Calories in excess of those needed for energy expenditure are stored in the body as fat.

Lack of exercise is one of the chief causes of overweight and, for most sedentary people, suitable exercise is one of the best means of weight control.

USDA has two publications to help consumers with weight control: Home and Garden Bulletin 74, "Food and Your Weight" and Agriculture Information Bulletin 364, "Calories and Weight—the USDA Pocket Guide."[3]

Moderation in Total Fat

There is no specific definition of moderation, but for most of us it means using less fat than we are in the habit of using. This applies especially to the fat we add to food during preparation and at the table. It is not unusual for fat to supply 45 to 50 percent of the total calories in an American diet. In a nationwide survey, fat supplied an average of 45 percent of the total calories in the diets of young and middle-aged men.

Some advocates of moderation believe that 38 to 40 percent of the total calories from fat is a reasonable goal. In most diets this reduction can be achieved by simply cutting down on the amount of visible or separable fat used.

Some advocates have a stricter definition of moderation and say that less than 35 percent of the total calories should be supplied by fat. This much reduction in fat intake is not difficult to achieve but requires some modification in food choices and methods of preparing food.

It is important to remember that fat is an important constituent of the diet and is important to health in many ways.

Fat is the most concentrated source of food energy. It supplies 9 calories per gram; protein and carbohydrate, the other two sources of food energy, supply 4 calories per gram. (Alcohol supplies 7 calories per gram.)

Fats are the chief sources of essential fatty acids (EFA's) as well as carriers of some essential vitamins, namely A, D, E, and K. Too little fat can result in a diet that is deficient in these nutrients. In addition, a diet too restricted in fat lacks flavor and satiety value; it is bulky because a greater volume of food is needed to satisfy the appetite and meet energy needs.

Variety in the Kinds of Fat or Fatty Acids

Fatty acids are the building blocks of fat. Three molecules of fatty acid combined with one molecule of glycerol constitute a molecule of fat. This is called a triglyceride, the form in which fat is stored in adipose tissue.

Fats are classified as saturated or unsaturated depending on the kind of fatty acids present. Most food fats are a combination of the different saturated and unsaturated fatty acids.

A chemist describes a fatty acid as saturated if its chain of carbon atoms

---

1. Prepared under the direction of Ruth M. Leverton, Agricultural Research Service (retired). Reprinted from a pamphlet published by the Agricultural Research Service, United States Department of Agriculture. Washington, D.C.: Government Printing Office, 1974.

2. Single copies available from Office of Communication, U.S. Department of Agriculture, Washington, D.C. 20250. Include your ZIP Code.

3. For sale by the Superintendent of Documents, U.S. Government Printing Office, Washington, D.C. 20402. Price $1.45.

contains all the hydrogen it can hold (or if there are no double bonds between carbon atoms). The most common saturated fatty acids are myristic acid and palmitic acid. Saturated fats are usually hard at room temperature. They occur in both animal and vegetable fats, but chiefly in animal fats.

A chemist describes a fatty acid as unsaturated if its chain of carbon atoms has one or more double bonds where hydrogen could be added. The process of adding hydrogen to a double bond in an unsaturated fatty acid to make it more saturated is referred to as hydrogenation.

Monounsaturated fatty acids have only one double bond where hydrogen could be added. Oleic acid is the most common monounsaturated fatty acid.

Polyunsaturated fatty acids have two or more double bonds where hydrogen could be added.

Polyunsaturated fats are usually oils and are most abundant in plant seeds and fish oils. Nearly all fats from plant sources are unsaturated; the only major exception is coconut oil, which is highly saturated.

The most common polyunsaturated fatty acid is linoleic acid. In general, the degree of unsaturation of a food fat depends on how much linoleic acid it contains.

Linoleic acid is an essential nutrient and must be supplied by food because the body cannot make it. It is involved in the metabolism of cholesterol and has other functions that are evident but have not yet been clearly defined. The body's need for linoleic acid seems to be met when about 2 percent of the total calories are supplied by linoleic acid.

Arachidonic acid, found in animal fats, is another essential polyunsaturated fatty acid. It is present in fats in relatively small amounts but can be synthesized from linoleic acid by the body.

Sometimes it is suggested that saturated, monounsaturated, and polyunsaturated fats should each supply about one-third of the total amount of fat

Table 1. Fat content and major fatty acid composition of selected foods (in decreasing order of linoleic acid content within each group of similar foods)

Food	Total fat	Saturated[2]	Unsaturated Oleic	Unsaturated Linoleic
Salad and cooking oils:				
Safflower	100	10	13	74
Sunflower	100	11	14	70
Corn	100	13	26	55
Cottonseed	100	23	17	54
Soybean[3]	100	14	25	50
Sesame	100	14	38	42
Soybean, specially processed	100	11	29	31
Peanut	100	18	47	29
Olive	100	11	76	7
Coconut	100	80	5	1
Vegetable fats—shortening	100	23	23	6–23
Margarine, first ingredient on label: [4,5]				
Safflower oil (liquid)—tub	80	11	18	48
Corn oil (liquid)—tub	80	14	26	38
Soybean oil (liquid)—tub[6]	80	15	31	33
Corn oil (liquid)—stick	80	15	33	29
Soybean oil (liquid)—stick[6]	80	15	40	25
Cottonseed or soybean oil, partially hydrogenated—tub[6]	80	16	52	13
Butter	81	46	27	2
Animal fats:				
Poultry	100	30	40	20
Beef, lamb, pork	100	45	44	2–6
Fish, raw:[6]				
Salmon	9	2	2	4
Mackerel	13	5	3	4
Herring, Pacific	13	4	2	3
Tuna	5	2	1	2
Nuts:				
Walnuts, English	64	4	10	40
Walnuts, black	60	4	21	28
Brazil	67	13	32	17
Peanuts or peanut butter	51	9	25	14
Pecan	65	4–6	33–48	9–24
Egg yolk	31	10	13	2
Avocado	16	3	7	2

[1] Total is not expected to equal total fat.
[2] Includes fatty acids with chains from 8 through 18 carbon atoms.
[3] Suitable as salad oil.
[4] Mean values of selected samples and may vary with brand name and date of manufacture.
[5] Includes small amounts of monounsaturated and diunsaturated fatty acids that are not oleic or linoleic.
[6] Linoleic acid includes higher polyunsaturated fatty acids.

in the diet. Although this amount of polyunsaturated fat would supply much more linoleic acid than 2 percent of the total calories, polyunsaturated fat may have a lowering effect on levels of cholesterol in the blood.

The fat content and the major fatty acid composition of commonly used sources of fat are shown in table 1.

Cholesterol

Cholesterol is a normal constituent of blood and tissues and is found in every animal cell. Some of the cholesterol in human blood and tissues is synthesized by the body and some is supplied by diet. The amount supplied by diet varies greatly depending on the kinds and amounts of foods included.

The amount of cholesterol in the diet is positively related to the amount of cholesterol in the blood. Ordinary diets are likely to supply 600 to 900 milligrams of cholesterol daily. A "low-cholesterol" diet usually provides about 300 milligrams of cholesterol daily. This amount is more difficult to achieve in the usual American diet and may well be lower than is necessary for a healthy individual on a well-balanced diet.

To date, studies have not shown convincingly that restriction of dietary cholesterol in the general population reduces the frequency of atherosclerosis. However, persons with atherosclerosis usually have higher blood cholesterol levels than persons without atherosclerosis; and persons with high cholesterol levels develop atherosclerosis more often than those with normal levels.

The approximate amounts of cholesterol in servings of selected foods are given in table 2. Foods of plant origin—such as fruits, vegetables, cereal grains, legumes, and nuts—do not contain cholesterol. They contain plant sterols, which have been shown to reduce blood cholesterol levels.

What We Know

It has been more than 15 years since the controversy over the role of fats in cardiovascular disease began. During this time, thousands of research studies have been made and many facts have been uncovered.

The utilization of fats in man is affected by many factors:

☐ By the food we eat all our lives and our state of nutrition.

☐ By our endocrine system—thyroid, adrenal, pituitary, ovarian, pancreatic, and other glands.

☐ By how active we are. Exercise increases the oxygen supply to the tissues, improves circulation, and relieves tension.

☐ By our emotional characteristics and our reactions to the modern, highly industrialized and technological environment.

☐ By our aging. Aging means that physiological processes slow down, enzyme mechanisms become unable to keep up with the usual pattern of eating, and some tissues throughout the body become less active.

☐ By our heredity. In some individuals a tendency to cardiovascular disease seems to be inherited. This does not mean that the disease is inevitable for those individuals. Neither does it mean that an apparent lack of a hereditary tendency guarantees the absence of the disease.

☐ By diseases that may interfere with the absorption and metabolism of fat.

We are certain that the body's utilization of fat and the role of fat in nutrition are affected by food constituents of all kinds and the interactions between them.

Diets high in fat can lead to above-

Table 2. Cholesterol content of common measures of selected foods (in ascending order)[1]

Food	Amount	Cholesterol (Milligrams)
Milk, skim, fluid or reconstituted dry	1 cup	5
Cottage cheese, uncreamed	½ cup	7
Lard	1 tablespoon	12
Cream, light table	1 fluid ounce	20
Cottage cheese, creamed	½ cup	24
Cream, half and half	¼ cup	26
Ice cream, regular, approximately 10% fat	½ cup	27
Cheese, cheddar	1 ounce	28
Milk, whole	1 cup	34
Butter	1 tablespoon	35
Oysters, salmon	3 ounces, cooked	40
Clams, halibut, tuna	3 ounces, cooked	55
Chicken, turkey, light meat	3 ounces, cooked	67
Beef, pork, lobster, chicken, turkey, dark meat	3 ounces, cooked	75
Lamb, veal, crab	3 ounces, cooked	85
Shrimp	3 ounces, cooked	130
Heart, beef	3 ounces, cooked	230
Egg	1 yolk or 1 egg	250
Liver, beef, calf, hog, lamb	3 ounces, cooked	370
Kidney	3 ounces, cooked	680
Brains	3 ounces, raw	more than 1700

[1] Source: "Cholesterol Content of Foods," R. M. Feeley, P. E. Criner, and B. K. Watt. J. Am. Diet. Assoc. 61:134 1972.

normal amounts of lipids in the blood. (Lipids include triglycerides, fatty acids, cholesterol, and other fatlike substances.) A high level of blood lipids—especially of cholesterol—is associated with atherosclerosis. Evidence of a causal relationship, however, is lacking.

Diets with as much as 10 to 15 percent of the calories supplied by polyunsaturated fats frequently lead to a lowering of elevated blood cholesterol levels.

Many nutrients are important in fat utilization, including calcium, magnesium, chromium, zinc, vanadium, niacin, biotin, pantothenic acid, vitamin B_6, and vitamin E. The involvement of these nutrients in fat metabolism has been established, although the specific action and quantitative requirement for some of them are not completely understood. For example, when the proportion of fat as polyunsaturated oils increases in the diet, the requirement for vitamin E increases.

The kind of carbohydrate in the diet can influence fat metabolism. Some studies have shown that a high sucrose intake can produce elevated blood lipid levels in laboratory animals and humans. However, some investigators do not think that the tissue changes which result from feeding high amounts of sucrose are characteristic of atherosclerosis.

There are still many things we do not know about the effects of dietary fat on health. Some aspects on which additional basic information is needed are:

☐ The body processes that control the handling of fat and cholesterol that come both from the diet and from synthesis in tissues.
☐ How these processes are influenced by diet and other factors, including emotional and modern environmental factors.
☐ The upper and lower limits of the amounts of polyunsaturated fats, cholesterol, and total fats needed in the diet for optimum health.

The Inter-Society Commission for Heart Disease Resources released a report in 1970 on "Primary Prevention of the Atherosclerotic Diseases."[4] This report recommends that people make some definite changes in their dietary habits, beginning in early childhood, in order to reduce the risk of coronary heart disease in later life.

The changes recommended include:

☐ Adjusting caloric intake to maintain optimum weight.
☐ Reducing fat intake so that fat supplies less than 35 percent of the total calories.
☐ A daily intake of less than 10 percent of the total calories from saturated fat and up to 10 percent from polyunsaturated fats, with the remainder of fat supplied by monounsaturated fats.
☐ A daily intake of less than 300 milligrams of cholesterol.

The report also urges the medicinal control of hypertension and the elimination of cigarette smoking.

The Inter-Society report has sparked a great deal of discussion and controversy. The only point of general agreement is the unquestioned importance of maintaining optimal weight at every age. The most controversial points are the proportions of total fat and different kinds of fat, the amount of cholesterol, and the efficacy of reducing the amounts of fat and cholesterol in diets of normal, healthy people.

The Committee on Nutrition of the American Academy of Pediatrics[5] has issued a statement recommending against the adoption of dietary changes for all children as urged by the Inter-Society Commission. The Committee believes that such dietary intervention is warranted only in special situations where children have been diagnosed as having elevated blood lipids, usually hereditary.

For children with diabetes or a strong family history of diabetes and children in families having a history of coronary heart disease, the Committee on Nutrition considers that no harm is known to occur from moderate dietary alteration along the lines recommended by the Inter-Society Commission, and there may be some benefits.

Progress has been made in defining abnormalities resulting in elevated levels of cholesterol and other fats in the blood, the significance of these different types in the development of atherosclerosis, and their treatment. Heredity plays an important role in the occurrence of the different types.

It is now possible for physicians to screen individuals to determine whether they have elevated blood lipid values, the type of abnormality, and whether dietary changes or medication are indicated. Many physicians and scientists think that specific diagnosis and medically supervised treatment hold great promise for reducing the incidence of and mortality from atherosclerosis.

The Food and Nutrition Board of the National Academy of Sciences-National Research Council and the Council on Foods and Nutrition of the American Medical Association issued the following joint statement on "Diet and Coronary Heart Disease" in July 1972:

Coronary heart disease is the major public health problem in the United States and in many other countries. In 1970, for example, some 666,000 Americans, of whom about 171,000 were under the age of 65, died of coronary heart disease (CHD) and many more were disabled by the same disorder. It is particularly disturbing that many relatively young Americans in their most productive years are killed or incapacitated by this disease.

Epidemiologic, experimental, and clinical investigations have identified a number of "risk factors" associated with susceptibility to CHD that can be manipulated. These include an elevation in plasma lipids, especially plasma cholesterol, high blood pressure (hypertension), heavy cigarette smoking, obesity, and physical inactivity. The evidence is not

4. *Circulation,* Vol. XLII, December 1970.
5. *Pediatrics,* Vol. 49, 305, 1972.

sufficient to quantitate the benefits that may be expected to come from modifying these various risk factors, but the seriousness of the situation demands that all reasonable means be used to reduce the conditions that contribute to risk of CHD.

There is abundant evidence that the risk of developing CHD is positively correlated with the level of cholesterol in the plasma. This risk, independent of other risk factors mentioned above, is relatively small at levels less than 220 mg/100 ml but increases progressively with each increment in plasma cholesterol above this level.

Approximately one-third of American men, and a less definitely known proportion of women, consuming their usual diets maintain plasma cholesterol levels at or below 220 mg/100 ml. There is extensive evidence that the level of cholesterol in the plasma of most people can be lowered by appropriate dietary modification.

Generally, such lowering can be achieved most practically by partial replacement of the dietary sources of saturated fat with sources of unsaturated fat, especially those rich in polyunsaturated fatty acids, and by a reduction in the consumption of foods rich in cholesterol.

Preliminary evidence suggests that faithful and continued consumption of a cholesterol-lowering diet over a period of years can reduce the coronary attack rate in middle-aged men. As would be expected in dealing with a chronic disease of this kind, early intervention appears to be more effective than intervention after the disease is evident.

Elevation of other plasma lipids (plasma triglycerides) also imposes an increased risk of CHD. The elevation of plasma triglycerides is often, but not always, associated with an elevation of plasma cholesterol. Plasma triglycerides can also be modified by dietary intervention. Although there are as yet no satisfactory epidemiologic data to support the conclusion that triglyceride-lowering diets can reduce the occurrence of CHD in persons with hypertriglyceridemia, the inference from clinical studies that such a reduction can be anticipated is strong.

In summary, the average level of plasma lipids in most American men and women is undesirably elevated. The importance of lowering the plasma cholesterol in any individual depends in large part upon his usual plasma cholesterol concentration.

The evidence now available is sufficient to discourage further temporizing with this major national health problem. Therefore, the Food and Nutrition Board and the Council on Foods and Nutrition recommend that:

(1) Measurement of the plasma lipid profile, particularly plasma cholesterol, become a routine part of all health maintenance physical examinations. Such measurements should be made in early adulthood, when coronary heart disease is still rare, and repeated at appropriate intervals. The potential impact of other risk factors should also be periodically assessed.

(2) Persons falling into "risk categories" on the basis of their plasma lipid levels be made aware of this and receive appropriate dietary advice. Such advice may vary somewhat with the nature of the blood lipid profile. [Frederickson, Levy, and Lees, N. Eng. J. Med. 276:34 (1967); Lees and Wilson, N. Eng. J. Med. 284:186 (1971); Report of Inter-Society Commission for Heart Disease Resources, Circulation XLII:A55 (1970); American Health Foundation Position Statement on Diet and Coronary Heart Disease, Preventive Medicine 1:255 (1972).] As indicated above, Americans should be advised to maintain a desirable body weight by an appropriate combination of physical activity and calorie intake. In "risk categories" it is important to decrease substantially the intake of saturated fat and to lower cholesterol consumption. In practice, this entails substituting polyunsaturated vegetable oils for part of the saturated fat in the diet.

(3) Care be taken to assure that the dietary advice given does not compromise the intake of essential nutrients. Desirable intakes of nutrients are indicated in the Recommended Dietary Allowances (Nat. Acad. Sci. Publ. No. 1694, 1968).

(4) Since the foregoing recommendations will be effective only if they can be accomplished with relative ease, modified and ordinary foods useful for this purpose be readily available on the market, reasonably priced, and easily identified by appropriate labeling. Any existing legal and regulatory barriers to the marketing of such foods should be removed.

(5) High priority be given to the conduct of studies that will determine reliably the extent to which the modification of plasma lipids, by dietary or other means, as well as modification of other risk factors, can reduce the risk of developing coronary artery disease.

Modifying Foods

A great deal of research is being done by USDA, universities, and food industries to develop ways to modify the kinds of fat, and especially to reduce the amount of fat, in meat and dairy products and in processed foods such as bakery goods and other convenience food items.

Many of these foods are already available in the market-place—lean meat; low-fat milk, cheese, and ice cream; and salad dressings with a high proportion of polyunsaturated vegetable oil. These foods offer increased variety to consumers and are of special help to persons with specific dietary needs. The acceptability of products and their continued use by consumers will determine their future availability and their effect on the diet and health of the population.

Appendix 10.4

Food and Nutrition Board, National Academy of Sciences—National Research Council Recommended Daily Dietary Allowances[a]

Revised 1979

Reproduced from: Recommended Dietary Allowances, Ninth Edition (1980), with the permission of the National Academy of Sciences, Washington, D.C.

[a] The allowances are intended to provide for individual variations among most normal persons as they live in the United States under usual environmental stresses. Diets should be based on a variety of common foods in order to provide other nutrients for which human requirements have been less well defined.

[b] Retinol equivalents. 1 retinol equivalent = 1 μg retinol or 6 μg β carotene. See text for calculation of vitamin A activity of diets as retinol equivalents.

[c] As cholecalciferol. 10 μg cholecalciferol = 400 IU of vitamin D.

[d] α-tocopherol equivalents. 1 mg d-α tocopherol = 1 α-TE.

[e] 1 NE (niacin equivalent) is equal to 1 mg of niacin or 60 mg of dietary tryptophan.

[f] The folacin allowances refer to dietary sources as determined by *Lactobacillus casei* assay after treatment with enzymes (conjugases) to make polyglutamyl forms of the vitamin available to the test organism.

[g] The recommended dietary allowance for vitamin B-12 in infants is based on average concentration of the vitamin in human milk. The allowances after weaning are based on energy intake (as recommended by the American Academy of Pediatrics) and consideration of other factors, such as intestinal absorption; see text.

[h] The increased requirement during pregnancy cannot be met by the iron content of habitual American diets nor by the existing iron stores of many women; therefore the use of 30–60 mg of supplemental iron is recommended. Iron needs during lactation are not substantially different from those of nonpregnant women, but continued supplementation of the mother for 2–3 months after parturition is advisable in order to replenish stores depleted by pregnancy.

	Age (years)	Weight (kg)	Weight (lb)	Height (cm)	Height (in)	Protein (g)	Vitamin A (μg RE)[b]	Vitamin D (μg)[c]	Vitamin E (mg α TE)[d]
Infants	0.0-0.5	6	1.3	60	24	kg × 2.2	420	10	3
	0.5-1.0	9	20	71	28	kg × 2.0	400	10	4
Children	1-3	13	29	90	35	23	400	10	5
	4-6	20	44	112	44	30	500	10	6
	7-10	28	62	132	52	34	700	10	7
Males	11-14	45	99	157	62	45	1000	10	8
	15-18	66	145	176	69	56	1000	10	10
	19-22	70	154	177	70	56	1000	7.5	10
	23-50	70	154	178	70	56	1000	5	10
	51 +	70	154	178	70	56	1000	5	10
Females	11-14	46	101	157	62	46	800	10	8
	15-18	55	120	163	64	46	800	10	8
	19-22	55	120	163	64	44	800	7.5	8
	23-50	55	120	163	64	44	800	5	8
	51 +	55	120	163	64	44	800	5	8
Pregnant						+30	+200	+5	+2
Lactating						+20	+400	+5	+3

Designed for the maintenance of good nutrition of practically all healthy people in the U.S.A.

| Water-Soluble Vitamins ||||||| Minerals |||||||
Vitamin C (mg)	Thiamin (mg)	Riboflavin (mg)	Niacin (mg NE)[e]	Vitamin B-6 (mg)	Folacin[f] (μg)	Vitamin B-12 (μg)	Calcium (mg)	Phosphorus (mg)	Magnesium (mg)	Iron (mg)	Zinc (mg)	Iodine (μg)
35	0.3	0.4	6	0.3	30	0.5[g]	360	240	50	10	3	40
35	0.5	0.6	8	0.6	45	1.5	540	360	70	15	5	50
45	0.7	0.8	9	0.9	100	2.0	800	800	150	15	10	70
45	0.9	1.0	11	1.3	200	2.5	800	800	200	10	10	90
45	1.2	1.4	16	1.6	300	3.0	800	800	250	10	10	120
50	1.4	1.6	18	1.8	400	3.0	1200	1200	350	18	15	150
60	1.4	1.7	18	2.0	400	3.0	1200	1200	400	18	15	150
60	1.5	1.7	19	2.2	400	3.0	800	800	350	10	15	150
60	1.4	1.6	18	2.2	400	3.0	800	800	350	10	15	150
60	1.2	1.4	16	2.2	400	3.0	800	800	350	10	15	150
50	1.1	1.3	15	1.8	400	3.0	1200	1200	300	18	15	150
60	1.1	1.3	14	2.0	400	3.0	1200	1200	300	18	15	150
60	1.1	1.3	14	2.0	400	3.0	800	800	300	18	15	150
60	1.0	1.2	13	2.0	400	3.0	800	800	300	18	15	150
60	1.0	1.2	13	2.0	400	3.0	800	800	300	10	15	150
+20	+0.4	+0.3	+2	+0.6	+400	+1.0	+400	+400	+150	[h]	+5	+25
+40	+0.5	+0.5	+5	+0.5	+100	+1.0	+400	+400	+150	[h]	+10	+50

CHAPTER ELEVEN
OTHER ITEMS IN THE BUDGET

We have discussed in sequence the major decisions households make about education, work, residence, saving, investing, and the major expenditures. As we go down the list, the things we spend money on involve smaller and smaller amounts of money and less commitment to the future, and so are worth discussing only if interesting or useful applications of economic principles are involved. We shall therefore not discuss every item in the consumer budget, but some important categories—food, clothing, transportation, recreation, recreational equipment, philanthropy, and repair services. Once again, some introductory discussion of principles is in order.

Priorities and Shopping

Having decided upon the amounts to be invested in self, durables, and savings, the household has an available sum of money to be allocated among its remaining consumption needs. A clear economic principle mentioned frequently earlier is that the cost of any expenditure is the value of the best alternative use of the money. Hence, I should push the expenditure in any one area up to the point where the added satisfaction from the next (marginal) expenditure in that area will produce less added satisfaction than an expenditure somewhere else. (The competing alternative of spending at some later time has already been taken care of in setting saving goals, although it may reassert itself at times.)

This way of looking at the choices is really simpler than asking "Is it worth the money?" because that shorthand rule assumes I always know what money is worth. But particularly in periods of inflation with differentially changing prices, I may have a distorted notion of whether something is a bargain. And besides, our rule places the decision to buy into a *choice* context, which properly deals with the costs involved.

The implication of this application of the principle of opportunity cost is that it is extremely useful to keep a rather comprehensive priority list of family needs, so that the priorities are set with forethought, and not by thinking about one need at a time. Indeed, opportunities for bargains are common enough that if one has a list of several high-priority next-needs, slight alterations in the order of acquisition may save substantial amounts of money. This is quite a different way of using sales from buying at bargain prices things that one had not even considered buying at all. Nothing is really a bargain if you do not need it.

A systematic listing and ordering of priorities also allows time to accumulate information on prices and qualities easily and efficiently in the course of other shopping, reading, or talking with friends. Setting such priorities, and even making sure that all the needs are simultaneously considered, will require some family discussion and collaboration. Adequate solutions to the problems of priorities among expenditures, and the compromising of the desires of different family members, probably make more difference in the total family satisfaction than shopping around for the best combination of high quality and low price. But shopping matters too. The ideal situation is to see something you need on sale, of a brand you have already decided is acceptable, and at a price you recognize as substantially less than has been available even at discount stores. A little systematic planning and a good memory can help make this happen.

Shopping includes the acquisition of information about a possible purchase, which, in turn, involves costs and benefits, not all of them easily measurable. Shopping costs are mostly time costs, plus some travel costs and perhaps the costs of books or magazines with information about the product or service in question. How much it pays to invest in shopping depends on expected benefits. The benefits may be partly psychic (e.g., the satisfaction of knowing that you got the lowest price), but even achieving the concrete economic benefits of a better quality or price requires the solution of a complex problem. By altering my idea of the actual quality and price variability, each additional bit of information I acquire can change the expected payoff to still more information (Telser). If I find that the first four stores I visit quote the same price, then I may decide that there are no bargains to be found and further search is not worthwhile. If I find a wide variety of prices, I may decide it is worth looking still further for an even better bargain.

Suppose I visited ten equally convenient and reputable appliance stores and was able to establish ten prices for several washing machines of equal quality. I would obviously take the one with the lowest price, and my savings would be the difference between the first price and the lowest one. Indeed, I could estimate the savings if I had gone only to the first two, or three, or four stores, etc., always taking the lowest price and comparing this with the cost of the extra visits (including a likely return visit to the best place). I would save less, of course, but how much less?

One can use the information more broadly, randomizing the order in which the shops *might have been* visited, to estimate the "expected value" of a second, third, etc., visit. One can then compare the average price (which is the *expected* price on a random visit to only one dealer) with the average, over all possible pairs, of the "lowest of two prices." The difference between these two averages is an estimate of the expected saving from making a second trip. Taking all possible triplets of prices, one can average the lowest prices, one from each triplet, and compare it to the average best deal from all possible ways of making two visits. The difference is the expected payoff to making a third visit.

As an illustration of this procedure, we can use the actual prices quoted by stores in the Ann Arbor, Michigan, area for a certain brand and model of single-lens reflex camera. These prices were: $335, $340, $280, and $336, which average to $323. The *expected* price for the first visit is just the average price of $323. Random visits to two stores would result in the following pairs of prices, with each pair having an equal chance of occurring:

Pair of Prices	Lowest Price of the Pair
$335, $340	$335
$335, $280	$280
$335, $336	$335
$340, $280	$280
$340, $336	$336
$280, $336	$280

The average of the lowest prices of the pairs is $308, so that the expected or average payoff to the second search is the difference between this average and the expected price from the first visit, or $323 − $308 = $15. This benefit must be weighed against the costs of the second visit plus the possibility of a need to return to the cheaper of the two stores.

It is easy to show that three-fourths of all possible combinations of visits to three stores would include the lowest priced store, while the remaining visits would have $335 as the lowest price. The expected price for three visits, then, is (0.75 × $280) + (0.25 × $335) = $294. So the payoff to the third search is $308 − $294 = $14. Visits to all four stores would, of course, produce the $280 price, and the expected payoff to the fourth search is also $14 ($294 − $280). So with this camera, the benefits to additional store visits are in the $10 to $20 range. The costs will depend upon whether these prices would be quoted over the phone and, if not, the time and money costs of the travel. It is hard to make general statements about the likely benefits of searching, but the dispersion in prices for many durable goods is often surprisingly large (Maynes). There is a statistical formula for estimating the lowest price among items in a sample of any size, using only the average and the standard deviation (Ratchford).

In a classic study of this type it was found that visiting more car dealers produced high but diminishing expected savings. More important, that study indicated that the bargaining skill of the purchaser had little to do with it. The implication is that it pays to shop around even if you are not good at haggling—and in the car market at that, where the conventional wisdom is that haggling is required (Jung).

There are a few general principles about when it pays to assume that large variations in quality or price exist. It always pays to shop around when other people typically buy a particular item or service in a hurry or in desperation (film), or on expense accounts (restaurants, hotels), or infrequently and without much expertise (cameras, hi-fi components), or where there is low turnover and great variety and hence high markups (furniture). Sometimes shopping does not help even here, if the demand fueled with other people's money (expense accounts) has simply driven up all the prices.

We turn now to some important categories of expenditure.

Food

We discussed the possibility of budgeting food expenditures and forecasting them in chapter 5, and the complexities of nutrition for health in chapter 10. Nutrition is a subject that repays further study, not just for health, but for lowering the cost of achieving it. The more one knows, the wider the range of substitutes possible and hence the more the bargains of the day can be seized.

When people begin to keep track of their expenditures and worry about economizing, it is usually food and clothing which get the most attention. Food seems to take the most money, and visibly each week. Clothing seems the most discretionary and postponable. On the other hand, food habits seem to be solidly fixed in childhood and appear difficult for most people to change. That is why we said it was so easy to predict future food budgets for a family—because standards do not change much, and because volume needs (calorie and protein requirements) change dramatically with the changing ages of family members (particularly boys).

Because most people's food preferences are relatively inflexible, there are real savings for those who are willing to be more flexible, not only in using less common foods, but in changing menus as prices change. Of course, this requires a good memory for prices. A good memory is in any case absolutely necessary in food purchasing. It is certainly not economical to visit several food stores each week looking for bargains, particularly if it turns out that the lowest prices are sometimes in the first store. What may pay, however, is to go to a different supermarket each week, buying what is cheaper in that particular store (memory again). Some investment in learning the layout of several stores is required to cut the shopping time costs. Food retailing profit margins are quite narrow, but there are differences between stores as to where they are reduced the most. Since margins are so narrow, it is quite unlikely that any one supermarket will consistently charge substantially less for a whole market basket than other supermarkets doing the same volume of business.

Margins, and prices, are of course higher in smaller food stores. It has been charged that they are also higher in poorer areas of the cities, but the evidence is mixed (Marcus; U.S. Department of Agriculture; U.S. Department of Labor). When one allows for differences in store size and in costs of pilferage and protection against it, it looks as though the price differences arise not from differences in profitability but from differences in costs and volume. The tendency of chains to take their markets *out* of low-income areas would reinforce this notion. Low-income people still end up paying more for their food, since they do not have easy transportation to alternative markets. They may also get worse service—as they do in other places that serve mostly poor—because they are less likely to complain, or less able to get their complaints to the right place.

Before the advent of the supermarkets in this country, and still in many countries of the world, food retailing exemplified the inefficiency of too much competition—many sellers and a "differentiated product." This situation is sometimes called monopolistic competition. Each store had to have large markups because it did not do enough business to spread its overhead costs, and yet no one store could expand, spread its overhead thinner, cut prices, and take over, because the other stores would meet the prices in the short run. Consumers, liking the convenience or friendly credit at the nearest store, did not respond to price differences. It is sometimes argued that this is not inefficient, but the price people pay for convenience or special service. Conceptually, one can distinguish between the two situations by asking whether it would be possible to get the customers to promise to patronize only a small list of large stores where they would get reduced prices, and then to get those few stores to reduce their prices on promise of getting all the business. In practice, the success of chains in finally breaking in, in spite of the nostalgic pleas to save the little family businesses, showed that people preferred the lower prices. Better roads and more cars also helped to get the high-volume stores going. And the food chains found they could imitate national brands and sell the store brand substitutes for 10 to 15 percent less in some cases.

Savings on the food bill, beyond those from finding the lower prices and adapting the menu to prices, depend heavily on the family's general mode of living. Some families do not plan ahead or manage carefully, and for them it pays never to buy more than is actually needed for the week. On the other hand, those who have a lot of willpower (or, rather, "won't power") can save by stocking up when prices are low, and buying economy sizes. It probably pays, however, to stock up mostly on necessities, not luxuries. In fact, one of the wisest things with which to fill a freezer is bread, which may even improve on freezing, can be toasted frozen, avoids the necessity for a trip to the store (when one usually ends up buying more than bread), and avoids the temptation to stock up on prime steaks. There are also costs of storage, of course: electricity and depreciation and foregone interest for the freezer, and foregone interest on the money invested in the stock of food. If food prices rise faster than the rate of interest on savings, there is no *real* foregone interest.

The price-shopping issue and the bulk-buying issue are interrelated. One can take substantial advantage of bargains only if one is willing to stock up on things when they are cheap or when one happens to be in the store which sells them more cheaply. But it pays to stock up only if one is not then tempted to use food more wastefully or live more luxuriously than one intended. For many families, the solution may be to stock up on bargains in necessities like bread, sugar, flour, etc., but never to stock up on luxuries, even at good prices, unless the family has some other control system for regulating its consumption of luxuries. Remember that in hoping to stock up on temporarily cheaper food, you are competing with large commercial operators whose storage costs are lower and whose knowledge of likely future prices is likely to be more accurate. The best economy may be to eat less, and there is evidence that you may also live longer eating less!

Both the growing and preparation of food offer opportunities for direct home production, economically speaking. But unless one values the exercise, or the recreational aspects, or particular qualities connected with fresh produce, the savings from growing one's own food, calculated as hourly earnings on the time spent, are likely to be rather low. For some of us, it is fun, and we do need the exercise, and the whole thing is a worthwhile challenge. With modern powered tillers available for rental, the backbreaking work of gardening is gone, and with modern hybrid seeds and good insecticides, the results are often excellent. You may even get along without expensive insecticides for a year or two in a new location. After that, at least some rotenone is likely to be required.

The same comment, with the added payoff that it may allow an expression of creativity, goes for investing more time in preparing foods at home rather than purchasing prepared things which already incorporate a lot of labor. The hard-headed economic way of looking at the investment of added time for preparation is to figure out how much you earn per hour by saving on the cost of food and to compare that with the value of alternative opportunities. Of course, if a parent does it while watching the children, the opportunity cost of the time may be nearly zero. Or if one feels a need for variety in one's tasks, one might argue that the opportunity cost is really low, or that there are other benefits.

As we said earlier about other do-it-yourself projects, the payoff depends on amortizing the investment in equipment and in learning how. In deciding whether to start, one must guess the learning costs and the potential use. In deciding whether to continue, the past investment costs should be ignored, so the returns per hour may well be quite high.

Going in the other direction, another way to buy your own time for leisure or fun is to eat in restaurants. Upper-income people and multiple-earner families do this a great deal, restaurant expenditures being highly "income elastic." Presumably one also gets entertainment and service as well as freedom from cooking and doing the dishes. At today's wages, it is still much cheaper to eat out than to have a hired cook at home. In response to the needs of people who are most interested in saving time, the speedy service drive-in has arisen, its major attraction being that one can get extremely rapid service and the low prices that production line food preparation makes possible. When a single chain can advertise that it has sold more than thirty billion hamburgers, it must be serving some need! It is quite possible, however, that the time saved is more important to the customers than the money saved.

Should food be cheaper? Consumer advocates have long railed about the wide price margins between what the farmer gets and what the eater pays. They have not always distinguished among the reasons: inefficiency, excess profits, real costs, and increased real services. The level of profits in food wholesaling and retailing has never been great, especially when compared with other industries. It is difficult to determine whether the distribution system could be made more efficient. But certainly there has been more and more processing of food, so that some of the wide and growing price spread reflects greater real contribution of processors in making the food easier to use, or better preserved. Those who think the extra processing costs too much must remember that in doing it themselves they are competing with a mass production industry with economies of scale.

Whenever there is inflation, consumers tend to focus their anger and concern on food. Recently this concern has led to pressures for unit pricing and open dating. And there has been criticism of the proposed system of computer check-out that uses a machine to read a set of markings on each package that would enable the computer (and register) to identify its current price. Although prices might be posted somewhere in the store, individual packages would no longer be marked. A reexamination of these concerns with the consumer in mind is useful, remembering that most of us have limited memories and limited ability to calculate in our heads.

Unit pricing advocates want everything priced in cents per ounce or pound or some other basic unit of measure instead of per package, because package sizes are so various. But for consumers who have learned the price ranges of some standard package sizes, like the twelve-ounce jar of jelly, the change would require learning a whole new set of norms. And after discovering that one package was cheaper per ounce than another, the customer would have to perform another multiplication in order to know how many *cents*, or what percentage, would be saved buying the cheaper brand, which is what matters to most of us. Perhaps more helpful to the consumer, and less costly to comply with, would be a law which required a translation of the price of any unusual package size into the equivalent price of the nearest standard-sized package. Any container size accounting for a substantial fraction of total volume of that product—where the consumers presumably have a memory of its price—would simply be priced as usual. But if a firm marketed a thirteen-ounce jar of jelly, or an eleven-ounce jar, the store would have to post a statement telling what its price would be—at the same price per ounce—in the standard size. The difference would tell the customer the approximate saving between the two jars. In addition to reducing the work (and costs) of the retail grocer, such a law would provide a great incentive to producers to reduce the number of sizes, and to stick with the common sizes. It would not arbitrarily restrict the number of sizes as some have proposed, but would allow freedom to change package sizes where technology or eating habits called for it. But unit pricing is clearly of some benefit to consumers.

Provided one can trust the implied shelf life in dating of the "use before Month, Year" type, or learn what it means, that too should help consumers arrange their food inventories.

Even the criticism of computer check-out and the lack of prices on each container may be misplaced. Research on cognitive processing of information indicates that it is extremely difficult for people to make comparisons by scanning many facts about each alternative and then going on to the next alternative. Try reading the nutrition information label on one cereal box and then going on to the next box and the next. You will find yourself doing the much easier task—comparing the whole set of boxes on protein content, then on price, then on whatever else is next in importance to you. What most of us do most easily is to rank the alternatives on the single most important dimension, then scan across the still acceptable alternatives on a second dimension, and so on. If this is really the way we can use information, printed price lists posted in the store would actually be easier to use than package labels for selecting purchases, because one could scan the list, one criterion at a time. In fact, since the information would all be computerized, the lists could give all kinds of other information, e.g., the average yearly price and the nutritive content. In addition, at the check-out counter, the printed tape could give the names of the products as well as their prices, so the customer would have useful records to keep at home for price comparisons or analysis of the food budget components. In other words, properly done, the computer check-out system could give the consumer far more usable information than is now available.

There have been for some time mandatory federal food standards, and some voluntary grade label standards. An official summary appears as appendix 11.1. States also have standards, sometimes stricter than the federal ones, as with the Michigan definition of what can be put into a hot dog. The standards are useful safeguards, the grade labels only occasionally helpful. With beef one must know which superlative is really best—they range up from Utility through Commercial, Good, Choice, to Prime. The best, Prime, is marbled with fat.[1] One study showed that people tended to choose the lower quality meat when it was all priced the same but that their satisfaction with it, reported later, was in agreement with the USDA grading (Lasley et al.). The lower grades had less fat and gave more meat per pound, but were less tender and tasty. That is one of the troubles with grade labels—agreeing on the criteria.

Clothing

The budget item most often robbed when things do not come out right is the clothing budget. We can postpone buying clothing if spending money is scarce, and it is difficult to predict clothing needs because they come in waves with the seasons. The distinction between depreciation and obsolescence (becoming out of style) is crucial in this area. If the only problem were physical depreciation, we should all buy the best quality clothing for the money, i.e., the most months of wear per dollar. But with most visible items, styles change with blinding rapidity. In this situation, it is hard to avoid the feeling that clothes need

1. With current concerns over cholesterol, the standards are being changed, marbling with fat given less weight as an indicator of quality.

not be durable, since they will be out of style before they wear out. On the other hand, most people are convinced that the really expensive clothes by good designers do not go out of style so quickly and so are a good buy, having both low depreciation and low obsolescence. We might also feel good in them because we know they are well made.

Clothing labels tell the content of the fibers or furs, but nothing of the quality of construction and nothing of the quality of the materials, which can vary within each type. Again, the household learns by experience, word of mouth, and occasional articles. Most articles on new fabrics appear in magazines which accept advertising from producers and sellers; for this reason, they tell what is good about each new product, but not what is bad. The customer has to learn through experience that 100 percent synthetic fabric shirts wear like iron but may also feel like it, that synthetic socks foster fungus infections of the feet, or that the "wash and wear" cotton and dacron-cotton fabrics are also impregnated with resin or similar substances and are quite uncomfortable for anyone with a tendency to perspire. What is needed is a better system for circulating information on what is wrong with new products—the producers will tell what is right with them—so that each household need not pay to find out for itself (see chap. 12).

Another problem is that manufacturers, particularly of men's clothing, have a tendency to produce the same limited set of styles and colors, changing them systematically as though a conspiracy existed to increase obsolescence as well as to make all men look alike at any point in time. For instance, men's raincoats come in black (which shows the dust) or light beige (which shows the dirt) or green (which is often ugly or clashes with suits). Only in the most expensive, custom made, lines is there real variety. Women sometimes face the reverse problem, with so much variety that a particular item is not available in their size when they want it.

The regular seasonal sales of clothing, particularly men's clothing with its slow style changes, are hard to explain. How can the stores sell at *other* times, when customers know that if they only wait a few months for the next sale, they can get at least 20 percent off? Apparently there are enough people who simply have to have something, or are afraid that the one item they like for color or style will disappear before it goes on sale. Smart buyers do a little scouting, then pick up what they want at the sales. The prior scouting also helps them avoid being "taken" by sales specials (bought or brought in for the sale and often not the same quality) or fictitious mark-downs.

Sales of men's clothes usually provide genuine bargains; for women, it is often a sign of change in style or season, so somewhat more risky. A woman with a sense of style, capable of guessing what will look right a year later, is thus better able to save money.

Children wear out some clothes before they outgrow them, and whether the optimal quality (durability) is worth the price differential may depend on whether there are younger siblings to take over the outgrown items. The large chains and catalog houses are an excellent place to buy children's clothing, because they are clear about what is in the fabric, offer a range of qualities, and deliver the purchase to your door. The larger catalog houses also test some of their clothing and will make good if things wear out too fast. Proper accounting for the costs in time and money of shopping locally may show that catalog shopping is cheaper, even with some mistakes to be returned and high postal rates.

Home production of clothing was for many years quite uneconomical. Clothing was being produced by mass production methods at relatively low wages. Recent years of climbing wages and rising distribution costs have driven many people back to the fabric shops and their own sewing machines. A big business in "simple" patterns fuels the drive. It may still not be worth investing in the skills to tailor men's clothes or such items as suits and coats, so it may pay best to make children's clothes—dresses, shorts, etc. Many a family has found it wise to provide a convenient place for the sewing machine. Skills at alterations and repairs are also handy in these days when it is difficult to get anybody to do anything cheaply (or at all).

An added advantage of some do-it-yourself home production is that in addition to providing tax-free income it may also save time. Altering clothing is an example, or repairing one's own appliances, where the alternative might be to take it somewhere and pick it up later. The extreme example is cutting the children's hair, where the job itself takes far less time than taking the children to the barber, and the equipment and training costs to be amortized are small.

A more complex economic consideration when one thinks of doing it oneself is the investment in equipment and training involved. It is not just a decision to invest time and materials in an individual act of sewing or gardening, but a decision to accumulate equipment and know-how, the return on which comes over many years of productive activity. The sewing machine, and learning how to use it, is a good example. The investment really pays off only if one continues to make use of the machine and the skills. In fact, since the necessary style and quality of clothing goes up as one gets older, most people are unlikely to make much of their own clothing after age thirty, unless they have by then acquired a rather high level of skill. The investment of time in learning the skills may well be larger than the investment in capital equipment, particularly since the equipment can often be rented.

One difficulty in learning skills is that the available printed materials telling how to do many of these productive activities are seriously deficient if available at all. The printed instructions on clothing patterns make sense only to those who already know pretty well what to do. A book on home gardens is not always adequate. Perhaps the best written instructional books are the cookbooks.

Finally, even though one may enjoy creative work as recreation, it pays to take the hard-hearted economic view first, then introduce these other considerations.

Transportation and Recreation

In the United States, the dominance of the automobile makes it necessary to consider transportation and recreation together. If the family needs a car for transportation, then that same car is available to reduce the costs of recreation, especially the vacation needs of large families. Indeed, the decision to buy a car, or to buy a newer one, involves an estimate of the payoffs both in transportation to work and stores and schools, and in making some kinds of recreation a great deal easier and cheaper.

The fact that cars can fulfill both transportation and recreation needs causes some budgeting problems, particularly if one attempts to keep separate account of transportation and recreation expenditures. The gasoline purchased on a pleasure trip belongs in the latter category, but the rest of the gasoline bill in the former. And how should one divide the other car costs, including depreciation and foregone interest, between the two uses? Perhaps we should allocate almost all of the costs to transportation, so that our recreation expenditures look smaller. Then we are induced into "economizing" by using the car, rather than airplanes, for vacations. It is correct economic analysis to consider only the marginal (added) costs in deciding whether to use the car for each purpose, of course, once the car is owned. Rising energy prices will affect all transportation, leaving choices still to be made, especially if gasoline taxes are raised to discourage the use of private cars.

The major transportation decisions have to do with the journey to work. Most people prefer to drive; except in the largest cities, they find they can get there faster and more conveniently by car. The convenience includes comfort, speed, privacy, and flexibility in timing. But the car costs more than alternative methods, particularly if one charges the full capital cost of the car to transportation, and the margin is greater when parking must be paid for. Most American families have more than one car. In households with two earners going to work in different places, the pressures are obvious. Even if the one car in a family is used for work, this leaves the other parent and children needing transportation to school, stores, etc. Given what we have already seen about the importance of depreciation and interest in the cost of a car, and the fact that a second car does not have to be used for highway travel, many families sensibly have one reasonably old car just for in-town transportation. The difficulty is that for family vacations a good, large car, usually a station wagon or van, is best, while for transportation to work, a smaller car, less expensive to operate and easier to park, seems optimal. Yet the cheapest way to get an older car initially is to keep your own old one when buying a new car. It costs a lot in trouble, risk, and dealer's margins to trade in a larger car on a more "economical" one. The result of this situation is that a lot of large cars are being used for driving to work. The inefficiency is only apparent, not real, for the individual family. Those large cars were originally the good, "family" car.

At various times, attempts are made to reduce the cost of the trip to work by the use of car pools, and various pressures will surely come to do more of this, but these pools tend to be inconvenient unless the members agree pretty well on time schedules and other details. If the schedule of drivers does not need constant adjustments, and if the driver phones each rider just before he leaves the house (not waiting for an answer), and if each rider then comes out promptly, the whole operation can be quite efficient. It avoids the need for two cars per family, and lowers the cost of getting to work every day. The sight of innumerable cars during the rush hours, a single person in each, testifies to the difficulties of cooperation and economy through car pools, and the value placed on privacy and flexibility.

One of the difficulties in any cooperative arrangement is keeping account of the relative contributions and preserving equity. Since car pools are essentially barter operations, there is bound to be some feeling of inequity, if not actual maldistribution of costs and benefits, unless prices are put on things and balances kept. One solution, used mostly in babysitting cooperatives, is to use "token" paper money designed for the purpose. Each member is given an initial sum of "token" paper money, and the services are then paid for in the "token" paper money at an agreed price or system of prices. This acts, just as real as money does, as an automatic method of balancing out; so long as you do not run out of the paper money, you know things are in balance. All that is needed in addition is a rule against accumulating too much of the money and hoarding it, which would cut off trade altogether. A similar system might be possible for a ride-sharing cooperative in cases where it was impossible for each rider to provide the pool car for the same fraction of the time.

There are hot public policy issues with respect to transportation, particularly in and around major urban areas. Interest is usually precipitated by increasing traffic jams, parking problems, threats of gas shortages, or the financial troubles of the public transit authority or the private bus line. Three major positions can be identified. One group wants to focus on public transportation, for its obvious physical efficiency, and keep the private cars out. Another more nostalgic and esthetically oriented group wants to decentralize the city, provide parks and greenbelts, and reduce the need for so much commuting. A third group, claiming to be more realistic about people's preferences and behavior and about the economics of geographic concentrations, argues for continuing the investment in expressways and parking facilities.

As in many such issues, there are considerations of economic efficiency and equity, as well as of esthetics. Since lower-income people are more apt to use public transportation, any improvement in it, particularly if it is somehow subsidized out of tax funds, benefits lower-income people more. On the other hand, if one values people's time according to their hourly earnings (and accepts the income distribution as reasonable), then careful economic calculations may not always come out in favor of public transportation. Regardless of the arguments, it has proven very difficult to convince people to give up the convenience and time saving of their private cars, and they seem willing to pay substantial sums for parking and other fees, and now gasoline.

If one combines these two considerations, it raises an interesting possibility. Suppose the government put a very heavy tax on *parking* in the city or on gasoline and used the money to provide *free* public transportation. The charges would be justified as a payment by those who wanted to drive, to encourage others to ride public transportation and not clog up the streets and parking places. Those willing to suffer the inconvenience of public transportation would be paid for this by getting it free. There are real economies, including speedier service, in not having to collect fares. Finally, it would be possible to experiment with routes and schedules during the transition, including express service from outlying parking lots for those willing to compromise and drive only part way. Enough users would justify sufficiently frequent service to make buses an acceptable alternative.

The critical thing to keep in mind is the economic aspects of these decisions. They must be interpreted both in terms of resource allocation and efficiency on the one hand, and in terms of fairness between different groups on the other. While neither can be considered totally separately, the conceptual experiment of trying to analyze both aspects is essential.

Careful economic analysis is required if even free public transportation is to be designed well enough to entice users. The user of public transportation cannot start from home, nor start exactly when he is ready, nor get to exactly where he is going. The costs of walking at both ends, and of waiting for the next bus, must be recognized. They involve the costs of a person's time as well as some energy expenditure. Frequent and dependable service can cut these costs, as can a wide variety of routes. If the schedule is not kept, then waiting time is increased, even on the average, because people have to allow more leeway to be sure of getting to work on time.

It is apparently easier politically to subsidize the capital costs than the operating costs of public transportation. This leads to disastrously large expenditures on rigid systems like the Bay Area Rapid Transit System in the San Francisco area. That system took years to build and services only limited areas. The same amount of money could have provided free bus service, from the beginning, for the whole area. Indeed, it is possible that the consumer would be better served by a variety of competing modes of mass transit, with less regulation and more competition. Individuals running jitney cabs and figuring out how to make money by serving real needs might well provide more flexible service more cheaply. Present regulations in many cities restrict the number of taxis, thus creating monopoly privileges that are bought and sold for substantial sums, and keeping fares higher than competitive fares. This is done presumably in return for some higher level of responsibility by the taxis. What do they do to justify their monopoly? With competition, would no taxis be available at the less profitable times and places?

The cost of public transportation cannot be directly affected by the individual consumer, but he can influence the cost of his own car and its operation in a number of ways. The simplest, already mentioned, is to keep each car longer, cutting the yearly cost of depreciation and interest. A second is to buy a secondhand car. Another is proper maintenance, a difficult thing when manufacturers' instructions vary so much and tend to suggest excessive caution and care.

Do-it-yourself maintenance and repairs, for those with some skill and interest, and a place to do it, can save a good deal. Perhaps even more with the car, there is an investment in equipment and in learning the necessary skills. Charges for simple things, that have been getting simpler, have been rising as wages rise and labor gets scarce and as fewer people think of doing it themselves. What used to be a complex job—greasing a car—now consists of applying grease from a pressure gun in less than a dozen places. A hand pressure gun is inexpensive and adequate. Changing oil and oil filters is an extremely simple, if dirty, task which costs dearly in labor charges plus inflated prices for the oil and filter. As it becomes increasingly inconvenient to have a car serviced or repaired, places having moved out to the edge of town where land is cheaper, the net benefits from doing it yourself get bigger; it may take no more time to do it yourself than to get the car to the garage and back again. Indeed, it is difficult to see the advantage of having the service garages so far out, thus requiring extra driving and time by each owner. Perhaps it is assumed that the owners will not take account of their time. But it is entirely possible that the garages which do try to save their customers' time will end up with most of the business.

Manufacturers issue a shop manual for each car they make, and these manuals can be purchased, making it easier to maintain and even repair your own car.[2] Secondhand parts from junkyards can often be used at great savings; on the other hand, repair garages get discounts on the parts they use, so some of the savings get dissipated in heavier charges for parts.

A substantial number of people do some work on their own cars. They are mostly middle-income people. The highest-income people are too busy, and the opportunity cost of their time is too high; lowest-income people may not have the confidence, skills, or ability to use written instructions easily, or may be working such long hours at such hard work that they cannot take on more tasks.

One major cost of any car is the tires, and they present one of the most confused and cut-up markets of any major consumer product. There are seasonal sales, and special cheap lines, and "discount tire stores." There are also places which recap tires with new tread, or sell such tires. The cheap tires are frequently no bargain, wearing through most of the tread in a year or a few thousand miles, and having such a weak carcass that they puncture easily. On the other hand, some of the most expensive tires can be justified only for high-speed, long-distance trips over bad roads, and perhaps even then a somewhat less fancy tire would do. The tubeless tire, a great product for good roads, has turned out to be a nightmare for anyone using a car on bad roads. It develops small leaks around the rim and elsewhere, and are difficult or impossible to patch. The steel-belted radial tire does wear longer, doesn't heat up in use, and increases gas mileage. It is still something of a luxury and should not be mixed with other tires on the same car since its dynamic properties are quite different. When it comes to buying tires, little can be said that is not obvious. Of course, it pays to shop around, and yet to stick to known brands of known quality, and to try to identify the quality lines of each brand when their names keep changing.

Another tire problem in areas requiring snow tires is the twice-a-year changing operation. One solution is to purchase a secondhand rim and then to change wheels, not tires, which can easily be done at home. One of the wheels with snow tire serves as a spare in summer, and one of those with a regular tire as a spare in winter. Again, it may take no more time to switch the two rear wheels oneself than to take the car somewhere, have it done, and pick it up. At present charges, a consumer could save several dollars a year and some time, minus the cost of an extra rim, plus the savings of not keeping an unused spare tire. (One needs only four regular tires and two snow tires.)

More complex car repairs often need extensive equipment. Rental businesses have sprung up all over the country that will rent such equipment, including portable hoists with which you can remove a motor or transmission. And since some specialized repair services often operate independently of the general repair garages, one can remove a piece, have it rebuilt or repaired, and replace it, without much skill.

While a few individualists will get around on bicycles, motorcycles, boats, or even on foot, most of us use either our own car or public transportation. Public transportation for the journey to work is only rarely adequate, and then mostly in cities which became large before the advent of the motor car. Even in those, and even with subsidies in some of them, it has a difficult time competing (Lansing, Hendricks). For longer journeys, the railroads, once the favorite or the only method of travel, were on a

---

2. Indeed, more and more manuals are appearing which spell out a step-by-step strategy for diagnosing the causes of trouble.

persistent decline, reinforced by reductions in frequency and quality of service. One might think that with expressways, the long-distance buses could compete with private autos, with all the economies and convenience of their size. But getting to and from the center-of-town terminals remains a problem. At present, buses tend to serve the people who live in the center of town, have low incomes, and perhaps do not have cars. Gas shortages and higher gas prices may reverse the declines in rail and bus service, perhaps even permanently.

For more extensive travel, the consumer faces greater unknowns as to the costs and quality of the alternatives. Car rental costs vary widely, and can be quite deceptive if they are quoted as so much per day plus so much per mile or kilometer. The quality, and even prices, of hotels is difficult to determine in advance, except in Europe, where relatively complete guides are published. Guides on how to get along cheaply in foreign lands are often useful, but quality can fall and prices rise between the time they investigate and the time the reader gets there; this is a common problem with something in limited supply. Better information about quality can rapidly eliminate the bargains. The ordinary traveler should be happy for such better information even if he does not use it, because it makes it less and less likely that he is missing any bargains, or hitting any bad buys.

What complicates the picture most is the growing use of package vacation tours, which not only can afford to invest in better information, but can negotiate bargains unavailable to the individual traveler. For the lower price, one trades the freedom to select schedules or activities, and gains freedom from worry and from having to do a lot of individual negotiating and decision making.

As hourly earnings rise, the opportunity cost of vacation time also rises, and the natural tendency is to find recreations which use more money relative to the time they take. The rapid rise in vacation air travel can be interpreted in this light.

The choice between car and bus or airplane involves tradeoffs between convenience, speed, and cost, which vary with the size of the family and the distance traveled, and whether each end of the trip is near a major airport. For a single person, air travel costs per mile are roughly equal to the real costs of travel by car if one includes depreciation and wear and tear. Remember that time is valuable, so one should not compare only out-of-pocket costs.

Even when the trip is a vacation trip, it consumes both time and money to produce enjoyment, and calculations should involve both. If the trip is by car, the drive itself may be enjoyable, depending on where it is and on the individuals. Children seem to find long drives boring. But some people manage to break up long trips so that the trip itself, and the activities along the way, are part of the vacation and not just a cost of getting to it and back.

Recreational Equipment

More and more recreational activities involve not only time and money but the use of equipment. Part of the cost, then, is either the rental cost of such equipment, or the depreciation, interest, and maintenance costs of owning the equipment. People own or rent boats, tent trailers, vacation trailers, snowmobiles, skis, summer cottages, fishing equipment, and so on. The advantages of owning such equipment are obvious. But to own a piece of equipment that is used only for a week or two of the year is clearly an expensive luxury, compared with renting it. The costs per use depend on the amount of use and the length of time over which the fixed costs can be spread.

The industries producing recreational equipment have innovated rapidly, produced a bewildering and changing variety of items at the cost of never achieving the major economies of mass production. There is mass production of some components, but until the consumers settle on a few standard lines and concentrate on looking for better prices, the situation seems unlikely to change. It is particularly chaotic in recreational vehicles.

In deciding whether or not to own a piece of recreational equipment, the rate of depreciation is clearly important. Things like tents and canoes and trailers, properly cared for, depreciate very slowly, since there is little to wear out and little obsolescence. So they may be worthwhile owning even if used only a little each year.

Such considerations affect the relative costs of the vacation trailer pulled by the family car, the "camper" that sits on a pickup truck, and the "motor home," which has the living quarters and the power source in the same unit.

The second alternative is more expensive than the first, because of the more rapid depreciation, unless one has use for the pickup truck during the rest of the year. On the other hand, because the pickup truck is a utility vehicle bought mostly by hard-headed businessmen and artisans, it may be cheaper than a car. The third alternative, the motor home, is quite expensive unless it is used for other purposes, or amortized over a good deal of camping. The cost is not just in interest and depreciation on the motor, extra wheels, etc., but also in maintenance on idle equipment that has moving parts. They are not produced in volume, so the original price is also high. Hence, if one wants the convenience of a motor home, it may well be cheaper to rent one, even at what seems like high rent, than to own one if it is to be used only a few days per year.

Another compromise is joint ownership in some cooperative arrangement with one or more other families. Differences in standards of upkeep and conflicts over scheduling may be tolerable if the savings are substantial. A more common procedure with a large item like a summer cottage or a motor home is to rent it out during the times when the owner is not using it. This leaves the responsibility for maintenance in one place.

Much recreational equipment, particularly boats and trailers, also requires capital facilities where it is to be used: docks, marinas, campgrounds, trailer parks. For years the production of the equipment has outpaced the creation of the facilities. One outstanding example was the production of "self-contained" vacation trailers, campers, and motor homes, with toilets whose tanks had to be emptied into some sewage treatment system if proper sanitation were to be maintained. Yet the number of dumping stations lagged far behind. Now, some gasoline service stations advertise such facilities, and the better state park systems are providing it in their campgrounds. A similar problem exists with yachts; there is a great temptation to dump a few miles from port, a solution that is socially acceptable only when not too many people do it.

Remembering again that a vacation requires both time and money, one can interpret the advantages of various kinds of camping equipment in those terms. For instance, as one goes from a regular tent to a tent trailer and then to a camper, trailer, or motor home, the amount of time required to unpack, set up, break down, and repack, gets smaller and smaller. (And it is also smaller than staying in motels.) For people on long trips, staying at a different place each night, the difference in free time for enjoying the scenery, fishing, etc., may be substantial. Of course, some people enjoy the work, and think it gives the family something to do together, although casual observation of American campgrounds reveals father and mother doing most of the work. A trailer or camper or motor home saves time also in food preparation, since everything is available in cupboards, and there is water at the sink and a protected table at which to eat. With children, there are added advantages: stops for lunch can be made when convenient, next to a park or playground.

Some overnight facilities for trailers are now appearing on major turnpikes and expressways or right at the exits, for those on long trips, saving them the time and costs of looking off the highway for a place to spend the night.

In all vacation and recreation decisions there are "non-economic" considerations. For those unable or unwilling to plan ahead and engage a summer cottage, the flexibility for last-minute decisions of camping equipment or a trailer may be worthwhile. One can even make last-minute decisions to go or stay home, depending on the weather prospects, although crowded conditions of American campgrounds in recent years have reduced that possibility. The ownership of such equipment may even encourage the family to take vacations it would not otherwise take, by cutting the marginal costs. A trailer or motor home facilitates visiting relatives, since the visitors can use it as a traveling guest room, not invading the relative's home except for meals and conversation. As campgrounds get more crowded or expensive or less pleasant, the "self-contained" equipment provides more flexibility as to where to stop.

The appearance of limited access highways across the country removes one of the disadvantages of elaborate vacation equipment, since even a substantial trailer can be pulled at highway speeds with little difficulty if the road has no steep grades or required stops. However, the joint effects of pollution control devices on cars, which lower both their horsepower and their gas mileage, and of rising gas prices have made it substantially more costly to haul heavy stuff on the highway. So the trend toward larger and heavier and more luxurious recreational vehicles may have to give way to smaller, simpler equipment. Indeed, in a world facing growing pressures on a limited and exhaustible fuel supply, it is already bad manners and very costly, and may soon be illegal, to be lavish with fuel.

It is the large family that finds tents and campers and trailers most economical and convenient, so most of the recreational vehicles are made to sleep six or more people. Multiplying a bus or train or plane fare by five or six makes family travel by public transportation very expensive. At the same time, airlines are experimenting with family plans and excursion fares which for some trips make air travel a competitive choice even for family trips. Like any sensible, discriminating monopolist, an airline needs to secure more business, even at lower rates, without allowing much of its present business to get away with paying less.

The future of recreational expenditures of time and money will depend on the way people respond to rising rates of earnings and changing prices for fuel and transportation. So far, people have seemed to prefer the extra money to the possibility of more leisure. But this may be a cultural lag, reinforced by institutional restrictions like a standard work week, and by psychological forces like the memory of the great depression of the 1930s. A new generation may well decide that one of the best things to do with extra money is buy one's own time back so as to have enough leisure to enjoy life. If this happens, we are in for an explosion of recreational time, and perhaps also an explosion in recreational expenditures. And certainly the *type* of recreational activities people choose will depend heavily on the mix of time and money they are prepared to invest. As people's time becomes increasingly valuable (in terms of opportunity costs of earning), they are likely to use it economically (with more money input) on vacations, even if they take longer vacations. On the other hand, the increasing numbers of retired and unemployed with more time than money should demand more facilities for leisure activities.

Recreational Facilities

There are some important social policy problems connected with the provision of recreational facilities. In many cases there are scarce natural resources involved. Competing uses, or even competition among many for the same use, can cause problems or even spoil the whole thing. Water skiers, speed boaters, sailors, swimmers, fishermen, and bird watchers tend to get in each other's way.

Where large investments are required to provide facilities like beaches and campgrounds, the issue arises of how they should be paid for. The desire to make them available, at least up to capacity, argues against service fees, particularly where the cost of a few more users is near zero. But if only a minority of the people in a state use its parks, it is difficult to argue that everyone should pay for them through taxes, including low-income city dwellers who are without cars or unable to afford vacations. In many areas, where the volume of use approaches capacity, problems of allocating a scarce resource arise, and charges, or limitations on how long one can camp in one place, become justified. In many cases, scarce opportunities have been rationed by ignorance (most people did not know they were available) or by long waiting lines, or by limits on how long one could stay. In the interest of sanitation, many state parks now send people away when the camp is full, arguing that the toilet facilities can stand no more. And there are problems when one state builds facilities and finds them heavily used by people from other states. Sometimes they charge out-of-state users more. Some states (Ohio) and some national parks (Tetons, Virgin Islands) have very elegant facilities, at prices to match.

Philanthropy

Giving can be considered a consumption expenditure, without denying the virtue and benefits of altruism and compassion. Like any other expenditure of time and money, charity can stand some thought and planning and even shopping. There may be little choice about gifts to relatives or individuals in need, but with charitable organizations one might like some comparative information. There is an organization set up to provide that information, telling you whether a charitable organization meets certain minimum standards and roughly what they are doing with their money. For a small annual fee, you have the right to ask for evaluations of charities to which you are thinking of giving (The National Information Bureau, 419 Park Avenue South, New York, New York 10016). If a charitable organization does not have audited financial statements, uses unusually large amounts of money for management and fund raising, has no unpaid board of directors, or simply shows little evidence of getting anything done, The National Information Bureau will so inform you.

The United States Treasury has a large catalog listing all the organizations deemed charitable so that gifts to them are deductible from your income for tax purposes—if you are itemizing deductions. The Treasury accepts or rejects applications for such status, and there is no independent review or appeal procedure. An organization can qualify as nonprofit, with some tax advantages, but only a subset of them also qualify as charitable so that gifts to them are deductible by the donor. The general rule is that organizations primarily engaged in political activity or lobbying do not qualify as charitable, but the boundary line is hazy; some organizations avoid the problem by setting up a separate foundation that can qualify for exempt status. So we have the Sierra Club and the Sierra Foundation, or the Southern Christian Leadership Conference and the Southern Christian Leadership Foundation.

As we saw in chapter 1, tax considerations have important implications for philanthropy. If your marginal tax rate is 35 percent, then it costs you only $65 to give $100 to charity, but $100 if you give it to a needy friend or relative. There are partial tax savings only if you provide more than half the total support of the relative for a year, and are paying taxes and itemizing. In addition, gifts to charity of appreciated assets (within limits) allow you to deduct the current market value of the asset from taxable income without paying any capital gains tax on the appreciation. Hence, anyone with appreciated assets such as stocks is well-advised to give them to charity instead of cash. Appreciated assets are often owned in amounts larger than you might want to give to any one charity. Fortunately, some stockbrokers have set up accounts for a number of local charities so that you can have the brokers divide your shares of stock among several charities, letting the charities decide whether they want to keep the stock or have it sold and take the proceeds. Technically, you have given the stock to charitable organizations and can consider its market value as a tax-deductible contribution.

Why should philanthropic organizations and churches be given favored tax status? They are not so favored in most other countries. The situation allows an individual to give money, some of which would otherwise go to the government in taxes, to the individual's own favorite charities. Those charities may be appreciated only by the giver and a few friends, or only by wealthy people. Public finance experts use the term "tax expenditures" to refer to such special tax treatments, which they interpret as a use of tax money for special purposes.

The answer in general is that the country needs a variety of individual initiatives in religious and charitable activities and that this facilitates the separation of church and state. Such shining examples as the Rockefeller Foundation's work with hybrid seeds and medical research, the earlier development of neighborhood centers, and the present United Way activities seem to justify some encouragement. Recent studies seem to show that the efficiency with which "tax expenditures" lead to charitable giving is relatively high. The incentive works, a dollar of "tax expenditure" stimulating a dollar or more of additional giving.

But the incentive is not equal for all of us; it ranges from zero for those who do not itemize, or have enough other business deductions to be paying the minimum tax anyway, up to 70 percent for upper-income people, and even more for upper-income people giving away appreciated assets. Someone in the top bracket who gives away $1,000 worth of stock for which he paid $100 years ago, has his taxes reduced by $700; if he had sold the stock, he would have had to pay capital gains taxes of $225.[3] So his gift of $1,000 cost him $300 compared with holding the asset, or $75 ($300 − $225), compared with selling it. For families who pay no taxes or do not itemize, the gift of $1,000 worth of stock costs $1,000.

It has been suggested that there ought to be a tax *credit*, rather than a tax *deduction*, for philanthropic contributions. This would reduce everyone's taxes by the same fraction of the amount they give, and thus it wouldn't depend upon whether someone itemized, or their marginal tax rate. This still provides no incentive for the few who pay no taxes, so some have suggested that the government match charitable gifts directly, giving a matching grant

---

3. A dollar of capital gains income adds $.40 to taxable income and 0.4 × MTR cents to taxes, where MTR is the marginal tax rate.

to charities upon receiving proof that any individual has given. That suggestion raises questions of privacy, policing, and general concern about potential government interference with private charities.

Other Expenditures

There is little more that can be said about the other kinds of expenditures, except that it is useful to distinguish, both in your mind and in your record keeping, those which are deductible or potentially deductible for tax purposes. The Internal Revenue Service provides average amounts for state sales taxes, by income and family size, which you can use without keeping records, but records may prove that you spent more than that. You may even want to bunch certain deductible expenditures in alternate years, if you are close to the boundary where itemizing pays, so you can take the standard deduction every other year, and have lots of deductions in the alternate year. For example, you could make one year's charitable contributions in January, the next year's in December of the same year, then skip a year.

You may also want to keep track of certain luxury expenditures, like vacations, in order to keep them under control, and to know how much you could save for other urgent purposes by cutting out some discretionary items.

Services (Particularly Repairs)

In many respects, consumer products are much easier to deal with than consumer services. With consumer products, there are sources of information about quality, enough continuity so that one can learn from experience, and some standardization. When it comes to *services*, the problems are much worse. We have already discussed the need for a personal doctor who can serve as a guide to whatever other medical services one needs. And we indicated that the likelihood of finding a good advisor on financial affairs and investments was unlikely.

In spite of all the advice about seeing your lawyer to avoid trouble, selecting a lawyer and deciding when to use one are difficult problems. There is a *Martindale-Hubbel Directory* available in most libraries, which lists most of the lawyers in the United States and gives some ratings. There may be conflict of interest problems if you ask your insurance agent or banker, so it is often suggested that you rely on friends' or clergy or relatives' advice about a lawyer. This has the disadvantage of piling the business on a few well-known lawyers who are already too busy and perhaps expensive. The standard advice is to ask beforehand what the charges will be, but you are likely to be told an hourly charge (plus expenses), so only some initial consultations or small jobs will reveal what costs are actually like. It is probably somewhat easier to change lawyers than doctors, but there is cumulative benefit from a lawyer who knows your situation. What most of us would like is a lawyer who will tell us when we do *not* need his or her services.

Many elaborate devices for making money or saving taxes involve heavy use of lawyers, often repeatedly, so that their net benefits depend heavily on whether the gains outweigh the legal fees. At any rate, there are some books to help the innocent layman use lawyers and the law more effectively, such as Martin J. Ross's *Handbook of Everyday Law* and Virginia Lehmann's *You, the Law, and Retirement*. Even these books, however, are written by lawyers and seem to the layman to encourage more use of legal counsel than is economically sensible for many people. Just as we are likely to encourage you to learn more about economics than you need, so a lawyer....

What can be said about repair services for the car, or appliances, carpentry, plumbing, or electrical work, and the like? Here there is no branded item, no professionalization, no simple standard of quality, no *Consumer Reports* magazine. And yet substantial amounts of money are involved, and there is a suspicion that there must be a wide variety of prices and qualities, not highly correlated with each other. There are some national franchises for things like muffler replacement and automatic transmissions, and at least one of the latter engages in some of the most unscrupulous practices since the Holland Furnace Company racket of years ago—and the same way. They disassemble your transmission instead of your furnace, then announce that it needs complete rebuilding or else a large charge to reassemble it.

An economic analysis, however, often shows that it is

far better to repair than to replace something in which you have little money tied up (if it has little market value) but which has large potential use value. Many of us replace things partly because of the difficulties of finding trustworthy repair service, and qualified repair people are so busy that they themselves frequently suggest replacement, or replacement of major parts, rather than simple repair. (Some are so busy they will happily tell you how to do simple repairs yourself.)

All of this speaks for investing at least in your own diagnostic skills and perhaps also in repair skills. It also speaks for watching the repair person and asking to keep any replaced parts. But it still leaves the problem of how to select the outfit to do the repair. It is not much help to have occasional reports of tests that show the variety of charges made for a simple repair, or the variety of repairs made on the same simply disabled test car or TV. It makes us uneasy but does not tell us what to do. Those who reveal the problems usually call for licensing, or bonding, or other regulation. In fact, the sorry history of most such legislation should give us all pause:

> Though most government regulation was enacted under the guise of protecting the consumer from abuse, much of today's regulatory machinery does little more than shelter producers from the normal competitive consequences of lassitude and inefficiency.[4]

The history, which will probably be repeated in the case of state licensing of auto mechanics and television repair people, is that the bonding and licensing requirements serve to keep people out, not to police the honesty or effectiveness of those who are in. And the regulations are enforced by those in the business, whose motives are always mixed between assuring quality and restricting competition. It seems clear that better information and more competition would do much more to improve the correlation between price and quality in repair services. But single market tests of the sort commonly run are not fair or adequate information for judging individual vendors, and it would be inordinately expensive to expand them until they were. Relying on consumer complaints does not offer much hope either. They include a large component of misunderstanding and human relations, and tend to reflect the problems of the intellectual affluent rather than the poor, who do not complain much.

I can always just ask a lot of friends and neighbors where they have their repairs done, or by whom, and what their experience has been. I can then weigh this information by knowing how demanding, perceptive, critical, and similar to me each informant is. Even if they are satisfied or dissatisfied for various reasons, including the personality of the repair personnel, I am likely to be satisfied or dissatisfied for the same reasons, so the information may even be better than the impossibly costly precise information on the mechanical quality of the service.

Indeed, it should be feasible to systematize the collection of the kind of information I erratically collect from friends and neighbors, and make it available to improve the working of the local market mechanism for repair services. If I knew that a significantly larger fraction of customers of Shop A were satisfied with the price and quality of the repair work than the customers of Shop B, and if I knew the difference was persistent and not associated with a particularly demanding or hostile collection of customers, it would be enough to help me choose where to have the item repaired. Indeed, this is the one place where information might be a salable commodity, since continual updating would be necessary. Only if vendors improved so rapidly (by using the same information) that price and quality became very highly correlated, would it cease to be worth my while to pay for the information; and in that case the justification for subsidizing such a service out of community funds (tax money) would be clear. The reason such experiments have not been tried is that they required a substantial initial investment simultaneously to assemble a large mass of information, process it, and develop dissemination techniques so that people can use it (Maynes et al.). A crucial element would be probability samples of people, not reliance on potentially biased volunteered information, or special groups of reporters. But the same process that repeatedly surveyed a community for its experiences could also find out how the information was affecting the market, and the efficiency of service outlets. The increased confidence of consumers might well expand the total amount of repair business substantially.

In the meantime, you can read the "how-to" books,

---

4. Lewis A. Engman, "Inflation and Regulation," *Antitrust Law and Economics* 7 (1975): 38–39.

accumulate neighborhood intelligence informally, and find your own reliable repair services, or do it yourself (Till).

With appliances, some careful attention to symptoms can ease the diagnosis problem substantially. Indeed, with the diagrams and parts lists that come with most appliances, one can often locate the offending part, send for another, and replace it.

With more complex things like additions and repairs to the house, a process of negotiation about details, and securing bids, is often involved. The difficulty is that bids almost never really specify the details, and there is often a great deal of leeway. A good outfit will tend to do a little extra if things go well; any outfit will cut corners and omit little things if things have gone badly or cost more than expected. All this is usually obfuscated by the likelihood that you may want to change things or add a few extras in the middle. All changes should have a separate bid to prevent the contractor from charging whatever extra he likes for them. Indeed, any questions about detail as the work progresses should be clearly sorted by agreement into those that change the work and the price and those that do not.

All this is easier said than done, particularly since there are human personalities involved.

More Information?

We can give only illustrative references because of the variety of products and services, and the overlaps between discussions on nutrition in chapter 10, on medical care and food discussions in this chapter, and expected food expenditures for budgeting in chapter 5. A few classics on consumer foibles are included even though most of them are exaggerated and devoid of useful implications.

Bloom, Murray Teigh. *The Trouble with Lawyers.* New York: Simon and Schuster, 1963.

Carman, James N. "A Summary of Empirical Research on Unit Pricing in Supermarkets." *Journal of Retailing*, Winter 1972–73, pp. 63–71.

Cobb, Hubbard, and Cobb, Betsy. *Vacation Houses: All You Should Know Before You Build or Buy.* New York: Dial Press, 1973.

Cross, Jennifer. *The Supermarket Trap: the Consumer and the Food Industry.* Bloomington: Indiana University Press, 1970.

Deutsch, Ronald M. *The Nuts Among the Berries: an Expose of America's Food Fads.* Rev. ed. New York: Ballantine Books, 1967.

Engman, Lewis A. "Inflation and Regulation." *Antitrust Law and Economics* 7 (1975): 38–39.

Evans, T. C., and Greene, David. *The Meat Book, a Consumer's Guide to Selecting, Buying, Cutting, Storing, Freezing, and Carving the Various Cuts.* New York: Charles Scribner's Sons, 1973.

General Motors. *General Motors Diagnosis and Repair Manual.* Southfield, Mich.: Creative Universal, 1977.

Hightower, Jim. *Eat Your Heart Out.* New York: Crown, 1975. (food profiteering)

Hutchinson, T. O. *Consumers' Knowledge and Use of Government Grades for Selected Food Items,* U.S. Department of Agriculture, Economic Research Service, Marketing Report #876. Washington, D.C.: Government Printing Office, 1970. (Little knowledge in a national sample of 3,000)

Jacobson, Michael F. *Eater's Digest: the Consumer's Factbook of Food Additives.* Garden City, N.Y.: Doubleday, 1972.

Jung, Allen F. "Price Variations Among Automobile Dealers in Chicago, Illinois." *Journal of Business* 32 (1959): 315–26.

Katz, Harvey. *Give: Who Gets Your Church Dollar.* Garden City, N.Y.: Doubleday, 1975.

Keats, John. *The Insolent Chariots.* Philadelphia: Lippincott, 1958.

King, Charles W., and Sprules, George B. *Fashion, Innovation, and Diffusion.* New York: Free Press, 1974.

Kinney, J., and Kinney, C. *How to Get 20 to 90 Percent Off.* West Nyack, N.Y.: Parker Publishing Company, 1966.

Lansing, John B., and Hendricks, Gary. *Automobile Ownership and Residential Density.* Ann Arbor: Institute for Social Research, 1967.

Lasley, Fred G.; Kiehl, Elmer R.; and Brady, D. E. *Consumer Preferences for Beef in Relation to Finish.* Research Bulletin 580. Columbus, Mo.: University of Missouri, College of Agriculture, Agricultural Experiment Station, 1955.

Lehmann, Virginia. *You, the Law, and Retirement.* Washington D.C.: Government Printing Office, U.S. Department of Health, Education, and Welfare, Administration on Aging, 1973.

Lenahan, R. J.; Thomas, J. A.; Taylor, D. A.; Call, D. L.; and Padberg, D. I. "Consumer Reactions to Nutritional Labels on Food Products." *Journal of Consumer Affairs* 7 (1973): 1–12.

Marcus, Rubton H. "Similarity of Ghetto and Nonghetto Food Costs." *Journal of Marketing Research* 6 (1969): 365–68.

Maynes, E. Scott; Morgan, James N.; Vivian, Weston; and Duncan, Greg J. "The Local Consumer Information System: An Institution-to-Be?" *Journal of Consumer Affairs* 11 (1977): 17–33.

Packard, Vance. *The Hidden Persuaders.* New York: McKay, 1957.

Packard, Vance. *The Status Seekers.* New York: McKay, 1959.

Packard, Vance. *The Waste Makers.* New York: McKay, 1960.

Packard, Vance. *The Naked Society.* New York: McKay, 1964.

Ratchford, Brian T. "The Value of Information for Selected Appliances." *Journal of Marketing Research* 17 (February, 1980): 14–25.

Rainey, Jean. *How to Shop for Food.* New York: Harper & Row, 1972.

Readers Digest. *You and the Law.* Rev. ed. New York: Readers Digest, 1973.

Ross, Martin J. *Handbook of Everyday Law.* Rev. ed. Greenwich, Conn.: Fawcett, 1967.

Schlink, F. J. *Eat, Drink, and Be Wary.* New York: Covici-Friede, 1935.

Selden, Joseph. *The Golden Fleece: Selling the Good Life to Americans.* New York: Macmillan, 1963.

Siegel, Edward. *How to Avoid Lawyers.* Greenwich, Conn.: Fawcett, 1969.

Simonds, Lois. "Variations in Food Costs in Major Ohio Cities." *Journal of Consumer Affairs* 3 (1969): 52–58.

Smith, Victor. *Linear Programming of Human Diets.* East Lansing, Mich.: Michigan State University, 1964.

Till, Anthony. *What You Should Know Before You Have Your Car Repaired.* New York: Signet, New American Library, 1972.

U.S. Department of Agriculture, Economic Research Service. *Food Dating: Shoppers' Reactions and the Impact on Retail Food Stores.* Marketing Research Report No. 984. Washington, D.C.: Government Printing Office, 1973.

U.S. Department of Agriculture, Economic Research Service. *Food Prices Before and After Distribution of Welfare Checks—Low Income Areas, Seven Cities, 1969.* Marketing Research Report No. 907. Washington, D.C.: Government Printing Office, 1970. (No simple differences, but more errors)

U.S. Department of Agriculture. *Family Food Buying: A Guide for Calculating Amounts to Buy and Comparing Costs.* Rev. ed. Washington, D.C.: Government Printing Office, 1969.

U.S. Department of Agriculture. *How to Buy Food.* Rev. ed. Washington, D.C.: Government Printing Office, 1969. (A packet of nine leaflets)

U.S. Department of Agriculture. *How to Use USDA Grades in Buying Foods.* Rev. ed. Washington, D.C.: Government Printing Office, 1969.

U.S. Department of Agriculture, Consumer Marketing Service. *How to Buy Lamb.* Home and Garden Bulletin 195. Washington, D.C.: Government Printing Office, 1971.

U.S. Department of Labor, Bureau of Labor Statistics, National Commission on Food Marketing. "Retail Food Prices in Low and Higher Income Areas." In *Special Studies in Food Marketing.* Technical Report No. 10. Washington, D.C.: Government Printing Office, 1966.

U.S. House of Representatives, Committee on Government Operations. *Economic Report on Food Chain Selling Practices in the District of Columbia and San Francisco.* (A Staff Report to the Federal Trade Commission.) Washington, D.C.: Government Printing Office, 1969. (Minor price and quality differences)

Warland, R. H., and Herrmann, Robert O. "The New Wave of Imitation Foods: Problems Ahead?" *Journal of Consumer Affairs* 4 (1971): 56–69. (1,157 telephone interviews in Philadelphia area revealed stereotyped beliefs.)

Winter, Ruth. *A Consumer's Dictionary of Food Additives.* New York: Crown, 1978.

Winter, Ruth. *Beware of the Food You Eat.* New York: New American Library, 1971.

Wright, Robin. *The Day the Pigs Refused to be Driven to Market: Advertising and the Consumer Revolution.* New York: Random House, 1974.

Young, Agnes Brooks. *Recurring Cycles of Fashion, 1760–1937.* New York: Harper & Brothers, 1937.

Some Projects to Learn More

1. Make a list of the items purchased in a week or two of food shopping, and their prices. See if you can price the same list in several other stores. What problems of quality comparison arise? For the items where quality is comparable, how much could you save by (a) sticking to the best store, (b) shopping around (including going back), and (c) rotating among the stores, stocking up on the nonperishable items when you were in the store where they were cheapest?

2. Select one appliance, or a particular car and accessories, and price it in ten places. Then estimate the marginal payoff (randomized) from going to a second, third, fourth, etc., dealer, and the costs of the extra time and travel, including return to the cheapest one. What if you had visited the stores in a different order?

3. Compare the prices of oil, oil filters, and grease with the cost of having your car greased and the oil changed. Estimate the time and capital equipment costs of doing it yourself and compare with the time and costs of having it done. What other things would affect this choice?

4. Compare rental charges with the cost of owning the following items: boat and outboard motor, canoe, sewing machine, skis and ski boots, power lawn mower, power garden tiller, tent trailer, vacation trailer, motor home, summer cottage, tent. How much would you have to use it in order to save by owning

rather than renting it? (Estimate depreciation by finding out about secondhand prices, less dealers' margin.)

5. Compare the prices for the following items as between the authorized dealer, a large auto parts store, and an auto junkyard (secondhand), for a three-year-old car of some particular make: generator, starter, battery, headlamp, taillight lens, bumper, extra wheel (for snow tire). Discuss the implications for strategy.

6. Use a newspaper file for the past few years to make an annual calendar of citywide sales, other sales, etc., with indications of the size of advertised markdowns, and whether end-of-season items, specials, or regular stock. What are the implications? To what extent are savings offset by costs and risks of storing until the next season?

7. Collect some estimates, perhaps from your own states only, of trends over the last few years in (a) the number of vacation trailers registered with the license bureau, (b) the number of boat trailers so registered, (c) the number of campground spaces available in the state, and (d) the number of boat launching sites. Implications? What are the current charges for camping sites?

8. Investigate the present public transportation services and subsidy, if any. Suppose that if the service were free, the total cost (net of savings from not collecting money) would remain constant. Estimate the number of cars parked in the city not on the owner's property during the day, and hence the added parking fee per year per car necessary to provide this free public transportation. Now suppose that the number of cars parked went down by 25 percent, and the added use of public transportation raised its cost by 25 percent (probably an exaggeration). What would be the required parking fee?

9. Secure some how-to-do-it books in one area (sewing, home gardening, painting). Evaluate their clarity and dependence on the assumption that the reader already knows a lot. Talk with someone who actually does such projects about the tricks and pitfalls. How many of these are in the books?

10. Imagine three specific vacation trips, to places 100, 500, and 2,000 miles away. Estimate the costs for a couple, and for a family with two children, of going by car, plane, train, and bus, including time, difference in meal cost on the way, etc.

11. Visit a fabric store or two, talking with some of the clerks and customers about whether people really save money, or dress better, by doing their own sewing. Can you find some examples of savings, and time taken, and hence estimate returns per hour? How much does experience cut down the time required so that the costs of learning how pay returns over the future?

12. Compare various ways of preparing a meal, using components with different degrees of prefabrication, from fresh vegetables to frozen, or even to frozen whole dinners. Estimate the difference in hours required for preparation, and the differences in costs of the materials, and calculate the amount one earns per hour doing more of the food preparation oneself. To what extent would this depend on (a) accumulated experience, and (b) the size of the family to be fed?

13. Calculate the costs and expected savings from a food freezer. If you can find information on annual variation in meat prices, assume you pruchase meat at low price periods and use it evenly during the year. Or find out the difference in price for meat bought in large quantities. Do the expected savings equal or surpass the depreciation, interest, and operating costs?

14. Examine the menus of some expensive restaurants. Are there any low-priced entrees for those not on expense accounts?

15. Investigate the range of prices in your area for one of the following products: gasoline, mufflers, hi-fi equipment, cameras, records and tapes, books, wines, lumber, paint, auto tires, air flights, typewriters, ten-speed bicycles, liquor (if not price-controlled in your state). Do they differ enough so that it would pay to shop around?

Appendix 11.1 Federal Food Standards[1]

All over the United States, if you buy mayonnaise, you can be sure you're getting essentially the same product. And if you buy USDA Choice beef, you can be sure it's the same quality.

The various kinds of food standards set by the Federal Government make this possible.

Just as Federal standards for weights and measures established by the National Bureau of Standards define how long a foot is (so measurements of distance are the same from coast to coast), standards of identity set by the Food and Drug Administration define what certain food products are, and U.S. Department of Agriculture grade standards define levels of quality for various foods.

FDA food standards of identity are mandatory or regulatory. They set requirements which products must meet if they move in interstate commerce. They protect against deception, because they define what a food product must consist of to be legally labeled "mayonnaise," for example.

USDA grade standards for food are voluntary. Federal law does not require that a food processor or distributor use the grade standards. The standards are widely used, however, as an aid in wholesale trading, because the quality of a product affects its price. The grade (quality level) also is often shown on food products in retail stores, so consumers can choose the grade that best fits their needs.

Food standards established by the Federal Government usually fall into two general classes—voluntary or mandatory. A third class consists of standards recommended for adoption by State and local governments.

Here is a brief listing of the principal kinds of Federal standards for food.

1. U.S. Department of Agriculture, Agricultural Marketing Service, publication no. AMS-548. Slightly revised November 1977.

Voluntary Standards

I. U.S. Department of Agriculture Grade Standards
Under authority of the Agricultural Marketing Act of 1946 and related statues, USDA has issued grade standards for some 300 food and farm products.

Food products for which grade standards have been established are: beef, veal and calf, lamb and mutton; poultry, including turkey, chicken, duck, goose, guinea, and squab; eggs; manufactured dairy products, including butter, Cheddar cheese, and instant nonfat dry milk; fresh fruits, vegetables, and nuts; canned, frozen, and dried fruits and vegetables and related products such as preserves; and rice, dry beans, and peas. U.S. grade standards are also available for grains, but not for the food products, such as flour or cereal, into which grain is processed.

USDA provides official grading services, often in cooperation with State departments of agriculture, for a fee, to packers, processors, distributors, or others who wish official certification of the grade of a product. The grade standards also are often used by packers and processors as a quality control tool.

Federal law does not require use of the U.S. grade standards or the official grading services. Official grading is required under some State and local ordinances and some industry marketing programs.

Products which have been officially graded may carry the USDA grade name or grade shield, such as the familiar purple "USDA Choice" shield seen on cuts of beef or the "U.S. Grade A" on cartons of eggs. Grade labeling, however, is not required by Federal law, even though a product has been officially graded. On the other hand, a packer or processor may not label his product with an official grade name such as Grade A (even without the "U.S." prefix) unless it actually measures up to the Federal standard for that grade. Mislabeling of this sort would be deemed a violation of the Food, Drug, and Cosmetics Act.

II. National Marine Fisheries Service Grade Standards
The U.S. Department of Commerce's National Marine Fisheries Service provides grade standards and grading services for fishery products similar to those provided by USDA for other foods. To date, 15 U.S. grade standards have been developed for frozen processed fishery products, covering such products as semi-processed raw whole fish, fish blocks, cut fish portions, steaks and fillets; breaded raw and precooked fish portions and sticks; raw headless and breaded shrimp; raw and fried scallops. Such products when produced and graded under the U.S. Department of Commerce inspection program may carry the USDC "Federally Inspected" mark and/or the U.S. grade shield. However, as under the USDA grading programs, grade labeling is not required by Federal law, even though products are officially inspected and graded.

Mandatory Standards

I. U.S. Department of Agriculture Standards of Composition and Identity
USDA has established minimum content requirements for Federally inspected meat and poultry products (usually canned or frozen) under the Federal Meat Inspection Act and the Poultry Products Inspection Act.

To be labeled with a particular name—such as "Beef Stew"—a Federally inspected meat or poultry product must meet specified content requirements. These requirements assure the consumer that he's getting what the label says he's getting. They do not, however, keep different companies from making distinctive recipes. The USDA minimum content requirement for beef stew specifies the minimum percentage of *beef only* (25 percent) that the stew must contain. It doesn't keep the manufacturer from using combinations of seasonings or increasing the amount of beef to make his product unique.

USDA has also established complete standards of identity for these products: chopped ham, corned beef hash, and oleomargarine. They go further than the composition standards, setting specific and optional ingredients.

II. Food and Drug Administration Standards

The Federal Food, Drug, and Cosmetic Act provides for three kinds of mandatory standards for products being shipped across State lines: standards of identity, standards of minimum quality, and standards of fill of container. All these standards are administered by the Food and Drug Administration of the U.S. Department of Health, Education, and Welfare. The law sets forth penalties for noncompliance.

A. Standards of Identity. FDA standards of identity (like USDA's) establish what a given food product *is*—for example, what a food must be to be labeled "preserves." The FDA standards of identity also provide for use of optional ingredients in addition to the mandatory ingredients that make the product what it is. Standards of identity have eliminated from the market such things as "raspberry spread"—made from a little fruit and a lot of water, pectin, sugar, artificial coloring and flavoring, and a few grass seeds to suggest a fruit product.

FDA has standards of identity for a large number of food products (excluding meat and poultry products, which are covered by USDA).

Types of products for which standards of identity have been formulated by FDA include: cacao products; cereal flour and related products; macaroni and noodle products; bakery products; milk and cream products; cheese and cheese products; frozen desserts; food flavoring; dressings for food; canned fruits and fruit juices; fruit butters; jellies, preserves, and related products; non-alcoholic beverages, canned and frozen shellfish; eggs and egg products; oleomargarine and margarine; nut products; canned vegetables; and tomato products.

B. Minimum Standards of Quality. FDA standards of quality have been set for a number of canned fruits and vegetables to supplement standards of identity. These are minimum standards for such factors as tenderness, color, and freedom from defects. They are regulatory, as opposed to USDA grade standards of quality, which are for voluntary use.

If a food does not meet the FDA quality standards it must be labeled "Below Standard in Quality; Good Food—Not High Grade." Or, words may be substituted for the second part of that statement to show in what respect the product is substandard. The label could read, "Below Standard in Quality; Excessively Broken" or "Below Standard in Quality; Excessive Peel." The consumer seldom if ever sees a product with a substandard label.

(When USDA grade standards are developed for a product for which FDA has a minimum standard of quality, the requirements for the lowest grade level USDA sets are at least as high as the FDA minimum. USDA grade standards for canned tomatoes, for example, are U.S. Grades A, B, and C. U.S. Grade C is comparable to FDA's minimum standard of quality.)

C. Standards of Fill of Container. These standards tell the packer how full a container must be to avoid deception. They prevent the selling of air or water in place of food.

Recommended Standards

Under the Public Health Service Act, FDA advises State and local governments on sanitation standards required for prevention of infectious diseases.

The most familiar and widely adopted standards deal with production, processing, and distribution of "Grade A" milk. In contrast to USDA quality grade standards for food, the PHS standard for Grade A milk is largely a standard of wholesomeness. The Grade A designation on fresh milk means that it has met State or local requirements, which usually follow provisions of FDA model ordinances.

USDA has issued recommended minimum standards of quality for manufacturing milk and recommended standards for the manufacture of frozen desserts, which are for adoption by State regulatory agencies.

["USDA Standards for Food and Farm Products" (AH-341) lists all USDA grade standards and tells how to obtain them. For a copy of AH-341, write to Office of Information, U.S. Department of Agriculture, Washington, D.C. 20250.]

CHAPTER TWELVE
CONSUMER DECISION MAKING, CONSUMER INFORMATION, AND CONSUMER PROTECTION

So far in this book very little attention has been paid to either of the two main topics found in most consumer economics books—wise shopping and consumer protection. The application of good economic analysis to setting priorities and budgets and deciding what to buy is more important and more difficult than mere shopping, although shopping has been discussed where it seemed appropriate.

This final chapter is really about "the consumer interest," but understanding what is best for consumers requires more than good will and just being a consumer. We need to understand how we all make decisions, and something of our own departures from how experts say decisions should be made. We need to know why consumer information and consumer insight are crucial if a market economy is to function properly. We need to know under what circumstances the consumer interest is best served through government protection, regulation, or government operation, rather than market competition. And finally, we need to realize that evaluating any situation, policy, or outcome in terms of its effects on consumers is a complex task with frequently ambiguous results. A great deal of regulation, much of it intended to protect or assist consumers, can be shown to have injured them. A movement away from government enterprise (public housing) and government regulation (airlines, trucking, railroads) and toward competition is in progress, but it requires careful watching and alert, informed consumers if the expected benefits from competitive markets are to be realized. Before getting into the discussion of consumer information and consumer protection, we need to consider human motivation and family decision making. Once again, we start with some theory.

Motivation

The great conceptual contribution of economics to the discussion of decision making has been the focus on choices among alternatives. The value of any one alternative has meaning only when compared with the next best choice. The second best choice measures the opportunity cost—i.e., what must be given up to get the best. But in the discussion of the value of any single alternative, economic theory is relatively empty, assuming that there is some unique utility attaching to that alternative, or some pattern of preference among various alternatives, without going beyond the notion of a single-dimensioned utility.

A theory of consumer decision making is needed to predict consumer behavior, analyze it, or assess the quality of actual decision making, our own or someone else's. Such a theory must be based on knowledge of what the consumer is doing. The simplest assumption is that consumers maximize satisfaction. If so, a theory based on that assumption needs to be based on knowledge of the sources of satisfaction.

We can borrow some notions from psychology to make the discussion more realistic. First, there are at least four main motives, or potential sources of satisfaction: .

1. Power over the environment, that is, the right to the basic physical needs like food and shelter. In a money economy this usually means money.

2. Power over other people, and independence from having to do what they say.
3. Affiliation, the giving and receiving of affection. We get satisfaction from seeing other people happy.
4. Achievement, the sense of accomplishment from the overcoming of obstacles through one's own efforts.

There is an elaborate literature in social psychology about such motives, particularly the last one, since it is in many ways the most interesting and the most crucial for the progress of the world (Atkinson).

Each of these motives can be thought of as a source of satisfaction to the individual, the amount of satisfaction depending on the general level of the motive and on how fully or recently it has been satisfied. In other words, one can think of a utility curve for each motive, and a marginal (added) utility at any point in time reflecting the current incentive value of more rewards of that type. In the case of physical needs like food, the notion of incentive value is obvious: the more one has eaten and the more recently, the less motivating is any current activity directed at eating more food.

In an uncertain world, where the choices are actions that are expected to lead to satisfaction of the various motives, a third dimension enters: the probability (subjective) that a particular action will actually lead to the desired result. Will working harder at some task actually make success more likely? Psychologists use the term "expectancy" for this notion of subjective probability. The final attractiveness of some alternative is then stated to be the product of the strength of the basic motive, the incentive value (marginal utility), and the expectancy (the probability that the desired outcome will occur).

We now have a complex theory, which says the total incentive value of a single alternative choice is the sum of its potential values in satisfying each of the four basic motives (power over things, power over people, affiliation, and achievement). Each of the values is affected by the current level of satisfaction of that motive, and by a subjective probability that the choice will have the desired outcome. The same calculations are required for the competing alternatives if one is to select the best.

These motives do not always lead directly to actions.

There is a great deal of inertia in human behavior, so that we mostly continue to do what we have been doing until some alternative develops sufficient incentive value to overcome that inertia. A person has to become aware of some problem or better alternative; before he is willing to go through the complex and demanding process of decision making, he has to pay attention to the problem.

Furthermore, many constraints narrow the range of alternatives. There are limits on one's financial power (income plus assets plus credit); limits on one's time (twenty-four hours a day); laws and institutions and customs; and ignorance of facts, of alternatives, or of the way things work. Major differences between countries and cultures may well result not from different human motivations at work, but from different restrictions placed on people's choices by law, custom, and institutions.

In addition, one's own major decisions can put constraints on one's minor decisions. There is a hierarchy of choices, and it is frequently possible to make sure that many minor decisions are at least passably good by making certain major decisions that constrain them. For instance, the choice of house and neighborhood will tend to establish one's general living standards, and a carefully chosen location will make it easier to stay within the budget on other things. A decision never to stock up on luxuries may assure that a conscious choice must be made each time a luxury item is consumed and needs replacement, and thus make it easier to avoid excessive indulgence. The use of installment credit as a self-disciplining device to keep one conscious of depreciation and to encourage spacing of expenditures on durables is another example.

Finally, in a dynamic situation, social psychology makes another contribution to the theory of consumer choice, pointing out that individuals learn and can therefore change their preference patterns. There is some disagreement about whether experience can change people's basic motives. Some argue that the level of a person's achievement motivation is a stable dimension of personality, determined mostly by early training in childhood and not much altered after that. Others argue that basic motives can be changed through experience or education.

Whether or not basic motives can be changed, people's subjective beliefs, about the kinds of satisfactions to be derived (and with what probabilities) from some choice of action, can certainly be altered by experience, information, and new insights. If a person tries hard and succeeds, the assumption that hard work pays off should grow stronger. If one tries a new product, or observes someone else using it, and likes what it does, one's notion that it will satisfy needs is likely to be affected. The belief in the payoff to avoiding risk, planning ahead, deliberation, and information-seeking in making choices, all are learned from successful experiences (or perhaps from the punishment when one fails to plan, avoid risk, or be deliberate). As we suggested in proposing money-handling procedures, effective learning requires early rewards, so long-term planning probably comes after some success at short-term planning.

Given all this, the notion in conventional economic theory of an unchanging preference function for an individual is clearly inappropriate, and what we need most in thinking about consumer behavior is a better theory of learning and of aspiration levels. At the same time, it is important to distinguish genuine choices, where motivation is important, from habitual or random actions in nonsalient areas, where the individual is not making choices in any psychological sense. A few studies have been done of deliberation and information-seeking in consumer decisions, and they show a wide variety of behavior. It is not always the amount of money involved that matters—sometimes style or the wide range of options stimulate deliberation (Katona and Mueller; Newman and Staelin).

The economist's tradition of deducing optimal behavior on the assumption that choices always aim at maximizing utility causes him to characterize as "irrational" any behavior that does not seem to fit this pattern. But the term has little meaning unless one can show that the individual's behavior is not meaningful in terms of his own purposes, information, and insights. Many discussions of what the "economic man" should do smack of the imposition of one person's set of values on another. The only behavior that might genuinely be considered irrational is the continued making of the same decision despite failure or regret, and this falls into the category of abnormal behavior. We can ask whether people have some reason, persuasive to them, if not to us, for what they are doing. And we can ask whether they would regret their decision if they had some information or insights that are easily available.

Family Decision Making

Even the best theory of individual decision making does not tell us what a family will do. A family is made up of individuals with different personalities and needs and, consequently, different sets of personal preferences. Ideally, each one gets some satisfaction from expressing affiliation (love) and hence puts some of the desires of the other members of the family into his own preference function. In spite of the fact that the preferences of family members may conflict, families make decisions all the time, and most of them do it well enough so that the family stays together, reasonably content. How do they do it?

We must remember first that family decisions are not simple conflict resolution. There are advantages to a family in staying together, even if the benefits are not shared equally, and even without the legal sanctions that hold them. There are economies of scale in feeding and housing. It takes two parents to produce children, and it helps to have both parents raise them. The actual solutions, then, may be sloppy rather than optimal in some sense, even if we could define optimal.

Communication and Consensus

Before any discussion of family decisions, we must look at the extent to which family members are aware of one another's desires and preferences, and the extent to which these desires are congruent rather than competitive. Remember that one motive is the desire to express affiliation by doing what makes the others happy. Too much focus on this single purpose can lead to trouble also, as in the clever "tea in the garden" episode in *The Screwtape Letters*, where the result of everyone trying to do what the others wanted was trouble all around (Lewis; Morgan, 1961).

If we assume that each spouse has worked his or her way through the alternatives, assessing their potential contribution to his or her satisfaction (through satisfying one or more of the four basic needs discussed earlier), then each has some set of priorities for alternative courses of action. They may or may not agree; in fact, the partners may not even have accurate information on what the other wants.

There have not been many studies of family decision making, family sociologists concentrating mostly on conflict and its resolution, and market researchers studying buying plans and focusing either on perceived power (who makes the decisions) or on which spouse best predicts actual behavior. Interestingly enough, while self-ratings on who makes the decisions in the family fit the popular stereotypes, these stereotypes do not agree with the findings of the one study which investigated whether husbands or wives actually predict real family decisions best (Wolgast). The study found that wives generally predicted better, even in areas where other studies found both spouses agreeing that it was the husband who made the decision. One explanation is that the wife has better empathy or intuition and so can provide a better prediction of what the family will do when they finally must reconcile their differences, even where the husband dominates the deliberations. (Or perhaps the wife really dominates the decision making after all.)

In a small study focused more directly on communication and consensus in the family, it appeared that husbands and wives were not very accurate in assessing each other's preferences or plans for specific actions, but were pretty well in agreement on each other's basic personality on a more general level (Morgan, 1968). Even if we were to think of conflict within the family as a power struggle, the whole concept of power is a very complex one. There are various kinds of power; even some studies of organizations indicate that power itself is not a constant sum allocated among antagonists, but that it is possible for everyone in a group to feel he has, and actually to have, power (Cartwright; Tannenbaum).

Social Optimum

Given that families can reach a consensus on the goods and services they want, under what conditions will the economy provide them efficiently? Most economists are fond of pointing out that, under certain conditions, firms in a profit-oriented, competitive environment will produce exactly the amounts of goods and services that people want, and at the least possible cost! It is startling to think that thousands of firms, acting with no central direction whatsoever and motivated by the desire for profits, will benefit anyone. And yet economists contend that the result of these independent actions is a situation in which it is impossible to reallocate labor, machines, or raw materials among firms to produce more of one product or service without cutting back on another, or to redistribute the goods and services among consumers so that some are better off without making others worse off.

The key to this result is that all consumers respond to the prices of the goods and services they consume and that firms respond to the product and input (factors of production) prices that they face. How do consumers respond to prices? They are assumed to purchase goods and services to the point where the added utility or satisfaction from spending one more dollar on any given good or service is equal to the added satisfaction from spending that dollar on something else. How much that dollar will buy depends, of course, on its price, so an alternative way of stating this result is to say that the ratio of the added benefit to the price is equal for all goods and across all consumers. If prices change, then consumers will reallocate their income, and will generally tend to consume less of the goods that have become relatively more expensive. By responding to prices in this way, consumers act so that the prices of goods and services reflect the added benefits that consumers attach to them, i.e., price = marginal (social) benefit to consumers in general.

In a competitive economy, producers are seen as slaves to the desires of consumers and to competition in the product market. Profit-maximizing firms will produce to the point where the production of one more unit of goods or services will add as much to their costs as to the revenues from the sale of that additional unit of the goods or services. (If these marginal costs were *less* than the marginal revenue, then firms could add to their total profit by expanding output; the reverse is true if marginal revenue is less than marginal cost.) Since the additional revenue from the sale of one more unit of output is just the *price* of that output, we have price = marginal revenue = marginal cost. Consumers "police" firms, in the sense that firms attempting to charge more than the going price will lose business and be forced to reduce prices back to competitive levels. Firms in industries with above average profits will find that the entry of new firms will drive away excess profits.

Finally, we must assume that firms compete with one another for the inputs to production, i.e., the manhours of labor, the machinery, and the raw materials needed to produce the output. Each firm will want to produce its output at least cost, and so will respond to changes in the prices of inputs and rearrange its use of these inputs just as consumers rearrange their purchases in response to product prices. The result of many firms competing against each other for the various factors of production is that these factors are used in accordance with the value placed on them by consumers demanding the products that use these inputs. The resulting cost of producing the good or service will reflect the opportunity cost to society of using those inputs instead of letting them be used to produce something else. Combining these results with the others, we have the following set of equalities:

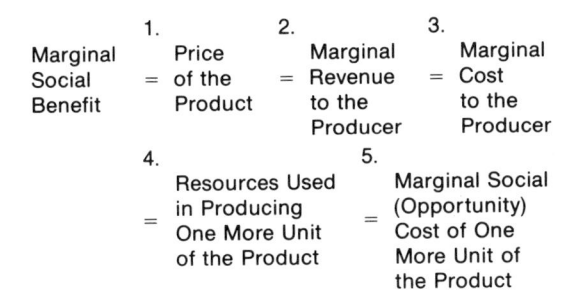

$$\begin{array}{l}\text{1.} \\ \text{Marginal} \\ \text{Social} \\ \text{Benefit}\end{array} = \begin{array}{l}\text{Price} \\ \text{of the} \\ \text{Product}\end{array} = \begin{array}{l}\text{2.} \\ \text{Marginal} \\ \text{Revenue} \\ \text{to the} \\ \text{Producer}\end{array} = \begin{array}{l}\text{3.} \\ \text{Marginal} \\ \text{Cost} \\ \text{to the} \\ \text{Producer}\end{array}$$

$$\begin{array}{l}\text{4.} \\ \text{Resources Used} \\ \text{in Producing} \\ \text{One More Unit} \\ \text{of the Product}\end{array} = \begin{array}{l}\text{5.} \\ \text{Marginal Social} \\ \text{(Opportunity)} \\ \text{Cost of One} \\ \text{More Unit of} \\ \text{the Product}\end{array}$$

That a competitive market system produces this result leads many people to recommend competition in markets as a better form of consumer protection rather than regulation. But before discussing such policy matters further, let us examine the conditions under which the equalities really hold.

1. When is the marginal social benefit reflected in the price people will pay?

☐ When families make optimal decisions for all the individuals within the family.

☐ When they are well-informed, know what they want, and can compare prices and qualities.
☐ When the income distribution is sufficiently fair that we are willing to count dollar power as a measure of utility, whoever is spending.
☐ When there are no "externalities" in consumption, i.e., when the costs or benefits to others of consuming the goods or services are included in the price. If the costs of cleaning up my litter are not reflected in the price I pay for a can of soda pop, then the price of soda pop overestimates its social benefits.

2. When is the price equal to marginal revenue?

☐ When there is enough competition in selling the product that no seller restricts production to get a higher price and higher profit.
☐ When product differences that keep sellers inefficiently small reflect real preferences for variety and not artificially created "monopolistic competition."

3. When is marginal revenue equal to marginal cost? When each firm maximizes its profits. This is the easiest assumption of all to make, and it is hard to find believable exceptions.

4. When is the price of the extra resources equal to the marginal cost of producing one more unit? When there is competition in the purchasing of factors of production. Associations of employers, on the one side, and labor unions, on the other, may lead to departures from this equality. A union, for example, may drive wages above the level that would prevail in the absence of a union. A one-company town may have very low wages.

5. When does the price of the extra resources used in production reflect the marginal social cost of the increase in production?

☐ When the same first four equations hold in all other lines of production, so that the competing demands for each resource also reflect their contributions to social benefit.
☐ When there are no "cost externalities," that is, when all the social costs of production are included in the private costs. When a firm is not charged for the pollution of air or water that it causes, the total cost to society of expanding production exceeds the private (input) costs to the firm.

It can be seen that there are a number of ways in which the market system may not lead to optimum resource allocation. Economists have given a great deal of attention to some of them—particularly to the failure of competition through various restrictive practices, and to the externalities in costs or benefits which accrue to others than the producer or consumer of the particular product. And economists have been quite aware of the critical importance of a reasonably fair distribution of disposable income, after all the tax deductions and transfer supplements.

But far less critical attention has been given to the assumption that the market purchases of a household actually reflect the benefits received. This requires not only reasonably good solutions to the consensus problem within the family, and adequate decision-making processes, but it also requires that households have good economic information and insights. They must understand the kinds of economic principles discussed in the rest of this book and have the current information with which to apply them. Hence, we now turn to the problem of household economic information.

Household Economic Information

There are some commodities which cannot be produced and sold in the marketplace because they can be enjoyed by additional people without cost. These are sometimes called social goods. Clean air is an often-cited example; I cannot benefit from antipollution expenditures without sharing the benefits with my neighbor. As a result, there is no "market" for clean air, in the sense of everyone paying for the clean air that they want. The shared benefits create a "free-rider" problem; if left to individual decision, there would be too little aggregate antipollution spending. Consumer information is another example of a social good, because it can be given away without being given up, i.e., you can give information to another person and still have it yourself. As with spending for clean air, a free-market approach to information would result in too little of it being purchased.

We have already seen that there are compelling social reasons why consumers need to be well informed. The problem is how the necessary information can be assembled, interpreted, and disseminated to them. Discussion of this problem will be easier if we distinguish consumer insights and permanent information from various kinds of current consumer information.

Permanent Insights and Facts

Some of the things households need to know are relatively permanent items of understanding, insight, or facts that do not change rapidly. Most of this book has been devoted to this kind of information and insight. Households need to be able to use facts and to know what facts they need. The necessary understanding requires working through some rather complex problems. The number of books that focus on the selection of facts and the sophisticated analysis to understand them is relatively small, and they do not sell well. There are many more books that rail passionately against the mendacity of sellers or the stupidity of consumers, but while muckraking may sell books, it is doubtful that it produces consumers with insight or information (Crowther; Keats; Packard; Wagner).

Judicious use of the library can, however, produce a great deal of useful information, and the search appears more nearly worthwhile if one remembers that this lasting sort of information and insight accumulates. It is a kind of capital investment that may pay off in a number of future decisions. Some of the sources are likely to give only one side of the story, such as the official or unofficial journals of various business or labor groups (*Printer's Ink, Tide*, labor union periodicals). Magazines with advertising tell the good points of new products, but negative information on their drawbacks is harder to acquire.

The *Journal of Home Economics* reflects a more direct concern with household economic problems. Its annual review of research may lead the reader to more extensive studies, often published in obscure places like the agricultural extension service bulletins or research bulletins of the agricultural experiment stations. These government publications are not adequately indexed, although references to them do appear in the United States National Agricultural Library, *Bibliography of Agriculture* and in publications of the United States Office of Experiment Stations. There are also technical journals of nutrition, medicine, and public health.

Legal information is more difficult, since a professional association jealous of its prerogatives is involved. But articles in law journals are often useful. The technicalities and variation from state to state are such that the admonition to see a lawyer rather than trust a book may be justified. Do-it-yourself books on legal problems do appear from time to time, in spite of the illegality of practicing law without a license (Dacey). The technicalities of garnishment, repossession, and bankruptcy are unlikely to interest those of us who do not think we shall ever need to know them; but for those who do need to know, the literature is quite deficient.

Medical information, in spite of many publications, is still a problem because the technical journals are not written for the layman. Books on insurance abound, some of them good (Belth; Consumers Union).

Perhaps the highest quality informational material for the household is in the cookbooks, although even they have not kept up with progress. For instance, they generally give times and temperatures from a period when things were cooked as fast as possible in order to minimize the time spent watching them. Now that we have good temperature regulators, people might prefer to cook things longer at lower temperature in order to get a moister roast, or to adjust work schedules, so it would be useful to know how one can trade a lower temperature for a longer cooking time. Actually, a good cook understands how to handle interlaced tasks so that their timing is right; in industry, the same problem is dignified with titles like "systems analysis" or "critical path analysis."

There are thousands of specialized "How to..." books available. Much of the general, permanent, consumer information we have been discussing probably belongs in the curriculum of the secondary schools, and some is already there. Since it is a social necessity that consumers be intelligent, and since information is difficult to market and often complex, society owes it to itself to see that it is taught to each new generation. Some parts of it are salable in the marketplace, although sometimes the books that sell do so because they provide convenience, or scapegoats, and not primarily information.

Current Information

When we come to the more perishable information about quality and prices of the goods and services on the market, we cannot depend upon the public schools, or on books, which would quickly become obsolete. It is difficult for governments to get involved at all, since it is the fates of private sellers which may be affected by better-informed consumers. Our government's inability or unwillingness to deal with clearly harmful products like cigarettes, and the conservative, even secretive, history of the National Bureau of Standards, are not encouraging. Yet France, Sweden, and Germany all have government-aided consumer information publications (Thorelli and Thorelli).

What households need is information about the choices they are currently about to make, up-to-date information on the alternatives available, their prices and quality, and some renewed insights on how to interpret the information. Unemployment and low incomes, or high and rising prices, usually stir up waves of concern about the plight of the consumer and new attempts to do something about it. In the depths of the Great Depression this led to books like *Your Money's Worth, 100,000,000 Guinea Pigs, Eat, Drink and Be Wary,* and also to the formation of Consumers Research, devoted to testing products and reporting their qualities. Disputes about labor standards (whether to allow the employees to organize, and whether to report the labor conditions under which the tested products were made, since there was no Fair Labor Standards Act then) led to a schism and to the formation of Consumers Union, which answered both questions "yes." Consumers Union's *Consumer Reports* magazine has since far outstripped Consumers Research *Bulletin* in circulation and in quantity and quality of information.[1]

With circulation of two million, *Consumer Reports* has a substantial effect on consumers and producers. The benefits spread far more widely, because there are many more readers than subscribers, because the news travels beyond readership, and because the increased price-quality correlation makes it more likely that even the uninformed consumers will get what they pay for.

In this respect, it should be stated clearly that there is a great difference between buying clubs, which secure benefits for their own members, often at the expense of other consumers, and consumer information services, which increase competition, make it possible for better producers and retailers to survive, and improve things for everyone. If price were a perfect reflection of quality, then I would

---

1. This happened in spite of the fact that for some years the former was on the House Un-American Activities Committee's *List of Subversive Organizations*. It was formally removed from the list in 1953, and never was on the more carefully prepared Attorney General's list.

need only to decide how much quality I wanted (and could afford). And I would not need to shop around. In fact, price and quality often have a surprisingly low correlation with one another (Maynes). Informed buyers will increase the correlation in the market between price and quality. A common way sellers take the sting out of consumer information organizations is to offer discounts to their members. After a short time, such organizations usually lose their drive, and the sellers can quietly remove the privilege. Even if it remains, other consumers do not benefit.

But what product testing and other market information organizations sell is as much convenience and a sense of belonging as it is information. A consumer could always get the same information by borrowing a copy of *Consumer Reports*, or reading it at the public library. Even that convenience is useful only for those with long memories, long horizons, or the ability to keep a library of journals and look up the relevant parts when some choice has to be made.

Technically, the problem is that the magazine format forces the information to be batch-processed, printed, and allowed to get out of date before the same subject is taken up again. The consumer thus finds that the information he wants is neither easily accessible, nor up to date, nor well tailored for his needs. He may be interested only in a particular type or a particular price range. Or he may want to scan the options.

An easy, but inadequate, solution would seem to be to keep all the information in a computer and allow consumers to address their questions to the computer. Experiments with this procedure have revealed that such interchanges take up time and energy unnecessarily. Something intermediate is required, with continuous updating of the information bank, not just so that the information is as fresh as possible, but so that it is salable. People will not then rely on getting the information secondhand, because it would be just old enough to be possibly inferior to the latest information. Such a system of providing selected subsets of information from a constantly updated file is potentially a self-supporting and economically viable way of using the marketplace to sell consumer information of the more perishable sort. There would be substantial development costs in getting the procedures set up for assembling, processing, and selling the information, particularly since it would all have to be developed simultaneously.

Whether the developing and processing of consumer information continues in its present mold (largely benefiting the well educated, who can plan ahead and handle their own libraries), or in some new form, there remains a question of public policy: should the government provide any financial support? We assume that it is not proper to have producers or sellers provide the information (although that happens in some countries, through producers' associations or the acceptance of advertising). The possibility of conflict of interest is too great. The answer to the question of government support depends on whether political pressures would be applied on the government by sellers or producers, or whether the government would be willing to provide funds for a completely independent product testing agency, as the West German government has done with great success.

A problem arises because consumer organizations have traditionally done more than report price and quality of goods and services. They have also been interested in government policies that affect the consumer, and in evaluating products whose design or utility was felt to be doubtful. Such functions are *not* properly subsidized by government, particularly if they might lead to lobbying in Congress for improved legislation. What would seem to be an appropriate government contribution to consumer information would be the funding of an independent consumer information service until it was able to become self-financing.

Local Consumer Information

There is a third kind of consumer information: facts about the price and quality of locally produced goods and services (chap. 11). Here, none of the economies of scale of a national organization will help, for the information is not only perishable but local. Yet some of the lowest correlations between price and quality are at the local level. There have been some magnificent examples of what can be done among the local groups of the British Consumers Association. They have examined and rated the sanitation practices of local restaurants and collected information on catering services, laundries, etc. All of this takes work, not simply the pooling of already available information. Many local groups form and enjoy immediate benefits from sharing the pool of knowledge the members already have. But lacking any procedure to stimulate the production of more information, they soon deteriorate. It is worth reconsidering a consumer information system, sharing information rather than expanding consumer protection systems and grievance-handling machinery. Consumer information systems can lead to several possible outcomes in terms of the fortunes of the sellers. Depending on the capacity of the "best" vendors to expand without sacrificing quality, they may either take over larger market shares or gain little. Depending on the capacity of the worst to improve, they may either go out of business or improve and expand.

A local consumer information system also provides three levels of benefits to consumers:

1. To the individual using information he asked for and paid for.
2. To others who got the information free, by accident, or because it had hit the rumor mill.
3. To others who still operate without information, simply because the correlation between price and quality has improved.

So the social value is considerably larger than the market value of the information to the seller of the information. Indeed, if the third effect is large enough, the value of information to the individual drops to zero, because the buyer can go into the marketplace uninformed and still do well.

The social equity arguments are strong for such an information system, particularly if there are wide differences in consumer capacity for, and interests in, processing information. A relatively small number of informed and mobile consumers can "rationalize" the marketplace so that the rest do not need to worry. This may, however, require a continual flow of new information, at least to a few, as the world keeps changing. There is reason to believe that better information might actually encourage people to have more things repaired, increasing the total amount of repair business and conserving resources by reducing unnecessary scrapping and replacement.

In comparing information systems with complaint-handling systems, it should be kept in mind that the former have very great economies of scale, while the latter have few or no such economies. Handling individual complaints is an expensive process (often subsidized today), and the cost per complaint is practically constant. Information, on the other hand, involves largely the overhead costs of accumulating the information and building the system; the dissemination costs are small, and the more people who use the system, the further the information spreads by word of mouth.

It might seem that the kind of information that could be elicited from people would be subject to large errors and idosyncracies, but this does not matter much. If eight of ten people report some dissatisfaction with one repair service, and only two out of ten with another, it is a reasonably good indication of some difference in their capacity to satisfy customers. When it becomes eighty out of one hundred, it is an even better indication. Questions for eliciting revealing facts could certainly be developed, such as whether the bill agreed with the estimate, how long the job took, and whether the item had to be returned for further work.

Information for Consumer Records

There is a fourth type of consumer information useful for record keeping, taxes, and watching trends in prices, namely records of one's own transactions and related flows.

We have already mentioned some possibilities with computerized checkout in food stores, but the principle extends elsewhere—more information is made possible. The consumer interest in modern computer developments toward a cashless, checkless society is far more in the information possibilities than in some small loss of free interest provided by present delays in billing and paying. Consumers need better records of where their money is going, and if the new systems pay attention to that need, they can provide it at little or no cost.

Once all the information is computer-readable anyway, it should be easy to provide the consumer with a detailed, itemized billing that would make his own record keeping much easier. Employers could provide to the bank with information on employer direct contributions to Social Security, pension funds, insurance, etc., as well as payroll deductions; this information would be passed along with the bank report on other bills paid by the bank or on a bank credit card. In the same way, utility bill information on dates, physical consumption, and rates could also be transmitted, and even the grocery store or department store bill could be itemized, since the information is entered for inventory control anyway.

This would enable consumers to keep proof that particular bills were paid, or particular items purchased from a particular store on a particular date. It would allow price comparisons between grocery stores at leisure, and watching for trends in utility bills. Instead of a welter of check stubs, grocery and sales slips, utility bills, payroll check stubs, and scribbled notes, the consumer would have one systematic monthly list.

Sellers as a Source of Information

Those who market goods or services want to provide a selected kind of information to potential customers, ranging from the relatively complex individual counseling of the insurance agent through the newspaper ads for sales to the demure listing of professionals by speciality in the Yellow Pages. Properly balanced with other information and a consciousness of the special interests, such information can clearly be useful.

One of the justifications for advertising is that it provides consumers with market information. Certainly, the local food ads and notices of sales do provide price information. Combined with a good memory, that information can be quite helpful. Advertising that economists regard as unproductive is the more competitive sort, touting one of several similar products and forcing competitors to spend money to do the same. The total result may be no larger sales, no greater competition, but higher costs.

It is useful to note where "sales" are advertised, the sales may be of several different kinds:

☐ Getting rid of things that would not sell because of overpricing or lack of customer interest.
☐ Getting rid of seasonal items to avoid having to store them until the season comes around again.
☐ Spreading sales over the year by keeping the store busy during slack seasons.
☐ Keeping profitably high prices for those more interested in style, or having what they want right away, but cutting them during seasonal sales to pick up the more price-conscious buyers—a form of price discrimination. Those who buy at the sales get it at less than what they would have to pay if there were no sales, thereby benefiting at the expense of those who buy when they need it.
☐ Enticing customers into the store with a "bait bargain," then getting them to buy something else, or something more, that provides some profit.

Government as a Source of Consumer Information

There is a variety of consumer information available, much of it in the form of free or inexpensive pamphlets, from many government agencies. Although some new activities of interest to consumers spring up in the most unexpected places, result in a few publications, and then wither away with a change in personnel or administration, there have been a number of relatively persistent sources issuing information. The United States Department of Agriculture, the Food and Drug Administration, and the Administration on Aging are three. The state agricultural extension services and their experiment stations also issue bulletins. Recently the General Services Administration has been issuing two indexes of selected government publications, one called *Consumer Product Information*, and the other *Consumer Information*. The President's Office of Consumer Affairs issues a variety of publications. The *Monthly Catalogue of U.S. Government Publications* of the Government Accounting Office is also helpful, although not everything government agencies publish gets listed.

There is a bewildering variety of Congressional committees that solicit reports and research and publish them. In general, however, the government seldom gives information about products by brand name, and this includes even the armed services and the National Bureau of Standards, both of which buy or test many products. Attempts have been made (but with limited success), particularly since the Freedom of Information Act, to pry from the government information it has that would be useful to consumers. For example, under the Aging Americans Act, nursing homes must be inspected at least once a year in order to qualify for Medicare or Medicaid. Attempts to secure access to these inspection reports has been discouraging. Similarly, it took a protracted suit by Consumers Union to secure the results of hearing-aid tests from the National Bureau of Standards, and then the information was out of date. It seems likely that the government will continue to be a better source of general consumer information than of information about individual brands.

There are a number of other agencies, mostly private, which provide a mixture of consumer information and protection: the American College of Surgeons; the American Dental Association, Council on Dental Therapeutics; the American Medical Association, Council on Pharmacy and Chemistry, Council on Physical Therapy, Council on Foods and Nutrition, Committee on Advertising of Cosmetics and Soaps, and Bureau of Investigation; the American Institute of Laundering; Better Business Bureaus; Underwriters Laboratories (which test the safety of electrical appliances); and the Major Appliance Consumer Action Panel (with a "hot line" for complaints).

There is probably more consumer information in the Sears, Penneys, and Wards mail order catalogs, and more protection through their testing programs and refund policies, than many other sources offer. Certainly the "seals of approval" of magazines that accept advertising from producers (such as *Good Housekeeping*) are of dubious value. The difference between a magazine like *Consumer Reports*, whose revenue comes solely and directly from consumers, and one whose main revenue is from sellers' advertising is important to remember.

Another procedure tried by consumers to protect themselves has been to form cooperatives. In some areas they have been moderately successful, as in credit unions and the newer burial cooperatives. In food retailing they have been unable to do much better than the large chain stores. With consumer durables, they have usually ended up becoming buying clubs for the exclusive benefit of their members. It is probably not a solution to consumers' problems to attempt to go into business, except in rare situations of insensitivity to consumer wants or restrictive practices and very high margins. We discussed housing cooperatives in chapter 4.

Shopping and Bargaining

One of the great historic advances in merchandising, often attributed to the United States, is the open posting of prices. Economists as well as ordinary consumers applauded it because it increased competition, made it easier for consumers to know the choices they faced, and seemed fairer. Even where prices are posted, however, bargaining still goes on in many places. It is easy to locate examples of substantial savings from careful shopping and from bargaining, and we have already mentioned the price-quality frontier that one tries to approach (Maynes).

Whenever I need to buy something, I have to add to my accumulated stock of general knowledge about quality and past prices some up-to-date information about what is available now, at what prices, and whether any bargaining is going on. The bargaining may take the form of variable trade-ins, even on useless broken-down things that the seller simply scraps. Or the seller may "throw in" something extra. There is a vast difference, however, between shopping and open determination of best buys, on the one hand, and secret negotiation for the best bargains, on the other. The former increases competition, rewards the most efficient producers and distributors, and improves things for all consumers. The latter makes the market less effective and less equitable for customers who do not have the skill, patience, and fortitude to bargain. The more we individually demand special deals, the more we move back to the haggling system of the Middle Ages, which made the most profits for the shrewdest and most cunning sellers, not for those with the lowest prices for the quality.

Just as there are few economies of scale in settling individual complaints and disagreements, so it is unlikely that the advantages of bargaining would generalize. If every customer haggled about the price, the total costs of distribution would certainly go up because of the time and manpower involved!

With this in mind, I must still attempt to obtain the best price and quality I can, but I can at least attempt to broadcast all the information I get about the actual (bargained) prices, so that they tend to become the market norm, available to everyone. This is why we have stressed the information-getting aspects of shopping throughout this book rather than the bargaining aspects, and proposed more systematic methods of assembling and redistributing the information about prices and qualities. The same principle applies to services, even though the definition of the "service" is less precise.

Consumer Protection by Government

There is a long history of government protection for individual citizens, against such things as foreign invasions; robbery, rape, and violence; pollution in air, water, and food; contagious diseases; fraud; dangerous foods, drugs, and other products; monopoly and other restraints on competition; and deception, misleading advertising, and poor-quality products.

We are so accustomed to much of that protection that we do not appreciate it. But as one proceeds down the list, the effectiveness of government protection diminishes, largely because the problems are not easily solved by legal and administrative rules and restrictions. This is not to say that improvements are not possible, as recent legislation on occupational health and safety and product safety indicates. We shall skip over the first four with the comment that the consumer as a citizen has the responsibility to support the improvement of such protections, so long as the benefits justify the costs. For example, it is not necessarily good economics to try to make the water everywhere fit to drink and raise trout, since rivers and lakes can absorb some waste; the costs of perfection can be prohibitive.

Fraud

Since fraud is illegal, the state Attorneys General had responsibility for helping defrauded consumers long before there were any state consumer councils or counsels or committees or offices. Most states have an office of weights and measures to minimize short-weighting or packaging (Gordon).

Yet consumer frauds remain. They rely sometimes on deception ("You have been selected," told to everyone in the neighborhood), or on false logic (Insurance is cheaper if you take it out when you are young). But mostly they rely on blinding avarice—the lure of something for nothing. The classic tricks of confidence men lead the sucker to believe he will get a large sum of money for nothing, subject only to his putting up some money of his own to prove his sincerity. He is left with a sack of cut newspapers in the "pigeon drop" version, or some letters from a prisoner in a foreign jail (promising to share his loot buried in the United States) in the Spanish-American Prisoner Hoax.

A few frauds work on careless customers who are in a hurry, or who are charging entertainment to an expense account, but most of them work best on less-educated, low-income people who can least afford the loss. People in affluent areas are not likely to listen to door-to-door solicitors, nor to believe they are getting a bargain when shown an ad for something at a high price reprinted from some obscure small-town newspaper. Low-income people do not as often read the periodic reports in newspapers about someone being bilked of lifetime savings, nor are they as likely to be exposed to other kinds of warnings. Once they have been defrauded, the legal remedies are usually ineffective even if the perpetrator is known. According to the first enforcement chief of the new New York City consumer protection agency, the law could not help in nine-tenths of the cases (Schrag). Indeed, a scanning of the lists of complaints that come to consumer protection agencies indicates that only a few are even clear fraud at all. Most involve deception (possibly unintentional), disagreement about the facts, shoddy products, slow service, or interpersonal problems.

More sophisticated consumers would help. One possible way to improve consumer sophistication might be to build into the plots of television plays some of the real economic problems people run into. It should be possible to make very exciting drama about door-to-door salesmen, garnishments, eviction, small-loan interest rates, and con men's tricks.

Where the mails are used to defraud, the United States Postal Service can prosecute, provided that the recipients of such mailings turn them over to postal authorities.

Dangerous Foods, Drugs, and Products

There are several government agencies engaged in protecting the consumer, ranging from the state health departments and state police in the case of illegal drugs, to the Food and Drug Administration and the United States Department of Agriculture. The latter is responsible for inspection of the processsing of foods, including meat, poultry, and fish. Any such ongoing activities can tend to become inadequate or careless, calling for someone like Ralph Nader to jack up the agencies or alert them to new problems. Only recently has there been a serious attempt to deal with dangerous toys and other consumer products. One difficulty is that we are not all agreed on how much protection we want—whether, for example, we would want to be told that we are allowed to buy only the safest lawnmower, which costs twice as much as any other.

Monopoly and Restraints on Competition

While the government actually supports some restrictive practices that injure consumers—such as agricultural price supports, tariffs, and exemptions from antitrust laws for agricultural cooperatives, shopping, banking, and export cartels, and labor unions—in general, the Anti-Trust Division of the Department of Justice tries to maintain competitive markets wherever it is possible. There is a growing feeling, arising from some years of both inflation and unemployment, that perhaps more attention should be paid to getting the competitive system to work more flexibly and adequately.

The Federal Trade Commission and Anti-Trust Division of the Department of Justice have to deal with concentration of market shares and the sheer power resulting from conglomerate mergers. An example of the former is the food retailing chains, where too few in any one city seems to lead to higher prices and higher profits (U.S. Congress).

But there are some areas where competition just cannot be relied upon, where there are natural monopolies. Usually this comes about because of the large "economies of scale" to be achieved when there is only one power company or telephone company, water supply, or natural gas pipeline. Protecting the consumer against the possible extortion that such monopoly allows can be done in one of two ways. Either the government regulates the prices and calls it a public utility, or the government provides the service. Both solutions have problems. Public ownership may lead to unresponsive bureaucracies, inefficiencies hidden in the accounting, and strange or inequitable financing partly through taxes. Private ownership with public regulation requires costly investigations and rate-regulating commissions, with duplicate accounting and the possibility that the commission ultimately becomes the defender and protector of the utility rather than of the consumers.

Regulatory commissions, such as the Interstate Commerce Commission, the Civil Aeronautics Board, and the state public utility regulatory commissions, have a delicate problem of steering between two reefs. If they set rates and adjust them frequently so as to keep profits at some fair rate of return on capital (6 percent), then the management of the utility has little incentive to improve or economize. Indeed, their incentive may be to maximize capital expenditures! On the other hand, if they adjust rates downward only after a long lag when profits rise, then the consumers are overcharged. The determination of a fair rate is a complex technical matter, and consumers need expert technical representation. A fair rate of return requires estimating the rate base (the investment on which a return is allowed to be earned), which requires agreement on depreciation rates and on the issue of whether to take account of much higher replacement costs, implicitly allowing the company to write off as depreciation (deduct from profits) more than it has actually invested. The definition of a fair rate is also ticklish, since the *average* return on more speculative ventures is hardly justified. Corporate complexities increase the problem. When a utility is owned by a holding company, with leverage, a 6 percent rate of return to the subsidiary utility may imply a much higher rate of return to the holding company.

Deception, Misleading Advertising, and Defective Products

It is when we come to deception, misleading advertising, poor-quality products, and similar problems that the role of the government is most problematical and difficult. The Federal Trade Commission has authority over misleading advertising and has recently been insisting that advertisers stand ready to prove the claims they make for their products. But it is not easy to prove that consumers have indeed been deceived; rarely has any government agency invested in the kind of research that would prove deception. Does the name *HI-C* imply that the product is as good as orange juice? And if the product contains plenty of (cheap) vitamin C but not some of the other good things in orange juice, like vitamin A, should people selling substitutes like *HI-C* be required to say so?

And if case-by-case activities are expensive and often inconclusive, what about regulations and restrictions? It is our view that they should be regarded as the last recourse when all else fails. The reason is that historically efforts at such regulation have largely ended up harming the consumer in a variety of ways:

1. *Sometimes they deprive him of alternatives.* Price or interest ceilings may prohibit sellers from meeting the demands of some special groups. For instance, usury laws have driven high-risk borrowers into the arms of illegal, gangster style lenders.

2. *They may restrict competition and lead to higher prices.* Many licensing arrangements, promoted as protection of consumers against poor quality, end up administered by a craft or guild or by the producers and are used largely to keep out competition. Price ceilings often become price floors. There is evidence that the failure rate on many of the professional licensing exams is higher when demand is slack and already-licensed practitioners do not want the new competition (Maurizi).

3. *They may lull consumers into a false sense of security.* The Securities and Exchange Commission requires that prospectuses be issued when new stock is sold, accurately and honestly describing the situation. But a lavish prospectus can accurately and honestly state that the stock is "watered" (i.e., the promoters were given stock for their wisdom, without putting up much money), or that the company is a pure vision, having produced nothing yet, and still people will buy the stock.

4. *They may raise costs and prices.* The complexities of FHA financing, with limits on the stated interest rate and "points" charged, have given rise to the "mortgage broker," who takes his cut, raising the effective interest rate to the borrower.

It is far easier for producers and sellers than for consumers to put pressure on governments, since their interests are more concentrated. It seems a fair summary of history to say that intense, sophisticated, and effective representation of the needs of consumers has been rare at all government levels, except for a few short periods, usually during a depression or a serious inflation. Much as we should like to have better consumer representation, it does not seem likely.

A listing of full-time "consumer advisers" in eight government agencies, all that could be found in late 1973, showed few with formal training or experience in economics, and a heavy concentration of those with experience in public relations, politics, merchandising, or business administration. The consumer interest in many areas of government activity is not easy to find; certainly more than enthusiasm and good will is required. Even those advocating more government representation, including a Consumer Affairs Department, are not always clear whether such a department should educate and inform consumers, conduct research on consumer problems and concerns, lobby for what is felt to be the consumer interest, or what. Congress is not likely to subsidize another department to tell it what legislation to pass, particularly if it threatens to be at odds with the interests of the Departments of Agriculture, Commerce, or Labor. Some have argued that the government should step in only where someone is likely to injure someone else (physically or economically), as in the case of fraud or monopoly. But others argue that even where a man may injure only himself the government should interfere, on the premise that no man is an island, that others are likely to be depending on him, and that in any case the government has invested a great deal in him through investments in education and public health.

Historically, however, interference in cases where a man is likely to injure himself is more likely where there is some moralistic objection to the behavior as well. The differential treatment of drugs like opium, tobacco, krebiozen, thalidomide, alcohol, marijuana, sleeping pills, and pep pills is instructive. The lumping of marijuana, where the evidence of addiction or physical harm is unclear, with opium, where it is clear, is an example. The reliance on taxes to discourage consumption of both alcohol and tobacco, when the problems are so different, is another.

In the end, governments can and must protect the consumer from fraud, dangerous products, monopoly, and outright deception, but it seems clear to us that more education and information for consumers, and the encouragement of competition in the market, will do more to eliminate deception, poor quality, and high prices than licensing and regulation and direct attempts to handle disputes.

If a consumer protection agency were formed, what would be its desirable characteristics?

1. The commissioners would be appointed for terms of ten years, or until they are sixty-five, whichever comes sooner. This

would keep them from thinking about a next job and make their commitment a serious one.

2. They would be prohibited from working for those they are regulating until at least five years after leaving their jobs.

3. They would have some training in economics, or some of them would.

4. They would have the funds for (a) a continuous polling of consumers for their experiences and problems; (b) monitoring of vendors who have appeared with more than usual regularity in complaints by consumers; and (c) publicizing cases of continued abuse after monitoring and warning (and perhaps also publishing the names of vendors with better than usual records according to customers).

5. They would file public "conflict of interest" statements yearly, listing major assets and other sources of income. ("Major" means accounting for more than 5 percent of income, or worth more than a year's income in asset value, and would include assets owned by spouse.)

Seduction of the Consumer

Many of the polemics about the horrors of motivation research as used by modern advertising focus not on fraud or deception but on the insidious creation of "false" wants. These are quite flattering to the advertising profession, attributing to them seductive powers they wish they had. Actually, the more careful students of consumer behavior and attitudes insist that people are basically shrewder than most people think, and are not really "taken in" for very long (Katona).

What remains, aside from the factual issue, is a philosophical one. If someone convinces a family that they will be happier with a television set, and having tried one they find it an indispensable part of their life, what can one say about whether they are better or worse off? Since their tastes have changed, there is no way even in theory to answer this. The only time one can really say a household was disadvantaged is when they regret a decision afterwards, the seduction having been only temporary. Or, since most people do not like to admit regret and tend to rationalize what they have done, one might want to infer a mistake from subsequent behavior.

Issues of rising standards of consumption in developing countries dramatize this same issue. If one brings in consumer goods to entice the natives to work harder and enter the cash economy, are they actually better off than in their more primitive state? Can we rely on their continuing behavior to tell us whether they are maximizing their satisfaction? Or can we impose some arbitrary values about what constitutes the "good life"? This is a subject for a different book.

It is interesting to note, however, that motivating people to work sometimes requires providing more consumer goods so they have something to work for. The Russians discovered that wage differentials were not enough to keep workers in Siberia, since there was too little there for them to do with the money. One perceptive study in Taiwan shows that the very families interested in and buying modern products were also those who seemed to be working the hardest, and also planning their families (Freedman).

It finally comes down to the individual household and what its priorities are. We may well be seeing a new generation which really believes that physical possessions have been valued too highly, and the quality of human relationships and the time to cultivate them not highly enough. Even at the national political level, we may be seeing a shift from emphasis on individual consumption to community expenditures to improve the total environment.

The Consumer Interest

There remain some areas of national or state or local policy where the consumer interest is involved, but where the only decisions the consumer has to make are how he feels, or votes, or whether he joins a protest group. Policy is made both in legislatures and in administrative agencies of governments, where the "consumer interest" is generally rather poorly represented, even when the administrative agency is supposedly protecting consumers. Periodically someone exposes the extent to which such commissions or other administrative agencies have failed to function or have even become the defenders of the industries they were supposed to regulate. Ralph Nader's activities are a recent and brilliant example of such exposés. Unfortunately, the pressures from business communities or labor or farmers are steadier and are even supported by official and well-financed government agencies like the Department of Commerce, the Department of Labor, and the Department of Agriculture. We have already pointed out that a number of restrictions of competition are sanctioned by law: resale price maintenance, agricultural price supports, tariffs, etc. Each is a complex economic problem, with some justification for interference with free market forces, but consumers are generally unaware of the facts and of the impact of what goes on.

The most glaring examples are in areas where the government creates monopolies by various licensing or restrictive devices, but without recapturing for the government the monopoly profits. This varies from local restrictions on the number of taxi licenses (they are reported to sell for $20,000 in cash in New York City), to limited routes for bus lines, or limited numbers of television stations, where again the license alone has a monopoly value. Land with a right to grow tobacco also sells at a huge "monopoly" premium, although the gains from the monopoly may go only to the owner at the time the monopoly was created. Aside from the temptations to fraud and corruption, and the issue of whether the restriction and high costs to the consumer are really necessary, there is the equity issue as to who gets the profits. Economists argue that in most cases it would be possible to auction off the licenses, so that the government got the profit and used it for the general public welfare. In most cases it is quite easy, at least in theory, to vary the number of licensed sellers by auctioning licenses good for limited periods; the fewer the licenses, the greater their auction value. Problems arise, of course, where long-term investments must be made and the risk of having one's license bid away discourages investment. Procedures might be developed for allowing some security of tenure but adjusting the annual prices based on market values of those that do change hands, to avoid leaving monopoly values to the licensees. In general, economists agree that it is better to stimulate a new activity by a temporary direct subsidy than a permanent monopoly privilege.

Sometimes the purpose of regulation is to stablize prices rather than to avoid excessive and wasteful duplication. The classic example is milk price control, done in various ways in each major milk marketing area. It is just one example of how complex the analysis is if we are to identify the "consumer interest" and propose policies. The basic economics justify some attempt to stabilize prices. The demand for fluid milk is highly inelastic (unresponsive to price), and milk is an essential food—shortages or excessive prices even for short periods are unacceptable. The supply is also very inelastic in the short run, because the equipment is specialized, including the cows (you cannot sell a cow for much if the price of milk has collapsed). In addition, milk is unusual because fluid milk has a limited market geographically and an inelastic demand, and all the other milk products, including butter, ice cream, cheese, and casein, have a wider market and a much more elastic demand. The natural solution in such a case is to stabilize the price in the local market (for fluid milk, usually called the Class I market) and let the surpluses, which vary over the year, be sold for what they will bring in the wider (Class II) market. In the process of regulation, the price of fluid milk is usually set higher than that for the other milk uses, so that the prices of milk products no longer reflect their real social costs. The consumption of fluid milk is thus discouraged (though perhaps not much if demand is really insensitive to price), and the consumers of ice cream and butter are subsidized. If the price of fluid milk, and the general profitability of milk production, is raised too much, then more people enter the business, the price has to be still higher (because a larger proportion of the milk has to be sold at the lower national prices), and yet the farmers are still just breaking even. Nor is there any easy way to reverse the process. There are also problems with the bargaining power of the large dairies relative to the large number of farmers who are often not well organized. And there are abuses when sanitary regulations, or restrictions on delivery of milk from outside the area, are used to buttress excessive restrictions.

Most of these price-stabilizing or price-supporting systems steer a narrow course between insufficient stability and farm poverty, on the one hand, and excessive exploitation of consumers, and prices that distort resource allocations, on the other. The original purpose of most agricultural price supports was to keep the small family farm in business; yet the bulk of the benefit now goes to large commercial farms, many of which could survive without it. Yet there do remain smaller farms that might fail without the supports. Once again, the consumer must be rather sophisticated to understand not only his own interest but the other problems involved in any change.

Given the complexity of many of these problems, what consumers need is persistent, sophisticated representation on the various regulatory commissions and administrative agencies and in the halls of legislatures when consumer interests are involved. The problem is probably more serious at the state level, too distant for local groups but not sufficiently visible or important to enough people for their representatives to get involved. Occasionally an elected representative takes his responsibility to consumers seriously, but it does not often appear politically profitable. The inadequate pay of state legislators tends to restrict the jobs to people with other income sources, such as insurance salesmen, realtors, lawyers, and union officials, all of whom have closer ties with various business or labor interests than they do with consumers. Administrators of commissions are secondary recipients of some of these pressures. The administrator of worker's compensation in one state added to his annual report a table showing the average number of days delay from work accident to first insurance payment, insurance company by insurance company. It led to some rapid improvements in speed of handling compensation claims, but the individual did not remain administrator very long.

Another area of public policy where the consumers' interests are involved as well as the issues of proper resource allocation and equity has to do with pricing of goods and services with large fixed costs and low marginal costs. The dramatic example is the choice between freeways and toll roads, but the price structures of public utilities are also an example. Our optimum equations said that production of any commodity or service should expand until the marginal social benefit equaled the marginal social cost. The marginal social cost of allowing additional cars on an expressway is close to zero until one gets traffic jams. But charging the users nothing, while it might provide optimum use of the highway, does not solve the problem of how the highway gets paid for. Considerations of equity might argue for the toll—let those who benefit pay. Considerations of resource use would argue for no tolls, but for a taxing system that generally put the burden mostly on those who benefited. Where the road was largely used locally, an annual charge on the users might be possible. Some toll bridges charge full tolls for out-of-state users but provide cheaper weekly passes for the commuters who might otherwise be discouraged from using it. A state like Michigan, which has an extensive system of freeways, can use the gas tax effectively to charge the users without discouraging them from using the expressways.

With public utilities, the solution has been to charge more for the first bit, or for the right to any service at all, but a lower rate for additional amounts used. Equity problems arise when some low-income people are precluded from using the service at all, but in general, the system approaches the optimum more closely than flat rates. Today, however, with increasing demands being put upon exhaustible resources like fossil fuels, a pricing system that encourages the use of light and power is no longer so appealing.

Overall regulation cannot really come to grips with the adequacy of the actual treatment of consumers in the case of such public utilities as railroads and power companies, or such service agencies as the Postal Service, Social Security, welfare, Internal Revenue Service, police and fire departments. The one thing all these have in common is that they have no competition and allow very little feedback from those they serve. If a store or repair service treats me badly, I can complain, or look for another, but there is only one Postal Service, and in most cities only one garbage collection service.

Most government attempts at accountability have consisted of collecting administrative records, and regulated utilities seem to be more interested in attitude surveys than in systematic samples and relatively specific reports from customers about their treatment. As more and more functions are performed in a noncompetitive way, the need for some substitute for the discipline of the market is clearly in order. The vast difference in treatment of (mostly high-income) airline customers, on the one hand, and (mostly low-income) bus travelers, on the other, shows how the lack of individual clout and insistence on service affects the outcome. (The railroads also treat customers shabbily, but they have an excuse—they are broke.)

Just as it is difficult to make the provision of consumer information a viable business, so it has proven difficult to establish enduring organizations that would represent consumers with legislatures and administrative agencies, or monitor consumer treatment by government agencies and public utilities. The gains to any individual consumer are small, the issues complex, and critical issues arise intermittently and not in a steady flow. Attempts to create government agencies to handle the problem have not been successful, falling victim to changing political dominance or incurring the wrath of the legislature in some cases. As the electorate becomes more sophisticated in economic matters, heeding the consumer interest may become better politics.

Research on Consumer Behavior

Even research designed to serve the consumer, such as product testing, needs to be based on some prior understanding of the consumer, his wants and desires, and his habits. Product evaluation requires measuring various attributes, and then weighting the scores on each attribute according to its importance. If I do not care about small differences in electricity consumption, but have a lot of difficulty keeping the vegetables crisp in the refrigerator, with attendant expensive spoilage, then I am interested primarily in buying a refrigerator with good moisture control, not merely with low electricity consumption.

Some basic research on consumer attitudes and behavior, properly translated, is relevant to understanding consumer problems. We have already talked about learning and the process by which success leads to rising aspiration levels, and perhaps higher expectancies of future success, and wider horizons. On the negative side, we know that we are all subject to two problems, self-deception and a tendency to conform. The major example of the former is our failure to be critical of our own past decisions; originally called rationalization, it is now more appropriately called "dissonance reduction," the process of making the world seem congruent with our own past decisions (Festinger). Of course, it is healthy within limits not to spend time regretting past mistakes, but it is not healthy to ignore them entirely or to distort reality in order to make them fit. Indeed, a revealing difference between people who are careful consumers and those who are not is the willingness of the former to admit their mistakes and profit from them (Janis and Mann).

Conformity is more difficult to discuss, because the evidence is less clear and the interpretation more subject to dispute. Dramatic experiments, in which pressure was put on one individual to agree with the judgments of the rest of the group, all of whom were stooges, show that people will disbelieve even the evidence of their own eyes (Asch). But in real life, the people we associate with are not stooges. If we behave the way others do, it can be argued that this is not really their influence, but a reflection of the fact that we have common backgrounds and interests (that is why we associate in the first place), or a result of a flow of information (we found out about the product by seeing it in use, or we figure that if Jones, whom we know to be a knowledgeable and careful buyer, picked that brand, it must be a safe selection).

This is not to say there are not pressures to conformity, but that they are mixed up with other things, and demonstrating influence is much more difficult than showing that groups in fact act or think alike.

Survey Research

While it is possible to find data about consumer behavior, sometimes in individual market areas, or before and after some change in prices or income, such semi-aggregated data do not carry us very far in understanding consumer behavior. The most powerful tool for this purpose is survey research. The results of such research are used in marketing and in helping decide issues of public policy, so it is important for the informed consumer to understand a little about the process to be able to spot poor quality research, and to interpret research findings sensibly.

The big advantage of survey research is that information from a small representative sample can tell us much about a whole population. Survey research on human populations is a relatively recent addition to our arsenal of scientific tools. Any research method becomes scientific only if it produces quantified and reproducible findings. And it can have its findings extended beyond its immediate data only if those data come from a representative sample. Three innovations have converted the process of asking people questions from a journalist's art to a scientific method:

First, one must have an unbiased representative sample in order to use survey results to talk about some whole population or subpopulation. Completely random selection is not crucial. Rather, the key is to know the probability of selection of every eligible respondent, family, or unit being sampled. There are unbiased ways of selecting probability samples which are far more efficient and less likely to vary from the true population than a simple random sample (Kish). It is crucial, of course, that a high proportion of the sample be interviewed successfully, because even the best sample can become biased through differential nonresponse.

One important fact about sampling is counterintuitive: the precision of survey results depends on the actual size of the sample and on its design, but hardly at all on the size of the population being sampled or on the percent of the population interviewed! This means that it takes nearly as large a sample to say something about one small town as it does to speak about the whole country. As sample size increases, the variability of sample estimates falls roughly in proportion to the square root of the number of cases, so doubling a sample size reduces sampling "errors" by about 40 percent (1/1.414).

Second, obtaining reliable information requires methods of interviewing and analysis that are reproducible and not biased by the procedures or the attitudes of the interviewers. The basic requirement here is to ask the same question in the same words of everyone, and controlling the interpretation of the responses. Responses other than "yes," "no," some amount, or a choice of a few stated alternatives require that answers be written down and analyzed in a central office under controls, including recoding to assure consistency. When this is not done, there is a disturbing tendency for the replies to questions on attitudes or public policy to vary, depending on the sponsorship of the study or the kind of organization doing the work. It is useful for the ordinary reader of survey results to know just what questions were asked—biases are sometimes apparent in the questions—and something about how the answers were treated.

Third, analysis of survey data requires finding relationships that are not spurious. Are women paid less than men even if we take account of education, years of experience, and age? Modern computers and statistical analysis make it easier to tackle such questions. The basic procedure is simple, however. If one looks separately at many small groups with the same age, education, and job tenure within a group, are the men paid more than the women within each group? If the wage differences between men and women remain until we take account of the exact job being done, then disappear, we know that it is access to jobs (or self-selection to jobs) that is crucial and calls for investigation.

For the user of the results of survey research, an assessment of the quality of the data requires answers to questions like:

1. Was there a probability sample, and of what population? (A large sample of a limited population may not be generalizable, e.g., a probability sample of people in one city or state.)
2. Were the questions asked exactly as they appear on the questionnaire and do they seem to be reasonably unbiased? (A request to agree or disagree with some statement or opinion is not unbiased, because people tend to agree to anything, particularly if they have little education or are authoritarian.)
3. Are the relationships shown a possible spurious artifact resulting from joint relationships with some third factor, like age or income?
4. Are the findings "statistically significant," that is, unlikely to have arisen from pure chance? (Even if statistical tests are used, or sampling variances given, the results may still be deceptive if the authors made a large number of tests. But aside from that, the concept of sampling variance is based on the notion that if one had a whole set of similar samples, there would be a range of findings, of which the sample at hand is one. The variability of that range of findings tells us something about the meaning of the one we have.)

How Survey Research Can Benefit Consumers

There are three different ways in which information elicited from consumers can benefit them. One, already discussed, is the redissemination to consumers of sampled experience of other consumers with local repair service and quality, with local price and availability of products, or with quality of products nationally.

A second use of survey data informs producers or retailers about problems consumers are having, or desires that are not being met. While it is true that most market research is an attempt to discover how to sell something, some of it does, and more of it could focus on improving product design or service.

A third use is to inform elected representatives and government administrators about the quality of what the government does and about people's needs and desires that might call for new government initiatives. As more and more of our resources are allocated by decisions to tax and spend on social priorities, rather than by individual purchase decisions in free markets, we can no longer rely on prices and sales as indicators of what people want and what satisfies them. Elected representatives have to make decisions, and systematic, genuinely representative, information from the voters would help. An occasional election is not enough. Where governments or large bureaucracies like the public utilities are serving consumers directly, surveys can even monitor the quality of that service. Wherever consumers have no choice of alternative services, they need a way of letting people know whether they are satisfied, or whether some new services are needed. To each consumer there is only one Internal Revenue Service, Social Security system, welfare department, Postal Service, electric company. Systematic survey evidence would seem a more powerful way of improving such services than occasional incidents or dramatic journalism.

Summary

This has been a long and varied chapter, starting with some theory about consumer behavior and motivation, and decision making in the family.

We then indicated why informed consumers are crucial and mentioned some of the problems of providing and distributing consumer information, ending with some proposed new alternative solutions.

We looked at various sources of consumer information, then turned to consumer protection by government, treating it as a last alternative when all else fails, for reasons we spell out.

We then discussed the consumer interest and problems of determining it and representing it. This led us logically to a discussion of research on consumer attitudes, desires, and behavior, and how to read and evaluate the results of such research. There are exciting possibilities for making better public policy decisions based on such research.

More Information?
There are more printed words on consumer information and consumer protection than we can manage. The many books that blame it all on someone else have little use, since it is our own decisions we can do something about. The thousands of "how to" books of substantive consumer information cannot be listed here, nor evaluated, though a suspicion remains that many of them tell me just enough to get me into trouble, but not enough to get me out.

We have included a few basic books on individual motivation and behavior and on decision making in the family, since they are important in understanding consumer use of information or need for protection.

Aaker, David A., and Day, George S., eds. *Consumerism: Search for the Consumer Interest.* New York: Free Press, 1971.

Arrow, Kenneth. *Social Choice and Individual Values.* New York: John Wiley and Sons, 1951. (Same impossibility of an optimal solution applies to family as to society.)

Asch, Solomon. "Studies of Independence and Conformity: A Minority of One Against a Unanimous Majority." *Psychological Monographs* 70 (1956), no. 416.

Atkinson, John. *An Introduction to Motivation.* Princeton, N.J.: D. Van Nostrand, 1964.

Baker, Sam Sinclair. *The Permissible Lie: The Inside Truth About Advertising.* Lawrence, Mass.: Beacon Press, 1971.

Balk, Alfred. *The Free List: Property Without Taxes.* New York: Russell Sage, 1971. (Property tax exemptions)

Been, Eugene R., and Ewing, John S. "Business Appraises Consumer Testing Agencies." *Harvard Business Review* 32 (1954): 113–26.

Better Business Bureau, Education Division, 430 N. Michigan Avenue, Chicago, Illinois. (Sundry pamphlets on consumer awareness)

Brandt, William K.; Day, George S.; and Deutscher, Terry. "Information Disclosure and Consumer Credit Knowledge: A Longitudinal Analysis." *Journal of Consumer Affairs* 9 (1975): 15–32.

Brecher, Edward M., and the Editors of Consumer Reports. *Licit and Illicit Drugs.* Boston: Little, Brown, 1972.

Canada, Ministry of Consumer and Corporate Affairs. *Consumer Contact.* (Periodical free from The Consumer, Box 99, Ottawa, Ontario, Canada)

Carson, Rachael. *The Silent Spring.* Boston: Houghton Mifflin, 1962.

Cartwright, Dorwin, ed. *Studies in Social Power.* Ann Arbor: Research Center for Group Dynamics, Institute for Social Research, University of Michigan, 1959.

Chase, Stuart, and Schlink, F. J. *Your Money's Worth.* New York: Macmillan, 1934.

Childers, Thomas. *The Information-Poor in America.* Metuchen, N.J.: Scarecrow Press, 1975.

Consumers Union. *Consumers Union Report on New City and County Consumer Protection Agencies.* Mt. Vernon, N.Y.: Consumers Union, 1972.

Consumers Union. *Guide to Consumer Services.* Rev. ed. Mt. Vernon, N.Y.: Consumers Union, 1979.

Creamer, J. Shane. *A Citizen's Guide to Legal Rights.* New York: Holt, Rinehart, and Winston, 1971.

Crowther, Sam, and Winehouse, Irwin. *Highway Robbery.* New York: Stein and Day, 1966.

Dacey, Norman. *How to Avoid Probate.* New York: Crown, 1965.

Dick, Charles H. "The Way to a Consumer's Heart." *FDA. Consumer*, September 1972. Washington, D.C.: Government Printing Office. (A description of FDA role in aiding consumers)

Donnelly, V. Paul, and Ehrle, Lynn. *Consumer Rights, Battle in the Marketplace.* Detroit: Consumer Alliance of Michigan, 1970.

Engman, Lewis A. "Inflation and Regulation." *Antitrust Law and Economics* 7 (1975): 35–46.

Epstein, Samuel S., and Grondy, Richard D. *The Legislation of Product Safety.* 2 vols. Cambridge, Mass.: MIT Press, 1974.

Feldman, Laurence P. *Consumer Protection: Problems and Prospects.* 2d ed. St. Paul, Minn.: West Publishing Company, 1980.

Festinger, Leon. *A Theory of Cognitive Dissonance.* Evanston, Ill.: Row Peterson, 1957.

Forming Consumer Organizations. Washington, D.C.: Government Printing Office, 1972.

Freedman, Deborah. "The Role of Consumption of Modern Durables in Economic Development." *Economic Development and Cultural Change* 18 (1970): 25–48.

Gaedeke, Ralph M., and Etcheson, Warren W. *Consumerism: Viewpoints from Business, Government, and the Public Interest.* San Francisco: Canfield Press, 1972.

Garman, E. Thomas, and Eckert, Sidney W. *The Consumer's World: Buying, Money Management, and Issues.* New York: McGraw-Hill, 1974.

Goodman, Charles S. *Do the Poor Pay More?* Philadelphia: Wharton School, The University of Pennsylvania, 1967.

Gordon, Leland J. *Weights and Measures and the Consumer.* Mt. Vernon, N.Y.: Consumers Union, 1970.

Haemmel, William Gordon; George, B. C.; and Bliss, J. J. *Text-Cases-Materials on Consumer Law.* St. Paul, Minn.: West Publishing Company, 1975.

Hapgood, David. *The Screwing of the Average Man.* New York: Bantam Books, 1975.

Harmer, Ruth Mulvey. *Unfit for Human Consumption.* Englewood Cliffs, N.J.: Prentice Hall, 1971.

Harrell, Gilbert D.; Hutt, Michael D.; and Allen, John W. *Universal Product Code: Price Removal and Consumer Behavior in Supermarkets.* MSU Business Studies. East Lansing, Mich.: Michigan State University, Graduate School of Business Administration, Division of Research, 1976.

Harris, Richard. *The Real Voice.* New York: Macmillan, 1964.

Hirschleifer, J. "Where Are We in the Theory of Information?" *American Economic Review* 63 (1973): 31–39.

International Organization of Consumer Unions. *Consumers Directory, 1976.* The Hague, Netherlands: International Organization of Consumer Unions, 1975.

Jacoby, Jacob; Szybillo, George J.; and Busato-Schach, Jacqueline. "Information Acquisition Behavior in Brand Choice Situations." *Journal of Consumer Research* 3 (1977): 209–16.

Janis, Irving L. and Mann, Leon. *Decision Making, A Psychological Analysis of Conflict, Choice, and Commitment*, New York: The Free Press, 1977.

Kallet, Arthur, and Schlink, F. J. *100,000,000 Guinea Pigs.* New York: Vanguard Press, 1938.

Katona, George. *Psychological Economics.* New York: Elsevier, 1975.

Katona, George, and Mueller, Eva. "A Study of Purchase Decisions." In *Consumer Behavior*, vol. 1, edited by L. Clark. New York: New York University Press, 1944.

Katz, Carol Hecht, ed. *The Law and the Low-Income Consumer.* New York: New York University School of Law, 1968.

Keats, John. *The Insolent Chariots.* Philadelphia: Lippincott, 1958.

Kish, Leslie. *Survey Sampling.* New York: John Wiley and Sons, 1965.

Kohlmeier, Louis. *The Regulators.* New York: Harper & Row, 1969.

Lerner, Abba. *The Economics of Control.* New York: Harper, 1944.

Lewis, C. S. *The Screwtape Letters.* New York: Macmillan, 1944.

Martindale-Hubbell Law Directory. 7 vols. Summit, N.J.: Martindale-Hubbell, annually. (A list of lawyers, rated by ability and reputation)

Matthews, Douglas. *Sue the B ST RDS—the Victim's Handbook* (How to Get Even in Small Claims Court—Cheap, Quick, and Without a Lawyer). New York: Arbor House Publishing Company, 1973.

Maurizi, Alex. "Occupational Licensing and the Public Interest." *Journal of Political Economy* 82 (1974): 399–413.

Maynes, E. Scott. *Decision Making for Consumers.* New York: Macmillan, 1976.

Monroe, Kent B., and LaPlaca, Peter J. "What Are the Benefits of Unit Pricing?" *Journal of Marketing* 36 (1972): 16–22.

Morgan, James N. "Household Decision Making." In *Household Decision Making*, edited by Nelson Foote. New York: New York University Press, 1961.

Morgan, James N. "Some Pilot Studies of Communication and Consensus in the Family." *Public Opinion Quarterly* 32 (1968): 113–21.

Morris, Ruby Turner, and Bronson, Clare Sekulski. "The Chaos of Competition Indicated by Consumer Reports." *Journal of Marketing* 33 (1969): 26–34.

Nadel, M. *The Politics of Consumer Protection.* Indianapolis: Bobbs-Merrill, 1971.

National Consumers Union. *Codebook.* Rev. ed. Prospect Heights, Ill.: National Consumers Union, 1971. (Aid to decoding packaged goods dating)

Newman, Joseph W., and Staelin, Richard. "Prepurchase Information-Seeking for New Cars and Major Household Appliances." *Journal of Marketing Research* 9 (1972): 249–57.

Nizer, Louis. *My Life in Court.* New York: Doubleday, 1961.

Packard, Vance. *The Hidden Persuaders.* New York: McKay, 1957.

Packard, Vance. *The Status Seekers.* New York: McKay, 1959.

Packard, Vance. *The Waste Makers.* New York: McKay, 1960.

Packard, Vance. *The Naked Society.* New York: McKay, 1964.

Paulson, Morton C. *The Great Land Hustle.* Chicago: Henry Regnery, 1972.

Peter, Paul, and Tarpey, Lawrence X., Sr. "A Comparative Analysis of Three Consumer Decision Strategies." *Journal of Consumer Research*, June 1975, pp. 29–37.

Rowatt, Donald C., ed. *The Ombudsman (Citizen Defenders).* Toronto: University of Toronto Press, 1965.

Russo, J. Edward. "The Value of Unit Price Information." *Journal of Marketing Research* 14 (1977): 193–201.

Schlink, F. J. *Eat, Drink, and Be Wary.* New York: Covice-Friede, 1935.

Schrag, Philip G. *Counsel for the Deceived: Case Studies in Consumer Fraud.* New York: Pantheon Press, 1972. (First enforcement chief of New York City Consumer Protection Agency found the law couldn't help much.)

Shapiro, Howard, and Denenberg, Herb. *How to Keep Them Honest.* Emmaus, Pa.: Rodale Press, 1974.

Spring, John L. *Consumer Swindlers and How to Avoid Them.* Chicago: Henry Regnery, 1970.

Stanford Law Review Note. "The Persecution and Intimidation of the Low-Income Litigant as Performed by the Small Claims Court in California." *Stanford Law Review* 21 (1969): 1657–84.

Tannenbaum, Arnold. *Hierarchy in Organizations: An International Comparison.* San Francisco: Jossey-Bass, 1974.

Telser, L. G. "Searching for the Lowest Price." *American Economic Review* 63 (1973): 40–49.

Thorelli, Hans B., and Thorelli, Sarah V. *Consumer Information Handbook: Europe and North America.* New York: Praeger, 1974.

Thorelli, Hans B.; Becker, Helmut; and Engledow, Jack. *The Information Seekers* (An International Study of Consumer Information and Advertising Image). Cambridge, Mass.: Bellinger Publishing Company, 1974.

Troutman, C. M., and Shanteau, J. "Do Consumers Evaluate Products by Adding of Averaging Attribute Information?" *Journal of Consumer Research* 3 (1976): 101–6.

U.S. Civil Aeronautics Board. *Air Travelers' Fly Rights.* Washington, D.C.: U.S. Civil Aeronautics Board, 1973.

U.S. Congress, Joint Economic Committee. *The Profit and Price Performance of Leading Food Chains, 1970–1974.* Washington, D.C.: Government Printing Office, 1977.

U.S. Department of Agriculture. *A Consumer's Guide to USDA Services.* Washington, D.C.: Government Printing Office, 1966.

U.S. Department of Agriculture. *Food Dating: Shoppers' Reactions and the Impact on Retail Foodstores.* Washington, D.C.: U.S. Department of Agriculture, 1973.

U.S. Department of Health, Education, and Welfare. *Programs and Services.* Washington, D.C.: Government Printing Office, 1966.

U.S. Department of Health, Education, and Welfare, Office of Consumer Affairs. *State Consumer Action, Summary 1974.* Washington, D.C.: Government Printing Office, 1975.

U.S. Federal Trade Commission. *Report on the Task Force on Warranties and Service.* Washington, D.C.: Government Printing Office, 1968.

U.S. General Services Administration, Consumer Product Information Coordinating Center, in Cooperation with the Office of Consumer Affairs, Executive Office of the President. *Consumer Product Information* (An Index of Selected Federal Publications on How to Buy, Use, and Take Care of Consumer Products). Washington, D.C.: Government Printing Office, 1971.

Waddell, Frederick E. "Consumer Research and Programs for the Elderly—the Forgotten Dimension." *Journal of Consumer Affairs* 9 (1975): 164–75.

Wagner, Walter. *The Golden Fleecers.* New York: Doubleday, 1966.

Warford, Jeremy J. *Public Policy Toward Aviation.* Washington, D.C.: Brookings Institution, 1971. (Unwarranted subsidy to small planes)

Warland, Rex H.; Herrman, Robert O.; and Willitts, Jane. "Dissatisfied Consumers: Who Gets Upset and Who Takes Action." *Journal of Consumer Affairs* 9 (1975): 148–63.

Wasserman, Paul, ed. *Consumer Sourcebook.* Detroit: Gale Research, 1974. (Directory to organizations and bibliographic material)

Winter, Ralph K., Jr. *The Consumer Advocate Versus the Consumer.* Washington, D.C.: American Enterprise Institute, 1972. (Questions the benefits)

Wolgast, Elizabeth. "Do Husbands or Wives Make the Purchasing Decisions?" *Journal of Marketing* 23 (1958): 151–58.

Zedeck S. *Information Processing and Decision Making as Influenced by Product Proliferation. Technological Change, Product Proliferation and Consumer Decision Processes,* vol. 3. University of California, Berkeley, and Columbia University, New York, 1974. (Survey of literature shows there really is little known about how the consumer deals with the proliferation of new products.)

Some Projects to Learn More

1. Choose some appliance or item that costs enough to justify careful selection in buying. See how much you can find out about the brands and models available, good and bad qualities, prices, and discounts available. Talk to dealers, repairmen, recent purchasers if you know any. Search the library, particularly the *Consumer Reports, Consumer Research Bulletin*, hobby magazines, *Popular Mechanics*, etc., for information.

2. Find several articles in magazines on the same consumer subject, purporting to inform consumers. Compare and evaluate them as to their hard information content, usefulness, etc.

3. Find out in some community what help is available to a customer who feels he has been defrauded. Is there a Better Business Bureau, a Legal Aid Clinic, a City Attorney, a Frauds and Rackets Division?

4. Read the last few annual reports on the Antitrust Division of the Justice Department and of the Federal Trade Commission, and any other recent publications of these agencies. Or try the Food and Drug Administration. Look for their press releases and categorize their activities. Perhaps check to see which of their press releases actually appeared in your local paper.

5. Visit the state Public Utilities Commission and find out what you can about their activities, and perhaps write up the details of a recent rate case.

6. Watch the newspapers for ads of suspiciously good bargains. Rush down and see whether these are "bait advertising," customers being switched to something else, or deceptive, or limited in supply, or real bargains.

7. Select some local service, like car repair or dry cleaning, and see what information you can collect from talking to friends and neighbors about the quality of the individual businesses. Could you quantify this information and collect it systematically? Would it be useful to consumers?

8. Find out how the price of milk is set in your area, and the price differential to farmers between Class I and Class II milk. Talk to a local dairy and the milk producers' association about how it works.

9. Check the *Monthly Catalogue of (United States) Government Publications* (using the annual index) for publications of use to consumers. Try to find some of them in your library. Evaluate them.

Glossary

Abstract—A summary of the history of the legal title to a piece of property.

Actuary—An expert in the mathematics of risk, probability, life expectancies, and insurance. It takes a special examination to become a licensed actuary.

Administrator of an estate—A person appointed by a probate or surrogate court to manage and distribute the assets of an estate if the decedent (one who died) did not leave a proper will appointing a proper executor or executrix.

Adverse selection—A propensity for those with a higher than average probability of collecting to carry insurance. It makes the insurance a bad buy for the average person.

Amino acids—The components of protein essential for nutrition.

Amortized loan—A loan repaid by a series of constant payments which repay both a portion of principal and interest on the remaining balance.

Annuity—A stream of annual payments, either accumulating with compound interest, or being repaid with interest on the remaining balance, or both.

Appraisal—An evaluation of the market value of a property (house and lot).

Assessed value—An administratively assigned "market value" assigned by the property tax assessor for tax purposes; often some fraction of true market value. It must be multiplied by the property tax rate to find the property tax, which can then be related to market value of the house.

Assigned risk—A high-risk person who is assigned to an insurance company at random. Some states do such assignments to assure that insurance is available even to high-risk people.

Assignment of property—The transfer of a right or interest in property by one person to another.

Attachable—Subject to being taken to pay debts.

Attractive nuisance—A legal concept making you liable for damages if you have an attraction, e.g., swimming pool, even if you post a sign, "No swimming."

Balloon note—A loan with some amortizing payments, but a substantial balance to be paid off at the end of the period.

Bankruptcy—A legal procedure under federal law for distributing remaining assets among the creditors of a person or business and wiping the slate clean of indebtedness. Cannot be repeated within seven years. *See* Title 13.

Beneficiary—One who receives property that someone who dies has willed to him or her.

Bequeath—To give property upon the death of the giver.

Betterment tax—A tax on increased property value resulting from government actions (in Britain).

Binder—A receipt for money paid to secure the right to purchase real estate upon agreed terms.

Book value—The value of a business according to its accounting records. Since assets are valued by purchase price less accrued depreciation charges, current market value is often much greater than book value in inflationary periods.

Call—A right to purchase shares of a specified stock at a specified price at any time within a specified period.

Capital—Something purchased or created at some present cost that provides a stream of services, benefits, or output in the future, usually depreciating in the process. Sometimes used casually to refer to assets.

Capitalized value—The present value of a future stream of net benefits. For a constant everlasting stream of $X per year at interest rate r, it is X/r.

Cash surrender value (of a life insurance policy)—A prestated amount, in a policy with a savings feature, that is returnable to you if you cancel the policy. It is smaller than the amount you can borrow on the policy if you keep it in force, and smaller than the cash reserve (of your money).

Certificate of title—A paper signifying ownership of a house, usually with a legal description of the house and its land.

Chattel mortgage—A loan with security for repayment of the loan, transferring title of some personal property if the loan is not paid.

Cholesterol—A fat-like substance found in every animal cell that tends to accumulate in the body if one consumes too much saturated fat or gets too little exercise.

Closed-end fund—A mutual fund that does not accept additional investments and reinvest them in the stock market, but merely manages the original fund. Shares are usually bought and sold like any other stock, rather than through agents or through the fund. *See* Open-end fund.

Closing costs (or settlement costs)—Costs in addition to the price of a house, including title search and insurance, transfer of ownership charges; so called because they are paid when the sale is "closed," i.e, when the actual transfer of money and property takes place.

Clustered sample—A multi-stage survey sample where subareas are listed and sampled for sequentially smaller fractions. The result is a saving in travel and cost greater than the loss in precision, and no bias is introduced.

Codicil—A change or addition to a will, added separately (since you cannot alter a will).

Coinsurance—1. A provision of an insurance policy by which you bear some fraction of the cost of loss, to provide an incentive for economy. 2. In fire insurance, if you insure for less than the market value, the increase in the fraction of a loss you must pay (or coinsure). 3. Sometimes, sharing by insurance companies of a large risky policy.

Commodity futures—Rights to buy or sell commodities (e.g., wheat, cotton) at some future date.

Compound interest—A form of interest which pays on previously-earned interest as well as on principal.

Condominium—One of a group of apartments or houses, owned by an individual, along with an undivided shared ownership of common areas and facilities.

Conflict of interest—A situation in which economic self-interest may distort a person's decisions or judgments in another area.

Contingent fee—An arrangement in tort law by which a lawyer is paid only if he or she succeeds in securing a damage award for the client.

Contributory negligence—A defense, if you are sued for negligence, that the other person was also negligent.

Cooperative housing—A group of apartments or houses owned in common by the residents. Individuals own shares of stock in the total enterprise.

Cost—A real using up of assets; or expense; often confused with the financial amount in some transfer, such as the cost of welfare.

Credit bureau—An organization keeping records on individuals to establish their credit rating, i.e., the likelihood that they will pay their debts. Businesses pay bureaus for checking whether it is safe to lend to a customer.

Credit life insurance—A small amount of life insurance sufficient to pay off a debt if you die. This protects the lender.

Custodian account—Assets given to minors and managed by a responsible adult (custodian) until the children are eighteen years old.

Decedent—A dead person.

Declining balance depreciation—A bookkeeping method whereby an asset is depreciated by a fraction of the current value rather than a constant amount each year.

Decreasing term insurance—A policy which pays a stated amount per month for the remainder of a stated period, hence an amount of insurance that drops to zero value over time.

Deductible—An insurance provision where you pay a stated portion of a loss, the insurance company the rest.

Demographer—A specialist in population, birth and death rates, net reproduction rates.

Depletion allowance—A tax provision allowing deduction from taxable income for depletion of an exhaustible resource; often cited as a tax loophole.

Depreciation—The wearing out and using up of a piece of capital in the course of producing goods or services.

Devise—To give real property, as in a will.

Disability waiver of premium—A small amount of disability insurance added to a life insurance policy sufficient to pay the life insurance premiums if you become disabled.

Discount—To convert a future sum to the present amount that, with interest, would cumulate to that future sum.

Diversification—In investment, the spreading of risk across a variety of investments to reduce the overall risk.

Dividend—1. A distribution of a share of a company's earnings to holders of its common stock. 2. The return at the end of each year of part of an insurance premium, in "participating" policies.

Double declining balance depreciation—A rapid depreciation charge allowed for tax purposes on investments including rental real estate, converting income into capital gains. The depreciation is a fraction of the remaining value, so is largest at the beginning, and is twice the usually allowed rate.

Earnest money—A deposit by buyer to seller, usually of real estate, applied against the purchase if the deal goes through and otherwise forfeited.

Easement—The right of a land owner to use the land of his neighbor, as in common driveways, or any right to use another's property, view, etc.

Efficiency—The allocation of resources to produce the desired output in the most effective way.

Efficiency frontier—The best available combinations of price and quality.

Elasticity—The percent change in something, e.g., output or sales, resulting from a 1 percent change in something else, usually price or income.

Eminent domain—A legal right of governments to condemn and purchase property for public use, at a court-determined price.

Endowment insurance—A policy that rapidly accrues a cash value equal to its face value, so that it can be converted to cash.

Equity—In accounting, a right to ownership of part of something; in economics, the fairness of the distribution of income or rights to the goods and services of society.

Escrow funds—Funds given to a third party to hold until all conditions in a contract are fulfilled.

Excess condemnation—Use of eminent domain by government to take more land than it needs for a project, the excess then being sold in an attempt to capture some of the capital gains produced. Of doubtful legality and historically ineffective.

Executor, Executrix—Someone named in a will to take charge of the estate and distribute it. See Administrator of an estate.

Expected value—The probability that an event will occur times its value (positive or negative) if it does.

Expenditure—A paying out of money, which may or may not involve an expense (cost).

Expense—A using up of goods and services, or incurring of obligations or costs, which may or may not involve expenditures.

Face value—The amount paid to a beneficiary upon the death of the holder of a life insurance policy.

Family income (insurance) policy—A combination of ordinary life insurance and a decreasing term insurance policy, with the face value declining to a base which is then constant.

Fee splitting—A payment by a specialist to the person who referred the customer to him or her. Clear conflict of interest.

FHA loan—A loan approved and insured by the Federal Housing Administration.

Fiduciary—A person who because of his or her position or relationship owes a duty of trust and confidence, as a guardian or trustee.

Garnishment—A notice or proceeding which requires an employer to pay part of an employee's wages to the employee's creditor.

Generic drug—A drug that is not patented and may be sold under brand names as well as (more cheaply) by its generic chemical name.

G.I. insurance—Life insurance available to veterans of the armed services through the government.

Gini coefficient—A measure of inequality in some quantity (e.g., income, wealth) based on the Lorenz curve.

GRAS list—A list of about 800 substances *generally recognized as safe*, and so exempt from testing required by the Food Additives Amendment.

Group insurance (life or other)—Insurance, usually handled by an employer who makes a single payment to cover a large group, that allows economizing on costs and sometimes compromising on rates paid by employees with different risks.

Group practice—A sharing of location, records, referrals, and equipment by a group of doctors, for greater efficiency.

Growth stock—Stock in a company that reinvests most of its earnings, and for this or other reasons is expected to grow also in size, earnings, future dividends, and the price of its stock.

Guardian—A person appointed to protect the interests of a minor.

Health Maintenance Organization—A combination of group practice and prepaid health care intended to focus on the maintenance of health rather than the care of illness.

Hedge—An investment with a risk opposite to a risk already being borne, so the two risks cancel.

Hire purchase—British term for installment credit.

Holder in due course—The purchaser of a commitment to pay, such as an installment credit contract, who is usually held to have a right to collect regardless of problems with the original product or service.

Holographic will—A will in the handwriting of the maker.

Human capital—Skills (education, on-the-job training) acquired through a process of self-investment. This concept views a human being like a piece of capital in the sense that investments increase future productivity.

Imputed income, interest, rent, or consumption—Estimated flows, when no cash expenditure or receipt occurs, representing real earning or consumption. Depreciation is an imputed consumption, included in the imputed rental income and rental consumption of an owned home. Interest cost of money tied up in a car is an imputed consumption.

Income—A real flow of accured rights to goods and services resulting from labor, ownership of capital, or transfers.

Indemnity—A reimbursement for a loss sustained.

Inflation—A general increase in prices and thus in the cost of living.

Insider trading—Purchase or sale of stock in a company by officials of the company that must be registered with the Securities and Exchange Commission. Some think such trading gives the investor clues about future earnings.

Interest—Payment for the use of money, as when money is loaned by passbook account holders to banks or when money is loaned by the bank to its customers.

Intestate—A person who dies without leaving a will.

Insurance—A contract in which, in return for a small fee, a company pooling the risks guarantees to reimburse you for losses from specified causes.

Investment—1. The financial act of purchasing securities or other rights to capital. 2. The real act of using resources to create or improve capital.

Investment trust—A financial arrangement which invests your money in a diversified portfolio of things, usually stocks. Same as a mutual fund.

Joint tenancy—Equal ownership interest in the same property. Usually specified "with rights of survivorship and not as tenants in common," so that either person can dispose of the property and claim it as a survivor, thus keeping it out of probate.

Land contract—A method of purchasing real property in which title does not pass until the final payment is made, avoiding need for foreclosure in case of default. Payments are amortized as in a regular mortgage, but often the seller holds the contract; he can, however, sell it to an investor.

Legal reserve life insurance—Insurance policies that maintain level premiums while accruing a reserve of the policyholder's money.

Legatee—Beneficiary of a legacy or bequest in a will leaving personal property.

Level premium life insurance—A type of policy that maintains a constant annual premium, usually by accumulating and using a reserve fund and earnings on the fund.

Leverage—Having the use of more assets than one owns, in order to increase potential earnings; the fixed borrowing commitments increase risk as well.

Lien—A claim filed against the property of another.

Life insurance—Insurance which compensates survivors of a named individual when the individual dies.

Lifetime annuity—A contract paying a guaranteed amount per year as long as you live. Insures against the risk of living too long and running out of money.

Loading—The portion of an insurance policy cost that is not used to pay benefits, but is retained by the company as expenses, profit, or unused "reserves." More generally, the expense and profit fraction of any situation, e.g., a mutual fund.

Loan value of a life insurance policy—The amount, usually less than the reserve (of your money), that you can borrow on the policy at a stated interest rate.

Lorenz curve—A representation of the distribution of income that plots the cumulative fraction of aggregate income against the cumulative proportion of families, arranged in order by income.

Marginal benefit or utility—The added benefit from a little more, which may not be the same as the average benefit (total divided by the number or amount).

Marginal cost—The cost of one unit more.

Marginal tax rate—In the federal income tax structure, the fraction of an additional dollar of income that would be taxed away.

Mechanic's lien law—The law which allows workers in the building trades to place a lien on property on which they worked (your house) for unpaid wages, even though you may already have paid the contractor. When paid, they will sign a *waiver of lien*.

Mortgage commitment—A written notice from a bank or other lender stating that it will advance a specified amount to enable you to buy a particular house at some interest rate.

Mortgage discount points—A one-time charge assessed by the lender in order to supplement the interest stated in the mortgage. A way of getting around FHA limits on mortgage interest rates. Officially paid by seller, who adds it to the price.

Mortgage protection insurance—Declining term life insurance sufficient to pay off the remaining mortgage on your house.

Mortgagee—The lender in a mortgage contract.

Mortgagor—The borrower in a mortgage contract.

Mutual fund—A company that reinvests your money in a diversified portfolio of investments, usually common stocks.

Negligence—A failure to take due precautions, leading to injury to another, for which you can be sued under the law of torts.

Net reproduction rate—A measure of population growth more precise than birth rate.

No-load mutual fund—A mutual fund having no difference between buying and selling price, i.e., no agent's fee. Sold directly by the fund or, if closed-end, on the stock market for the usual stockbroker's fee.

Obsolescence—Decline in value not from use but from becoming out of date or out of style.

Open-end mutual fund or investment trust—A fund that accepts additional investments after the initial investment, reinvesting in a portfolio, usually of common stocks.

Opportunity cost—The cost of any choice, measured by the value of the next best foregone alternative.

Option—A right to choose a course of action, e.g., to renew a lease or insurance policy, or to buy something within a stated period at some price. Often purchased as insurance against a rising price or unavailability.

Ordinary life insurance—A life insurance policy that combines life insurance with a savings account. This type of insurance has level premiums, constant face value, and a declining amount of pure insurance.

Outlay—An expenditure, not to be confused with an expense.

Pareto optimality—A situation where it is not possible to make anyone better off without making someone else worse off.

Participating insurance policy—A policy that pays dividends at the end of each year (actually a refund of part of the premium).

Participating preferred stock—Preferred stock that can also share in extra profits.

Points—*See* Mortgage discount points.

Policy loan—A loan with your life insurance reserve as security.

Portable pension—A pension that can be taken with you if you leave the company.

Preferred stock—Ownership share in a corporation with prior claim on earnings before common stockholders get anything.

Premium—The annual charge for an insurance policy.

Present value—The value now of future sums to be paid or received.

Prescriptive easement—The right to use another's property because you have been doing so in the past without his or her objection.

Price/earnings ratio—The ratio of a current stock price to the company's last year's earnings per share.

Principal—In a loan, the amount owed, not including interest.

Probability sample—A sample, each element of which has a known probability of selection.

Probate court (or surrogate court)—The court that probates wills.

Probate of a will—A judicial procedure to determine if a document is a valid will that can be enforced to dispose of the estate according to its provisions.

Progressive tax—A tax that tends to take a larger fraction of income the higher the income, and hence is redistributive.

Put—An option to sell a specified stock at a specified price within a specified period; the opposite of a call.

Random sample—A sample in which every element in a population has the same, independent probability of being selected.

Real estate, real property, realty—Land, buildings, and any other attached improvements.

Receipts—Money received, whether income or not.

Regressive tax—Tax that tends to take a larger fraction of income from those with lower incomes.

Real estate investment trust (R.E.I.T.)—A trust which invests your money in a portfolio of real estate instead of stocks.

Relatives' responsibility laws—Laws making individuals responsible for the financial support of needy relatives.

Renewable term insurance—Pure life insurance, renewable periodically without another medical exam (at higher rates, to reflect the higher probability of dying as you get older).

Repossession—The resuming of possession by a creditor of property that was security for a debt, if the debtor defaults.

Reserve—An accumulation of excess premiums and interest in a life insurance policy that reduces the amount of pure insurance and earns further interest.

Residuary trust—A trust to hold that part of an estate outside the marital exemption and deduction, on which estate tax has been paid; used to care for the surviving spouse, but can be transferred to the children when the spouse dies, to avoid another estate tax.

Revenue (or income)—Accrual of rights to goods or services, including earnings, interest, dividends, rent, and transfers, whether received in cash or not.

Risk—A chance that some (usually bad) event will happen; the term ordinarily implies some knowledge of the probability; in contrast with uncertainty, where the probability is unknown. Risks can be insured against.

Risk-adjusted yield—A way of comparing yields of investments with different levels of risk.

Rule of 72—The approximation that, in compound interest, an amount doubles when the interest rate times the number of years reaches 72.

Sampling variance (often called sampling error)—The amount an estimate based on a sample might differ from a value based on the whole population.

Savings bank life insurance—Life insurance available at savings banks to residents in New York and Massachusetts. It has lower premiums because of the lower selling costs.

Settlement options—Alternative ways of paying death benefits of a life insurance policy.

Special assessment—A tax on property for a specific purpose of local benefit, such as new sewers or sidewalks or the first paving of a street.

Stock dividend—An issue of extra shares of stock to stockholders, often instead of money.

Stock split—Same as a stock dividend.

Straight life insurance—Ordinary life insurance, with level premiums, a constant face value, and the accumulation of a cash reserve which, with accrued interest, reduces the amount of pure insurance.

Striking price—The price at which a call or put option allows you to buy or sell the stock.

Subrogation—A substitution of creditors, as when your insurance company collects compensation for damages from another person for you, subrogating your claim. The company may even collect from you for benefits paid by them and also from another source.

Tenancy in common—The kind of joint ownership requiring signatures of both parties to change anything, unlike joint tenancy, where either party can sign for both.

Term insurance—Pure insurance for a period of time at a price, with no tied-in saving program.

Testamentary trust—A trust set up by a will.

Testate—A word used to describe a person who died having left a will.

Testator, Testatrix—A person who leaves property by a will.

Time averaging—Investing a constant amount regularly in stock regardless of its price.

Title insurance—Insurance against discovering that the title to your land is incomplete, which covers any losses involved.

Title search—A check back through the various transfers of title to your property before you got it, ideally back to a valid owner.

Title 13—A provision of the Federal Bankruptcy Act allowing the insolvent person to turn his assets and income over to a lawyer for scheduled repayments of part or all debts to creditors. It avoids formal bankruptcy, saves credit rating, and can be repeated without waiting seven years.

Tontine—An ancient alternative to an annuity, wherein the last man alive got it all.

Tort law—The law dealing with injury to another through negligence or malice.

Transfer income—Income not currently earned, though there may have been earlier contributions, as with retirement pensions. Includes welfare and Social Security benefits.

Trustee—An individual who receives and administers the property of a trust and is personally liable for its management.

Twenty-year net cost—A method of pricing life insurance which ignores interest and thus can be misleading. It is twenty years of premiums minus dividends minus the cash value at the end.

Uncertainty—The possibility of bad or good events to which no probability can be assigned and thus for which no insurance is possible.

Variable annuity—An annuity whose accumulated funds are invested in stocks or other things calculated to hedge against inflation by rising in value or yield with the price level.

Variance—A statistical measure of dispersion equal to the summed squared deviations around the mean.

Vested interest (in a pension)—Pension rights that an individual cannot be deprived of, although he or she may have to wait until age sixty-five to start receiving them.

Waiver of lien—A statement signed by members of the building trades that they have been paid for their work on a particular house; it ensures that they will not place a lien on it later for unpaid wages.

Waiver of premium—A provision that under certain conditions an insurance policy will be kept in full force without further payment of premiums. *See* Disability waiver.

Index

Publications providing more information on specific topics which are referred to throughout the text are listed alphabetically by author's name at the end of each chapter.

Accounting, 65; principles of, 74–77
Adverse selection, 141, 156, 245
Advertising, 230, 233
Aging Americans Act, 230
Aid to Families with Dependent Children, 27, 32, 37
American Medical Association, 173
Amino acids, 167, 188, 245
Amortized loans. See Loans
Annuity, 18, 21, 68–73, 143, 245; calculation tables, 18, 20, 142; joint or survivor, 69, 73
Anti-Trust Division of Department of Justice (U.S.), 233
Assessed value, 56, 245
Assets, 78, 122, 145, 153; capital costs of depreciating, 21, 127–28; income tax implications of, 35; insurance aspects of, 153; and life insurance needs, 145; and philanthropy, 212; ownership patterns of, 153; and transfer payments, 37
Attorney's funds, 51
Attractive nuisance, 159, 245
Automobile insurance, 153–56; avoidable accidents and costs of, 154; coinsurance, 155; collision, 156; liability, 153–56; "no-fault," 155–56; purchase of, 156–57; theft, 156; unavoidable accidents and costs of, 154
Automobiles: and commuting, 206; depreciation of, 129–31; insurance (see Automobile insurance); maintenance of, 207–8; market value vs. use value of, 130; rental, 209; style obsolescence of, 131; timing of purchase of, 131; trading costs of, 129

"Bait advertising", 135–36
Balance sheet, 74
Balloon note loan. See Loans
Bankruptcy, 97–100, 103, 245; Title 13 provision of, 98
Bankruptcy Act of 1978, 98

Bargaining, 231
Bathtub theorem, 65, 79. See also Budgeting
Bequests, 68, 245. See also Estate planning
Betterment tax, 58, 245
Blue Cross, 158, 174, 175
Bonds, 105–9, 112; coupon payment, 105; government, 112; guaranteed redemption of, 112; ratings of, 112; tax implications of, 34; yield curve of, 106, 117
Book value (of stock), 114, 245
Borrowing, 91–104. See also Credit; Debt; Loans
Budgeting, 65–67, 74–82; accounting principles of, 74; bathtub theorem and, 65; expenditure monitoring and, 80–81; expenditures vs. expenses and, 65; guidelines, 73; and monitoring consumption, 79–80; receipts vs. income and, 65; sources of income and, 77; sources of savings and, 77

Calls, 118, 245
Calorie requirements, 30, 80, 191
Capital, 7, 245; account, 74; budgeting aspects of, 66; defined, 7, 245; transactions, 66. See also Financial capital; Human capital; Physical capital
Capital gains and losses, 34, 58, 106, 110; of bonds, 106; of housing, 42, 43; and investments, 113; and philanthropy, 212
Capitalized value, 18, 105, 245; applied to housing costs, 52; effects of property tax on, 57; of income stream, 105
Career choice, 13; on-the-job training and, 23–24
Car pools, 206
Cars. See Automobiles
Casualty losses. See Losses, casualty
Categorical assistance, 37
Charitable contributions: capital gains tax on, 120. See also Philanthropy
Charitable trust, 163
Chattel mortgage, 97, 245
Checking accounts, 119
Chicago Board of Options Exchange, 118
Children: cost and benefits of, 26–28; public policy aspects of having, 27
Cholesterol, 193, 245

Closed-end funds. See Mutual funds
Clothing, 204–5; budgetary aspects of, 81
Coinsurance, 155, 157, 159, 246
Collision insurance. See Automobile insurance
Commodity futures, 118, 246
Common stocks. See Stocks
Common tenancy, 110, 249
Condominiums, 49, 246
Constructive eviction, 51
Consumer attitudes and expectations, 84
Consumer durables. See Durables
Consumer information. See Information
Consumer information systems, 214, 229–30
Consumer interest, 221, 235–38
Consumer protection, 232–35
Consumer Reports, 132, 135, 157, 173, 227, 231
Consumers Research, 227
Consumers Union, 95, 132, 135, 149, 157, 169, 177, 227, 230
Consumption, 66
Contingent fee, 153, 246
Contributory transfers, 33
Cooperatives, 49
Corporate profits tax, 34
Credit, 91–104; cards, 94–95; counselors, 99; rating, 97; unions, 94, 130. See also Borrowing; Debt; Loans

Debt, 91–104; costs of, 96; macroeconomic aspects of, 100. See also Borrowing; Credit; Loans
Debt adjusters, 99
Deception, 233
Department of Health and Human Services (U.S.), 174
Depreciation, 113, 127–28, 129–31, 246; of automobile, 129–31; budget aspects of, 77–78; declining balance, 246; double declining balance, 113; of durables, 127–28; of housing, 42; implications for investments of, 113
Diet. See Nutrition
Diet for a Small Planet, 168
Disability insurance, 141; waiver of premium, 149, 246
Discounting, 9, 92, 246; on loans, 92. See also Present value
Dissonance reduction, 238

Dividends, 107-9, 246; effects on stock prices, 107-9
Divorce: economic implications of, 29; implications for insurance needs, 145
Do-it-yourself repairs, 134
Dowry, 26
Drugs, 173, 177, 232
Dunning letters, 97
Durables, 96, 127-38; benefits of, 132-33; budgeting aspects of, 67, 136; capital theory aspects of, 127-28; consumer behavior regarding, 136; market value vs. use value of, 127-28; owning vs. renting of, 133; repair aspects of, 134; repair records on, 132; shopping for, 132; sources of information on, 135; timing of purchases of, 96, 136

Easement, 50, 246
Economies of scale: defined, 25-26; implications for family needs of, 30-31
Economy of fear, 76
Economy of love, 76
Education, 7-17, 176; budgeting aspects of, 68; costs and benefits of, 7; effects of college quality on, 12; financing of, 15; medical, 176; payoffs to, 11; policy aspects regarding, 15-16; rate of return on, 10-13; social vs. private costs and benefits of, 14-16
Efficiency, 224; conditions for, 224; defined, 4, 246
Efficiency frontier curve, 132, 246
Employee Retirement Income Security Act, 71-72, 110
Equity, 27, 225; defined, 4, 246. *See also* Fairness
Estate planning, 121, 161-63; investment aspects of, 121; marital deduction and, 121. *See also* Bequests
Estate tax, 36, 73, 110, 162
Excess condemnation, 58, 246
Exercise, 169
Expectancy, 222
Expected price, 200
Expected value, 10-13, 106, 107, 139, 160, 200, 222, 246; applied to bond prices, 106, 107; applied to gambling, 160; applied to payoff to shopping, 200; defined, 2, 246; in theory of motivation, 222
Expenditures, 65, 246

Expenses, 65; defined, 74, 246
Externalities, 225

Fair Credit Reporting Act, 97, 103-4
Fairness, 4. *See also* Equity
Family composition: economic implications of, 29; effects of public programs on, 29
Family decision making, 223-24
Family planning, 27. *See also* Children
Family well-being, 28-29
Federal Credit Union Act, 94
Federal Deposit Insurance Corporation, 111
Federal Housing Administration, 47, 59; mortgages, 55
Federal income tax. *See* Income tax
Federal poverty needs standard, 29, 30-31; calculations of, 30; economies of scale and, 30; levels for 1978, 30
Federal Real Estate Settlement Procedures Act, 47
Federal Savings and Loan Insurance Corporation, 111
Federal Trade Commission (U.S.), 98, 173, 178
Federal transfer tax, 162
Fee splitting, 171, 246
Financial capital: in household balance sheet, 74. *See also* Capital
Financial planning, 65-89; long-range goals and, 67-68
Fiscal policy, 84
Flight insurance, 140
"Float," 100
Food, 203; costs, 30; expenditures, 201-4; open dating of, 203; standards, 218-19; unit pricing of, 203
Food and Drug Act, 179
Food and Drug Administration, 178, 179; minimum standards of quality, 219; standards of identity, 219
Fraud, 232
Freedom of Information Act, 230
Fringe benefits, 25
Funerals, 161
Future value, 9, 18. *See also* Present value

G.I. insurance, 152, 247
Gambling, 160
Garnishment, 33, 93, 97-100, 153; defined, 97, 247; use of, 98
Gift tax, 162
Gini coefficient, 31, 247
Good Housekeeping, 231
Grade standards (USDA), 218
Group practice, 173, 247

Health care. *See* Medical care
Health maintenance organizations, 173, 175, 247
Hedge, 109, 247
Hire purchase, 100, 247
Holder in due course doctrine, 99, 247
Home ownership, 48. *See also* Housing
Home production, 25
Hours of work, 24
Household insurance, 43, 159; coinsurance and, 159
Housework, 25; valuation of, 83
Housing, 41-63, 113, 134; additions and repairs to, 134; appreciation, 42; as an investment, 113; costs of, 41-57, 60; depreciation, 42; design and style considerations of, 54; legal considerations of, 50-51; neighborhood considerations, 52-53; owning vs. renting of, 41, 42, 44-49; policy aspects regarding, 54-55; property taxes on, 55-57; tax effects of, 34-36; transactions, 51-52
Human capital, 7, 74, 247; in household balance sheet, 74. *See also* Capital

Imputation, 2, 3
Imputed cost, 2
Imputed income. *See* Income
Imputed interest. *See* Interest
Income, 65, 247; as a measure of family well-being, 28-29; defined, 74, 247; imputed, 2, 34, 43, 56, 77, 83, 247; inequality, 31; nonmoney, 28; ratio to needs, 28-29; redistribution, 32-38; sources of, 77; total family money, defined, 28
Income account, 74
Income protection life insurance. *See* Life insurance
Income tax, vi, 76, 96, 110, 112; advantages for homeowners, 45; credit vs. deduction, 33; deductions, 34, 36; effects on behavior, 36-37; effects on costs and benefits, 2; effects on do-it-

yourself activity, 25; effects on family composition, 29; effects on home production, 45; effects on house closing costs, 48; effects on housing choices, 43–44; effects on investment, 120; effects on market work, 24; implications for casualty insurance, 156; implications for debt, 96; implications for financial investments, 110; implications for philanthropy, 212; income exempt from, 34; loopholes, 35–36; major features of, 33–36; marginal tax rate (*See* Marginal tax rate); marriage penalty, 35; standard deduction, 34, 35; state, 35; tax exempt government bonds and, 112; treatment of capital gains and losses, 34
Income test, 37
Individual Retirement Account, 73, 110
Inequality: effects on saving, 82; measures of, 31
Inflation, 109, 118, 128, 130, 151, 247; effects on saving goals, 68; effects on durable goods, 128, 130; effects on housing costs, 44; effects on life insurance needs, 151; investment strategies against, 109, 118
Information, 225, 226; from government, 230; implications for efficiency of, 225; insights and, 226–27; on local services, 229–30; and record-keeping, 229; from sellers, 230; social good aspects of, 226; sources of, 226
Information systems, 214, 229
Insurable interest, 140
Insurable risk, 139
Insurance, 94, 139–61, 172, 175–76, 247; availability, 140–41; budgetary aspects of, 76; experience rating, 158; face value vs. real amount of, 148; household behavior and, 159–60; implications for redistribution of income of, 33; optimal amounts of, 140; policy aspects of, 160; premium cost vs. real cost of, 148; principles of, 139. *See also* Automobile insurance; Disability insurance; Flight insurance; G.I. insurance; Household insurance; Life insurance; Malpractice insurance; Medical insurance; Theft insurance; Title insurance; Worker's compensation
Interest, 247; imputed, 2, 247. *See also* Interest costs; Interest rate
Interest costs, 91, 127; of durables, 127; of housing, 42; of housing closing charges, 46; pattern of, in an amortized loan, 91
Interest rates, 91, 92, 105, 106, 128, 143, 149, 247; of bonds, 105; calculation on loans, 91–92; effects on bond prices, 106; effects on life insurance costs, 149; of financial investments, 105; real vs. nominal (market), 2, 8–9, 20–21, 42–43, 128, 143; relationship with inflation rate, 8–9; shopping for, 93; true annual, 92; use of 3 percent rule and, 20–21
Internal rate of return, 18; defined, 9–10; relationship to present value, 9–10
Investment, 105, 109–12, 117, 119, 122, 247; in art and antiques, 120; aspects of home ownership, 43–44; behavior, 121–22; in bonds (*see* Bonds); budgetary aspects of, 66; calculation of net benefits of, 9; characteristics of, 109–12; in commodity futures, 118; in debentures, 119; in human capital, 7; information and management costs of, 111; information considerations of, 121; liquidity considerations of, 109; in money market funds, 119; in mutual real estate investment trusts, 120; in on-the-job training, 13; in options market, 118; in preferred stock, 119; principles of, 105; protection against inflation by, 109; in real estate, 112; risk considerations of, 109; in small businesses, 119; social and ethical considerations of, 111; social aspects of, 122; tax considerations of, 110, 120; timing of, 117; in trusts, 115–18. *See also* Stocks

Joint or survivor annuity. *See* Annuity
Joint tenancy, 110, 121, 163, 247

Keogh plan, 110

Labor supply, 24–25; implications for family well-being of, 31–32
Land contract, 50, 247
Lawyers, 213; information sources on, 213
Leverage, 109, 114; applied to housing investment, 48; defined, 114, 247

Licensing, 214, 236
Lien, 50, 247. *See also* Mechanic's lien laws
Life insurance, 141–53, 247; cash surrender value of, 146, 246; costs of, 149–50; decreasing term, 146; disability waiver of premium for, 149, 246; face value of, 146, 246; family income, 148, 246; family life-cycle needs and, 143; income protection, 148; interest-adjusted net costs of, 149; mortage protection, 148, 149; needs for, 141–44, 144–45; nonparticipating policy, 148; "paid up," 148; participating policy, 148, 248; present values and, 21; renewable term, 146, 248; return on savings in, 149; rules of thumb, 150, 151; savings bank, 152; term, 146–47, 249; term vs. cash value, 146–49; twenty-year net costs of, 149; whole, 146–49
Liquidity, 109
"Loading," 160, 247; on mutual fund, 115
Loans, 91–104, 130; amortized, 91, 245; balloon note, 130; calculation of interest rate on, 91; defaulting on, 93; sources of, 94. *See also* Borrowing; Credit; Debt; Packing; Sum of digits method
Loopholes. *See* Income tax
Lorenz curve, 31, 247
Losses, casualty: tax deductibility of, 156
Lotteries, 160, 161
"Low balling," 135–36

M-Reit, 120
Macroeconomic policy, 83, 84
Malpractice, 172; insurance, 172
Marginal tax rate, 3, 34, 112, 247; defined, 3, 247; effects on bond yields, 112; effects on housing costs, 44; implications for casualty insurance of, 156; implications for philanthropy of, 33, 212. *See also* Income tax
Marriage, 25–26; career choice implications of, 26; implications for financial planning of, 73; legal aspects of, 26
Martindale-Hubbel Directory, 213
Means test, 37
Mechanic's lien laws, 50, 248
Medicaid, 174, 230

Medical care, 167–82; costs of, 172; drugs and, 173, 177; fee-splitting in, 171; group practice in, 173; information about, 171; insurance (see Medical insurance); malpractice, 172; and mental health, 170–71; paying for, 174; policy aspects of, 171, 176–78; preventive, 169–70
Medical insurance, 66, 157–58, 174–75, 175–76
Medicare, 174, 175, 230
Mental health. See Medical care, and mental health
Milk price control, 236
Minimum Daily Requirements, 189
Monetary policy, 84
Money market funds, 119
Monopolies, 233, 236
Monopolistic competition, 201, 225
Moody's Investors Service, 116
Mortgage, 93; brokers, 55; budgetary aspects of, 78; calculation of payment, 44–45; calculation table, 46, 48; commitment, 248; costs of, 46–49; effects of extending length of, 46; income tax considerations of, 34; payments, 42; points (see Points); savings aspects of, 45
Motivation, 221–22
Mutual funds, 115–18, 248; no-load, 116, 248; open-end, 116, 248; selection strategies for, 116

National Bureau of Standards, 227, 230
National Housing Agency, 59
National Marine Fisheries Service, 218
Needs standard, family, 28–29, 30
Negative income tax, 38
Neighborhood: effects on house prices of, 52–53
No-fault. See Automobile insurance
No-load mutual funds. See Mutual funds
Nominal interest rate. See Interest rates, real vs. nominal (market)
Noncontributory transfers, 32
Nonmoney income. See Income
Nutrition, 167–69, 186–90, 191–95, 203; cholesterol and, 193; fats and, 191–93; labeling of foods and, 186; protein balance and, 168; salt intake and, 168

On-the-job training, 13, 23–24
Open dating, 203
Open-end mutual funds. See Mutual funds
Opportunity cost principle: applied to consumption choices, 199; defined, 248
Opportunity, alternative, 3
Option value of education, 10
Options market, 118
Owning a home. See Housing, owning vs. renting of

Packing, 93. See also Loans
Payout ratios, 108
Pensions, 67, 69, 71, 72
Philanthropy, 33, 76, 120, 163, 211–13; budgetary aspects of, 81; tax expenditures and, 212. See also Charitable contributions
Physical capital, 7. See also Capital
"Pigeon drop," 232
Points, 55, 248; conversion to interest costs, 48; defined, 47–48, 248; See also Mortgage
Poverty line. See Federal poverty needs standard
Prescription drugs. See Drugs
Prescriptive easement, 50, 248
Present value, 2, 8–10, 18–21, 105, 106, 127–28, 143, 248; applied to on-the-job training, 23–24; of bonds, 106; calculation table, 18, 19, 20, 142, 143; of depreciation, 127–28; discounted, 18; of financial investments, 105; of foregone interest, 127–28; of life insurance needs, 143; rule of thumb, 18
Price-earnings ratio, 107–9, 115, 248
Probability samples, 239, 248
Property tax, 36, 43, 55–57
Protection. See Consumer protection
Public Health Service, 178
Puts, 118, 248

Rate of return, 105. See also Internal rate of return
Real estate investment trust (R.E.I.T.), 120, 248
Real interest rate. See Interest rates, real vs. nominal (market)
Realtor's fee, 51

Receipts, 65, 248
Recommended Daily Allowances, 187–89
Recreation, 205–11
Recreational equipment, 209–11
Recreational facilities, 211
Redistribution: effects on behavior, 36–37; policy aspects of, 38
Redlining, 59
Reforms: tax, 37; welfare, 37
Registrar of deeds, 51
Regulation, 233–34, 236
Relatives' responsibility laws, 37, 248
Renting. See Housing, owning vs. renting of
Repair services, 213–15
Repossession, 97–100, 248
Residence requirements, 37
Retained earnings, 107; effects on stock prices, 107
Retirement: annuity, 21; savings implications for, 69–72; sex differential, 88
"Riding the yield curve," 106
Risk, 106, 107, 109, 139–40, 248; effects on bond prices of, 106, 107; of investments, 109
Rule of 72, 19, 112–13, 120, 248

Safety, 169; of investments (see Risk of investments)
Sales, 230
Sales tax, 36
Sampling errors, 239
Saving: amount of needed for retirement, 69–72; behavior, 82–83; budgeting aspects of, 66; goal setting, 68; goals, 78; long-range goals, 67–68; macroeconomic aspects of, 83; sources of, 77; statistics on, 82
Savings and loan associations, 111
Savings bank life insurance, 249
Savings banks, 111
Savings bonds, 35
Securities and Exchange Commission, 116, 234
"Seduction of consumers," 235
Services, 213–15
Shopping, 199–201, 231
Small claims court, 97
Small-loan companies, 97
Social optimum, 224–26

Social Security, 34, 73, 76, 84–87, 100, 105, 140, 141, 143–44, 145, 151, 175; budget aspects of, 66–67, 78; as component of family income, 28; as contributory transfer, 33; disability benefits, 141; effects on family composition of, 29; estimation of benefits from, 72; financing issues, 87; implications of for cost of children, 27; implications of for financial planning, 72–73; implications of for life insurance needs, 143–44, 151; implications of for savings goals, 68, 69, 71; insurance aspects of, 76, 140, 145; principles of, 84–87; treatment of women under, 88; trust fund, 85
Spanish-American Prisoner Hoax, 232
Standard and Poor's, 116
Stocks, 107–9, 113–15; book value, 114; dividends, 114–15, 249; price averaging, 117; prices of, 107–9; principles of, 107–9; splits of, 114, 249; striking price of, 118, 249
Store brand substitutes, 202
Striking price. *See* Stocks
Sum of digits method, 92
Sunk costs: applied to automobiles, 128; defined, 2

Supplemental Security Income, 32
Survey research, 238–40

Tax-free cash flow, 113
Tax. *See* Estate tax; Federal transfer tax; Gift tax; Income tax; Property tax; Sales tax
Taxpayer number, 35
Tenant's rights, 50
Term life insurance. *See* Life insurance, term
Theft insurance, 156
Title insurance, 46, 51, 159, 249
Title search, 46, 249
Title 13. *See* Bankruptcy
Tort law, 153, 249
Transfer income, 28, 249; contributory vs. noncontributory, 32–33; policy aspects of, 37
Transportation, 205–9. *See also* Automobiles
Trusts, 110, 121, 162; investment aspects of, 121; relative to income tax, 35; testamentary, 249
Truth in Lending Act, 91, 93, 94

Uncertainty, 13, 106, 107, 249; effects on bond prices of, 106, 107; relationship with expected value of, 2
Unemployment, 24
Uniform Credit Code, 99
Uniform Gift to Minors Act, 35
Unit pricing, 203
Urban development, 58
USDA grade standards for food, 218
Usury laws, 97
Utility costs, 43

Vacations, 209
Veterans Administration, 47, 174
Vitamins, 168, 183–85

Well-being. *See* Family well-being
Whole life insurance, 146–49
Wills, 162
Worker's compensation, 76, 158–59, 174

Yield curve (of a bond), 106, 117; risk adjusted, 248

Zoning laws, 53

DATE DUE

DEC 1 7 1998			

DEMCO 38-297